# CELEBRITY COOKBOOK

by

## Johna Blinn

Edited by
**Malvina G. Vogel**

Illustrated by
**Mel Mann**

**MOBY BOOKS**

**PLAYMORE, INC. Publishers**
Under arrangement with **WALDMAN PUBLISHING CORP.**
New York, New York

To the celebrities who have given
generously of their time in conversations
about food and foodstyles, and to my
husband and children who have been
denied my time in order for me to travel
across the country and the world to record
these celebrity foodprints.

CELEBRITY COOKBOOK. Copyright © 1981 by Johna Blinn.
Drawings copyright © 1981 by Waldman Publishing Corp.
All rights reserved. Printed in the United States of
America. No part of this book may be used or reproduced
in any manner whatsoever without written permission except
in the case of brief quotations embodied in critical
articles and reviews. For information address Waldman
Publishing Corp., 18 East 41st Street, New York, N.Y. 10017

MOBY BOOKS is a trademark of
Waldman Publishing Corp.
18 East 41st Street, New York, New York 10017

# Introduction

*"Bad men live that they may eat and drink, where
good men eat and drink that they may live."*

– Socrates

This is a cookbook, certainly, but it is more. It is a forum in which celebrities echo time, revealing their own unique, provocative selves through their views on food.

In face-to-face interviews in celebrity homes, on movie sets, in television studios and on locations as varied as the posh Beverly Hills Hotel in Southern California to the New Mexico desert at midnight to the sunny Bahamas to a gold mine in South Africa, to London, Paris, Montreal, Mexico, Honolulu, I get people to talk about food to get the flavor of the person.

By reporting on these conversations with famous people, I hope to bring a new dimension and renewed enthusiasm to the humdrum stuffs we have to eat in order to survive. That is why each subject is more than merely a recipe with biographical notes taken from a file of clippings. Even the celebrities who look on cooking as a spectator sport talk with great zest of food, and their favorite dishes can be fun to make and create in any kitchen.

I feel I know people by their "foodprints" as well as if we took their fingerprints. I have found that people reveal their true feelings about themselves by what they eat, with a decided celebrity preference for fresh fruits and vegetables, less red meat, more fish. Stars seemed to discover good nutrition before the rest of us. Most also like simple foods, broiled, simmered, steamed, and they have a definite aversion to junk foods. Because of the long hours when they work, most have liberated themselves by using convenience equipment (crock pots, freezers, microwave ovens, etc.) to produce make-ahead dinners.

Above all, celebrities are sensitive to good food and service and enjoy the communion of eating with friends and family. Everyone stressed the importance of eating in a relaxed atmosphere. Typically, they would tell me, "I'd rather cook an egg for myself and eat alone in my dressing room or hotel than eat out in an elegant restaurant and be hounded by autograph seekers."

All the recipes of the stars I've talked to could not be included because of the limitation of space, but I believe the book is a good cross section of the people I interviewed. I have also tried not to duplicate dishes so that you would have a wide selection of recipes as well as a compendium of famous lifestyles and food views. Also, it should be noted that the interviews included here are presented the way they were at the time we talked. It's as if you were there, too, I hope. Some circumstances concerning certain celebrities may have changed – a change of residence or marital status. But these changes have not changed the person's foodprints, and to update each case would not only be a fruitless race with time, it would deny you the authenticity of the moment.

– Johna Blinn

# The Author

To the stars, Johna Blinn is herself a celebrity. Even the publicity-shy ones are happy to meet with her over a savory dish and disclose their innermost food loves, their secret lives at the range ... because she treats them as fascinating dinner companions, not as icons to be blasted and exploited.

Blinn, an expert in the culinary arts, kitchen-tests each recipe for accuracy and star quality. Thus you can count on serving a tasty dish with the one-up cachet: "This is Paul Newman's favorite salad!" or "Farrah Fawcett's 'pedigreed' sausage and peppers!"

Blinn is a former assistant food editor of *LOOK* magazine, an associate editor of *Forecast*, the professional magazine for home economists, and food editor of *American Weekend*. She wrote the first syndicated foreign food column which appeared in many papers here and abroad (*Yomiuri Shimbun, Toledo Blade, Montreal Gazette, Chicago Sun-Times, Washington Post, Boston Globe, Houston Post, Philadelphia Inquirer, St. Louis Post-Dispatch* and others). Her "Celebrity Cookbook" column is syndicated to more than 150 newspapers around the world by the Los Angeles Times Syndicate. She is the author of a number of books, including *The Shangri-la Cookbook*, and is currently at work on her first novel and screenplay.

A graduate of the State University of Iowa (B.A. in home economics), Blinn did graduate work at the University of Wisconsin and taught home economics in schools in Hampton, Virginia, Keokuk, Iowa and Long Island, New York.

She is married and the mother of two children. The family lives in Los Angeles.

# Contents

## DESSERTS

## HOLIDAYS

# Appetizers

# Eddie Albert

While I was lunching with actor Eddie Albert and his actress wife, Margo, she said, "If more people knew how to grow vegetables, picked them fresh, felt them, and arranged them like a still life, more people would realize how beautiful what they are eating really is. Instead of string beans that are limp and gray-green, they would be emerald, crisp and gorgeous!"

"Listen, I'll give you a recipe for an elixir that's a hell of a drink," Eddie said. "Get a mixer, take an egg and beat it in, shell and all."

"Don't scare people," his wife chided.

"But," continued Eddie, "it's really a tasty, delicious drink, very much like a thick malted milk. And the calcium from the shell is good for you. The egg should be organic. I have it for breakfast, and you can throw vitamins in there. And what you don't drink, you can put in the freezer."

Eddie's main concern with food is directly related to his concern for man's survival in our polluted environment. His latest project of creative excitement is the mini-garden program he has sponsored across the country. Under this program and with the cooperation of local recreation directors, children are given seeds and a plot of ground where they can grow their own vegetables in city-sponsored projects.

"Vegetables from a 15- by 20-foot plot can go a long way toward feeding a family," he added, "especially in the South, where they can grow more than one plot a year."

# Margo Albert's Guacamole

Makes about 2½ cups

1 small clove garlic,
    peeled
2 large, ripe avocados
1 small tomato, peeled,
    seeded and chopped (drain
    off any excess liquid)
2-3 tbsps. finely minced
    onion or scallions or
    chives
salt to taste

2 tbsps. farmers' cheese
    or small curd cottage
    cheese (optional)
about 1 tbsp. fine-grade
    olive oil or safflower oil
2 sprigs fresh coriander
    or ½ tsp. dried
    coriander
freshly ground black pepper
    to taste

1-2 Mexican chili peppers (the kind that come pickled
    in small bottles), seeds removed and finely minced

1. *Rub mixing bowl with garlic.*
2. *Peel and mash avocados with fork, but be sure you have small chunks of avocado left in bowl.*
3. *Add remaining ingredients and mix until guacamole is thick and light.*
4. *Serve at once with fried tortilla chips or as a dressing for green salad.*

*NOTE: Margo's guacamole is grainy and beautifully flavored. She advises, "Be certain each ingredient retains its character and texture so it can be seen as well as savored. Remove seeds from Mexican chili peppers, otherwise you will fly to the moon! For Texans, I sometimes add just a touch of chili powder." Guacamole can be made in advance, adding a few drops of lemon or lime juice to prevent it from turning dark. Cover tightly and chill before serving.*

# Lucille Ball

Lucille Ball does most of her cooking when she and her husband, Gary Morton, are in Aspen, Colorado, where they go to ski. "I like to cook there because of my nice, cozy kitchen. In Aspen, I can easily cook for 8, 9, even 10 people," she said, breaking into the dazzling smile that has bewitched millions on movie and TV screens for over four decades.

Seated in her pretty house in Beverly Hills, Lucy was looking even better than she does on the tube. "Listen," she said, leaning closer, "I cook – but Gary doesn't necessarily eat what I cook! Eating doesn't interest me all that much, but I like the warmth and nice feeling that comes from having something good to serve my family and friends. That's what's important to me about food."

Her antics in the kitchen were the source of many funny incidents in the well-loved "I Love Lucy" series. "I've pulled a lot of boners in the kitchen, like the time I cooked rice, using 1 cup of rice per person. It boiled all over the kitchen. There was enough rice for an army! We used that incident in one of the early 'Lucy' shows."

Lucy's cooking reflects her background. She lived much of her childhood with her grandparents near Jamestown, in upstate New York. "I make New England boiled dinners, legs of lamb, chicken, turkey, chops or baked potatoes." Lucy learned to cook from her mother and her maternal grandmother, Florabel Hunt. "My grandmother made everything from yellow corn bread to pies. She cooked and canned, and kept an orchard and a truck garden. My grandparents did all their own butchering, too."

Lucille Ball's energy and enthusiasm are amazing. "You cannot rely on your youthful energy," she said. "You must look ahead and build for the future with good eating and exercise, with the emphasis on good nutrition."

# Lucille Ball's Chopped Chicken Livers

Makes about 1½ cups

about ¼ cup chicken fat
½ lb. chicken livers, quartered
1 medium onion, peeled and
    finely minced
½ tsp. salt

¼ tsp. freshly ground pepper
2 hard-cooked eggs, yolks and
    whites minced separately
Melba rounds or whole
    wheat toast

1. *Melt chicken fat in large skillet.*
2. *Cook livers in hot fat about 8 minutes. Do not overcook livers, or they will get hard and unpalatable.*
3. *Lift livers from hot fat, drain, and cool to room temperature.*
4. *Chop livers with sharp knife, to the size of cornmeal.*
5. *Cook half the onion in the same fat livers have been cooked in until golden.*
6. *Add sautéed onion, remaining raw onion, salt and pepper to chopped livers. Mix well. Add more chicken fat if necessary to make mixture spreadable.*
7. *Arrange chopped liver on small serving dish. Put chopped egg white in center of separate dish; arrange yolks around white. Serve with thin rounds of Melba toast. Provide guests with spoons so they can add garnish of chopped eggs to appetizer.*

NOTE: *Lucy usually keeps a container of onion-flavored chicken fat in her refrigerator. But if she doesn't have any handy, she cooks the onion first in the chicken fat and then does the chicken livers. The mixture should be grainy in appearance, resembling cornmeal, rather than smooth, like a pâté.*

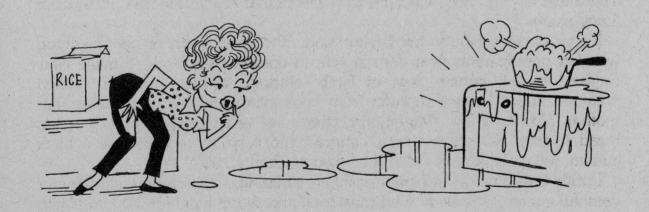

# LeVar Burton

"Roots" superstar LeVar Burton chatted happily in the sunny Malibu beach house of his personal manager. "I'm a magnet of positive energy," he laughed. "I suck it in. I draw on it. All the women in my family are great cooks – my grandmother, my mom and my two sisters. We always had lots of steak, potatoes, greens, cornbread. It's kinda the Southern thing, including fried chicken which I adore! I love deep-fried foods, especially shrimp. My mother makes shrimp in a special way by cooking them in beer. Every time I visit her, she fixes shrimp-fried rice.

"Some of my favorite foods are really bizarre. I like escargots and French foods. I try everything. I cook for myself – things like salads, eggs, steak and chicken. I love to deep-fry chicken. I throw everything I can find from the spice rack into the flour and shake it up. I make some of the best chili there is. I prefer more beef than beans, plus plenty of spices. I serve it over rice."

LeVar has no problems dealing with his own fame. "I still look at people the same way. I like people. The interactions between people are what makes life interesting and exciting."

# Le Var Burton's Shrimp Cooked in Beer

Serves 6

2 cans (12 ozs.) beer
2 bay leaves, crumbled
½ tsp. red peppers, crushed
½ tsp. cayenne or freshly
  ground black pepper

2 tbsps. mustard seed
1½ lbs. giant shrimp,
  shelled and deveined
¼ cup wine vinegar
1 large clove garlic,
  peeled

1. *In a saucepan, combine beer, bay leaves, seasonings.*
2. *Bring to boil and simmer 5 minutes.*
3. *Add shrimp and simmer 8-10 minutes or until shrimp turns pink.*
4. *Remove from heat. Add vinegar and garlic.*
5. *Let stand 30 minutes, then strain.*
6. *Chill well before serving. Great for appetizers!*

# Dyan Cannon

When Dyan Cannon throws a bash in her Malibu beach house, it's often a last-minute affair with plenty of good food, congenial company and the sounds of happy music! The pretty, three-bedroom, Spanish-style house is complete with swimming pool, warm open kitchen, hammock, colorful rugs from North Africa, myriads of comfortable pillows (so her guests can sit on the floor), and plenty of *vino* served up in huge blown glasses.

Dyan is a vegetarian, a real "raw-fooder," but she provides generous portions of chicken for her guests. Her housekeeper, Gabrielle, is a prize. "Food is my last great addiction!" Dyan said as she busily rolled sweet potato puffs between her fingers and covered them with pecans. Dyan seemed totally unperturbed by the fact that her guest list had stretched to include 18 people. "Gabrielle is a little worried and suggested that some of my guests bring along some pizza," Dyan said, with her ringing infectious laugh that seems to start deep in her body.

Dyan did a lot of cooking when she was married to actor Cary Grant, but these days, she is more interested in raw or health foods. "I've hated meat ever since I was a kid," she said. "My folks used to worry and pay me money to eat meat, but I couldn't keep it down. Just the idea of eating part of an animal's tongue or liver bothers me. I've really made a diligent study of food. Too many people treat their bodies like garbage cans; they just shovel in the food. I mean if you lifted that lid, just think of what you'd see! We should spend more time cleansing our bodies and less stuffing our faces!"

Dyan goes through periods during which she fasts. "I work better when I don't eat. My channels are clear." Her favorite fast is living on watermelon. "I wouldn't advise anyone to fast without a doctor's advice. But in my case, the weight comes off fast, and I feel marvelous because my body gets cleansed!"

# Dyan Cannon's Finger Lettuce Sandwiches

Makes 8 sandwiches

### For herbed dressing

4 tsps. olive oil
1½ tsps. vinegar
few drops fresh lemon juice

¼ tsp. dill weed
½ tsp. fresh basil, chopped
salt to taste

freshly ground pepper to taste

*Mix all ingredients thoroughly by shaking them vigorously in a glass jar with a tight screw top.*

### For the sandwiches

8 crisp romaine leaves
2 small ripe tomatoes,
   peeled and sliced

black olive rings
½ ripe avocado, peeled and
   cut in small pieces

1. *Arrange romaine leaves on a large serving platter.*
2. *Alternate tomato, avocado and olive rings on each leaf to form a decorative pattern.*
3. *Drizzle a few drops of herbed dressing over each lettuce leaf.*
4. *Pick up leaves in fingers to eat. Serve as buffet food or great with cocktails!*

# Phyllis Diller

Comedienne Phyllis Diller describes herself as a "gourmet cook," then added, "People come to my house and they just don't believe it. I serve a buffet every three days to get rid of all the food."

The "gourmet cook" was eating a typical dinner (spinach, cream of tomato soup and milk) as we talked. She seasoned the soup liberally with her favorite condiments: cracked black pepper, seasoned salt and grated Parmesan cheese. "I put Parmesan cheese in everything," she said. "In fact, I cook it into soup." Nearly a vegetarian, Phyllis relies on eggs "almost any way – the phosphorus is good for the brain." She likes Camembert or Liederkrantz cheese in lieu of meat.

Phyllis' secret passion is soup. "I adore soup for breakfast because a hot fluid is so nourishing in the morning." Her devotion to vegetables is attributable to their longevity properties. Her culinary achievements include deviled eggs, chili, Italian spaghetti and "garbage soup." The latter, a Diller invention, is so named because she says, "It calls for leftovers and I hate waste." Her favorite cuisine is Polynesian food. She said, "I adore tiny bits of meat but not a great big cow."

Her biggest complaint regarding food is, "After years of being on the road, every menu in America is alike. It's either lobster or steak, and I hate steak." Her favorite drink is vodka mixed with fruit juices, particularly a "salty dog" (vodka and grapefruit juice served in a glass frosted with salt). She proudly displayed two albums of herbs and seasonings sent by her children to liven up her meals on the road.

# Phyllis Diller's Stuffed Mushrooms

Serves 4-6 as hors d'oeuvres

3 tbsps. onions, minced
1/4 clove garlic, minced
1/2 tsp. butter
1 can (4 1/2 ozs.) deviled
  ham
2 tbsps. Parmesan cheese,
  grated

2 tbsps. bread crumbs
1 egg yolk, beaten
2 1/2 tbsps. parsley, chopped
pinch freshly ground pepper
1/8 tsp. seasoned salt
12 mushrooms
paprika

1. *Sauté onion and garlic in butter over very low heat until onion is transparent. Stir often.*
2. *Combine remaining ingredients except mushrooms and paprika. Add onion mixture.*
3. *Remove stems from cleaned mushrooms. Fill caps with ham mixture. Dust tops with paprika.*
4. *Place in a greased pan and bake at 375° F. 15-20 minutes, or until mushrooms are tender.*

# Farrah Fawcett

"I love to cook," actress Farrah Fawcett said, nibbling on a chicken leg. "Sunday nights, I fix chicken or a roast, make a salad and cook some kind of vegetable – broccoli, for instance. I don't usually make sauces for my vegetables, not because they take more time, but because I've found I don't seem to want rich food anymore."

Farrah learned how to cook in Houston, where she was born and raised. "Basically, I'm a Southern cook. I love to make chicken-fried steak, baking powder biscuits and red-eye gravy. I only use a cookbook for certain types of cooking. I'm experimental when it comes to seasonings. For example, I don't particularly like nutmeg or cinnamon, so if a recipe calls for one of them, I'll substitute curry powder or oregano.

"Dinah Shore's cookbook, *Someone's in the Kitchen with Dinah,* is my favorite. She's one of the world's greatest cooks – I particularly like her Italian recipes. One night, she fixed sausages and peppers and they were delicious! She originally got the recipe from Frank Sinatra, who gave it to her while they were driving to the airport. It's the best thing! It can be an appetizer or a main dish. I'm getting hungry just talking about it!"

Watching Farrah munch on sunflower seeds, a hunk of cheese and a slab of carrot cake, one had to wonder why this elegantly slim creature wasn't as wide as a barrel. "Oh, I never watch my weight. With the long hours I work, I burn it all off. I'm a garbage disposal," she said cheerfully. "I eat everything!"

# Farrah Fawcett's "Pedigreed" Sausage and Peppers

### Serves 4

3 large, green bell peppers
3 tbsps. olive oil
¾ cup dry red wine

salt to taste
freshly ground pepper to taste
1 lb. hot Italian pork sausages

1. *Wash peppers and remove stem ends and seeds. Cut into large chunks.*
2. *Pour olive oil into an oven-proof, flameproof baking dish.*
3. *Sauté pepper chunks in olive oil until they begin to soften.*
4. *Sprinkle with salt and pepper to taste.*
5. *Remove peppers from dish and set aside.*
6. *Brown sausages in same dish used for peppers.*
7. *Add wine and cover. Bake in preheated 350° F. oven 40 minutes.*
8. *Uncover and add sautéed green peppers. Bake 30 minutes longer.*
9. *Serve at once in the same baking dish.*
10. *Delicious as an appetizer or as a main dish, served alone or with hunks of Italian bread spread with butter, plus tossed green salad and dry red wine.*

# Leonard Frey

"Oh, world, give me some sun," actor-clown-chef Leonard Frey sang, peering skyward as we "coffee'ed" at a sidewalk café near New York's Lincoln Center. Leonard was rehearsing nearby at the Beaumont Theatre.

"How did you celebrate birthdays as a kid?" I asked. "Was it an affair of the heart?"

"Usually my parents took me to the Statue of Liberty," he answered succinctly. "That was the first woman I was ever in love with – the tall, but very strong type. I get very attracted to that kind of woman."

I had questioned him about birthday celebrations because he's the famous birthday boy in the movie *The Boys in the Band*.

Leonard grew up in the Flatbush section of Brooklyn, the son of a food wholesaler. "My brother is now in the business too, so it's Charles Frey & Son. My brother turned into a fantastic cook. He only does the hard stuff. He made a beef Wellington a couple of weeks ago when I was over there that was better than any I had in England. One Christmas he cooked a goose. He filled it with oranges, nuts, rice. Ummm. . . . There's nothing better in the world than goin' in an English pub around lunch time. Some very crisp-lookin' lady is always behind the bar. For lunch they put a spankin' white cloth on the bar. You can get a beautiful slab of cold roast beef – it's so bloody rare, with a little care you can revive the damn thing. That, plus a Scotch egg (hard-boiled eggs done up a crusty kind of a thing) and some very crisp, beautiful salad came to about $1.20."

# Leonard Frey's Scotch Eggs

Makes 8 halved eggs

4 hard-cooked eggs
3 ozs. mild-flavored fresh
   pork sausage, in bulk
pinch fresh parsley, minced
few gratings freshly ground
   pepper

¼ tsp. lemon rind, finely
   grated
pinch dried sage, thyme
   or savory
1 egg, beaten
fine breadcrumbs

vegetable oil

1. *Strip shells from hard-cooked eggs. Set eggs aside.*
2. *Combine sausage, parsley, pepper, lemon rind and sage. Mix well.*
3. *Roll out on lightly floured board. Divide into four portions.*
4. *Enclose each hard-cooked egg in seasoned meat mixture, dip in beaten egg, and coat in breadcrumbs.*
5. *Cook in oil until crisp and golden.*
6. *Serve whole, or slice in half across the center. Place each half on a piece of fried toast.*
7. *Serve as an appetizer, a savory (a salty tidbit consumed by the English in lieu of dessert), or a supper dish.*

*NOTE: Leonard's favorite "pub fare" can be made many ways: with forcemeat (ground ham, minced suet, lemon rind, breadcrumbs, parsley and sweet herbs) or pounded anchovies. For a supper dish, eggs can be oven-browned and served with an herb-flavored tomato sauce.*

# Joel Grey

"I don't think I'm an exceptionally good cook. Often I do some good things, and often they're mistakes!" said Joel Grey, appraising his cooking improvisations.

A pint-sized actor, with gargantuan talent, Joel looked like a jolly Hummel figure, gowned in a floor-length sapphire blue velvet caftan, created by his next door neighbor in Malibu, where Joel, his actress wife, Jo Wilder, and their two children live.

Joel thrives on change, like his exchange of New York living for California. He explained, "We're still New Yorkers, but for this period of our lives we're refreshed by the change in environment."

Mexican cooking (Joel's favorite) is easier in California, too. "We can get fresh flour tortillas. I make tostados, fried on both sides in raw, sweet churned butter. Adele Davis' favorite dairy just happens to deliver to us so we have all the raw milk and sweet butter we can use. I use a special 12-inch *cazuela* (casserole) pan. Say, if you have a wok and *cazuela* pan, then life's a cabaret!" he said, laughing wickedly.

"Sorry about that. If I were going to have my *last* supper, it would be Chinese. I'd have stuffed lettuce leaves! Whatever ability I have in cooking comes from mother, who's a genuis with cooking, Chinese or otherwise. One of my favorite Chinese recipes is curried chicken, because I love Indian food too. I serve it with cold bean sprouts, a little rice vinegar and coarse salt, that's all. Those ten-course things are not for me."

# Joel Grey's Tostados

Serves 4-6

## For the guacamole

1 medium-sized, very ripe
    avocado
1 small, ripe tomato, peeled
    and finely chopped
½ small onion, very finely
    grated
few drops oil from pressed
    garlic, more if desired

1 tsp. juice from canned
    Jalapeño chiles
about 1 tsp. salt
½ tsp. fresh lemon juice
½ tsp. fresh lime juice
1 tbsp. chili powder
ground coriander, to taste

1. Mash avocado with fork.
2. Add other ingredients to make a paste, but not too smooth. If you want to make it ahead of time, put avocado seed in spread to keep it from turning brown, wrap tightly with foil, and refrigerate until ready to use.

## For the tostados

6 12-inch fresh flour tortillas
    (available in Mexican
    foodshops, otherwise
    use frozen or canned)
sweet butter

½ lb. Monterey Jack cheese,
    cut in julienne strips
1 can (4 ozs.) roasted,
    peeled green chili peppers
dairy sour cream, chilled

1. Lightly brown tortillas in melted butter on flat griddle; turn and brown on other side.
2. Lift out from pan; drain well on absorbent paper.
3. Arrange layer of cheese on half of half-cooked tortillas.
4. Drain chiles; remove most of seed from chiles, leaving a few to give a peppery taste.
5. Cut chiles into strips; arrange on top of cheese strips and roll up.
6. Brown stuffed tortillas on heated griddle over medium heat until crispy and cheese is nice and gooey on the inside.
7. Cut with pizza cutter or sharp knife.
8. Serve with gaucamole with a dab of sour cream on top.
9. Serve at once as appetizer or as midday snack with Margueritas or Mexican beer.

# Ken Howard

Actor Ken Howard of TV's "White Shadow" says he and his wife, Margo, happily share the cooking chores. "I'm kind of a good cook," he said. "I can do everything except the delicacies. Margo excels at anything 'cooked under glass.'"

The towering ex-basketball player got into cooking after he married Margo and inherited a ready-made family. Margo, the daughter of syndicated columnist Ann Landers, with three children from a previous marriage, is currently hard at work on a book about her mother and aunt, Abigail ("Dear Abby") Van Buren.

"I knew about cooking before, but never did it," Ken explained. "This seems to be part of us. We're so well-matched."

Ken's cooking repertoire consists of leftovers, breakfast and ham-and-cheese on rye or "deli" foods. "Margo's great with caviar mousse or caviar pie. She makes a terrific cold rice salad with kasha. For main dishes, she makes incredible manicotti or fantastic lemon garlic chicken. It's always something she throws together in a hurry."

The Howards like to entertain simply, preferably one couple at a time. They enjoy their life, secluded in their house, which sits behind a large garden gate. "We hide," Ken said. "Pacific Palisades is a beautiful place. I can even pretend I'm in New Hampshire."

Their most frequent guests are actress Blythe Danner and her writer-producer husband, Bruce Paltrow. It was Bruce who suggested that Ken play a basketball coach. "Someone you can relate to," he told Ken. Bruce wrote the pilot script and worked with Ken to create the role of "White Shadow," a nickname given to Ken when he starred as the only white player on a champion basketball team for Manhasset High School on Long Island.

# Caviar Pie, House of Ken Howard

Makes 12-14 hors d'oeuvres

8 hard-boiled eggs, shelled
¾ stick butter, melted
3 cans (1 oz.) fresh caviar

½ cup white onion or
   scallions, chopped
½ cup dairy sour cream

1. *Put hard-boiled eggs through strainer or food machine.*
2. *Combine eggs with melted butter.*
3. *Cool to room temperature, then press into a 9-inch pie plate.*
4. *Freeze 1 hour.*
5. *When ready to serve, spread egg-butter crust evenly with caviar, sprinkle evenly with chopped onion, and frost with sour cream.*

*NOTE: Margo suggests, "This makes an unusual appetizer. It can be expensive if you use the finest quality caviar. Choose a less expensive grade."*

# Fernando Lamas &
# Esther Williams

Fernando Lamas claims to be a gourmet, but not a cook. He has, however, taught his wife, beautiful Esther Williams, how to cook, particularly Italian and Spanish specialties.

"I'm a spectator cook," he said. "I can tell you how to make certain Spanish or Italian dishes because I hung around the kitchen when I was a kid." Dressed casually in an open-neck knitted shirt and matching slacks, Fernando said his role of cooking coach began when he married Esther Williams in 1961. Esther, who never claimed expertise in the kitchen, was a "stew girl" from Inglewood, California, until her encounter with the "Argentinean gourmet."

Their joint culinary efforts began with mastering *crêpes suzettes*. "Esther makes them magnificently now. *Crêpes* must be so thin that you're able to see through them. At first, hers were like a round cushion you sit on," Fernando said with a straight face. "I ate them, saying, 'They're very good.' The next time she made them, it was like eating half a cushion. We kept progressing until now they're incredible. It's the same with everything she prepares. When we moved to Europe, Esther learned to make wonderful pasta. Italian food is my favorite. That's what I call soul food — something you eat and your teeth fall out on the table because it's so strong and marvelous."

This Argentinean gourmet is cunning in the way he gets his wife to prepare his favorite dishes. "I have to encourage her. Otherwise, she'd quit on me," he said slyly. "She's very good at a tricky thing made in Latin America and Spain called *empañadas*. They are little, half-moon-shaped cakes. The secret is to make the dough very thin. With all her strength as a swimmer, she still swims 50 laps every day. Esther's great with a rolling pin."

# Esther Williams's Empañadas

Makes 20

## For the pastry

scant cup all-purpose flour
½ tsp. baking powder

1½ tsps. sugar
½ tsp. salt

3 tbsps. butter, melted

1 egg
¼ cup sherry

1. In a bowl, mix togther flour, baking powder, sugar, salt.
2. Make a well in center; add egg, sherry, melted butter.
3. Mix quickly with spatula, forming smooth dough.
4. Knead lightly on lightly floured board. Cover and refrigerate 1 hour.

## For the filling

1 small clove garlic, mashed
1 lb. lean ground beef
1 medium onion, peeled and
  finely chopped
1-2 tbsps. olive oil
1 medium green pepper, finely
  chopped
1 medium tomato, finely chopped

salt to taste
black pepper to taste
pinch of oregano
pinch of basil
2 hard-cooked eggs, finely chopped
½ cup raisins
1 egg white, beaten
safflower oil for deep fat frying

1. Sauté garlic, beef and onion in olive oil until beef begins to turn light.
2. Add green pepper, tomato, seasonings and herbs, stir-cooking over low heat for few minutes.
3. Add hard-cooked eggs and raisins. Heat through.
4. Skim off and discard fat that forms on top. Mixture should be dry.
5. Cool; refrigerate 1 hour.
6. Roll out dough to ¼-inch thickness on lightly floured board.
7. Using coffee can lid for cutter, cut out rounds and lay them carefully on waxed paper.
8. Cover circles with additional waxed paper to prevent drying.
9. Lightly brush circles with egg white.
10. Place a spoonful of cold filling in center of each circle. Spread evenly; fold over to form crescent. Dab fingers with cold water; press and seal edges.
11. Heat oil to 375° F. and drop in empañadas. Cook 3 minutes or until golden brown and puffy. Turn them over and cook.
12. Remove carefully with slotted spoon and drain on absorbent paper. Serve piping hot, lightly dusted with grated Parmesan cheese and red wine.

# Liza Minnelli

An over-sized, over-fed, nondescript dog sprawled on the deep, plush carpet in the green and gold suite at the Waldorf, his well-gnawed bone lying under the couch.

Then Liza, in sweater and slacks, entered, clutching a guitar under her arm. "I've just come from the second half of my second guitar lesson!" she proudly announced. She greeted her canine companion, offered me a choice of refreshments and expertly whipped up her own chocolate soda from the generous scoop of chocolate ice cream in a nest of shaved ice. "This is my secret for bad skin," she said, grinning. "I've had a terrible sweet tooth. I can talk if you think it doesn't sound too awful!"

The dog jumped into Liza's lap while she kicked off her shoes and crossed her legs, assuming a Buddha position. "My mother (the late, legendary Judy Garland) taught me to cook. She used to love to cook. She cooked everything from shepherd's pie to chocolate soufflé and big pot roasts. I love Hungarian spices very much and Yugoslavian food. I know it sounds strange, but I love thyme and rosemary on meats. And dill in salads is great. I love savory foods! I love comfort foods!"

Liza is well known for her *pièces de resistance* and often cooks elaborately. She excels at soufflés, particularly the Grand Marnier variety. "I love orange flavor. It's delicious in cooking. Cherry brandy-kirsch is good on meats like veal chops, braised with kirsch in a cream sauce. Or steak done with mustard sauce and kirsch is really good. But you see what happens is when you burn it, the alcohol goes out and only the flavor remains."

A culinary contribution made by Otto Preminger is one that Liza describes as "something that's fun to do and so good! It's potato shells stuffed with sour cream, spiked with caviar and a nuance of vodka. You eat it like a hot dog."

# Liza Minnelli's Potato Shells

Makes 8

4 small long, slender baking
  potatoes
about 4 tsps. sweet butter
salt to taste

1 cup dairy sour cream
  (more if needed)
4 tbsps. caviar
1 jigger vodka

freshly ground pepper to taste

1. *Scrub and dry potatoes. Rub skins lightly with fat.*
2. *Bake in preheated 425° F. oven about 1¼ hours, or until inside is soft and skin is crunchy.*
3. *Cut potatoes in half lengthwise. Remove about half of the potato, put ½ tsp. butter in each shell with a light sprinkling of salt and freshly ground pepper.*
4. *Fill each shell with sour cream. Top with 1 tbsp. caviar and sprinkle with vodka.*
5. *Serve at once as finger food to go with cocktails.*

NOTE: *Liza's potato shells can be made as a dinner accompaniment by removing all the potato, flavoring it with butter, salt and pepper, then restuffing and double baking it before adding sour cream, caviar and vodka.*

# Carroll O'Connor

Actor-writer Carroll O'Connor's idea of a terrific evening "is relaxing over dinner with some of my writer pals like Hal Holbrook."

The ruddy-faced gentleman with the liquid-green eyes, who the world knows best as Archie Bunker of CBS-TV's "All in the Family," grew up in New York and is a man of many talents. He writes, sings, speaks four languages, and loves the life he shares with his wife, Nancy, and their son in their Italian-styled house in Westwood, California.

"I wouldn't say I'm a cook, but I can roast a bird if someone else prepares the stuffing," said Carroll. "Or I can roast a loin of pork or beef roast. I just learned by watching the women around the house doing it and helping out occasionally."

Most of Carroll's eclectic taste in food was cultivated when he and Nancy lived abroad in Ireland and Italy. "I like the food in Ireland in certain selected places like the Royal Hibernian and the Shelbourne, but their everyday cooking is not memorable. They overcook their vegetables. I like how the Italians cook their vegetables *al dente*."

Carroll rates his wife as "a very good cook. Nancy prepares many veal dishes or a lot of things with chicken or fowl. I don't like duck, but I love her turkey divan. She's very good with fish like abalone or red snapper. We enjoy entertaining at home, but don't like big parties. Our dinner parties are for eight, or no more than ten people at the most. Nancy does a lot of brunches. Sometimes our brunches go on until three in the morning! Our guests never go home, but it's fun and we have a good time! Nancy usually has a buffet with two or three hot things."

# Carroll O'Connor's Tarragon Mushrooms

### Serves 6

1 lb. fresh mushrooms
1½ cups dairy sour cream
2 tbsps. fresh lemon juice
1 tbsp. onion, finely grated

1½ tsps. tarragon leaves,
  crumbled
1½ tsp. salt
¼ tsp. ground white pepper

1. *Rinse, pat dry, and halve fresh mushrooms.*
2. *Combine the rest of the ingredients. Add to mushrooms and toss to coat.*
3. *Cover and refrigerate at least 1 hour.*
4. *Serve on lettuce leaves, if desired. Serve as an appetizer or salad.*

# Danny Thomas

"A candy butcher was a title or expression for people or young kids who sold refreshments years ago in burlesque theaters, carnivals or circuses," said Danny Thomas, the forlorn-faced comedian with the famous nickle-pickle nose, recalling his first taste of show biz. He waved a jumbo-sized cigar as if it were a baton and explained how candy butchery led to his becoming the "bologna" man, and inevitably, the funnyman.

Danny, who was headlining at Irving and Marge Cowan's Diplomat Hotel in Hollywood, Florida, recalled his days as a bologna buff in Rochester, New York. "When I went to the Gaiety Theater in Rochester, I was still in knee-pants. I was 13 years old and applied for the job as a candy butcher. So this fella gave me a chance, and I ate bologna and buns and drank a pint of milk for lunch every day that entire school year. Working in burlesque, I, subliminally, was educated for my business today. I still like bologna."

The Thomases have homes in Palm Springs and Beverly Hills. "Without my wife, I'm really a bum," he said. "Years ago Rose Marie was upset when she heard the plans to entertain the General Foods people at a posh hotel in Beverly Hills, followed by dinner at Chasens. She remembered that when her father was a worker at the Ford plant in Detroit, you didn't *take* your boss out for dinner, but you brought him to your home. Within a day and half, she'd made plans and had dinner in our home for 50 people. And although it was a catered affair, she prepared all the appetizers."

Despite Rose Marie's natural leanings toward ravioli and other Italian dishes, she has mastered many Middle Eastern dishes.

# Danny Thomas's Lamb Pies

Makes 6½ dozen

## For the dough

1 pkg. (¼ oz.) active dry yeast
dash sugar
2½ to 3 cups lukewarm water

about 8 cups unsifted all-purpose
flour
1 tbsp. salt

3 tbsps. olive oil or vegetable oil

1. Sprinkle yeast and sugar over ½ cup of the water and stir until dissolved. Set aside for 5 minutes.
2. Mix flour and salt in large bowl. Make a well in the center, add yeast mixture, olive oil and remaining water. Mix well, adding more water if needed. Dough should be rather stiff.
3. Knead dough on lightly floured surface until smooth and elastic.
4. Place in large oiled bowl, turn over dough, and cover with damp towel.
5. Let rise in warm place until doubled in bulk, about 1½ hours.

## For the lamb filling

3 lbs. ground lean (uncooked)
　lamb
4 medium-size onions, minced
⅔ cup yogurt
⅔ cup fresh lemon juice

¾ cup pine nuts, sautéed
　lightly in butter
2 tsps. salt
¼ tsp. freshly ground pepper
dash allspice

1. Mix all ingredients in bowl and chill while dough is rising.
2. Divide dough into four parts. Roll out each part on a lightly floured board until it is about ⅛ inch thick.
3. Cut dough into 3-inch rounds. Place a heaping tablespoon of lamb filling in the center of each round. Wet edge of dough with water, bring dough up over meat filling, and pinch edges together to form a triangle. Leave a small opening on top.
4. Place meat pies on oiled, foil-lined baking sheets. Brush with oil.
5. Bake in preheated 375° F. oven 40 minutes, or until golden brown. Serve warm.

NOTE: Dough may be rerolled if it's first allowed to rise again. If there is any lamb filling left, shape into balls and brown in butter or vegetable oil.

# Soups & Salads

# Edward Albee

Edward Albee is a playwright, composer, painter and a fine cook! His food tastes, like his plays, are subtle, unusual, and subject to a change of theme. Whereas he used to entertain his friends at small dinners based on French *haute cuisine* in the posh townhouse he owned in Greenwich Village, he now prefers the simple fare he creates in his Walden-type home in Montauk, Long Island. "I like anything delicate," said Edward. "I invented a great soup the other day. It's a combination of several things and is, in a way, related to one of those Chinese clear soups."

Edward's been known to create a beautiful omelet for friends (taught to him by the "omelet king," Rudy Standish) and other excellent fare. "I do *sashimi* (Japanese raw fish dressed with soy sauce, ginger root and seaweed) a good bit. I'm very fond of Japanese food. It's immensely subtle, sophisticated but simple. I prefer it to most Chinese food, except for some of the Northern Chinese cooking. I use white fish most of the time because I don't eat red meat. It's too heavy and it's not good for you. That, plus the fact that you get beautiful fresh fish out there, and fresh garden vegetables, makes Japanese cooking a simple, healthy way to eat. You don't fill yourself up with nonsense things like, for example, sandwiches."

# Edward Albee's Chicken-Tomato Soup

Serves 4-6

1 lb. chicken parts
2 scallions
1 piece fresh ginger root,
   2-inches long
1 chicken carcass
1 tsp. salt
2 quarts water

1 large beefsteak tomato,
   peeled, seeded, and
   chopped very fine
½ oz. bonito flakes, shaved
   and dried
½ oz. dried *daikon*
   (Japanese radish)

soy sauce to taste

1. *Wash chicken parts, slice into pieces.*
2. *Chop scallions and ginger into thin, 1-inch-long pieces.*
3. *Place chicken, carcass, scallions, ginger, salt and water in large saucepan. Bring to a boil; reduce heat and simmer about 1 hour, or until chicken is tender. Skim fat off the surface several times as it simmers.*
4. *Cool, cover and chill to remove layer of fat that congeals on the surface. Strain through cloth to obtain clear broth.*
5. *Reheat. Add tomato, bonito flakes, daikon (hydrate in water according to package instructions, drain well and cut in small pieces), and soy sauce to taste.*
6. *Heat through, stirring until soup simmers long enough for flavors to blend, about 15 minutes.*
7. *Serve at once for luncheon or for first course of dinner.*

NOTE: *Edward's soup is a beautiful color, subtle and delicious in flavor, and a boon for dieters! Dried bonito flakes (called* hanagatsuo, *available in small packages) and dried* daikon, *the Japanese white radish (sold packaged as* seengiri-daikon), *are easily obtainable in Oriental food shops or through mail-order houses.*

# Fred Astaire

"People didn't know the word cholesterol when I was growing up. We didn't know about vitamins, either. Nowadays, everyone talks about cholesterol. They're afraid to look a chicken in the eye and they don't dare think about eating an egg for fear their hearts will stop beating. That's a lot of nonsense!" said Fred Astaire, flashing his famous lopsided grin. Seated in the den of his handsome modern house in Beverly Hills, Fred looked exactly like he looks on the screen: lithe, athletic and trim. "I think everyone eats far too much."

When he's working, Fred often totes his lunch to the studio in a brown paper bag and carries a Thermos of hot soup. "I like to have a sandwich or a cup of soup, but I never have lunch if I have any work to do in the afternoon. It bogs me down. In fact, I sometimes go without eating altogether. I think it's healthy."

Fred rarely entertains because "good cooks are hard to find." He enjoys being at home, however, and likes to play billiards with his cronies at the huge billiard table in his den.

When his wife, Phyllis, was alive, they often entertained at small dinner parties at home. Fred claims he never goes near the kitchen. "I suppose I could boil an egg or make some consommé from a cube if I had to," he said with a laugh. His mother, who died in 1975 at the age of 96, was a good cook. "She was amazing!" he said. "She made everything from scratch, including the noodles for her wonderful soup." Fred still likes soup prepared the way his mother fixed it, very carefully in the old-fashioned way. "I like simple foods best. I love chicken noodle soup and chicken pie."

# Fred Astaire's Chicken Soup with Homemade Noodles

Serves 6-8

## For the noodles

½ tsp. salt
2 eggs, slightly beaten

2 scant cups unsifted all-purpose flour

1. *Add salt to eggs; add eggs to flour. Mix thoroughly with wooden spoon until dough leaves the sides of the bowl. (Dough should be fairly stiff.)*
2. *Turn out on lightly floured board; knead lightly until smooth and elastic.*
3. *Roll out dough with floured rolling pin to ⅛-inch thickness. Let dough stand until noodle sheet feels dry, about 30 minutes.*
4. *Use a sharp knife to cut dough into narrow strips. Cut a few at a time, tossing lightly to separate strands. Allow to dry completely, about 1 hour, before storing in covered glass jar or plastic bag.*
5. *When ready to use, drop in rapidly boiling salted water or soup. Cook about 10 minutes.*

## For the soup

1 plump dressed chicken, weighing 4 to 5 lbs.
2 cleaned chicken feet (optional)
about 4 quarts water

8 peppercorns, bruised
2 cloves
1 small yellow onion, peeled and chopped
1 tbsp. salt

6-8 sprigs parsley
2 stalks celery
2 bay leaves
2 eggs (with shells)
1 tbsp. ice water

1. *Wash chicken; cut into serving pieces. Scald and skin chicken feet.*
2. *Put chicken and feet in cold water; bring to a boil. Skim thoroughly.*
3. *Simmer until chicken is tender, about 1½ hours.*
4. *Add remaining ingredients except eggs and ice water. Cook 15 minutes.*
5. *Strain and cool. Remove and discard chicken feet, reserve chicken. Refrigerate until ready to use.*
6. *Remove layer of congealed chicken fat that forms on the top; reserve fat for cooking or flavoring liver pâté.*
7. *Reheat broth and clarify by adding 2 beaten eggs and broken eggshells to the stock. Place over low heat and stir constantly until the broth is simmering. Boil 2 minutes.*
8. *Add 1 tbsp. ice water; set aside for 10 minutes. Then strain through a double thickness of cheesecloth placed over a fine strainer.*
9. *Reheat broth, adding noodles; simmer until noodles are cooked. Taste soup to correct seasonings.*

# George Burns

"My diet is simple: I eat anything that makes a noise in my mouth – bacon, carrot sticks or cottage-fried potatoes! If it makes a noise, I feel like there's applause, and as I eat, I can take bows!" said George Burns, the amazing octogenarian with a huge appetite for life. We chatted in the comfortable family room of the Beverly Hills home where he has lived for over 40 years.

"Ya wanna know what else I like to eat?" he said, leaning closer, peering through his glasses. "I like food that you can eat with a spoon. If you've got to cut food with a knife, you should get paid for eating it! My food has always got to be stove-hot. I always tell the waiter, 'If you can carry the food in, I don't want it!' That's how I like my food."

George admits that his late wife, the beloved Gracie Allen, was not the best cook in the world. "When we first worked together, she made spaghetti for my brother Willie and me. She was in love with another fellow and he wanted to marry her. She put hot white peppers in the spaghetti, like my mother used to, only my mother would put in only four peppers and leave them whole – you know how hot they are! Gracie put in eight peppers and split them in half. When we tasted that spaghetti, there was smoke coming out of our ears! Willie said, 'You have to eat it or Gracie will marry the other guy!' It was the worse meal I ever had, but I ate ever bit of it!"

George is well cared for by his Belgian cook, Arlette, and her husband. "Now I like soup! Arlette makes delicious chicken soup with rice and thin tomato-rice soup and great vegetable soup."

George eats his main meal at night. "I like to have steak, hamburger or broiled fish. I'm not keen on vegetables, but I like endive or asparagus salads. I don't like fresh asparagus, but I do like canned white asparagus, served ice cold with a nice French dressing."

# Chicken Vegetable Soup, House of George Burns

Serves 6

2 lbs. chicken parts: breasts,
   thighs or drumsticks
5 cups water
1 tbsp. salt
4 celery stalks with leaves
1 small onion, peeled and sliced
3 whole cloves or 1 small
   carrot, peeled and sliced

4 whole peppercorns
1 tbsp. fresh parsley, minced
⅓ cup rice
¼ lb. mushrooms, sliced
1 cup cooked green peas or
   broccoli spears or raw
   spinach leaves (cleaned,
   drained, and torn into bite-
   sized pieces)

1. *Place chicken pieces in deep pot with water, salt, celery, onion, cloves, peppercorns and parsley. Cover, simmer 1 hour or until chicken is tender.*
2. *Remove chicken. Strain broth, discarding vegetables.*
3. *Cool chicken slightly and remove meat from bones. Cut into strips. (If broth and chicken are not used immediately, cover and refrigerate.)*
4. *Bring stock to boil. Add rice, chicken strips, and mushrooms; cook 10 minutes. Add peas. Cook until vegetables are heated through.*
5. *Taste to adjust seasoning. Serve at once.*

*NOTE: This soup is excellent for the dieter! Remove congealed fat that forms on broth when it is refrigerated. If desired, dish can be expanded into a complete meal; leave chicken in large pieces and add more vegetables. Soup is also terrific as a first course before broiled fish or roast leg of lamb and a simple dessert of fruit and cookies.*

# Art Carney

"When I get home from work, I like to kick off the shoes, don slacks and sport shirt, and just be informal," Art Carney said. "I wouldn't put on a necktie for the King of England!" And, as he introduced his attractive wife, Barbara, he added, "We don't have formal dinner parties. I want to give people what they like to eat. I don't want to make a big thing out of it. Above all, I don't want to make people feel uncomfortable."

Sometimes, Art Carney doubles as cook and host. "I'm not exactly what you'd call a chef. I used to fool around the kitchen. In fact, I like to toss a few salads."

The Carneys' friends are not limited to the entertainment arts. "It's more relaxing to have friends outside show biz. There are other things people want to talk about, like Pittsburg Plate Glass, the traffic, the forest and the trees, babies or old people," he said with a straight face.

Basically, the Carneys are steak lovers, Barbara said. Art has typical American food tastes. "In Florida," he said, "I liked the pompano, grouper or stone crab in mustard or butter sauce." A fish lover, he praised the oyster stew he found at the Oyster Bar in Grand Central Station and New England clam chowder. He believes there is truly a genuine American cuisine of ham and steak, hot dogs and French fries and hash browns.

# Art Carney's Avocado-Grapefruit-Endive Salad

Serves 4

### For the sour cream dressing

7 tbsps. salad oil
3 tbsps. dairy sour cream
1 tbsp. wine vinegar

salt to taste
freshly ground pepper
  to taste

1. *Add salad oil to sour cream, 1 tablespoon at a time. Mix well.*
2. *Add vinegar. Blend well.*
3. *Add seasonings. Set aside.*

### For the salad

2 white grapefruits
2 avocados, ripe but firm
1 wedge lemon or lime

2 endives
several sprigs fresh dill,
  chopped

1. *Peel and section grapefruits, removing outer skin.*
2. *Peel avocados, cut in small pieces, and squeeze with lemon to prevent fruit from turning brown.*
3. *Wash endive carefully and shake well in salad basket to dry thoroughly. Discard any discolored leaves.*
4. *Arrange grapefruit sections, avocados and endive in large salad bowl. Pour sour cream dressing over all. Garnish with dill. Serve at once.*

# Joanne Carson

"I tried to learn how to cook when I first married Johnny", said Joanne Carson, referring to her marriage to Johnny Carson. "Johnny always said, 'I didn't marry Betty Crocker!'

"A Betty Crocker, I'm not. I would copy a recipe from the book, look at the picture of the dish and make my own version. There was no way those two even looked like they were the same animal! Finally, I got so discouraged I just gave up!"

Joanne makes up for her cooking failures by her enthusiasm. She said her present cooking repertoire is still limited to meat loaf and steaks. "I've always been very safe with that. I even managed to do very good Swiss steak at one time, but finally Johnny said, 'Enough of the Swiss steak.' He said he didn't need the flour in his coffee either. He used to walk out in the morning, turn on the fan and the flour would blow all over the kitchen.

"After I dropped the Swiss steak from the menu, I was down to two dishes, plus barbecued chicken I used to get at the delicatessen downstairs when we lived in New York. I could cheat with that. And I was great with frozen food. I only had to turn on the oven. Johnny would come home at night and ask, 'What did you defrost tonight for dinner?'

"I still get very nervous in the kitchen because once I was burned trying to make fried chicken. We were in the boat and I had on my bikini and was frying chicken. The chicken dropped and spattered me, and I got third-degree burns. Cooking in the buff is very dangerous. Even now, anything that makes noise gets me very nervous. If it's a salad, I'm fine!"

One of Joanne's favorite guests, Academy Award winner Shelley Winters, provided her with a prize recipe for Caesar Salad.

# Joanne Carson's Caesar Salad
## à la Shelley Winters

Serves 4

2 tbsps. wine vinegar
6 tbsps. fine grade
 olive oil
1 tsp. dry mustard
2 dashes original Worces-
 tershire sauce
freshly ground black pepper

2 heads Bibb or Romaine lettuce,
 cleaned and well-chilled
1 cup croutons
1 clove garlic, crushed
½ can anchovies, mashed
½ cup Parmesan cheese,
 freshly grated

1. *Combine vinegar, olive oil, mustard, Worcestershire and pepper in screw-top glass container; shake well.*
2. *Put lettuce, croutons, garlic, anchovies and Parmesan cheese in salad bowl.*
3. *Mix dressing well before sprinkling over salad.*
4. *Toss well; serve at once.*

# Bette Davis

"One of my greatest passions in life is New England boiled tongue and spinach. I'm insane about it," said Bette Davis. "On a chilly day back home, I cook – it's the greatest therapy I've ever known. If I'm ever in a mess or feel blue, I take to my kitchen!"

Bette was curled up on a beige chaise lounge and her voice crackled with enthusiasm. Somewhere in between making over 80 films, Bette learned how to become a sensational cook. "I've never done needlepoint," she said, lighting her cigarette with a kitchen match, "but I learned to cook when my children came along." She has three grown children: daughters B.D. and Margot, and son Mike.

The actress lived in a cozy house in Weston, Connecticut, before moving to California. "I haven't cooked in nearly six weeks and I can't wait to get home and start cooking again! Cooking's very creative, but I need lots of time. I marvel at the meals my host turns out – he comes home and in 15 minutes, turns out a fabulous meal. I get my best recipes from the newspapers. I'm bringing back three or four new recipes, including one for a marvelous avocado sauce."

Bette clings to her old recipes, which she keeps in a loose-leaf notebook. "A lot of the pages are black or half missing," she said, "but I still treasure my recipes."

# Bette Davis's Mustard Gelatin Ring

Serves 6-8

4 eggs
¾ cup sugar
1 envelope (1 tbsp.)
   unflavored gelatin
1½ tbsps. dry mustard
½ tsp. turmeric
¼ tsp. salt

1 cup water
½ cup cider vinegar
½ cup whipping cream
cole slaw mixed with canned
   pineapple chunks
chicory, watercress or other
   feathery greens

1. *Beat eggs; set aside.*
2. *Mix together sugar and unflavored gelatin; stir in mustard, turmeric and salt.*
3. *Add water and vinegar to the beaten eggs; stir in sugar-gelatin mixture.*
4. *Cook in double boiler over boiling water until slightly thickened, stirring continuously.*
5. *Cool until mixture is thick.*
6. *Whip cream and stir in. Pour mixture into a 1½-quart ring mold. Chill until firm.*
7. *Unmold and, if desired, fill center with cole slaw-pineapple mixture.*
8. *Garnish with chilled greens. Delicious with baked ham.*

NOTE: *Bette comments: "The sweet and sour flavor contrast is marvelous."
Lovely for buffet table with baked ham, particularly in summer.*

# Doris Day

One good, close-up look at Doris Day, and any of her fans will be scurrying to load up on natural foods! "I don't like to cook, but I sure like to eat," she said, enthusiastically putting away what she described as "a potpourri of good things" (a chickpea and tuna fish salad) and a cup of steaming Manhattan clam chowder. She was lunching at one of her favorite haunts, the Old World Restaurant, which specializes in natural foods. Doris flashed her famous smile as she looked around the cozy restaurant, a stone's throw from the UCLA campus in Westwood.

"My dentist, who is a nutrition buff, sent me here. While he fills your teeth, he always gives you the whole rundown on nutrition and vitamins. The last time I was there, he said, 'You're going to the Old World Restaurant!' I told him I had some things I had to do, but he insisted. 'You are going to have the best ice cream in this world.' So off I trundled with Ruth, who is my housekeeper, secretary and friend. We like to eat out, and once we started coming in here, we just kept on. I love their food. I come here for Sunday brunch to have their Belgian waffles and I often drop by for a hamburger!"

Her fondness for ice cream contributed to her "Miss Goody Two-shoes" image, Doris said. Before the death of her husband, Marty Melcher, she was often photographed concocting sensationally delicious and highly caloric ice cream confections at the soda fountain in her Beverly Hills home. "Whenever we entertained, our guests made their own desserts. We had everything you could think of – whipped cream, chopped nuts, cherries, all the toppings and every kind of ice cream! We made sodas, milkshakes and the most fabulous banana splits!"

# Doris Day's German Potato Salad

Serves 4

6 medium-size potatoes, well
  scrubbed
1 large stalk celery, chopped

4 slices lean bacon
⅔ cup water
½ cup cider vinegar

3-4 scallions (white part only), chopped

1. *Cook potatoes in their skins until tender.*
2. *Cool slightly, peel and slice into a large bowl.*
3. *Add celery and scallions.*
4. *Cut up bacon into small strips and fry in saucepan until crisp.*
5. *Add water and vinegar to bacon in saucepan.*
6. *Pour over potato-celery-scallion mixture; toss lightly.*
7. *Cover and marinate thoroughly several hours or overnight before serving.*

NOTE: *For more "sour" flavor, add more vinegar to marinade. Can also be served with dollop of sour cream or mayonnaise, if desired (add after draining off marinade).*

# Robert Evans

Movie producer Robert Evans has exquisite food tastes that reflect his fondness for beauty and luxurious surroundings. "I can cook anything from pheasant to roast beef," he said. "I find it very creative. Unfortunately, I don't get to cook as much as I'd like to anymore, because I don't want to do it when my mind isn't on it."

Typically, Bob puts in a 16-hour working day, preferably at home – a palatial, 16-room French Regency house in Beverly Hills, complete with two acres of carefully manicured trees and shrubs and a lovely guest cottage that has housed such famous visitors as Henry Kissinger and Teddy Kennedy.

Bob's menus are as elegant as his beautiful art collection, which includes Dalis, Modiglianis, Renoirs and pre-Columbian art. "I like to begin a meal with jellied madrilene, topped with sour cream and imported caviar. Roast duck served with wild rice and carrots makes a terrific entree! I'll follow that with endive-watercress salad and finish with a delicious *crème* brûlée (burnt sugar dessert) and grapes."

Bob likes to serve top-grade, imported caviar accompanied either by Bloody Marys or well-chilled Polish vodka. One of his favorite company menus is as filling as it is delicious: chicken tarragon, salad, cheesecake, good wine and lots of good conversation!

# Robert Evans' Jellied Madrilene

Serves 4

1 tbsp. unflavored gelatin
¼ cup cold water
3 cups tomato juice

2 tsps. Angostura aromatic bitters
2 tsps. fresh lemon juice
parsley or chives, chopped

1. *Dissolve gelatin in cold water.*
2. *Heat tomato juice to boiling; remove from heat.*
3. *Add softened gelatin, stir until dissolved.*
4. *Cool. Add Angostura bitters and lemon juice.*
5. *Chill for 3 hours.*
6. *Break with fork. Pile lightly in bouillon cups to serve. Garnish with parsley or chives.*

*NOTE: For gala, caloric, expensive touches, add sour cream and caviar!*

# Hal Holbrook

Actor Hal Holbrook can sail a boat as deftly as he can prepare a feast on board with his day's catch from the sea! The lean, lanky gentleman, who looks offstage very much like his popular onstage Mark Twain character, lives in Santa Monica, California. He does most of his cooking on board his 32-foot ketch.

"I've made a lot of wonderful feeds for myself," said Hal. "I love to broil a good steak, and I make a terrific salad! Sometimes I have fresh corn on the cob, but I can't do that, of course, when I go out for more than a few days at a time. Many times, I just open up a can of something, like stew. Any kind of food tastes good out there!"

Hal got hooked on sailing when he chartered a boat in St. Thomas some years ago. "There's something quite fascinating about it." Hal's boat, of course, is complete with galley. "It's a proper boat that can go anywhere in the world," he says with pride. "I usually sail off to Catalina, preferably the ocean side, because there are fewer boats there. If I want to cook on deck, I have a barbecue device that hangs over the side. Or I can boil up some clams or lobsters! The other day, I cooked some fillet of flounder, using Carol's (wife Carol Rossen) instructions. She's an excellent cook." Carol always cooks her fish quickly, pan-frying it no more than two minutes, with butter and lemon.

The Holbrooks entertain often. Their most frequent guests are Carroll O'Connor and his wife, Nancy. "We've known them since they first lived out here years ago. Carol lived in their garage when she first came to Hollywood to become an actress!"

# Hal Holbrook's Spinach Salad California

Serves 4

## For the salad dressing

6 tbsps. fresh lemon juice
⅓ cup salad oil

salt to taste
pepper to taste

1. Combine lemon juice and salad oil in glass jar.
2. Add salt and pepper to taste.
3. Cover jar tightly with screw lid; shake well just before using.

## For the salad

1 lb. fresh spinach
2 hard-cooked eggs, peeled
   and shredded

1 large, ripe, California avocado,
   peeled and cut in strips
cherry tomatoes (optional)

1. Wash and pick over spinach carefully.
2. Drain spinach well on paper towel.
3. Arrange spinach, eggs and avocado in large salad bowl.
4. Pour salad dressing over all; toss lightly.
5. Garnish with cherry tomatoes as desired.

# Ross Hunter

When we first talked in 1966, producer Ross Hunter told me, "I have a quirk about food. Wherever I go, I head for the kitchen in search of recipes. I've collected them from every city of the world. Someday soon, I'll have enough to fill a cookbook."

Recipe madness isn't his only quirk: Ross is a self-confessed lemon lover. In the place of honor in his office hangs a lovingly rendered oil painting of a lemon. Whenever he entertains, the color scheme is based on – what else? – lemon yellow! "I'm addicted to lemons," he cheerfully admits. "And I love to use them in my cooking. As a matter of fact, I'm quite famous for my lemon chicken."

The Hunter face is leaner than it was more than a decade ago, but he still possesses the boyish enthusiasm that makes him one of Hollywood's most popular producers. Lately, he's turned his talents to television. Ross has little time for entertaining or even eating these days. "I find myself eating less lately. I feel better and I've lost a lot of weight. I'm eating less meat and more chicken, fish, vegetables and fruit."

In spite of his tight schedule, Ross is still one of Hollywood's most celebrated hosts at his sumptuous Trousdales Estates mansion. Ross's house is straight out of the movies. Nestled between the Sunset Strip and Beverly Hills, it's replete with marble swimming pool, three massive fountains, bridge room and movie projection room.

# Ross Hunter's Quick Saffron Soup

Serves 4

2 cans (10½ ozs.) condensed
   cream of chicken soup
1 soup can milk
⅛ tsp. saffron threads
1-2 tbsps. lemon peel, cut in
   large pieces

2-3 tbsps. hot water
salt to taste
freshly ground black pepper
   to taste
¼ cup dairy sour cream
chopped chives

1. *Combine soup and milk; heat to simmering, stirring often.*
2. *Combine saffron thread, lemon peel and hot water; stir into soup.*
3. *Simmer gently 10 minutes to blend flavors. Remove from heat.*
4. *Remove lemon peel by straining.*
5. *Season with salt and pepper to taste.*
6. *Serve piping hot with a dollop of sour cream and chives to garnish.*

NOTE: *A longer version of the soup can be made by cooking a chicken slowly in stock flavored with pieces of cut lemon, parsley and a small amount of chopped carrot. Strain soup, add saffron thread, dilute with cream, and reheat a few minutes to develop saffron flavor.*

# Bel Kaufman

"I have enormous respect for food. I was a little girl in Russia during the famine. I don't think anyone who has lived through a famine can ever look at food without enormous respect," said blonde, vivacious Bel Kaufman, author of the best-seller *Up the Down Staircase,* over lunch at New York's Metropolitan Museum of Art. "We even had green bread made by grinding dried pea shells because we didn't have any flour."

Digging into some cherry pie, Bel recalled, "There's something I've never tasted in this country: dumplings made with sour pitted cherries and sour cream. There's something about the warmth of the dumplings, the coldness of the cream and the tartness of the cherries that's hard to imagine. We had a villa on the Black Sea. We had the dumplings there during cherry harvest. The dumplings, or *Varenki*" – she penciled the name in Russian – "is made from noodle dough and plunged into boiling water to cook.

"I've always been at a disadvantage in the kitchen. My mother had a housekeeper. Mother was a writer and when it came to cooking, she was impatient and occuped with other things. I envy people who have a creative feel for cooking; it's a great talent. Women who become great cooks are the little girls who hung around the kitchen growing up.

"I'd say I have a healthy regard for food," Bel added. "When my children were small, I never did any of the things parents do to coax their children to eat, like standing on their head. If my children pushed the food away from the table, I'd say, 'I'll eat it if you don't want it,' and I did, even if it was pablum that tasted like white cement," she said, laughing.

# Bel Kaufman's Russian Borsch

Serves 12-15

2½ or 3 lbs. stewing beef
2 marrow bones, cracked
about 6 cups water
1 can (12 oz.) V-8 juice
2 bay leaves
2 pinches basil
1 clove garlic or ¼ tsp.
  garlic salt
1 tbsp. salt
6 bruised peppercorns
4 carrots, chopped and peeled
4 stalks celery and leaves, cut
  in 1-inch pieces
1 medium sweet white onion,
  chopped

1 leek, chopped
1 small green pepper, diced
1 can (16 oz.) stewed tomatoes
½ cup lemon juice
2 tbsps. sugar
1 small head cabbage, shredded
2 large potatoes, peeled and
  diced
1 can (16 oz.) pickled beets,
  drained and cut in large
  pieces
1 can (16 oz.) shoestring beets
½ cup parsley, minced
3 tbsps. fresh dill, minced
dairy sour cream

1.  *Put meat and bones in an 8-quart soup pot. Add enough water to barely cover the bones.*
2.  *Bring to a boil. Skim off and discard foam.*
3.  *Add V-8 juice, bay leaves, basil, garlic, salt, peppercorns and remaining water.*
4.  *Bring to a boil and start adding chopped carrots, celery, onion and leek.*
5.  *Cover and simmer 1¼ hours.*
6.  *Add green pepper, tomatoes, lemon juice and sugar. Cook 30 minutes longer.*
7.  *Add cabbage, potatoes and pickled beets. Cook 45 minutes longer or until potatoes are tender.*
8.  *Add undrained shoestring beets, parsley and dill. Simmer 20 minutes.*
9.  *Remove meat to platter, cut in thick slices, and put back in soup pot.*
10. *Serve borsch piping hot with a side dish of chilled sour cream and slices of dark Russian bread spread with sweet butter.*

NOTE: *Bel Kaufman suggests, "Don't attempt to prepare borsch in smaller quantities than given in the recipe. The flavor improves the next day and can be varied by the addition of string beans or navy beans."*

# Janet Leigh

A veteran of almost 60 movies, Janet Leigh burns up her food, never diets and, more often than not, has had a problem putting *on* weight, rather than taking it off. She's a sports enthusiast, prefers to be a participant rather than a spectator and excels in tennis, swimming, water and snow skiing, golf and bike riding.

"Food interests me, but not the preparation," said Janet, seated in the den of the modern house she shares with husband Robert Brandt, a successful Beverly Hills stockbroker. The house was once part of the Norma Talmadge estate in a woodsy area off Benedict Canyon. "I can eat anything, except coconuts, but I like fresh green salads, vegetables, especially artichokes, and lovely fruits in lieu of gooey, rich confections.

"I love to entertain informally," Janet added. "For example, we have a tennis group over for swimming. We might have a poolside party, a light summer buffet. Sometimes we have a lobster salad, or shrimp, and we have a tray of crackers, Triscuits, and a little cheese and fruit. There are people who live to eat. I'm the opposite. I'm moderate. I enjoy what's good, but I don't have to have quantity."

Janet and Robert divide their vacation seasons between Sun Valley for skiing and Paradise Island in the Bahamas for tennis and beach life. Janet loves the Bahamas, including the Caribbean food. "I'm not big on fishing myself," she explained, "but I like grouper. You have to fish for grouper at dusk because during the day, they're so big, they go way deep and you'd never get them. At dusk they come up to feed."

# Janet Leigh's Fruit Salad with Daiquiri Dressing

Serves 4

## Daiquiri Dressing

Makes about ½ cup dressing

⅓ cup corn oil
½ tsp. lime peel, grated
1½ tbsps. lime juice

1½ tbsps. rum
½ tsp. salt
dash sugar

1. *Combine all ingredients and blend well.*
2. *Set aside.*

## For the salad

1 head western iceberg
   lettuce
1 large orange
2 bananas

1 papaya
4 slices fresh or canned
   pineapple
brown sugar

1. *Core, rinse and thoroughly drain lettuce. Chill in disposable plastic bag or crisper.*
2. *Pare and section orange.*
3. *Peel bananas, cut in halves lengthwise, then in halves crosswise.*
4. *Cut papaya in half; remove seeds and peel fruit. Cut in thick slices.*
5. *Arrange fruits in shallow pan. Pour Daiquiri Dressing over fruit.*
6. *Marinate for about an hour.*
7. *Just before serving, drain off dressing and reserve.*
8. *Sprinkle fruit lightly with brown sugar.*
9. *Broil about 4 inches from heat 5 minutes, or until lightly browned.*
10. *Meanwhile, cut 4 crosswise sections from lettuce and arrange on individual salad plates. Arrange warm broiled fruit on lettuce rafts and spoon dressing over all.*

*NOTE: If desired, a few drops of rum extract may be substituted for rum.*

# Liberace

"When I'm home, I like to dine elegantly, whether it's by myself or with company," said Liberace, respendent in a gold and black tapestry suit, black shirt and velvet loafers.

Lee often takes to the kitchen to prepare meals for friends or family. His menus and settings in his Palm Springs house vary from elaborate, seven-course dinners complete with candelabras and crystal to suppers for one. "I love to serve a dish in the same utensil it's been cooked in. I make a fantastic stew, but I have one problem with it. Every time I make it, it costs me a pot. Everybody loves the stew, but they're not content with the recipe. They always say, 'Where did you ever find that pot?' So I wind up giving it away."

Lee's favorite way to cook involves his collection of sizzling platters. "They're made of stainless steel and they can be used on top of the range, in the oven or under the broiler. After they come off the stove, you set the platters in wooden trays, and the food stays hot for a long time. Each wooden tray has two wells, for salad and baked potatoes. Cooking on a sizzling platter is mainly a matter of timing," Lee stressed. "You must be careful not to overcook the food. For example, if you want a rare steak, you have to take it out underdone, because the meat continues to cook on the platter after it comes out of the broiler. If you're preparing breakfast, just cook the ham or bacon on the platter and draw off the fat. Break a couple of eggs onto the platter after you take it off the stove, and by the time you serve it the eggs are cooked.

"For dinner, I like to roast individual game birds – pheasant, quail or Rock Cornish hens – with a chewy stuffing made from meat, nuts and water chestnuts, spiked with a deep red wine."

# Liberace's Meatball Soup

## Serves 8

1½ lbs. ground beef
⅛ lb. lean ground pork
3 tbsps. parsley, chopped
1 cup onion, chopped
4 tbsps. flour
2 eggs

1 tsp. salt
¼ tsp. pepper
2 quarts salted water
1 bay leaf
¼ tsp. ground allspice
½ cup light cream
boiling potatoes

2 slices bread, soaked in milk and squeezed dry

1. Mix together beef, pork, parsley, half the onion, 1 tbsp. flour, eggs, bread, salt and pepper.
2. Shape into spheres the size of golf balls.
3. Simmer in salted water with bay leaf, allspice and remaining onion for 30 minutes. Thicken broth with additional flour.
4. Remove ½ cup broth and mix with remaining flour until smooth.
5. Return to pan and blend well.
6. Simmer for several minutes.
7. Remove from heat and stir in cream. Serve over boiled potatoes.

NOTE: This soup is a delicious, hearty, meal-in-one dish. Complete menu with a bowl of crisp salad or cole slaw.

# Jack Lord

"I want to be buried in lasagna," said a laughing Jack Lord, the man most people think of as the humorless chief of "Hawaii Five-O." Jack went on to explain, "For my wife, Marie, and I, Italian food is soul food. Just yesterday we imported five pounds of Romano and Parmesan cheese, mixed half-and-half, because we can't get good Italian cheese in Honolulu."

Jack talked of his love for good food while relaxing in his personally designed mobile dressing room – a virtual land yacht built on a 30-foot, 330-h.p. bus chassis. The dressing room, decorated in avocado-greens and lemon-yellows, is an air-conditioned oasis on the main "Five-O" lot, away from the tropical sun outside.

Jack's shyness shows despite his articulateness. He enjoys cooking and admits to "trotting out four or five things that are kind of flashy." But, he says, "My wife really is a brilliant cook. We read cookbooks together the way we also read novels. When I find a new cookbook, I bring it home and we read it aloud. I cook very good custards. I make very good mayonnaise. And I make one or two veal dishes – including very thin scallopini and cream – even though it's pretty hard to get white veal here."

Asked why so many people in the performing arts are such outstanding cooks, Jack replied, "I think it's all part of the same process. Isn't it the creative thing? We like to start from scratch and make something. We're all hams in the kitchen. We like to perform and, as either cooks or actors, we need our applause."

# Jack Lord's Watercress Soup

### Serves 4

1 large bunch watercress
4½ cups water
1¾ lbs. baking potatoes,
   peeled and cut in large pieces

½ cup milk
3-4 tbsps. butter
salt to taste
white pepper to taste

1. *Remove leaves from watercress, wash, and place in colander.*
2. *Break off tender part of stems, cut into smaller pieces and put in blender, adding 1½ cups water, a little at a time, until stems are dissolved.*
3. *Pour liquid through a sieve.*
4. *Boil potatoes in remaining water until tender.*
5. *Put potato water, potato, watercress liquid and watercress leaves in blender; whirl until just blended; then add milk.*
6. *Heat slightly; add butter, salt and white pepper to taste just before serving. If desired, serve with homemade croutons (cubes of French bread lightly sautéed in small amount of butter until golden).*

# Myrna Loy

"I've always known a lot about food, but I've never done much cooking. In fact, I'm just now learning," said actress Myrna Loy, gazing out into the bleak winter sky from her East Side Manhattan penthouse apartment. "On the road, I got very tired of eating out and craved home-cooked food, so I got an apartment.

"Cooking requires using your mind and gets you interested in the basics of life. The only things I really enjoy cooking are lengthy affairs like a *cassoulet*. It's a very difficult dish and takes days to prepare. I'm reminded of the marvelous *cassoulets* I had one winter in Paris when I was making a film. I was there from October to February, and the Parisian winters can be very long. I used to dine in a tiny Basque restaurant. I can still see the copper braziers filled with those aromatic sauces. The waiters would bring in steaming earthenware *cassoulets* filled with beans and pungent sausage smelling so marvelously."

Myrna credits her parents for her interest in excellent food. "My father was a gourmet. Mother came to her marriage unable to boil water."

Of Welsh, Scottish and Swedish descent, the freckle-faced actress was born Myrna Williams in Radersburg, Montana. Her father's parents came from Wales. "My maternal grandmother came from the lowlands near Glasgow and made marvelous shortbread and scones."

One of Myrna's fondest memories is of her mother's fruitcakes and mince-meat. "I remember the mincemeat sitting in huge crocks in the pantry," she recalled. "She put down all that meat and laced it with lots of brandy. It smelled so good. Maybe I will try making it someday."

# Myrna Loy's Quick Chicken Pimento Soup

### Serves 4-6

1 quart homemade or canned
  chicken soup

1 jar (2 oz.) pimento, drained
  and chopped

½ cup heavy cream, whipped
salt to taste

freshly ground black pepper
  to taste

2 chicken breasts, cooked, skinned, and cut in Julienne strips

1. *Heat chicken soup with chicken; season to taste with salt and pepper.*
2. *Ladle soup into individual soup bowls; top with dollops of whipped cream.*
3. *Garnish with chopped pimento.*

# Dean Martin

Off camera, Dean Martin puts aside his drawl and hangs up his liquored image as easily as his hat. Dino's really a simple guy, good-natured, extremely loyal to old friends and very candid. His food style reflects his Italian family background. He's a good cook, but only on occasion. "I don't like pizza made with a thick, doughy crust: the crust should be nice and crisp," said Dean. "I like cheese pizza or the kind made with pepperoni or sweet Italian sausages and I love Bruno's (a Los Angeles restaurant) sourdough rolls, served with a side order of green peppers and sausages, prepared in spaghetti sauce!"

Dino is also particularly fond of Bruno's antipasto and *calzone imbottito* (means "stuffed stockings"). A *calzone* is a large turnover made with pizza dough and filled with a delicious mixture of ricotta cheese, chopped salami, diced ham, parsley, egg and herbs.

"Listen, I'm shy and hate parties," Dino said. "If I walk into a party, I go into a corner, looking for someone I know. I don't like small talk! I'm just an honest guy who doesn't want to bother anybody and likes it when nobody bothers me. Frank Sinatra is my dearest friend, and has been for over 30 years. I kid about him on stage and he kids about me!"

Sinatra often cooks for Dino. The pair frequently play golf together. "I love being outdoors," added Dino. " After you've walked five miles, you get relaxed and you're ready to sit down and really eat!"

Dino's apt to start his days with his biggest meal of the day: hotcakes, eggs and sausage. He attributes his great flow of energy to "being happy at what I'm doing! You can't retire. Frank found that out. You can't get out of bed and just do nothing."

# Dean Martin's Antipasto Bruno

Serves 4

### For the marinade

⅓ cup olive oil
2 tsps. red wine vinegar,
  more if desired

½ tsp. pickling spices
2 scallions, chopped
salt and pepper to taste

OR a good quality bottled Italian dressing

*Mix all ingredients together and set aside.*

### For the salad

1 head Romaine lettuce
2 heads Bibb lettuce
1 can (10 ozs.) garbanzo
  beans, drained
½ lb. salami, sliced
8 slices provolone cheese
8 slices mozzarella cheese

1 can (3-4 ozs.) pickled
  mushrooms, drained
8 black olives
8 green onions
8 radishes, cut in roses
4 anchovy fillets
8 slices tomato

1 can (8 ozs.) artichoke hearts in oil, drained

1. *Wash, drain and crisp Romaine and Bibb lettuce.*
2. *Pour marinade over drained garbanzo beans.*
3. *Cover and refrigerate 3-4 hours.*

### To assemble

1. *Arrange Romaine leaves on large oval platter.*
2. *Top with mound of Bibb lettuce.*
3. *Cover with salami, provolone and mozzarella.*
4. *Arrange artichoke hearts around the edge.*
5. *Drain beans and place in center of platter.*
6. *Arrange mushrooms, olives, onions, radishes, anchovy fillets and tomato on plate to form an attractive pattern.*
7. *Serve alone or with hot toasted sourdough bread and sweet butter.*

*NOTE: If desired, fresh mushrooms may be added (marinate with same dressing as beans). For tasty, colorful tidbits, include: slices hard-cooked egg, pimentos, vinegar peppers, celery hearts. Makes an excellent meal in one. Dino likes a good dry red Italian wine with his antipasto!*

# Lee Marvin

"Yeah, sure I cook. I throw a fish on a fire – or a lobster, whatever's at hand . . . I burn a steak and do all those dumb things . . . and once in a while, I really do a ham up with pineapple, corn syrup and all that kind of junk," said Lee Marvin as he talked about a potpourri of subjects, including chow. His soft, silky, prematurely white hair contrasted sharply with his tanned good looks. He wore a tan suit with a beautiful gray-green paisley tie that looked, in his words, "like it could have been ripped off the back of some old lady's chair."

Other first impressions: an enormously polite man, affable, gracious and attentive, the complete antithesis of the rough and tough "gung-ho" guy he portrays so brilliantly on the screen. But very much the man who likes his privacy.

Lee's favorite spot of privacy (in addition to his home at Malibu, where he walks the beach at night for relaxation, collects shells and bottles, for the most part shuns the company of actors and prefers to spend his time with working people at bars like the Cottage and the Raft) is Palau in the Pacific, Lee's island in the sun.

Producing some colored prints of his 45-foot big game boat, the *Ngerengchol*, complete with galley, Lee explained, "We don't really cook very much. What we do is catch a tuna and just *sashimi* him: Take some soy sauce, throw it on a pieplate, throw some *wasabi* (Japanese horseradish) in there which really heats it up and then eat the fish right now just raw, and the fresher the better!"

Returning to cooked chow, Lee said, "Once in a while I get a sackful of lentils and make a nice lima bean soup. I use just anything I can find around." Nowadays the actor won't be cooking in solitude. He married Pamela Feeley, a long time friend from Woodstock, New York.

# Lee Marvin's Lentil Bean Soup

### Serves 6

1 lb. dried lima beans or split
    peas or lentils
2-3 quarts water
1½ lb. butt end of ham or
    6 oz. piece salt pork,
    bacon or turkey carcass
1 large onion, peeled and
    coarsely chopped
small carrot, chopped

2 large stalks celery with
    leaves, chopped
bay leaf
salt to taste
pepper to taste
dash cayenne or Tabasco
2-3 tbsps. butter (depending
    upon what kind of meat
    used for seasoning)

1. *Soak beans overnight in water.*
2. *Drain and put in a large saucepan with water.*
3. *Add all the ingredients except butter.*
4. *Simmer uncovered about 3½ hours, adding more liquid if needed.*
5. *Strain through colander.*
6. *Chill to remove congealed fat. Discard fat.*
7. *Reheat and taste to correct seasonings. Add butter for flavor.*

*NOTE: At the beach, fish scraps (head, tails) can be used. Use a pinch of thyme, slice in a tomato or two, use clam juice in lieu of water. If desired, lentil soup can be thickened by blending 2 tbsps. flour with a little soup (cooled to room temperature) before adding to the saucepan. Lee's delicious soup makes a hearty accompaniment to gargantuan rye bread sandwiches made with huge slabs of his Malibu ham, Swiss cheese, dill pickles, horseradish-mustard and beer.*

# Ricardo Montalban

"My wife is not a fancy cook. She cooks the way I think it should be done. Simplicity is the ultimate," says Ricardo Montalban. Almost 60, the reed-slender actor and host of TV's "Fantasy Island" looks years younger. We sat in the posh den of his Hollywood Hills home. Over tea served with tiny morsels of homemade fruitcake, Ricardo leaned back, relaxed, and played the perfect host.

For all his success and worldwide travel, Ricardo remains home-and family-oriented. He and his wife, Georgiana, who is Loretta Young's younger sister, once lived on a pretentious scale. But 15 years ago, they elected to move to a smaller house. Furnished with beautiful antiques, paintings and organic touches such as oversized plants and trees, their house has an interesting indoor-outdoor atmosphere.

Ricardo's food tastes are eclectic. He enjoys Mexican, Japanese and Italian dishes. Admittedly a spectator in the kitchen, Ricardo said, "I'm a great appreciator. Georgiana prepares wonderful Mexican food. The beauty of Mexican cuisine is in its freshness and the ingredients that complement each other."

A purist at heart, Ricardo went on to say, "If I order fish, I want it to taste like fish. If I order veal, it must taste like veal." He disdains "sauces that hide or camouflage food" and prefers simpler, tastier food. "I'm hooked on *sashimi* (raw fish). The way the Japanese prepare it is so simple. I crave it twice a week. *Sashimi's* very healthful food. I'll eat anything: sea urchins, eel, octopus, yellowtail, red snapper, mussels," he said, laughing.

# Mexican Calves' Brain Soup, House of Ricardo Montalban

Serves 6

### For beef stock

1 large marrow bone, cracked
4 lbs. short ribs of beef
   or other beef with bones
2-3 quarts cold water

1 small clove garlic, peeled
   and mashed
salt to taste
1 tsp. peppercorns, crushed

1. *Place bones and beef in large kettle. Cover with cold water and bring to boil.*
2. *Cover and simmer 1 hour, or until meat is half-cooked (for browner stock, first sear meat in small amount of oil).*
3. *Add garlic, salt and peppercorns. Simmer uncovered over low heat 3-4 hours, skimming surface often to remove scum. Strain and reserve meat.*
4. *Cool, cover and refrigerate. Remove and discard layer of surface fat. (This may be used for any recipe calling for beef stock.) Makes about 2 quarts.*

### To prepare calves' brain soup

2 pair calves' brains
1 tsp. salt
1 tbsp. vinegar
1 quart boiling water
½ medium-size yellow onion,
   peeled and minced

¼ cup butter
2 large potatoes, peeled
   and thinly sliced
3 large leeks, thinly sliced
2 quarts beef stock
Monterey Jack cheese, grated

1. *Wash brains, remove arteries.*
2. *Add salt and vinegar to boiling water. Add brains.*
3. *Cover, reduce heat; simmer until tender, about 20-30 minutes.*
4. *Drain. Cover with ice water. Let stand 20 minutes, drain again.*
5. *Slice brains into small pieces; set aside.*
6. *Sauté onion in butter in large skillet. Add potatoes and leeks.*
7. *Cook over low heat until vegetables begin to tenderize.*
8. *Add beef stock. Simmer slowly 30 minutes.*
9. *Add brains, reheat only until meat is heated through (cooking longer toughens meat).*
10. *Spoon piping hot into soup plates. Garnish with grated cheese. Serve alone or with crisp green salad, tortillas or burritos, French bread and Mexican beer.*

# Rita Moreno

Actress Rita Moreno has a lusty appetite for life. She appreciates great food. In fact, she says, her eyes become crossed when she talks about good food! "Did you ever make *garbanzo* (chickpea) soup? It's so good. It's made with *chorizos* (Spanish sausage)," she said, her eyes becoming almost glazed.

When she cooks for special occasions, Rita loves to fix dishes from her native Puerto Rico. "It's fun to serve Puerto Rican dishes because you can get regular food everywhere. I'm about to prepare black beans and rice, and I may cook up a big pot of 'Old Clothes.' Isn't that a super name for a stew? They call it that because you shred the meat with forks so it looks like old shredded clothes!"

# Rita Moreno's Chickpea Soup

Serves 6-8

1 lbs. dried chickpeas,
   washed and picked over
water
1 carrot, peeled and diced
2 medium onions, peeled and
   sliced
2 tomatoes, peeled and chopped
¼ lb. cooked ham, minced

1 cup olive oil
3 cloves garlic, crushed
½ bay leaf, crushed
1 tsp. parsley
¼ tsp. freshly ground
   black pepper
salt to taste
3 quarts water

½ lb. *chorizos* (Spanish sausage)

1. *Cover chickpeas with water and bring to a boil.*
2. *Drain and discard water.*
3. *Sauté vegetables, ham and sausages in olive oil until tender.*
4. *Add chickpeas, herbs, seasonings and water. Simmer 3 hours, or until peas are tender.*
5. *Can be served this way or put through a sieve and served as a purée.*

NOTE: Soup can be made with navy beans or lentils, which require shorter cooking time. Wonderful as main dish fare served with buttered crusty bread.

# Paul Newman

"I probably make the best popcorn in the world!" Paul Newman said, grinning. Sitting in an East Side Chinese restaurant, with Moo-shu pork in Peking pancakes and a bottle of beer in front of him, Paul explained the high art of popping corn! "First, the best popcorn is the pop dry (available everywhere). And a popper with handles on the screen is the best kind. Secondly, get a great pot of melted butter and take the pan filled with corn and, with a knife, evenly spatter the melted butter over the top layer," he said, demonstrating the motions. "Then flip the pan like you were making an omelet so that you expose another layer of corn, and butter that the same way. But you mustn't shake it. You've got to flip it so it comes up and over."

Paul might sound like he's flipped out, but he can hold his own in the kitchen with as much expertise as he shows in front or back of the camera. He is also a champion hamburger chef. "My theory about meat is you don't touch it," he said. "I never put salt or onions or egg or breadcrumbs or anything in hamburger. Just take good chuck — not round, not sirloin but plain chuck — that's what makes a sensational hamburger!"

Paul thinks people too often "garbage" up food, especially steak. "They've got to put everything on it. I love to cook. Most of my cooking is done outdoors, but I do make bouillabaisse and various gumbos, and great gazpacho!"

Paul told the secret of the salads he makes: "The first bite usually brings tears to your eyes because of the onion." He laughed. Sometimes he uses leftover salad to make his gazpacho, throwing it into a blender with V-8 juice, adding green peppers and chopped tomatoes. "It could be called the day-before salad and day-after soup."

# Paul Newman's Salad-Gazpacho

Serves 5-6

2-3 cups leftover tossed
 green salad
2 cans (12 oz.) cocktail
 vegetable juice
½ tsp. salt
⅛ tsp. pepper
2 tsps. prepared mustard
1 tbsp. garlic-flavored
 wine vinegar

1 tbsp. salad oil
¼ cup sweet red onion,
 chopped
¼ cup cucumber, pared
¼ cup celery, chopped
2 tbsps. green pepper,
 chopped
2 cups iceberg lettuce,
 shredded

1. *Put leftover salad into blender.*
2. *Add 1 can vegetable juice, seasonings, vinegar and oil. Blend until smooth.*
3. *Add remaining vegetable juice, cover and chill.*
4. *Combine chopped onion, cucumber, celery and green pepper; chill.*
5. *When ready to serve, pour gazpacho into serving bowls. Garnish with chopped vegetables and shredded lettuce.*

### For leftover tossed green salad

*Use any tossed lettuce salad dressed with French-type dressing. It may contain tomato, onion, cucumber. If you do not have leftover salad, use 2-3 cups iceberg lettuce chunks, ½ cup diced, pared cucumber and ⅓ cup chopped onion with ¼ cup French dressing.*

# Louis Nye

"I used to do a character called 'Neville Nosher.' Neville was a gourmet and critic. He reviewed restaurants and new dishes very much like one would review a play. And I wrote about that on the so-called 'magazine of the air' (on the original 'Tonight' show with Steve Allen). It started with an idea I had because I like to cook. I can whip up a fine stew – beef or lamb – and steak tartar." The speaker: Louis Nye, a gentle, funny man.

"I like veal, if it's well done, but let's start with the fine art of making steak tartar – I've been making it a new way. First, the meat must be ground very, very well, or done in the old traditional way, it can be scraped. Chill the meat several hours so it's completely cold – until *rigor mortis* sets in. Take some capers, a few chopped anchovies, and lay them on top of the steak. Form the steak to look like a loaf of bread. To the mixture add an egg yolk and finely diced sweet onion – white onion, naturally. Then add salt, pepper, a touch of Tabasco and Worcestershire. Lemon is what really tops it off. It has a great cleansing quality and brings out the flavor. It also cuts down on the need for salt that causes fluid retention. That's the validity for eating a lot of grapefruit, too. It takes away the baddies in your tum-tum!

"I try to introduce people to spritzer. That's about the nicest drink you can order. A spritzer, 'as day say in da old country,' " he said in a heavy German accent, "is just white wine with a couple of ice cubes, seltzer and a twist of lemon.

"Do you know what would really bend your badge if you really like to cook? Sauerkraut soup! My mother used to make it. She was Ukranian and she said everyone who was poor ate a lot of sauerkraut. I didn't have a big thing for it, but as I've gotten older, I started to think sauerkraut soup couldn't be nicer."

# Louis Nye's Sauerkraut Soup

### Serves 8

2 lbs. beef flank
several marrow bones,
    split open
2½ qts. liquid (part
    sauerkraut juice)
2 large onions, chopped
bunch cleaned soup greens
    (1 celery root,
    3 sprigs parsley,
    1 carrot, chopped,
    1 stalk celery with leaves)

large clove garlic, chopped
1 tart peeled apple, chopped
1½ lbs. sauerkraut
2-3 tbsps. fat (butter or
    salt pork or bacon grease)
1 bay leaf
6 crushed peppercorns
juice from half a lemon
1 tbsp. salt
sugar to taste
fresh dill, chopped

1. *Put beef, bones and liquid (include sauerkraut juice squeezed from canned sauerkraut) in large pot. Let simmer about 1 hour, skimming off any scum or fat that forms on surface.*
2. *Sauté onion, chopped soup greens (cut in large pieces), garlic, apple and sauerkraut in hot fat.*
3. *Add to stock pot with beef mixture.*
4. *Add bay leaf, peppercorns, lemon juice, salt and sugar to taste. Simmer 1 hour longer, adding additional liquid as needed (preferably sauerkraut juice) so bones, meat and vegetables are well covered.*
5. *Remove meat from bones, remove meat from marrow bones and discard bones.*
6. *Taste to correct seasonings. Skim off excess fat.*
7. *Serve garnished with fresh dill, alone, or with crusty dark bread.*

NOTE: *This basic Ukranian favorite can be made many ways: by adding dried mushrooms to stock, adding tomatoes or serving with boiled potatoes or sour cream as personal tastes dictate. For a meatier flavor, add cooked, diced Polish sausage or salami to soup just before serving.*

# Sidney Poitier

"I learned to cook as a kid, but now I fix mostly health foods," Sidney Poitier said. "I eat the damnest-looking oranges, they're puny and wrinkled. I go for unsprayed vegetables and fruit and fish. There are too many chemicals and pesticides used in growing food. I've just read a book which is the scariest book I've ever read, called *Poison in Our Food*. On the cover is a hot dog with a hypodermic needle in it. The analysis of what goes into a hot dog is frightening!

"Or, take preservatives. In order to get a loaf of bread that can stay on the shelf for a week, they have to take the nutrients out of the bread, particularly the flour, because most of the important nutrients are found in the oily substance of the wheat. So, many of the fat-soluble vitamins are removed."

As a child, eating in the sunny Caribbean was easy for Sidney. "Food was usually seafood, root vegetables (cassava or yams) and fresh vegetables. We lived on that. We never used brown sugar or processed milk, and we ate fish we caught that day, or preserved it by 'corning' (drying) it in its natural state in the sun. The field stuff had to be eaten before it spoiled."

Sidney was the son of a Cat Island farmer. Fishing is still one of life's great pleasures for Sidney. "I fish like the Bahamians do, with a line on the ocean banks. You have to get about 100 yards before the drop-off where the fish gather for protection from the big boys, the sharks. And I catch a lot of fish: grouper, grunts, margarets, turbots (called steak-of-the-sea by Bahamians)."

Sidney still dons an apron and cooks occasionally, usually breaded chicken. "I bread my chicken with wheat germ and broil it. There's also a favorite Bahamian recipe, one I still love, but a bit involved. My mother used to prepare okra soup, using portions of cured fish, conch and land crabs."

# Sidney Poitier's Corn & Okra Soup

Serves 6-8

6 ears fresh corn
2 cups water
¾ tsp. salt
2 small live lobsters, each
 weighing about 1¼ lbs.
2 tbsps. vegetable oil or
 bacon fat
1 large onion, peeled and sliced
½ clove garlic, pressed
1 green pepper, minced
2 stalks celery, chopped

¼ tsp. thyme leaves
3 large ripe tomatoes, peeled
 and chopped
2 cups liquid, water or clam juice
½ cup carrots, sliced
1 bay leaf
1 whole red pepper
½ lb. okra, chopped
½ lb. scallops
salt to taste
pepper to taste

½ lb. jumbo green shrimp, shelled, deveined and cut in half

1. Remove husks and silks from corn. Cut kernels off cob (makes about 4 cups); set aside.
2. Heat water and salt to boiling point in large kettle.
3. Add lobsters; return to boiling point.
4. Cover, reduce heat, simmer 10-15 minutes.
5. Remove lobsters; set aside to cool. Reserve lobster stock.
6. Heat oil in large stock pot; sauté onion, garlic, green pepper, celery and thyme until vegeatbles are limp.
7. Add tomatoes, cook and stir over low fire until tomatoes become mushy.
8. Add lobster stock, liquid, carrots, bay leaf, red pepper. Cover and cook 15-20 minutes.
9. Remove lid. Add okra, reserved corn, scallops, shrimp, salt and pepper to taste. Cook 10 minutes.
10. Meanwhile, remove lobster meat from shell, cut into bite-size pieces, add to soup just before serving.
11. Serve alone or with hot buttered Johnny cake.

NOTE: Sidney's soup, known simply as "okra soup" in the Bahamas, is made in many ways. Traditionally, conch and crabs are used for the soup (but they are sometimes difficult to obtain in the U.S.) with a medley of fresh vegetables, ranging from cassava, yams, potatoes and cabbage, to snap beans. Fresh thyme from the branch is added to the soup and the corn-on-the-cob is cut in quarters and thrown in the pot. Leftover chicken can be added. American cooks may substitute hard-shell crabs for lobster.

# Robert Redford

"I think women are wonderful and it's terrific to treat them like women. I seek femininity in a woman because it's simply more romantic to me," said Robert Redford. "I'm not saying a wife's role is in the kitchen, but my wife, who loves to cook and look after our children herself, also has a very independent life of her own."

Lola Redford, seated in the wonderfully comfortable "country kitchen" she designed in the spacious Upper Fifth Avenue apartment where the Redfords live, is a deceptively fragile-looking blonde. The Redfords are not true vegetarians, but they love quantities of fresh fruits and vegetables. They've had a vegetable garden out in Utah, in the mountain-top summer vacation house they both helped build. "We eat more chicken and fish, except when we're in Utah," said Lola. "There we can get a lot of wonderful beef."

Bob takes his turn in the kitchen, particularly out West, and likes barbecuing rainbow trout. "Bob adores making salads, but he really doesn't have much time to do any cooking. He's marvelous to cook for because he loves to eat. I mean, he will sit down to a meal and eat anything. We live in our kitchen! We like to sit around the corner table," Lola said, pointing to the big round oak table in the corner.

The biggest hit with the entire family is Lola's wonderful, homemade, quick whole wheat bread. "We often have it when we've been out skiing in Utah," said Lola. "I just love the recipe because the bread doesn't have to raise. Bob and the kids can hardly wait for it to come out of the oven to put some butter on it! The recipe came from my mother, out of an old Mormon cookbook."

# Robert Redford's Terrific Olive Green Salad

Serves 6-8

1 pkg. (9 oz.) frozen
  artichoke hearts
  or small can
  artichoke hearts,
  drained
1 cup boiling water
1 head romaine, torn into
  bite-size pieces
1 cup ming bean sprouts or
  1 can (16 oz.) bean sprouts,
  drained

½ cup salad oil
¼ cup wine vinegar or
  3 tbsps. fresh lemon juice
4 tsps. fresh dill, chopped,
  or 1 tsp. dill weed
1 tbsp. fresh parsley, chopped
2 scant tsps. sugar
1 tsp. Dijon mustard
1 tsp. salt
¼ tsp. freshly ground
  pepper

1 cup small, whole, pimento-stuffed olives

1. *Plunge artichoke hearts in boiling water; remove pan from heat and let stand for only 2 minutes.*
2. *Drain and chill.*
3. *In large salad bowl, combine artichoke hearts, romaine, bean sprouts and olives.*
4. *In small jar with a tight-fitting lid, combine salad oil, wine vinegar, dill, parsley, sugar, salt, mustard and pepper. Shake well to combine salad dressing ingredients.*
5. *Just before serving, pour dressing over salad and toss until well-coated.*

NOTE: Robert Redford's salad is terrific with barbecue steak or grilled rainbow trout. If desired, the salad can be made with additional greens, such as escarole or endives.

# Della Reese

"I don't cook by one cup milk, one-half cup eggs. I just get in there: I throw it all in a pot. And I love it and I rub it and I chop it with affection. There's a lot of T.L.C. (tender loving care) in there. And it always comes out very well," said the very loquacious Della Reese.

Delloreese (her real first name) is a gal who thinks in terms of *pounds*. To prepare her favorite dessert, strawberry short cake made with homemade pound cake, the songstress-cook supreme uses a *pound* of flour, a *pound* of butter and a *pound* of sugar. That may be why lately she has been thinking in terms of shedding *poundage*!

Standing in the sunny kitchen of her cliffside Hollywood Hills home, Della was in the throes of preparing some of her favorite salads, tossing greens in an ancient wooden salad bowl with a crack in one side, but a treasured possession prized for the task at hand. "Listen, I just lost 28 pounds, honey, because I like my cooking. I eat all the while I'm cooking. Since I don't go by one cup this and one spoon that, I steadily taste it to see if it's coming out all right. When it's done, I sit down and eat more than anybody else. It doesn't really matter to me that anybody else doesn't like the cooking 'cause it's cooked to suit me and I eat like a mad dog in heat!"

Della claims she can tell a lot about people from their food tastes. "A person who only likes celery, lettuce and things that aren't too spicy is usually mild-mannered. People with hefty tastes are usually a little looser, whereas, those who like spicy things are often kind of sexy."

# Della Reese's Chicken Salad à la Grecque

## Serves 2

1 head iceberg lettuce
1 cup chicken stock
¾ cup dry white wine
2 tbsps. fresh lemon juice
¼ tsp. curry powder
¼ tsp. rosemary
1 bay leaf

1 whole chicken breast, split
2 tsps. corn oil
salt to taste
freshly ground black pepper
   to taste
1 cup seedless green grapes
2 tbsps. feta or Monterey Jack
   cheese

1. *Core, rinse and drain lettuce thoroughly; chill in disposable plastic bag (or plastic crisper).*
2. *Bring chicken stock, wine, lemon, curry powder, rosemary and bay leaf to a boil.*
3. *Add chicken breasts; cover and simmer 15 to 20 minutes until chicken is tender.*
4. *Cool in broth.*
5. *Remove skin, cut into large chunks.*
6. *Tear lettuce into bite-size pieces; toss with 2 or 3 tbsps. chicken broth, corn oil, salt, pepper and grapes.*
7. *Top with crumbled or cubed cheese.*
8. *Heat remaining broth to sip with salad.*

NOTE: *Della likes to toss a salad in a glass or wooden salad bowl. Her favorite salad bowl is a large, 12-year-old wooden bowl bought in New York. To prepare the bowl for salad-making, she suggests, "Let bowl soak in oil – any kind will do – for three days. Pour off the oil, wipe dry with paper toweling. After using, it can be cleaned simply by wiping dry with paper toweling. It should be rinsed with water only, never soap. Dry thoroughly before putting away." Della learned her "soak-in-oil" trick from her late mother.*

# Jean Seberg

"I don't particularly like *haute cuisine*," said the late blonde, beautiful actress Jean Seberg. "I appreciate it, but how can you possibly appreciate an 18-course banquet if you have to eat it every day of your life? If it's an evening at Maxim's once a year, beautiful. But it's like having to live with the Mona Lisa all the time: sooner or later, you're gonna say, 'Honey, your nose is dripping!'

"One of the things that shocked me after a long period of being abroad was seeing peanut butter and grape jelly mixed together in a jar. America must be becoming decadent," she said, stretching her long legs. Jean made frequent reference to her Midwestern origin.

Her historic rise to "instant" fame (as the "Saint Joan" chosen from thousands by Otto Preminger, when she was 17 years old) was one of the classic celluloid Cinderella stories. The land of plenty left an indelible mark on Jean's palate, and left it as unchanged as a Grant Wood painting. "You are what you eat and, for me, that's fat," she said, laughing. (At 5'4", 108 pounds?)

In one respect, Jean said, her life had been a life-long diet, precipitated at least in part by her fondness for peanut butter. She used to have a friend in Baltimore who regularly sent a dozen jars a year to Europe. When she first lived in Paris, what she missed most was not being able to find a pizza parlor, but added she knew where to get doughnuts. The actress had a Midwesterner's reluctance to use prepared mixes or convenience foods. "If you're going to make a pie, you've got to make it from scratch. There are just some things you can't cheat on."

# Jean Seberg's Cucumber Soup

### Serves 4-6

3 medium-sized cucumbers
¼ cup green onion, minced
3 tbsps. butter
2 cans (10½ ozs.) chicken
  broth
1 cup liquid: water, milk or
  dry white wine

salt to taste
white pepper to taste
2 tsps. fresh dill, minced
1 cup dairy sour cream
fresh chives or parsley,
  minced

1. *Peel washed cucumbers and grate on coarse side of a grater.*
2. *Put cucumber in saucepan with onion and butter. Stew until barely tender.*
3. *Put through sieve or electric blender. Set aside.*
4. *To sieved cucumbers add chicken broth (undiluted), liquid, salt and pepper to taste. Mix well.*
5. *Add dill and pour soup into jar.*
6. *Cover and refrigerate several hours to chill well.*
7. *Taste to correct seasonings.*
8. *To serve, spoon soup into soup plates and garnish with generous dollops of sour cream and chives or parsley. Serve at once, alone, or with rye or pumpernickel bread and sweet butter.*

# Mary Stuart

Actress-musician Mary Stuart is familiar to her TV fans as Joanne Vincente, the central character in the CBS-TV daytime drama, "Search for Tomorrow." She has played Joanne ever since the program premiered in 1952.

Mary lives in a comfortable, antique-filled, sunny apartment near Madison Avenue in New York. This lovely lady, as Scotch as her name implies, is a proud member of the Stuart clan. "I'm pure Scotch," she said, giving me a cook's tour of her apartment that started with the dining room. "I don't entertain much, except on Sundays. I like to serve Sunday suppers, but I never invite more than 10 people, since I can't seat any more at this table! I'm an instant cook, especially now that I'm living alone for the first time."

Since her children, Cynthia and Jeffrey, are now grown, Mary says she has become "Nancy Neat, running around emptying ashtrays! I love to cook, especially when I'm in the mood. Then I go in for the whole long process. During the Christmas holidays it was wonderful because I had someone to cook for almost every meal! I always serve one hot dish, and everything else cold."

Mary's favorite hot dish is a French potato leek soup. Her most recent holiday menu was cold roast ham, chicken liver pâté (she makes hers with chopped onion, a little butter, and mayonnaise for flavor) and a "super dessert" of strawberries Romanoff. Her baked ham is a favorite with her children. "I just stick whole cloves in it and smear the whole thing with orange marmalade. Of course, I make my own marmalade. That tastes super and looks so pretty, too!"

# Mary Stuart's Potato Leek Soup

Serves 6

## For the chicken stock

Makes about 2 quarts

1 broiler-fryer chicken,
  cut up and ready to cook
1 small stalk celery with leaves
1/8 tsp. peppercorns, crushed
1 small yellow onion, peeled
  and stuck with 2 cloves

2 small carrots, peeled
  and cut in serving
  pieces
1/2 bay leaf
2 large sprigs parsley
about 1 1/2 tsps. salt

water to cover chicken, about 3 quarts

1. *Cut chicken into serving pieces. Add chicken to large stock pot with remaining ingredients, with enough water to cover.*
2. *Heat to simmering, skimming off any foam that forms on surface.*
3. *Simmer 2 hours, or until chicken is tender and stock is tasty!*
4. *Strain stock, reserve chicken pieces.*
5. *Cool and skim off most of the fat.*
6. *Measure 4 cups chicken stock for potato leek soup. (Reserve remaining stock to flavor chicken casseroles, if desired.)*

## For the potato leek soup

4 leeks (white part only),
  minced
1 small yellow onion, peeled and
  minced
1 1/2 tbsps. butter or
  margarine
6 potatoes, peeled and sliced

about 1 quart homemade
  (or canned) chicken stock
2 tsps. salt
freshly ground black pepper
  to taste
1 1/2 cups light cream
1 cup milk

1. *Sauté leeks and onions in butter until vegetables soften.*
2. *Place leek-onion mixture in large stock pot with all remaining ingredients except cream and milk.*
3. *Bring to boiling point; reduce heat to simmer.*
4. *Simmer uncovered about 45 minutes or until potatoes soften.*
5. *Run through a sieve. Return strained stock to stock pot.*
6. *Taste to correct seasoning.*
7. *Add cream and milk; reheat to serve piping hot! If desired, garnish with grating of freshly ground black pepper or chopped chives.*

# Gloria Swanson

Gloria Swanson has retained her perennially trim figure without counting calories. "I don't advise people how to eat," she said. " I've gotten so I can watch people eat ground glass if they want to. As for myself, I believe in keeping the body clean inside by eating lots of natural foods, especially green leafy foods, rich in chlorophyll. Most Americans are pill happy and if they would eat good food raised in rich soil, they would be much healthier. But please distinguish between nutrition and diet. We should think in terms of nutrition and not diet: for most Americans the word diet means counting calories.

"I'm appalled by what Americans put in their tummies. If you're hungry for something, eat meat but don't mix it with clams, whipped cream and four martinis. And then many Americans wonder why they have poor complexions. I eat natural foods without salt. I do use grated rock salt on celery and salads, and lemon in place of salt to season vegetables, and a little sweet butter."

Gloria is no great steak lover, but prepares it at home, trimming off the fat before grilling. She eats fish if "I can see it caught with my own eyes." For dessert, she prefers fruit picked right off the tree. "I always have lots of fruit in my house, such as grapefruit, papayas and bananas. I like my fruit untampered (without added sugar)."

Her tonic for a natural cleanser, called potassium broth, she prepares from unsprayed vegetables flown in from California. "Drink the broth every few hours, hot or cold," she said. "It tastes sweet, as all the natural flavors of the food come out. It's one of the best cleaners I know."

# Gloria Swanson's Potassium Broth

string beans, chopped

outer green stalks of celery, chopped

zucchini, chopped

few leaves Swiss chard, chopped

spring or mountain water

1. *Wash all the vegetables.*
2. *Measure 1 cup chopped vegetables per 2 cups spring water. Do not use tap water.*
3. *Cover, cook in glass pan or pressure cooker, simmering until the celery is tender.*
4. *Allow the broth to cool to room temperature.*
5. *Refrigerate in large screw-type glass jars.*

# Liv Ullmann

"They say if you take fresh grapefruit with your meals, you don't have to worry about weight-adding," Norwegian actress Liv Ullmann said, ordering a "dieter's lunch" at the Warner Brothers commissary. There was no indication that Liv, looking cool and refreshed in a beige, form-fitting knitted dress, had been working since early that morning, filming outdoors on location in humid, 100° weather.

Liv, pronounced "Leave," looks even better in person than she does on the screen. She's blonde with beautiful clear-blue eyes. A big food lover, and never a dieter — she habitually walks off her food in her home city of Oslo — she finally settled for a high protein lunch of broiled lean chopped steak, cottage cheese and sliced tomatoes.

"Let me tell you about my favorite meal for company," she said eagerly. "It's not Norwegian, but a beautiful beef soup made with Japanese vegetables. It's my favorite way of cooking: you just pour everything into it, starting with delicious meat I marinate overnight and add bean sprouts and bamboo shoots."

Liv's idea of "heaven" is eating in "any good Chinese restaurant."

She seemed happy, too, about returning home, looking forward to her favorite Norwegian dessert of cloudberries, *multer med krem* (cloudberries with cream).

Liv Ullmann, who was touted as the new Bergman or Garbo, has made it on her own talent, her natural honesty and straight-forward manner. She shuns becoming a Hollywood star. "There are too many temptations that go along with that — suddenly you want all the money that goes with it and start picking things for the money and start believing in all this nonsense."

# Liv Ullmann's Fish and Mushroom Soup

Serves 8

½ cup soy sauce or oyster
    sauce
¼ cup water
3 tbsps. dry sherry
3 tbsps. white onion,
    minced
1 tbsp. rice wine vinegar
2 lbs. fish: 1 lb. abalone,
    fresh preferably, or
      1 lb. halibut steaks,
    fresh or frozen
½ lb. raw shrimp, fresh
    or frozen

½ lb. crabmeat, fresh or
    frozen
¼ lb. butter
1 lb. fresh mushrooms or 2 cans
    (6 to 8 ozs.), sliced and drained
1½ cups cabbage, finely
    shredded
1 can (1 lb.) bean sprouts,
    drained and rinsed
1 can (8½ ozs.) bamboo
    shoots, drained
1 can (8 ozs.) water chestnuts,
    drained and sliced

1. *Combine soy sauce, water, sherry, onion, and vinegar for marinade; let stand 10 minutes.*
2. *Cut abalone or halibut into strips. Throw fish strips, shrimp and crabmeat into marinade.*
3. *Cover and refrigerate 2 hours.*
4. *In large wok or skillet, heat butter. Add mushrooms; sauté 3 minutes.*
5. *Add cabbage; sauté 2 minutes.*
6. *Add fish and marinade; stir-fry 5 minutes.*
7. *Add bean sprouts, bamboo shoots and water chestnuts; stir-fry 5 minutes longer.*
8. *If desired, serve with rice.*

*NOTE: Liv's soup is as thick as a stew, therefore excellent as a main dish offering. If oyster sauce (available in Oriental food shops) is used, dilute slightly with water, as oyster sauce has a meatier, saltier taste than soy sauce. Abalone is available fresh on the West Coast, but otherwise in very limited supply in cans in other parts of U.S. Frozen clams, or any firm white fish make an interesting substitute for abalone or halibut. Since fish soup is meaty and richly flavored, serve with either a well-chilled red California wine or a good imported Beaujolais.*

# Meats

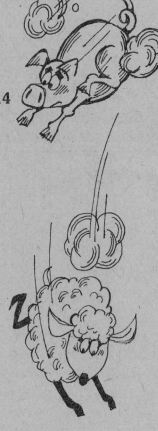

# Alan Alda

"I bummed around Europe for a year and had a terrific time. I often ran out of money until one day I had to push my Skoda (a Czechoslovakian car) into Rome. So all I had was a broken-down car and a loaf of bread on the seat beside me." Actor Alan Alda was describing what he called "the best year of my education in Europe."

Alda, the tall, lanky video doctor known as "Hawkeye" to millions of CBS-TV "M*A*S*H" viewers, reminisced about "being on my own" when he went to Paris to study at the Catholic Institute of Philosophy. "Most of the time I didn't eat too well. It was a pure case of mismanagement. I had something like $25 or $30 a week to live on, adequate if you didn't eat too much. It wasn't until years later, when I went back to France, I found how really great French food can be. I particularly love their famous sauces. I like my steak on the plain side, but *Steak au Poivre* (Pepper Steak) is a great favorite of mine, and I like Steak Diane, too, when it's made very well."

Alda works in California, but prefers living in a suburban New Jersey town, 15 minutes from New York. "Most of our best friends live in our small town. Arlene's (his wife) the real cook of our family, but if I have to, I can cook for myself. I make rubbery pancakes, horrible chili – and that's exactly what it is – and 'diet' pizza. But, my things doesn't interest anybody." That may be why this modest cook leaves the kitchen chores to his wife.

# Arlene Alda's Pepper Steak

Serves 4

2 lbs. top-grade steak,
   cut 1-inch thick
2 tbsps. peppercorns
salt to taste
3 tbsps. butter
1 tbsp. fresh parsley, minced

few drops oil from pressed
   garlic
3 tbsps. beef broth
3 tbsps. Cognac
watercress or parsley for
   garnish

1. *Dry steaks with a paper towel.*
2. *Crush peppercorns coarsely with a rolling pin or with a mortar and pestle. Rub and press crushed peppercorns into both sides of the steaks using your fingers and the heel of your hand.*
3. *Let steaks stand at room temperature for several hours, or until the meat absorbs the flavor of the pepper.*
4. *Pre-heat grill. Broil steaks 3-4 inches from source of heat until brown; turn and grill on reverse side about 5 minutes longer for very rare meat; longer for well-done steak.*
5. *Transfer steak at once to a heated platter and salt to taste.*
6. *Pour cooking juices from broiler pan into a small skillet, adding butter, parsley, garlic, beef broth and Cognac.*
7. *Cook over medium heat until sauce is reduced in volume by 1/2.*
8. *Pour sauce over steak. Garnish with watercress. Serve at once.*
9. *Lovely alone or served with French fries and a cool, crisp green salad.*

*NOTE: If desired, steaks may be pan-fried in a skillet. Use a mixture of half-salt and half-sweet butter to pan-fry steaks. If desired, a pinch of parsley or tarragon butter (flavored with a few drops fresh lemon juice and 1 drop garlic) may be added directly to steaks just before serving and sauce omitted in the preparation. Either way the steak is sensational!*

# June Allyson

"I say this without absolutely any modesty. I make the greatest stew you'll ever encounter. Richard (late husband Dick Powell) used to eat tons of it," actress June Allyson said while consuming *beaucoup* calories: asparagus vinaigrette and a gargantuan portion of a New York sirloin strip steak swimming in melted sweet butter. The actress would appear to be a gorger and/or compulsive eater. The truth is, June eats to keep her weight up and her nervous energies going. Dick Powell once threatened to market June's famous "Allyson Stew." As June explained, "We used to live out on our boat a lot. Habitually, I had to make this stew for Richard at least four times a week. Finally, when we got the freezers, I'd make barrels of it and just chuck it into the freezer. I love to cook and do simple things: lovely fillet of sole or halibut with lemon-butter. Fish is always delicate and lovely to eat. I have to eat a lot of fattening things now so I don't get too thin. You don't really get a lot of energy from potatoes and bread like you do from meat or fish."

June still has one habit that persists from her early movie days — that of always consuming all the food props that are used in eating scenes. "I did it recently, and they hated me for it. There's never any left for retakes. It must be a carryover from my childhood. We never had enough money for food and, boy, if food was there, I was going to eat it before somebody took it away! I had a breakfast scene where I wasn't supposed to be able to eat anything, but they were to serve me scrambled eggs. They thought, 'This will be simple. We only need one order because she's not supposed to eat it.' I fooled them and ate the eggs anyway!"

# June Allyson's Beef Stew
## à la Dick Powell

Serves 4-6

2 lbs. lean round or chuck
  steak
3 tbsps. butter
1 large onion, peeled and
  chopped
1 clove garlic, minced
2 cups carrots, sliced
2 cups potatoes, cut in
  large pieces
2 stalks celery, chopped

2 cups water or undiluted
  beef broth
½ cup vermouth
1½ tsps. salt
½ tsp. oregano
½ tsp. tarragon
1 bay leaf
2 cups green peas or string
  beans
1 cup corn, cut from cob

Parmesan cheese, freshly grated

1. Brown beef quickly in melted butter and remove to heated dish.
2. Brown onion and garlic in pan drippings over low heat.
3. Prepare vegetables; set aside.
4. Return beef and stock to pan with onion and garlic.
5. Add carrots, potatoes, celery, water, vermouth, seasonings and herbs. Cover and simmer about 1¼ hours, or until meat is tender.
6. Add green peas and corn. Cook 10 minutes, or until vegetables are tender.
7. Taste to correct seasonings.
8. Spoon into soup plates.
9. Garnish with Parmesan cheese at table.
10. If desired, stew can be thickened with flour, but it tastes best with just the natural juice of the vegetables and meat to flavor it.

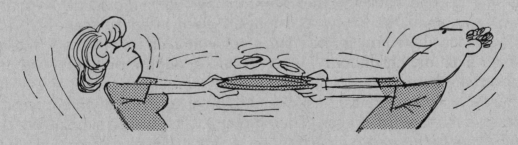

# Bill Anderson

Country music superstar Bill Anderson claims the three loves in his life are: "country music, sports and writing." After sharing a delightful evening with him over a Japanese dinner in a New York restaurant, I realized he had a fourth passion: great food!

Dining shoeless, seated on the floor in the Japanese manner, Bill wrestled his way through the intricacies of the Japanese menu. When some of the specialties of the house were not available, he responded to a friendly suggestion that he try dining in a nearby Korean restaurant with, "Sure, let's go get some Seoul food." He happily settled in the end for some delicious soy bean soup and *sukiyaki* (thin strips of steak, celery, onion, bamboo shoots and mushrooms simmered in a tasty, soy-flavored sauce).

It was plain that Bill was lonesome for his wife, Becky. "Becky is a marvelous cook!" he boasted. "Her corncakes are the greatest. She has a way of frying them in a skillet that's totally different from anything I've ever tasted. Her fried chicken is something else, too! I often cooked when I was alone, but I don't know if I can even still make a meat loaf! Occasionally, I cook dinner at home, but creative cooking involves a big time factor. While I'm sitting there waiting for the food to get done, I could be writing a song. I don't seem to have the patience real cooking demands."

# Becky Anderson's Beef Stew

### Serves 8

⅓ cup shortening

3 lbs. boneless beef,
    cut into 1½-inch cubes

2 medium-sized onions, peeled
    and chopped

6 cups water with 2 beef
    bouillon cubes, or 6
    cups beef broth

1½ cups dry red wine

1½ tsps. instant garlic
    flakes, minced

few sprigs fresh parsley,
    chopped

1 bay leaf

¼ tsp. thyme

2 tsps. salt

¼ tsp. freshly ground
    black pepper

10 potatoes, peeled and cut up

10 carrots, peeled and cut in
    large pieces

10 pearl onions, peeled

2 medium-sized green peppers,
    cut in large pieces

2 medium-sized tomatoes,
    peeled and cut in large chunks

1. *Heat shortening in large skillet or Dutch oven.*
2. *Brown beef quickly in hot fat.*
3. *Remove beef from skillet and set aside.*
4. *Brown onion in pan drippings; return beef to skillet.*
5. *Add water and bouillon cubes, wine, garlic, parsley, bay leaf, thyme, salt and pepper. Bring to boiling point.*
6. *Reduce heat. Cover and simmer about 1½ hours.*
7. *Add potatoes, carrots and onions; cook 45 minutes longer or until vegetables are tender.*
8. *During last 20 minutes of cooking time, add green pepper and tomato.*
9. *Taste to correct seasonings. Serve at once!*

NOTE: *Becky advises, "We particularly enjoy stew in fall and winter. You can make a big pot of it, eat part of it and freeze the rest."*

# Loni Anderson

Actress Loni Anderson is more than a casual cook. However, since starting her work in the CBS series, "WKRP in Cincinnati," she finds "fast cooking and a microwave oven a real godsend. But I love to cook." Loni spoke as she hungrily pulled leaves from a boiled artichoke at the out-of-the-way French restaurant, Le Petit Gourmet.

"And my husband's a real gourmet cook," she added, referring to actor Ross Bickell. "We share the cooking. Ross is always looking for new recipes to try. However, he doesn't want to be expected to cook. But neither do I."

Luckily, Loni has no weight problem, but Ross does. "When we first got married, I made all these heavy dishes — chicken and dumplings, Swedish meatballs, mashed potatoes and yummy desserts like rhubarb pie or cheesecake. I didn't gain an ounce, but Ross gained 20 pounds. Now, of course, he has lost the weight plus more and looks great."

Loni enjoys trying out new recipes. "I made a delicious new fettucine with shredded, sautéed zucchini and mushrooms, flavored with Parmesan cheese. It's so delicious and light."

# Loni Anderson's Gourmet Party Stroganoff

### Serves 14

4 lbs. lean boneless
   sirloin steak or
   tenderloin tips
about ½ lb. sweet butter
3 medium yellow onions,
   peeled and minced
1 lb. fresh mushrooms,
   washed, pat-dried and sliced
1½ tsps. fresh dill, minced

1 tsp. paprika
2 tsps. Dijon mustard
1 cup dry sherry or beef bouillon
2-3 drops Tabasco sauce
salt to taste
freshly ground black pepper
   to taste
1-1½ pints dairy sour cream
hot cooked wild rice

1. Prepare meat carefully, removing fat and gristle. Slice into 1½- x ⅜-inch strips.
2. Pound with meat hammer on chopping board to flatten and tenderize.
3. Heat heavy iron skillet to searing temperature.
4. Drop in part of butter, a few tablespoons at a time. Just before butter starts to smoke and burn, drop in meat, a few strips at a time. Brown meat quickly on both sides.
5. Remove meat to heated casserole. Butter is quickly absorbed, so keep adding it, heating as directed before browning remainder of the meat.
6. Reduce heat under skillet. Add more butter and sauté onions slowly until golden. Remove with slotted spoon to casserole.
7. Add remaining butter and sauté mushrooms over low heat. Remove from skillet to casserole.
8. Reduce heat under skillet to simmer and smoothly blend into pan juices dill, paprika, mustard, sherry, Tabasco, salt and pepper to taste.
9. Stir continuously and bring to low simmer. Turn heat down until bubbling stops completely.
10. Blend in sour cream. Add more seasoning to taste. (For thicker sauce, add more sour cream, seasonings.)
11. Add mushrooms, meat and onion. There should be enough sauce to coat each strip of meat.
12. Put in preheated 350° F. oven for 15 minutes. Serve piping hot over hot cooked wild rice.

NOTE: Loni's stroganoff is exceptionally rich, but wonderful! For sharper sauce omit dill, add accent of chili powder.

# Ursula Andress

"I love somebody who cooks for me. I love someone who reads to me. I'm always looking for that," said Swiss-born "sex-symbol" Ursula Andress. "If they read or play music for me, that's lovely. And if I find somebody who cooks fabulously, then, of course, I eat at home. But if I'm at home and the maid doesn't cook as well as I do, I cook. I love to cook."

This luscious actress looked the least-likely candidate for the kitchen as she swept into the room at mid-morning with the grand gesture. "If only I had lived during the golden era of films and been a great movie star," she said with a devious little-girl glint in her eyes. "I cook spaghetti and I like Chinese and Japanese food. I love American food – charcoal-broiled steak and a baked potato! You never get any better baked potato in this world. I adore that with the butter and the pepper and sour cream. I love that charcoal-broiled New York-cut steak. And I love sandwiches.

"The hot dogs and the different pastrami and roast beef sandwiches are delicious. So when I come to America, I don't come to eat French food, because it can't compare to the French food in France. I adore the scrambled eggs and the corn bread and the apple jam on it. I think Americans have the best breakfasts in the world."

Ursula offered a great Rumanian-Hungarian goulash recipe to me, explaining, "I use a lot of things. I go to the butcher and have him specially cut the meat. In Europe they cut the meat entirely differently."

# Ursula Andress's Hungarian Goulash

### Serves 8

3 lbs. top-grade beef steak:
   sirloin or Porterhouse
"seasoned" flour: flour, salt,
   pepper, Hungarian sweet paprika
2-3 tbsps. vegetable oil or butter
3 onions, peeled and chopped
2 large peppers, cut into large
   pieces
4 large ripe tomatoes, peeled
   and cut into quarters

1 clove garlic, pressed
2 tsps. salt
freshly ground black pepper
   to taste
2 heaping tbsps. Hungarian Sweet
   paprika
about 1½ cups liquid: beef
   stock mixed with ⅓ cup
   Cognac
handful chopped parsley

1. *Trim fat from beef; cut into 1½-inch cubes.*
2. *Sprinkle meat liberally with seasoned flour; set aside.*
3. *Heat vegetable oil in heavy Dutch oven; add onions and peppers.*
4. *Cook slowly until vegetables begin to soften. Remove vegetables and set aside.*
5. *Add more vegetable oil to Dutch oven, if needed, and brown beef quickly on all sides.*
6. *Return vegetables to Dutch oven with tomatoes, garlic, salt, pepper, paprika and liquid. Mix well.*
7. *Cover and cook over low heat about 1½ hours, stirring occasionally.*
8. *Remove cover and cook ½ hour longer to reduce stock. Correct seasonings.*
9. *Garnish with parsley. Serve with boiled potatoes, buttered noodles or sauerkraut.*

NOTE: *Ursula often prepares goulash with wine in lieu of Cognac, particularly when she serves it with sauerkraut (cooked with goulash or cooked as a side dish flavored with red wine, apples, bay leaf, onion and spices). Paprika can be substituted for sweet Hungarian paprika.*

# Ed Asner

"I'm not a cook, but I'm very much a consumer, as you can see." said jovial Ed Asner, rubbing his chest while drinking his morning coffee. Ed sat in the dining room of the Bel Air home he shares with his wife, Nancy, their three children and a menagerie of animals, including three dogs, two cats, turtles and tropical fish.

A huge teddy bear of a man, the two-time Emmy-winner is as funny and charming a "heavy" in real life as he is as the short-tempered but warm-hearted city editor Lou Grant on CBS. He exudes warmth, and his sharp, biting wit fades early, revealing very much the homebody he is. "Listen, my wife is a great cook!" the actor said proudly. "She does so much cooking and has so many standbys, I've forgotten all of their names. She's not worth a damn at breakfast or lunch, but, man, does she make up for it at dinner!" Ed's smile almost reached up to his balding brow.

Ed gave me the grand tour, starting in the U-shaped Spanish kitchen, where Nancy does "her stuff." It's a pretty but functional kitchen with white tiles, copper fishmolds and unique touches, like an old sign reading: "Rooms for Rent, No Theatricals." It has easy access to the dining room, which is outfitted with Mexican cane-bottom chairs and a cherrywood harvest drop-leaf table.

# Nancy Asner's Sweet-and-Sour Leg of Lamb

### Serves 6-8

1 butterflied boneless leg of lamb, weighing 6-8 lbs.

½ cup pineapple preserves · 1 tsp. salt

⅓ cup vinegar ¼ tsp. liquid smoke

¼ cup soy sauce 2 tbsps. cornstarch

¼ cup brown sugar ¼ cup cold water

1. *Put butterflied leg of lamb on rack of roasting pan and place in preheated 325° F. oven.*
2. *Combine all ingredients except cornstarch and water in saucepan over low heat.*
3. *Stir cornstarch into cold water until smooth, then add to saucepan, stirring constantly.*
4. *Cook and stir until mixture comes to a boil. Allow mixture to simmer 3 minutes, or until thickened and clear.*
5. *Baste lamb with sauce, and continue to baste every 10-14 minutes throughout roasting time (1½ hours, or until meat thermometer registers 170° F. for medium doneness).*
6. *Serve alone, or with new potatoes and minted garden peas.*

*NOTE: Have butcher "butterfly" boneless leg of lamb. Lamb may also be broiled or grilled over coals. For both cooking methods, place meat about 6 inches from source of heat and cook for 20-25 minutes per side, or until meat thermometer reaches 170° F. Baste with sauce during cooking time as directed above.*

# Bob Barker

Bob Barker grew up in the small town of Mission, South Dakota, where he spent his summers fishing in the river, cooking bullheads (freshwater catfish) over an open fire, and savoring baked potatoes he and his Indian buddies cooked by burying them in the dirt.

Seated in Michelangelo's, a new Beverly Hills restaurant, he dug into the specialty of the day: cannelloni, tender crêpes filled with a veal/spinach mixture and topped with a delicate Bechamel sauce. "My wife (Dorothy Jo) would love this," he said.

"I can eat or drink anything," Bob added. "My biggest decision of the day is: What will I drink tonight? I like martinis, bourbon and soda or vodka on the rocks. I'm the same about food. Dorothy Jo cooks beautiful Italian and Mexican food."

After lunch, we visited Bob's home. Dorothy Jo, who was in the midst of baking a prize-winning carrot cake, told us, "I love to prepare five-course dinners, but I can't find anyone to eat that way. Everyone's always on a diet. I like to begin with *seviche*, *gazpacho*, and my special Mexican salad."

The beef mole she prepares is a real winner, and part can be made ahead, frozen, and assembled just before serving. For dessert, she serves orange sections sprinkled with Cointreau, Tequilla and lime, which she describes as "a margarita without the salt."

# Dorothy Jo Barker's Beef Mole Antonio

### Serves 12-16

hot water
6 *ancho* (Mexican chili peppers)
4 *pisalla* (Mexican chili peppers)
4 *mulato* (Mexican chili peppers)
2 onions, chopped
4 cloves garlic, peeled and minced
1/3 cup peanuts
1/3 cup pumpkin seeds
1 tsp. sugar
4 tbsps. sesame seeds
1 tsp. cumin
1 tortilla (dry)
3 medium-sized tomatoes

1 can (1 lb.) *tomatillo* (green tomatoes, available in Mexican store or gourmet grocery)
1 cup of almonds, blanched
1/2 cup raisins
1/2 tsp. cloves
1/2 tsp. cinnamon
1/2 tsp. coriander
2 cups beef broth
2 circles of Ibarra brand Mexican chocolate (semi-sweet cooking chocolate flavored with cinnamon)
5 lbs. top sirloin, cut in bite-sized chunks
about 3 1/2 tbsps. shortening
salt to taste
freshly ground pepper to taste

1. *Put enough hot water over ancho, pisalla, and mulato to cover. Let soak 20 minutes or until chili peppers soften slightly.*
2. *Discard water, seeds, and veins from peppers. Leave skin on.*
3. *Combine all remaining ingredients except beef broth, chocolate, beef, shortening, salt and pepper. Put through blender. It will take 3 or 4 containerfuls to blend the entire mixture.*
4. *Heat 4 tsps. shortening in large skillet. Stir over low heat 5 minutes.*
5. *Add beef broth and chocolate. Cook until chocolate is melted, stirring over low heat. Combine with above mixture.*
6. *Sauté sirloin in separate skillet with remaining shortening. Use as little shortening as possible, as meat has its own fat.*
7. *Cook meat until brown and well done. Season to taste with salt and pepper.*
8. *Put meat in bottom of greased casserole dish; top with sauce. Heat in 350° F. oven until thoroughly heated through. Serve piping hot.*

NOTE: *Dorothy Jo likes to make and freeze the sauce in advance, leaving the broth, chocolate and seasonings to be added on serving day.*

# Ralph Bellamy

"I've always fancied myself a chili maker and I've made some that's pretty good," Ralph Bellamy said. "I used to make chili from scratch, but some friends sent me a packaged mix with everything except the meat – beautiful, beautiful chili!

"I like seasoning in food. Chili's often thought to be a Mexican dish. Actually, it's not at all, it's a Texas border dish." Ralph's not keen on using the fiery chili powder to excess. "You should perspire a little, but I don't think you should have to go around blowing your tongue for a half hour afterwards!"

He's equally adept at making an offbeat stew. "I've got a crazy recipe that defies every rule in the kitchen. It has no water, only wine. I just invented it one time and it's pretty good."

The veteran actor once excelled as a soda jerk when he was a high school lad in New Trier, Illinois. "I used to make a beautiful chocolate soda; put in the chocolate, ice cream and two kinds of squirt. I was finally eased out of that job because I was over-serving my friends too many scoops of ice cream and too many malted milks!"

Asked if he'd ever prepared game, Ralph answered, "Oh yes, venison is delicious. There are roasts, chops and steaks, but it's dry meat so you've got to use a little butter with it. The steaks and chops are really better fried in a skillet. They take a little cooking too, because it's pretty solid meat. First marinate it in wine, a little seasoning, onion and pepper. I'm drooling," he added, laughing.

Before leaving the set, I ran into Bellamy's director, George Schaeffer, packing a copy of Ralph's chili recipe in his briefcase along with the script for his nightly homework!

# Ralph Bellamy's Pork Vegetable Stew

### Serves 4-6

2½ lbs. pork chops
3 stalks celery with leaves, chopped
4 small onions, chopped
4 potatoes, peeled and cut in large pieces
6 medium-sized carrots, peeled and cut in large pieces
1 clove garlic, pressed

2 sprigs parsley
½ tsp. ground sage
large pinch dried thyme
1 bay leaf
1½ tsp. salt
freshly ground pepper to taste
about 2½ cups dry red wine
1 lb. cleaned spinach or 1 pkg. (10 ozs.) frozen leaf spinach

1. *Trim off excessive fat from pork chops and broil on both sides. Cool.*
2. *Drain off excess fat from broiler pan; reserve pan drippings to flavor stew.*
3. *Put rest of ingredients except wine and spinach in a large saucepan. Add 2 cups wine. Bring to a boil, cover, and simmer 45 minutes.*
4. *Dice pork, add to saucepan with bones and pan drippings from broiler. Add more wine if needed.*
5. *Cover and simmer 45 minutes longer.*
6. *Uncover, add spinach, and cook until barely tender and most of liquid is absorbed.*
7. *Taste to correct seasonings.*
8. *Serve alone or with tossed well-chilled green salad and your favorite libation.*

# Karen Black

Actress Karen Black is constantly dreaming up new recipes. Her latest interest is searching for ways to include honey and chili paste – a hot, garlicky ingredient typical of Szechuan cuisine, in her culinary creations.

"Lately, I'm really into health foods," she said. "I particularly like to use honey instead of sugar in my cooking. I've noticed if you eat sugar, you gain more weight than if you use honey to sweeten food. Honey doesn't seem to confuse body chemistry the way sugar does. Sugar is used in such idiotic ways, even in canned beans! You can find all kinds of dishes to make with honey if you look for them – for example, custards, pies, bread. I use honey to sweeten strawberries and other fruits.

"One thing I love is steak soup. You cut up a lovely piece of steak, brown it in a saucepan with a bunch of vegetables, add some canned beef broth, V-8 and beet juice, and you have a wonderful meal in less than half an hour!"

# Karen Black's 10-Minute-Tomato-Beef
# Chinese Number

Serves 4

1 cup celery, cut in thin,
  bias strips
salted boiling water
2 tbsps. safflower oil
1 lb. top quality, lean boneless Porterhouse or sirloin, cut in thin, bite-
  size strips

½ green pepper, diced
1½ cups cherry tomatoes,
  washed and stemmed
about 2 tbsps. tomato sauce
2 tbsps. soy sauce
freshly ground pepper
  to taste
cooked brown rice

1 small yellow onion, chopped, or couple tbsps. scallion, minced

1. *Pre-cook celery quickly in salted boiling water until barely tender.*
2. *Heat oil in wok or large skillet; brown meat and onion quickly on all sides.*
3. *Add celery, green pepper, cherry tomatoes, tomato sauce and soy sauce. Boil quickly, stirring often.*
4. *Taste to correct seasonings. Add in additional soy sauce and pepper as needed.*
5. *Serve very hot over cooked brown rice.*

# Joan Blondell

"Our mother did the cooking because we couldn't afford to eat out when vaudeville began to decline," said veteran actress Joan Blondell during an interview shortly before her death in 1980.

"Our father had rigged up a little portable stove. We had two pans that took care of frying steak and potatoes. My mother always put salt on the bottom of the pan to pan-broil the steak. With five or six sternos, there was enough heat to cook a steak. I don't know how she did it," the silver-haired Joan said as she sipped a spritze at Jack's at the Beach.

The Blondells stuffed cotton in the keyholes to keep the cooking odors from wafting through the boarding house. "Somehow, we all survived."

Joan has many wonderful food memories, including the food served on board the *Santa Paula*, the luxury liner on which she honeymooned with her second husband, the late actor Dick Powell. "We were always seated at the Captain's Table. I wish my grandchildren could have such a wonderful experience. That's why I'm working now. I want to put aside enough so they can go on a long, lavish trip. Being so family-oriented, I love to cook for others, but I'm really out of practice. Cooking is like dancing – you have to do it every day. Whenever my grandchildren come over, they always ask for spareribs. I don't know where my recipe came from. It's a favorite from our travels."

# Joan Blondell's Barbecued Spareribs

Serves 5-6

## For the ribs

5-6 lbs. pork spareribs,
  left whole
about 3 quarts water
1 small onion, peeled
  and chopped
1 large clove garlic, peeled
  and left whole

few sprigs parsley
1 small carrot, cut in
  large pieces
pinch dried thyme
½ tsp. salt
ground black pepper
  to taste

1 large bay leaf

1. *Choose top-quality lean spareribs. Place spareribs in large stock pot with remaining ingredients.*
2. *Simmer slowly about 1 hour or until meat is fork-tender.*
3. *Drain.*

## For the barbecue sauce

2 cups catsup
¼ cup white vinegar
½ cup brown sugar
1 cup very strong coffee

10 drops Tabasco (more if
  needed)
2-3 tbsps. butter or
  margarine

salt to taste

1. *Combine ingredients in saucepan and cook slowly over low flame about 30 minutes, or until sauce is reduced in volume one-fourth, stirring often to prevent scorching.*
2. *Rub both sides of ribs generously with butter and place on rack in flat roasting pan.*
3. *Roast in preheated 450° F. oven a few minutes, then begin basting frequently as ribs cook. Roast 20-25 minutes, or until ribs are crisp, glazed, browned and fork-tender.*
4. *Serve piping hot with mashed potatoes and a big bowl of homemade applesauce.*

NOTE: *Joan Blondell's barbecue sauce is the secret to her delicious spareribs. The coffee imparts a smoky flavor to the ribs. Barbecue sauce works equally well for ribs cooked outdoors over charcoal coals. Allow ¾ to 1 pound per serving. Sauce is excellent for barbecuing chicken, chops or steaks.*

# Helen Gurley Brown

"Cooking is just part of a girl's arsenal! It's only one of the implements a single girl can use to get a man into her life and have a better social life." So said Helen Gurley Brown, high priestess of the single-girl set.

Helen Gurley was a 37-year-old bachelor girl before her marriage to David Brown, a prominent motion picture producer. She said, "A single gal must have a man in her life to have a good life. As far as outright seduction goes, food can help lure a guy. Fix a wonderful meal, but you must look, sound, feel and smell good, too! It's sexy to be healthy, and cooking healthily means preserving the health value of the food."

She captures all the nutrients by including raw vegetables and fruits in her menus, cooking unpeeled vegetables in stews and cassoulets, and incorporating cooking juices from vegetables in soups and sauces. She injects a sense of humor into her cuisine by giving her specialties of the house sexy names, ranging from "libidinous lobster" (lobster *en brochette*) to "passionate pasta."

# Helen Gurley Brown's "Torrid Tripe"

### Serves 4-6

1½ lbs. honeycomb tripe
4 marrow bones, cut in
 1½-inch pieces
2 quarts water
½ cup beef bouillon
 (undiluted)
1 cup vegetable stock (from
 canned or fresh-cooked
 vegetables)
1⅓ cups fresh tomatoes,
 chopped
1 tbsp. blackstrap molasses
1 tbsp. vinegar
generous pinch savory

1 medium onion, stuck
 with a clove
generous pinch thyme
4 sprigs parsley
½ small bay leaf
1½ tsps. salt
½ tsp. freshly
 ground pepper
½ cup potato, diced
½ carrot, diced
½ cup yellow turnip,
 peeled and diced
3 tbsps. instant potato
 flakes

1. *Wash and shred tripe.*
2. *Add tripe to a large saucepan with bones, water, bouillon, stock, tomatoes, molasses, vinegar, onion, savory, thyme, parsley, bay leaf, salt and pepper.*
3. *Cover and simmer 2 hours.*
4. *Add diced vegetables; cover and simmer 1 hour longer, or until vegetables are tender.*
5. *Stir in potato flakes; cook 5 minutes.*
6. *Serve as main course alone, or with fresh rye bread and sweet butter.*

LIBIDINOUS LOBSTER     PASSIONATE PASTA

# James Caan

"I don't mind spending a lot of money for a fine dinner if I feel like it's been worth it!" is the way the very opinionated actor James Caan looks at food. The actor comes by his love for good food naturally, from his German-born parents, Arthur and Sophie Caan.

"My dad was in the meat business – he's retired now – and he knew about good restaurants because of being a meat purveyor. We always had good meat at home. I think Chinese food is probably my favorite food, either Mandarin or Szechuan.

"Let's say, I like food if it's good! I can cook for myself if I have to: like throw a steak on the fire or fry a hamburger. And I can call up the local pizza joint. My mother still makes things I love: potato pancakes, kugel, and her stuffed cabbage is the best! Cooking is still a hobby with my dad. He makes a great kidney stew. He can do wondrous things with chopped meat; he grinds it up with Worcestershire sauce, catsup, shredded onion, paprika and parsley."

Jimmy has become somewhat of a wine buff. "I'm a big fan of the Chardonnay Sauvignon of California. I think they're the best wines in the world. I'll match them with any wine in the world other than Lafitte Rothschild."

# James Caan's Kidney Stew

Serves 4

1½ lbs. veal or lamb kidneys
salted water
4 tbsps. salad oil, divided in half
¼ cup yellow onion
1 clove garlic, pressed (optional)
1 tbsp. tomato catsup

1 tsp. original Worcestershire sauce
salt to taste
freshly ground black pepper to taste
⅓ cup brandy or kirsch
hot, cooked potatoes, peeled
fresh minced parsley

1. *Remove all of the outer membrane and most of the fat, central fat and white tubes from kidneys.*
2. *Wash kidneys carefully in running water. Soak them in well-salted water about 30 minutes, changing water once (to remove the strong flavor).*
3. *Meanwhile, heat 2 tbsps. salad oil over low flame, adding onion and garlic. Cook, stirring, until onion is lightly golden.*
4. *Remove kidneys from water and dry well on absorbent toweling. Slice kidney into ½-inch slices.*
5. *In separate skillet, brown kidneys quickly in remaining salad oil until meat begins to turn white.*
6. *Add sautéed kidneys to onion-garlic mixture.*
7. *Stir in tomato catsup, Worcestershire sauce, and salt and pepper to taste. Simmer over low fire few minutes.*
8. *Pour brandy into a ladle that is hot (or hold ladle briefly over the burner).*
9. *Pour heated spirits over kidneys and flame. Do not flame longer than 1 minute or kidneys will toughen.*
10. *Serve at once with hot, peeled potatoes, garnished with fresh minced parsley.*

NOTE: *James Caan's father, Arthur, advises, "The whole dish is a short-process thing. If desired, use dry red wine (adding during the last 2 minutes of cooking). Also if desired, more spirits may be added to thin down the gravy."*

# John Cassavetes

"Men at work!" could have been the theme of the stag group that greeted me in the Sherry-Netherland Hotel suite. Blowups of the principals – Cassavetes, Falk and Gazzara – were scattered about the carpet and on virtually every chair. Peter Falk was absent, but Ben Gazzara paced the floor, kibitzing.

I interviewed director/actor John Cassavettes, an unpretentious guy, tieless, wearing a soft cashmere, sleeveless sweater. "Does your wife (actress Gena Rowlands) cook Greek dishes?" I asked. (Cassavetes is of Greek parentage.)

"Listen, I never promised to be loyal. She makes one Greek dish that she likes, but I don't particularly like," he replied amid lots of laughs and joshing from other cast members on the sidelines. "I didn't marry her for being a cook. But she's capable of cooking well. You know when I first married her, she promised she would never cook. She said, 'Let's go out to restaurants all the time and enjoy ourselves.' And then, of course, you have children and you have to cook for them."

Since Gena wasn't there to defend herself in the company of these men, I felt compelled to do that for her. So I asked about her specialties.

"She's terrific with sandwiches!" her husband said.

"She's trying pretty hard to cement this marriage, isn't she?" Gazzara wisecracked.

If you couldn't stand up under the teasing of these guys, you'd better fold your tent, tape recorder and go home *sans* story.

"Are you a veal man?" I asked.

"A veal man? No, I'm a leg man – a leg of lamb man. That's Gazzara's favorite dish, too." (The group that eats together stays together.)

# John Cassavetes' "Minted" Beef

### Serves 4

2 large yellow onions, chopped
2 tbsps. butter
1 can (16 ozs.) tomatoes
1 can water
½ tsp. sugar
salt to taste

freshly ground pepper
  to taste
1½ lbs. top round steak
2 tsps. fresh mint,
  crushed
2 eggs, beaten

### 1 cup rice, uncooked

1. *Sauté onions in butter until golden.*
2. *Add tomatoes, water, sugar, salt and pepper to taste. Simmer about 30 minutes, or until volume has reduced by ⅓, stirring often.*
3. *Trim and discard fat from steak.*
4. *Put meat through grinder twice with onion.*
5. *Add mint, eggs and rice.*
6. *With hands, form meat mixture into 1½-inch balls.*
7. *Drop meatballs into boiling sauce. Cook 10-15 minutes, or until rice is cooked. Add water so meatballs won't stick to pot.*

# Carol Channing

"I don't really have time to cook, but somehow you find the time to do the things you enjoy doing," Carol Channing said in her famous, squeaky-husky voice. The glamorous blonde used to be a regular Sunday cook in the days when her son, Chan, accompanied her on tour. "Most of the time we stayed in hotels and lived on room service, but on Sundays, we'd forego the hotel food and do our own cooking."

Although Carol's been consuming health foods almost exclusively for a number of years, even carrying her own food to swanky Hollywood or Manhattan parties, she still likes to prepare some old family favorites, particularly those she and Chan used to cook up. Carol looked terrific and was in a reminiscing mood. "My son and I used to adore cooking," she recalled. "We started when he was four." The family unit then consisted of Carol, Chan and his father, Charles Lowe, who is also Carol's manager. They kept their personal possessions to a minimum so there would be room to carry along all the kitchen gadgets they kept acquiring. The pair kept a book, *Lowe's Concoctions*, in which they recorded their cooking goofs and successes.

Carol's great love for sweets has more than once almost been her downfall. "My worst hang-up is cake," she said. "If I take a clothes hanger and twist it just right, I can reach into a fruit-filled cake and pull out the cherries and plums. One time, I gave a cake to a friend who served it that night at dinner. When he went to cut it, the cake collapsed. I had forgotten I'd pulled out all the cherries!"

Carol recalled that "Chan once wrote a composition about a typical day at home. When he wrote about the padlock we put on the refrigerator to stop my late-night eating, the teacher expressed surprise. I guess there's really no hope for me!"

# Carol Channing's German Pot Roast

Serves 8

4 lbs. beef brisket, all fat
  trimmed off
2 tsps. salt
1 tsp. ground ginger
1 clove garlic
½ tsp. dry mustard
2 cups red wine vinegar
1 cup water

2 medium yellow onions,
  peeled and quartered
2 bay leaves
2 tsps. mixed pickling spices
1 tsp. whole black peppercorns
8 whole cloves
⅓ cup sugar
2 tsps. fat or vegetable oil

6 ginger snaps, finely crushed

1. Rub meat with salt, ginger and cut garlic. Place in large bowl.
2. Combine remaining ingredients except fat and ginger snaps in a saucepan. Bring to a boil and pour over meat.
3. Cool, cover tightly, and place in refrigerator overnight, turning once.
4. Remove meat and reserve the marinade. Dry meat with paper towel.
5. Heat fat in a heavy skillet until sizzling. Sear meat on all sides.
6. Transfer meat to Dutch oven or deep, heavy skillet. Add 1¼ cups of marinade. Cover tightly, simmer on top of stove or braise in moderate oven for 3½ hours, or until meat is tender. Add more marinade as needed.
7. Remove meat to heated serving platter.
8. Strain liquid in pot and return to heat. Skim off excess fat.
9. Thicken with ginger snaps and season to taste with salt and pepper. Reduce gravy slightly, stirring constantly over low heat.
10. Slice meat diagonally and serve alone or with side dishes of gravy and new potatoes cooked in their jackets or potato dumplings or noodles.

NOTE: Carol's pot roast works well in the new "crock pot." Sear meat first as directed in recipe, then cook in crock pot at low oven temperature for 6-8 hours. Her dish is an old-fashioned delight, aromatic, delicious and memorable. Try it during cold, wintery days!

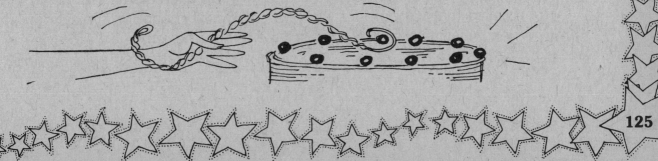

# Elisha Cook, Jr.

"Do I like stroganoff? I love it! This is delicious. I even ate some for lunch after I got killed." said Elisha Cook, one of Hollywood's most durable character actors. "I sure was glad to get my face out of the noodles though, because I couldn't breathe very well!" The "corpse" looked pretty lively after his dive, just minutes before, into a plate of stroganoff and noodles, where he had landed after he had been "shot"!

Certainly, the circumstances were unusual, but pure fun! The place looked authentic, an elaborate nightclub setting of the 30s, where even the food was real. Elisha was seated across from me at the same table where he'd just gotten bumped off on the set of *The Black Bird*, a spoof of *The Maltese Falcon*.

Elisha, who starred in *Falcon*, recreated his role of Wilmer Cook, the armed criminal in *Black Bird*. "Listen, I wouldn't bother cooking stroganoff," he said. "I like plain food. I do simple things like steak or trout. Tonight I'm taking some brook trout downtown to Bob Preston, who's performing in a play. He's gonna flip. He used to love to come up to a lake nearby where I live and camp out and fish. I smoke the trout in something special, but I'm not going to tell you what. Then people would go out in the mountains and rob the forest of the wood!"

# Elisha Cook Jr.'s Beef Stroganoff "Black Bird"

### Serves 6

2 lbs. top round steak
1½ tsps. salt
½ tsp. freshly ground
   pepper
2 tbsps. butter
1½ cups water

1 can (4 oz.) mushrooms,
   with liquid
1 onion, peeled and sliced
2 tsps. Angostura aromatic
   bitters
2 tbsps. flour

2 cups dairy sour cream

1. With a very sharp knife, cut beef across the grain into narrow 2-inch strips.
2. Salt and pepper meat on both sides and quickly brown it in hot butter in a skillet or Dutch oven.
3. Add water, mushrooms with liquid, onion and Angostura bitters.
4. Cover and simmer 45 minutes, or until meat is tender, stirring occasionally. Add additional water sparingly, if necessary, during cooking.
5. Make a paste with flour, using 2 tbsps. of pot liquid.
6. Add paste slowly to meat mixture, stirring constantly to prevent lumping. Simmer until gravy is thick.
7. Reduce heat to lowest possible level. Stir in sour cream and heat thoroughly, but do not boil, or sauce will curdle.
8. Remove to chafing dish. Serve alone or with hot, cooked noodles.

NOTE: Stroganoff makes a fabulous early autumn entrée to please your guests! Complete the menu with crisp green beans, cooked al dente, flavored with butter, a squeeze of lemon, small amount of grated lemon peel and a dash of white pepper. A green salad spiked with plenty of fresh, snipped parsley or dill completes the meal! For your favorite libation: well-chilled white or rosé wine!

# Bob Crane

"I'm a non-drinker and non-smoker, but I surely love to eat. One year I made over 265 personal appearances. I gained over 25 pounds. I swear I had gravy on everything, even the cornflakes," the late Bob Crane once told me. "It was the chicken circuit. My doctor told me to join the 'Y' and knock off the weight, which I finally did. My wife (he was then married to childhood sweetheart, Anne) laughs at me because I have skim milk in coffee, bypass the potatoes and then I'll have a chocolate nut sundae. I'm crazy about sweets. In our home in California, we have a cookie drawer. My son, Robert, has a great love for chocolate-covered cupcakes. But now he has the 'zits' (that's acne in California teen-age vernacular), so he's careful about the cupcakes.

"I cook an occasional steak, but Anne or my mother-in-law does all the cooking in our house. Our idea of a great dinner is shrimp cocktail, steak, fresh asparagus, a green salad and ice cream. Our entertaining consists of having a few good friends in, and we cook outdoors in an informal setting."

When asked about people who go in for food as a status symbol, Bob said, "The people who 'go Hollywood' are only a small minority. We just look at them and laugh and think, 'Why can't they be normal?' Of course, there are some people who have a genuine love for special foods." He cited director George Cukor, who has his own live-in French pastry chef. "He's one of the biggest directors out there, and he's basically just a nice guy with a great sense of humor."

# Bob Crane's Lamb Kebabs

### Serves 8

4 cups "boned-out" leg of
lamb, cut in 2-inch cubes

1/3 cup olive oil

1 cup wine vinegar

1 medium yellow onion,
sliced

1/8 tsp. garlic salt

1 1/2 tsps. salt

1/2 tsp. freshly ground
pepper

1/4 tsp. each dried oregano
and thyme

1 large green pepper, cut
in pieces

8 large or 16 small mushroom
caps

2-3 tomatoes, cut in quarters

1 onion, peeled and cut
in pieces

1 small jar whole drained
pimento

salt to taste

pepper to taste

1. Trim excess fat from lamb.
2. Prepare marinade by mixing together olive oil, vinegar, onion and seasonings.
3. Place meat in a bowl with marinade.
4. Cover and refrigerate several hours or overnight, turning meat occasionally.
5. Arrange lamb on skewers alternately with vegetables. Brush lightly with marinade.
6. Cook on outdoor grill over coals. Turn, basting frequently with marinade until meat is done – 15 minutes or longer, depending on size of cubes.
7. Season as desired.
8. Remove cooked lamb and vegetables from skewers onto plate. Great served alone or with rice pilaf and green salad!

# Walter Cronkite

"My work has broadened my waist and my palate," jovial TV newsman Walter Cronkite revealed, loading up his plate at the Copenhagen Restaurant in New York. Walter, a great appreciator of fine fare, has been eating there for 18 years. "I can pick out anything here from the *koldt bord* (cold table) and enjoy it, but what really attracts me most is the infinite variety of herring they serve – marinated, curried, sweet-and-sour, you name it."

Walter is two people. One, of course, is familiar – the dedicated, conscientious commentator. The other is the off-camera Cronkite – devoted father with a delicious sense of humor, fun-loving *bon vivant* who's been known to keep his wife Betsy out dancing until she's almost dead on her feet, and animal lover who once almost wrecked a car and himself to avoid running over a turtle!

A keen observer of the way people of different geographical and cultural backgrounds entertain and the food they serve, Walter noted that in dining with the "Eastern establishment" the food usually tended toward continental dishes, but was rather poorly prepared and in short supply. "I starve to death in the homes of famous people!"

In contrast, Walter favored "the Midwestern or Southwestern pioneer tradition which dictates that you overfeed everyone who comes to the door! If a businessman comes to town or if you just meet someone casually, you take him home to dinner. That's something that's not done in the East. Here, you select your guests very, very carefully. Then you *don't* feed them!"

Dining *chez* Cronkite is typically Midwestern. "Betsy overfeeds me," Walter explained. "She still gets into the kitchen, especially to fix food for our getaway weekends of sailing on the sloop. She's a great collector of cookbooks."

Betsy gave her recipe for lamb shanks. "Walter loves lamb," she said. "I was trained to use the inexpensive cuts of meat, and I haven't changed my cooking habits much over the years. I always have lamb for Walter's birthday dinner."

# Walter Cronkite's Birthday Lamb Dinner

Serves 4

4 large lamb shanks, bones
   cracked
2 tsps. paprika
1 tsp. salt
1/8 tsp. freshly ground
   black pepper
1 tbsp. vegetable oil
      water (small amount)

3 tomatoes, peeled and
   quartered
1½ cups water
8 small carrots, peeled and
   cut in 2-inch pieces
hot cooked brown rice
flour (small amount)

1. Season shanks with paprika, salt and pepper.
2. Heat oil in deep, ovenproof skillet and brown meat on all sides.
3. Add tomatoes and water.
4. Bake, uncovered, in preheated 350° F. oven for 30 minutes. Turn shanks and bake 30 minutes longer.
5. Add carrots, cover, and bake at 375° F. for an additional 45 minutes or until carrots and lamb are fork-tender.
6. Remove lamb and carrots to heated platter. Surround with hot, cooked brown rice.
7. Skim off excess fat from pan juices in skillet. Stir a small amount of flour into a small amount of water to form a smooth paste. Stir paste into pan juices and cook over low heat, stirring often until thickened.
8. Taste to adjust seasoning.
9. Spoon sauce over lamb, carrots and rice.

NOTE: Betsy's lamb dish is delicious and inexpensive. If desired, use small potatoes and peas in place of rice.

# Quinn Cummings

"I have my own weird recipes. For example, blueberry syrup and peanut butter sandwiches are very good," claims Quinn Cummings, who is the first to admit her kitchen failures.

Quinn lives in the Hollywood Hills in a 66-year-old house built by U.S. Grant III.

"You must have heard about my crêpes," she said sadly. "They came out two inches thick and burned black."

"They weren't that bad, she tried," said her mother, Jan, a pleasant woman who obviously has a good rapport with Quinn.

"We often eat at an Indian restaurant in Westwood," said Quinn. "They make a very spicy soup and delicious bread. I usually have lamb *tandoori*. I like that sort of stuff. It makes my eyes tear. It's made with a carload of spices, yogurt and lemon, and comes out an exquisite red-orange color."

It's small wonder Quinn rejects the the ubiquitous hamburgers, roast beef and hot dogs most kids her age devour. "I do what I consider survival cooking," her mother said. "I don't prepare gourmet food, but I do like to cook. I'm constantly looking for clever ways to disguise hamburger because hamburgers aren't eaten in this house. I cooked roast beef the other night and Quinn put mustard all over the top. Her eating habits don't inspire me to make anything fancy."

"I love your Greek stew," Quinn chimed in. "It's made with Greek feta cheese and walnuts," she said. Quinn Cummings is an extraordinary mixture of wit, animation and poise. Beneath the chatterbox exterior, though, is a very serious soul with a lot of common sense. "I'm a little loud, a little rude, a little annoying, a little of a lot of things. I'm like a stew that you make from leftovers – made up of a lot of things, but no one ingredient stands out."

# Greek Stew, House of Quinn Cummings

Serves 6

2 lbs. top or bottom boneless round, cut into
  1-inch cubes
2 tbsps. olive oil or butter
1 small yellow onion, peeled
  and chopped
small clove garlic, pressed
1-2 tbsps. tomato paste
3 cups beef broth or water

1 cup dry red wine
1 bay leaf
salt to taste
freshly ground black pepper
  to taste
12 pearl onions, peeled
1 cup feta or Mozzarella
  cheese
1 cup walnut halves

1. *Brown beef in olive oil, then lift out.*
2. *In same pan brown onion with garlic.*
3. *Return beef to pan. Add tomato paste, beef broth, wine, bay leaf, salt and pepper to taste.*
4. *Cover and cook over low heat about 1¼ hours.*
5. *Add onions and cheese. Cook uncovered 30 minutes longer, or until onions are tender.*
6. *Add walnuts. Heat few minutes longer.*
7. *Taste to correct seasonings.*
8. *Stew may be thickened, if desired, with a flour-water mixture. Great alone or with pita bread and tossed green salad.*

*NOTE: Feta cheese, a white goat cheese, is available in most supermarkets. Quinn's mother advises to feel free to ad-lib with recipe. Stew works well made in crock pot or oven. Other touches to give authentic Greek flavor to recipe: artichokes, ripe olives, dill or mint; or add vegetable of your choice (carrots or green peas).*

# John Davidson

During his bachelor days, singer John Davidson recalled his mother's most memorable meal. "It was kind of western goulash made with hamburger, noodles, green pepper, tomatoes and celery. We called it 'The Thing.' When I left home, I became somewhat fussier about food."

John likes hollandaise sauce on broccoli or asparagus and the shrimp and mustard sauce at the Four Seasons. "When I lived in New York, I tried my hand at cooking, but I wasn't very good at it. I'm a very meticulous person," he said.

Before his marriage, John Davidson resided in Hidden Hills, California, on a 2½-acre ranch. He's an expert horseman and a discerner of good grub. Naturally, his tastes in food have gone western. "When I barbecue outdoors, I like to have two kinds of salads: one with mixed greens and if I can get it, endive mixed with hearts of palm."

In the great food department, Davidson praised Peggy Lee's buttermilk pancakes. "After I'd sampled three helpings of them, I said, 'Peggy, would you make some a little more well done? These are a little rare.' I've always been used to flapjacks and didn't know the buttermilk kind is supposed to be so tender." The night of an opening, John recalled, "Peggy sent me a stack of her buttermilk pancakes with these words:

'I love your voice, as smooth as silk;
You love my pancakes of buttermilk?' "

# John Davidson's "The Thing"

### Serves 8-10

3 lbs. lean ground chuck
1 tbsp. butter
1 medium yellow onion,
  peeled and finely chopped
1 large green pepper, chopped
3 large stalks celery, minced
1 can (3 oz.) mushrooms,
  sliced and drained
¼ tsp. freshly ground
  pepper

½ tsp. salt
¼ tsp. garlic powder
1 scant tsp. curry powder
1½ cups marinara or
  spaghetti sauce, canned
1 can (1 lb.) basil-flavored
  Italian-style plum
  tomatoes
2½ cups elbow macaroni,
  cooked

1. *Sauté beef in butter in a large stock pot with onion, green pepper, celery, mushrooms, salt and pepper.*
2. *Cook over low heat, stirring with wooden spoon until meat browns and vegetables are transparent. Mixture should have a "loose" consistency.*
3. *Add garlic powder, curry powder, marinara sauce and tomatoes. Cook over low heat, uncovered, 10 minutes, stirring often to prevent sticking.*
4. *Add cooked macaroni and heat thoroughly.*
5. *Serve alone or with tossed green salad and garlic bread.*

*NOTE: For convenience, freeze the Davidson "Thing," adding more marinara sauce. To serve: thaw completely, place in greased ovenproof casserole, and heat in 350° F. oven for 30 minutes.*

# Sammy Davis, Jr.

"I love spaghetti and meatballs. But I swear it has nothing to do with Sinatra," said superstar Sammy Davis, Jr. "It dates back to when I was a kid."

Sammy joined his father and Will Mastin as a hoofer at the tender age of three. "We used to play a lot of roadhouses," he recalled. "They would give us salary plus room and board. And I guess spaghetti was the cheapest thing to feed an entertainer. Mostly, I like old-fashioned food, on the plain side."

Sammy described the meals he shares with his wife, Altovise. "We enjoy basic food, eating 12 or 15 dishes that intrigue us, such as roast beef, lamb (well cooked, he stressed, not in the European manner) and good pot roast."

Sammy still savors the Southern cooking of his grandmother, Rosa B. Davis. "Her ham hocks and pot of greens were the greatest. We still like fried chicken and black-eyed peas on Sunday."

Sammy and Altovise are known for throwing lavish parties. "Dining out is confined to two or three restaurants because, when it comes to food, I hate to experiment. These restaurants are like established friends."

Sammy doesn't pretend to cook. He said, "When people ask me what I can't do, I say I can't cook or swim!"

# Sammy Davis, Jr.'s Spaghetti and Meatballs

Serves 8

### For the sauce

2 large yellow onions,
   coarsely grated
1 large green pepper,
   coarsely grated
¼ cup olive oil
2 cans (8 ozs.) tomato sauce
2 cans (6 ozs.) Italian
   tomato paste

⅓ cup water
1 clove garlic, peeled
1 medium bay leaf
½ tsp. basil
½ tsp. oregano
1 tsp. sugar
¾ tsp. salt
½ tsp. freshly ground pepper

1. *Squeeze or strain onions, discarding juice and retaining the pulp.*
2. *Sauté grated onion and green pepper in olive oil 10 minutes, stirring often.*
3. *Transfer to cooking pan. Add remaining ingredients and mix well.*
4. *Cook over low heat about 45 minutes, stirring often to prevent burning.*
5. *Just before serving, remove garlic and bay leaf.*

### For the meatballs

1 large yellow onion,
   coarsely grated
1½ lbs. lean ground round
2 eggs, beaten

¼ tsp. garlic salt
1 tsp. salt
¼ tsp. freshly ground pepper
olive oil

1. *Combine all ingredients except olive oil. Mix well.*
2. *Form into balls.*
3. *Brown in olive oil, rotating to cook on all sides.*
4. *Drain on absorbent paper before adding to the sauce.*

### To assemble

1. *Cook spaghetti according to package directions.*
2. *Spoon the sauce and meatballs over the spaghetti.*
3. *Top with freshly grated Parmesan cheese.*

NOTE: *The amount of spaghetti needed varies according to your appetite! Meatballs are also excellent made with ground fresh turkey. If desired, add Italian-flavored breadcrumbs to meatballs to give added flavor.*

# Lesley-Anne Down

"The moment film people try to kill what I believe in, then I shall retire," said British actress Lesley-Anne Down. "I'll buy my house in Cornwall and start having children and raising dogs. I will bottle my pickles and make my wine."

The stunning beauty, dressed to the nines in a white silk suit, says she adores making films, but obviously finds more to life than having a full-time career. Lesley is a fascinating mix of contemporary girl and old-fashioned lady. She readily endorses equal pay for men and women but feels, "women's lib only alienates men and makes them wary."

She shuns discos in favor of staying home to read a good book or to cook up a sensational prawn (shrimp) or lamb curry. "I take hours to cook a good curry. If I plan to serve it to guests I ask, 'Do you like curry?' If they reply, 'Absolutely!' in go the hot chiles." Lesley prefers lamb and shrimp to chicken in the Indian classic. "Chicken meat doesn't curry very well."

Often she likes to prepare a Sunday roast: "Leg of lamb stuffed with garlic and rosemary, cooked with half a bottle of red wine poured over the top. You don't get roasted potatoes over here. I'm awfully fond of them. They are the most English of potatoes. I never stop eating," said the actress. "I love good food."

# Lesley-Anne Down's Lamb Curry with Vegetables

Serves 6-8

## For the lamb

2 lbs. boneless lean lamb,
  cut in pieces
3 onions, peeled
  and sliced
2 tbsps. clarified butter
2 tsp. salt

½ oz. minced green
  ginger root or 1
  tsp. ground ginger
¼ tsp. ground cloves
1 tbsp. curry powder
boiling salted water

freshly ground pepper to taste

1. Sauté lamb and onion in butter until lamb turns light brown.
2. Add salt, pepper, ginger root, cloves and curry powder; stir over medium heat.
3. Add enough water to cover lamb and vegetables. Simmer slowly to tenderize lamb (one hour).

## For the vegetables

3 lbs. mixed, chopped raw
  vegetables: onions,
  celery, red and green
  bell peppers, cauliflower
  or green beans
¼ cup flour

1 cup clarified butter
3 onions, peeled and chopped
1-2 tbsps. curry powder
1 tsp. vinegar
1 tomato, chopped
½ cup cream

2 cups stock (either lamb stock or
  vegetable-flavored bouillon)

1. Dredge chopped raw vegetables in flour and cook in all but 2 tbsps. of the clarified butter. Drain and reserve.
2. Cook onions in remaining butter until lightly browned.
3. Add curry, vinegar and tomato; let simmer 5 minutes.
4. Add stock (or bouillon); simmer 20 minutes.
5. Add vegetables and cooked lamb mixture (most of liquid should be reduced by cooking), and cook slowly, uncovered, another 10 minutes.
6. Just before serving, add cream.
7. Taste to correct seasonings. Serve over hot cooked rice.

# Fionnula Flanagan

"Nobody likes to talk about Irish food," says Emmy/Tony Award-winning actress Fionnula Flanagan. The attractive, auburn-haired, green-eyed actress is still very Irish at heart despite years of being away from her native Dublin. She admitted that she still hankers for "lovely Dublin Bay shrimp and smoked salmon."

Despite a sophisticated upbringing, Fionnula's food tastes are "very peasant. I can't understand why people here don't like crubeens or pig's feet," she said, laughing merrily.

The actress moved west six years ago when her psychiatrist husband, Dr. Garrett O'Connor, became an associate professor at UCLA. Her growing number of American fans remember her best from TV's "Rich Man, Poor Man."

When entertaining American guests at home, Fionnula often prepares colcannon champ, or stelk as it's known in Ireland. She shares cooking honors with her husband, especially when they entertain.

"I love good talk because I love to talk and to listen," said Fionnula. Afternoon tea, when she serves "tiny little cucumber-watercress sandwiches or wonderful Brie or cheddar from the cheese board, is a great way to talk to people."

When they entertain at dinner, Garrett often makes an unusual Madras curry with both beef and chicken. Their friends, many of whom have become vegetarians, or partial vegetarians, enjoy the curry because Garrett adds cauliflower, carrots, parsnips, potatoes or turnips. "They eat the juice of meat, but don't eat the meat."

# Garrett O'Connor's
# Beef and Chicken Curry

Serves 6

¾ lb. butter
2½ onions, chopped
2 cloves garlic, pressed
3 tsps. cinnamon
½ tsp. black pepper
½ tsp. salt
3 tsps. cardamon
20 whole cardamon seeds
3 bay leaves
2 tsps. mace
1 tsp. paprika
½ tsp. minced red pepper
  flakes

6 cloves
small pinch cayenne
1 tsp. ground ginger
1½ lbs. lean ground chuck or round
1½ lbs. lean stewing beef, cut
  into 1½-inch cubes
about 2½-3 cups cold water
3 tsps. curry powder
1-4 tsps. chili powder
6-8 chicken legs
choice of vegetables: 1 cup each cauliflower, carrots, potatoes and turnips (washed, peeled, chopped)

1. *Melt butter in large cast-iron pot. Add onions. Cook until soft over low heat.*
2. *Add garlic and all the spices and herbs, except curry powder and chili powder. Cook, stirring, over low fire 5-10 minutes.*
3. *Add ground and stewing beef. Cook over medium heat, stirring, until meat loses its redness.*
4. *Gradually add cold water and bring to boiling point.*
5. *Add curry powder and 1 tsp. chili powder. Gradually add remaining chili powder for a "hotter" taste.*
6. *Cook over low simmer, slightly covered, 1-1½ hours, stirring occasionally.*
7. *Add chicken legs and cook 45 minutes longer.*
8. *Add vegetables and cook 45 minutes longer, or until vegetables are tender. Taste to correct seasonings.*
9. *Serve spooned over hot cooked turmeric rice.*

*NOTE: Garrett comments: "Cooks should not be concerned if there is leftover curry because surplus curry mellows and ripens deliciously with age, and can be refrigerated or frozen and subsequently eaten, hot or cold." Curry is best eaten with mango and/or peach chutney, slivered almonds, ice-cold lime yogurt (spiked with pressed, thinly slivered cucumber) and "pickled" onion. (Mince ½ onion, sprinkle with 2 tsps. cayenne pepper, marinate several hours in ½ cup white vinegar.) "The onion can be garnished over the curry, or served on the side. It's a unique taste."*

# Henry Fonda

"I'm a good cook," said Henry Fonda. "In fact, in the days when Jim (James Stewart) and I first lived together in New York, I was the cook."

While the cameras rolled and Gene Kelly directed atop a ladder, and Jimmy Stewart, elegantly decked out in a cocoa-colored frock coat, tipped his hat across the street, Hank watched the proceedings and talked between takes of the western comedy, *The Cheyenne Social Club.*

"In New York, Jim and I used to bring back maybe 12 or 15 buddies to the apartment for dinner. I was famous for two things, Swedish meat balls and Mexican rice — both recipes I got from my mother." The actors were part of the University Players that worked on Broadway during the early thirties. "My mother was a good cook," Hank said. "Her meatballs were made with ground veal and beef and breadcrumbs soaked in milk. I still make them, as a matter of fact."

Hank was told that Jimmy Stewart had rated his Swedish meat balls as "terrible."

"He did!" Hank exclaimed, in false indignation. "I think he's just trying to make a funny story out of it because they were very successful and he always ate about 18 of them."

Hank talked about the great breakfast drink he discovered while on location. "Breakfast is always a difficult meal, as you know. It's not only a drag to eat, but it takes time. And if you are working on a picture, you have to get up at six. You can't get your cook up at home at that hour, because she's still going to be up at 8 o'clock at dinner. So you cook your own or do without. I used to throw two raw eggs in me and chase them with orange juice. When the makeup man saw me squeezing the oranges, he told me about the powder (lecithin) and gave me some. I've since bought a case of it," he said.

# Henry Fonda's Swedish Meatballs

Serves 4-6

½ cup breadcrumbs
½ cup milk
½ cup yellow onion,
   finely minced
3 tbsps. sweet butter
1 lb. lean ground beef

1 lb. ground veal
1½ tsps. salt
⅛ tsp. freshly ground
   black pepper
½ tsp. ground cinnamon or
   ¼ tsp. ground nutmeg

2 eggs, lightly beaten

1. Soak breadcrumbs in milk until liquid is absorbed. Mix with a fork to form a smooth texture.
2. Sauté onion slowly in 1 tbsp. butter until golden; remove onion to mixing bowl.
3. Add beef, veal, salt, pepper, cinnamon and eggs to bowl. Mix well with fingers.
4. Place bowl, tightly covered, in refrigerator for several hours.
5. When chilled, shape meat mixture into 2-inch balls with fingers.
6. Heat remaining butter in large skillet until butter begins to sizzle. Brown meatballs quickly over medium heat on all sides by shaking the pan.
7. Transfer meatballs to an ovenproof baking dish.
8. Add few tbsps. milk to skillet; deglaze skillet over medium heat, stirring.
9. Pour over meatballs in baking dish. Bake in preheated 350° F. oven about 15 minutes, or until meatballs are heated through.
10. Serve with mashed potatoes and sauce made from juices in casserole. (Blend with a little heavy cream over direct flame until slightly reduced in volume to make a thin sauce. Taste to correct seasonings.)

# Judy Garland

The hour is 2:00 A.M. Fans still linger on the sidewalk in hopes of catching a glimpse of their idol. Below, in the catacombs of Manhattan's famous Palace Theater, an interview with the late Judy Garland and two of her children, Lorna and Joey Luft, is underway.

Asked who cooks in the family, Lorna, then 14, replies, "Mama mostly, but I do, too, and enjoy it. I love messing up a kitchen!"

"Men are better cooks than women, I think," says Joey, opinionated when it comes to food. "I get in there when I can. Mostly I get thrown out of the kitchen. I used to get drafted to dry dishes."

"My children are my champions," says Judy, seated at her dressing table in a hostess gown of vibrant hues. "I never had to read Dr. Spock to know how to make friends with them. Each one is very different, but all three (Lorna, Joey, and Liza Minnelli) are full of sunshine and humor, and that's very gratifying. Lorna and I take turns in the kitchen. I'm a very good cook. I probably cook better than I sing. When both my daughters and I get into the kitchen, it's like one of those Pillsbury bake-off things. Joey's role is getting in there and stealing chocolate cake and cookies," she said, giggling.

"My mother (Ethel Gumm) was a hell of a cook. She never seemed to want us to be successful in the kitchen, so I sorta sneaked around and learned a little. I can now cook for 36 people, and I'm prouder of that than anything else I do! I can't eat certain foods. And I can't eat at least three hours before show times or for several hours afterwards."

She is finally asked about her shepherd's pie. "It's beautiful," she says. "It comes out looking like a birthday cake, all fluffy and delicious. Be sure to give yourself lots of time."

# Judy Garland's Shepherd's Pie Supreme

Serves 8-12

## Filling

5 lb. leg of lamb, bone in
2 chicken breasts, weighing
   1¾ lbs.
1 can (10¾ ozs.) chicken broth
1 can (10¾ ozs.) beef broth
3 tbsps. fresh dill, minced
½ tsp. salt

⅛ tsp. freshly ground pepper
1 can (10¾ ozs.) cream of
   mushroom soup
1 cup chicken stock
2 tsps. original Worcestershire
   sauce
½ tsp. onion juice

1. Place lamb on rack in roasting pan. Insert meat thermometer, being careful not to touch bone. Roast, uncovered, in preheated 300° F. oven 2¼ hours, or until thermometer registers 170° F. for rare lamb.
2. Cool slightly; trim and discard outer skin, fat and cartilage.
3. Chop or hand grind meat by putting it through coarse blade of meat grinder. Makes about 4 cups ground lamb.
4. Put chicken in saucepan; cover with undiluted chicken and beef broth. Cover and simmer about ¾ hour, or until tender. Cool on plate; reserve stock.
5. Strip meat from bones; put through coarse blade of meat grinder. Makes about 2 cups ground chicken.
6. Combine lamb, chicken, dill, salt and pepper in bowl. Mix well with hands.
7. Dilute mushroom soup with about 1 cup chicken stock, Worcestershire sauce and onion juice. Mix well with meat mixture. Divide mixture in half.
8. Butter 2 two-quart casseroles. Press mixture into each casserole.

## Topping

1 cup water
1 cup stock (from chicken)
½ cup milk
2 tbsps. butter
2½ cups instant potato flakes

1 cup dairy sour cream
1 tbsp. chives, minced
½ tsp. caraway or sesame seeds
salt to taste
freshly ground pepper to taste

1. Heat water and stock together until boiling; remove from fire.
2. Add milk and butter; stir in potato flakes, beating until light and fluffy.
3. Add sour cream, chives, caraway seeds, salt and pepper; blend well.
4. Top meat in each casserole with whipped potato mixture.
5. Bake in preheated 450° F. oven 20-25 minutes. Run under broiler to brown. (Reserve second casserole for encores, or cover tightly and freeze.)

# Kathryn Grayson

Actress Kathryn Grayson has been a chili *afficionado* for years; she is a former North Carolina state champion chili cook. "I think my all-American chili is the best in the world because I sing to it," she said with a laugh.

Kathryn talked in the cozy, book-lined den of her 19-room English Tudor house here. While we talked, her chili was cooking, filling the house with tantalizing smells and teasing the seven dogs who live with her! "You should have been here yesterday, when I was trying to cook with all seven dogs in the kitchen with me!" said Kathryn, laughing. "Mary, my wonderful housekeeper, who has been with me for years, was also busy in the kitchen, trying to get a turkey ready for the oven. All she said was, 'I sure wish you would get on with that chili!' "

Kathryn's chili was served on trays in the library with rice on the side, a tossed vegetable salad and wedges of honeydew melon. The chili was delicious — light and unusual. Her chili is thick and fine-textured because the meat is ground twice.

Kathryn's knowledge of cooking is as vast as her singing repertoire. "We grew up eating lovely soup, wonderful homemade breads and pastries. I've kept all my mother's recipes, and over the years, I've learned how to cook them all myself."

# Kathryn Grayson's All-American Chili

Serves 8-12

½ lb. fresh, hot chili
  peppers, about 2½-3
  inches long
salted boiling water
3 large yellow onions,
  peeled
2½ lbs. filet mignon
2½ lbs. lean, boneless
  flank or round steak
1 tbsp. salt, more if desired
½ tsp. freshly ground black
  pepper, more if desired
¼ tsp. garlic powder

2 eggs, beaten
1 cup unseasoned breadcrumbs
3 cans (15 ozs.) tomato purée
2 cans (14 ozs.) beef broth,
  homemade or canned, or
  water
¾ tsp. oregano leaves, crushed
¼ tsp. basil, crushed
2 tsps. ground cumin
2 large bay leaves
¼ cup chili powder
about 1½ tbsps. brown sugar
  or catsup to taste

1. Rinse chili peppers; place in saucepan. Cover with salted boiling water. Cover and cook over medium heat 10 minutes, or until tender.
2. Drain. Split peppers. Remove and discard stem ends and seeds from peppers. Scrape pulp from skin; place in large stock pot.
3. Mince 1½ onions finely and place in pot with chili pulp. Set aside.
4. Trim all fat and connective tissue from meat. Cut half the filet into bite-size pieces and set aside. Cut remaining filet and steak into 2-inch cubes.
5. Quarter remaining onions and put through fine blade of electric or hand grinder along with meat cubes. Season meat mixture as you grind it with 2 tsps. salt, half the pepper and garlic powder. Mix with hands. Grind meat second time and divide into two parts.
6. Add eggs and breadcrumbs to half the ground meat-onion mixture; knead well with fingers to blend. Shape into marble-size meatballs.
7. Broil meatballs a few seconds; set aside. Add remaining ground meat mixture to stock pot with chili pulp-minced onion mixture.
8. Add tomato purée, stirring to blend, plus beef broth, oregano, basil, cumin, bay leaves, chili powder and remaining salt and pepper. Cook and stir 1 hour over medium heat.
9. Add meatballs; cook 15 minutes longer, stirring.
10. Add filet bits; cook 30 minutes longer, stirring.
11. Add sugar or catsup to taste, and additional water or broth as needed. As chili cooks, taste, adding more chili powder or seasonings as desired.
12. Serve piping hot, alone, or with mounds of rice, macaroni or beans.

# Merv Griffin

"My wife thinks people look like food. She's very strange that way," said Merv Griffin. "Ask Julann about Doris Day and she'll say Doris looks like a bread stick!" Merv was in his executive offices, surrounded by a jungle of plants and a collection of photographs, including Rose and Bobby Kennedy, Martin Luther King and John Lindsay, when we talked in 1970, before he and Julann were divorced.

"What does Julann think *you* look like?" I asked Merv, who was comfortably clad in gray slacks topped with a maroon, short-sleeved T-shirt.

"Like a muffin," he said with a leprechaun's grin.

Merv doesn't relate people to food, but said, "I can walk into a restaurant and tell if the food's good by the salad. The greens must be crisp and cold."

The Griffins entertained often at huge sit-down farm house dinners. "What's really funny, though, is outside New York, people don't know what you're talking about if you use the word 'catered.' I never heard the word in California. But we even have it out at our farm on a Sunday when we'll have 150 or 200 people in for dinner. We call up the local Presbyterian church. One of the ladies will quote a price of so much per person and they'll deliver the food. They make a profit for their church. We set up all the tables and benches. There's nobody there that's not a good cook! The Presbyterian ladies arrive with turkeys, hams, fresh vegetables and homemade pies. I've never seen such food and the women serve it."

Merv is always a consumer and never a cook. "I couldn't wait until my kid was 9 years old, so I could teach him how to take out the garbage."

# Julann Griffin's
# Ham Loaf with Mustard Sauce

Serves 8

### For the mustard sauce

½ cup canned tomato soup
½ cup prepared mustard
½ cup vinegar
3 egg yolks, beaten

⅓ cup sugar
½ cup corn oil or
   melted butter
1 tsp. salt

freshly ground black pepper to taste

1. *Combine ingredients in top of a double boiler. Blend well using whisk.*
2. *Insert top into lower part of double boiler filled with water. Cook, stirring often until thick to prevent sticking.*
3. *Serve hot or cold, spooning sauce over ham loaf, baked ham or other meat dishes.*

### For the ham loaf

1½ lbs. ham
1½ lbs. lean fresh pork
3 eggs, beaten
1½ cups breadcrumbs
1½ cups milk

2 tsps. fresh onion,
   grated
freshly ground pepper
   to taste
½ can tomato soup

1. *Grind together ham and pork.*
2. *Add remaining ingredients except the tomato soup; mix well.*
3. *Form into loaf in baking dish lined with aluminum foil.*
4. *Insert baking dish in larger baking dish partially filled with water.*
5. *Bake in preheated 350° F. oven for 45 minutes.*
6. *Pour off grease which has collected and cover loaf with undiluted tomato soup.*
7. *Bake 45 minutes longer.*
8. *Slice to serve. Serve alone or with mustard sauce.*

# Buddy Hackett

"I talk great," said Buddy Hackett when asked to compare two of his most renowned talents – eating and talking. The comedian, whose face looks like Silly Putty gone wild, talked mostly about food while seated in a comfortable beige couch in the living room of his Beverly Hills home.

Buddy, who likes to cook *al fresco*, was roasting two golden chickens on the barbecue. He jumped up to baste them. "Oh, you succulent fowl," he said, then aside: "It's best to use tongs. It's a good way to beat off the guests.

"My mother made the worst food," he recalled. "Once when I was home on furlough, I said if the Army were exposed to her cooking, we would blow the war. She did do a couple of good things like split-pea soup, chicken fricassee made with meatballs, flanken and *tzimmes* (side dish made with carrots and sweet potatoes). She kept a kosher house, and so do we," he said, referring to his lovely wife, Sherry. "Kosher means respect for life," he explained.

"I have something I must show you," he said, leading the way into the kitchen. "I have 50 of these salamis flown out from the Stage (a delicatessen in New York) every month to give to friends." He opened the deep freeze and displayed salamis stacked like cordwood. "I have a special list of people I give them to, like Dinah Shore because she hates me so much," he said, his button eyes smiling.

"I'm really quite an unorthodox cook. One day when I was stuck in the kitchen like a mouse in a trap with only a can of bean sprouts, out came Chinese chili. When my friend, Jeno Paulucci, who used to own Chun King, heard how much I like bean sprouts, he sent me a hundred cases. I couldn't get through the door."

# Buddy Hackett's Chinese Chili

Serves 8

1 tbsp. safflower oil
3 lbs. lean ground beef
1 large yellow onion, peeled and chopped
1 large green pepper, diced
½ clove garlic, pressed
2 vegetable bouillon cubes
¼ cup boiling water
2 cans (6 oz.) tomato paste
about 3½ cups cold water
1 cup soy sauce
1½ tsps. oregano

2 tsps. chili powder (more if desired)
scant tsp. crushed red pepper flakes
1 tsp. salt
¼ tsp. white pepper
1½ cups canned water chestnuts, sliced
3 cans (1 lb.) Chinese bean sprouts
cooked white rice, dry noodles or corn chips

1 large handful Oriental mushrooms (available at Oriental food shops)

1. Heat oil in large skillet.
2. Add beef, onion, green pepper and garlic. Cook over medium heat, stirring until meat turns brown and is crumbly in appearance.
3. Pour off and discard excess fat.
4. Place meat mixture in large, deep stock pot.
5. Dissolve vegetable cubes in boiling water and add to the pot with tomato paste, cold water, soy sauce, oregano, chili powder, red pepper flakes, salt, white pepper and water chestnuts.
6. Cook over low fire about 45 minutes, stirring often to prevent burning.
7. Meanwhile, soak dried mushrooms in lukewarm water about 30 minutes.
8. Drain off water, squeeze out excess fluid, slice mushrooms thinly, and add to chili.
9. Drain bean sprouts and rinse carefully in cold water to remove canned taste.
10. Gradually add bean sprouts to stock pot. Heat through.
11. Serve at once over steaming mounds of cooked white rice, dry noodles or corn chips.

NOTE: Serve with tall glasses of cold jasmine tea.

# Gene Hackman

"This isn't a well put-together kitchen," said Gene Hackman, as he plugged in the coffee maker in the kitchen of his rented East Side apartment. The actor's a big guy – he's got a good face with a slightly mangled nose left over from his high school football days – and he looked out of place in the tiny kitchenette. Remnants of bachelor-type cooking were around him: jars of peanut butter and cheese on yawning cupboard shelves and store-bought cookies on the counter.

"New Yorkers tend to order food – even coffee – in a certain way," added Gene. "I once worked as relief counterman in drugstores all over the city, from Harlem to Brooklyn, and at first I wouldn't know what they were saying to me." He still remembers the lingo: " 'Grade A's' milk, of course! 'Stretch,' now that's a good one; that's Pepsi or a Coke. A 'burn' is a chocolate malted. Sandwiches were the worst. Like 'radio' is when you order a toasted sandwich. Or just toast is 'side down,' but if it's a toasted sandwich, it's 'radio down!' "

Gene likes to cook and is willing to take a chance on new dishes. "I feel, 'Let them try this thing. If they don't like it, they can go to Chock Full o' Nuts.' I've had good luck with Steak Diane and tempura, and I fix both often. I like *sashimi,* too, but I find when I do it myself and have to buy the fish and cut it up, it becomes a chore." Gene's version is seasoned with hot mustard and soy sauce.

# Gene Hackman's Steak Diane

Serves 2

1 lb. center cut beef
   tenderloin
1 clove garlic, cut
4 tbsps. sweet butter
2 tbsps. brandy

1 tbsp. original
   Worcestershire sauce
salt to taste
freshly ground black
   pepper to taste

3 tbsps. parsley, minced

1. Cut steak into 1-inch strips. Flatten by pounding to $\frac{1}{16}$-inch thickness.
2. Rub strips lightly with cut garlic.
3. Heat 2 tbsps. butter in skillet until foaming. Brown meat quickly on both sides.
4. Add heated brandy to flambé meat.
5. Add the remaining butter, Worcestershire, salt and pepper to taste. Stir well and heat.
6. Serve at once; garnish liberally with parsley.

NOTE: If desired, omit brandy and substitute minced fresh chives, mushrooms, or a good quality bottled sauce diable to sauce.

# Larry Hagman

"I cook in front of TV and watch the football games," said actor Larry Hagman, digging into some delicious Beef Bourguignon at the Chronicle, a charming, mid-Victorian-style restaurant. Hagman was accompanied by his attractive Swedish wife, Maj (pronounced My). The pair arrived separately, Larry on his "scooter," Maj by car.

The *bon vivant* and star of CBS-TV's "Dallas" loves to cook. "I make chili from a mix I buy in a bag," said Larry. "I fool around with it, flavoring it to suit myself."

"Larry makes very good spaghetti," chimed in Maj.

"I cook enough for an army," added Larry. "No matter how much I make, it's gone by nightfall. The secret to my chili is the seasoning and meat. I like to use plenty of cayenne and Hungarian paprika that's so hot, it blows your brains out. We buy it at a special Greek store downtown."

Maj is a sensational cook, according to her friends back in Malibu, including neighbor Burgess Meredith. She enjoys making Chinese dishes. "I can organize and prepare a meal in an hour, but if I stop and think about it, then things happen," she said.

Larry's favorite is Maj's marinated salmon, flavored with lemon juice and fresh dill. "It's sensational!" he exclaimed. "The marinade cooks the fish like *seviche* (a raw fish served with onion and garlic). You must have bricks to weight the fish."

Larry's mother, the immortal Mary Martin, never was a cook. "She still cooks fudge," he said. "I tell her, 'Who's going to eat it? Everyone's so weight-conscious now.' But she insists, saying, 'If I fix it, people will eat it.' "

Larry and Maj live in a beach home bought for $80,000 some years ago, but now probably worth a cool million. They travel back and forth often to Texas, where Larry is working on location for "Dallas."

# Larry Hagman's Hot and Spicy Spaghetti

Makes about 1½ - 2 quarts

¼ cup olive oil
2 medium-size onions, peeled
   and chopped
3 cloves garlic, pressed
2 lbs. boneless beef neck
   meat, fat trimmed, cut
   in small cubes
½ tsp. cayenne pepper
¼ cup flour
salt to taste
freshly ground black
   pepper to taste

2 cans (8 ozs.) tomato sauce
2 cans (6 ozs.) tomato paste
½ lb. mushrooms, sliced
1½ cups water or beef
   stock (canned)
1 large lemon, squeezed
1 tsp. oregano
2 tsps. basil
good handful parsley
1½ tsps. salt
¼ tsp. pepper
1 bay leaf

1 tbsp. Hungarian pepper (more or less to taste)

1. Heat olive oil in large skillet or stock pot.
2. Sauté onions and garlic until transparent. Lift out and reserve.
3. Shake meat in paper bag with cayenne pepper, flour, salt and pepper.
4. Brown meat on all sides in garlic-flavored oil.
5. Stir in remaining ingredients, blending well.
6. Cook, uncovered, simmering for 3 hours and stirring occasionally.
7. Toward end of cooking, add onions and garlic. Taste to correct seasonings.
8. Serve over hot cooked spaghetti according to package instructions.
9. Wonderful with French bread, green salad and your favorite red wine.

NOTE: If Hungarian pepper is not available, use red pepper flakes or chili pepper to give desired degree of "hotness" to sauce.

# Nicholas Hammond

"English cooks rely on the integrity of food itself rather than sauces to camouflage it. I suppose that stems from history," said actor Nicholas Hammond. "Centuries ago, particularly along the Mediterranean and African continent, people relied heavily on spices because their meat and fish spoiled so quickly. Consequently, they developed many saffrons and peppers."

The son of English actress Eileen Bennett and American Army Col. Thomas Hammond, Nick spent much of his childhood in London and Paris, where his father was stationed as an aide to Gen. Dwight D. Eisenhower.

"I love to eat," he said, despite the fact that he keeps his lithe, six-foot-one frame pared down to 160 pounds. Much of that is due to his self-discipline and his passion for tennis, sailing and horseback riding. "I cook everything, but I like Italian and French dishes best. Most of my relatives still live in Southern England. Many of them are farmers, so they serve hearty meals. Their breakfasts and teas are superb, and their roast beef, leg of lamb and seafood are unbeatable. The two greatest fallacies in the world are that English people are cold and that their food is not good. I've met some of the warmest, nicest, and most outgoing people in England. I've sampled food in their homes as well as in their restaurants. They do fabulous things with vegetables. With something as simple as plain boiled potatoes, they'll add a tiny bit of parsley and salt, and they are perfection."

Nick keeps no frozen vegetables in his Santa Monica apartment — "only ice cubes and a bottle of vodka! I prefer entertaining small groups at home, rather than going to restaurants. I'm not a party-giver or goer."

# Nicholas Hammond's Black Mushroom Tomato Sauce with Sausages

Serves 4-6

2 ozs. dried imported black mushrooms
2 small cloves garlic, peeled
2 tbsps. olive oil
1 can (28 ozs.) basil flavored Italian plum tomatoes, chopped
3 sweet Italian pork sausages

3 hot Italian pork sausages
½ cup dry red wine
½ tsp. basil leaves, crumbled
½ tsp. lemon pepper
soy sauce to taste
4 tbsps. Parmesan cheese, freshly grated

1. Soak mushrooms overnight; drain well.
2. Brown garlic in olive oil; remove and discard.
3. Chop mushrooms; sauté in garlic-flavored olive oil until well flavored. Place mushrooms in large saucepan with tomatoes.
4. Remove and discard outer skins from sausages; mash with fork and cook in same skillet used to sauté garlic and mushrooms. Stir with fork, cooking over low fire until sausages are half-cooked.
5. Add sausages to tomato mixture; discard fat left in pan.
6. Add wine, basil and lemon pepper. Simmer over low heat, uncovered, about 1½ hours.
7. Add soy sauce to taste after 1 hour. Stir often.
8. Reheat to serve; add grated Parmesan cheese to sauce. Spoon over hot cooked pasta.
9. Serve with bread sticks, green salad and dry red Italian wine. Finish meal with fruit and cheese.

NOTE: Nicholas traditionally uses funghi porcini (dried black mushrooms from northern Italy), available in Italian food stores or through mail-order houses. Other dried mushrooms from Europe, found in most supermarkets in the United States, may be substituted, but the flavor will be different. If sauce seems too thick, just add a little more tomatoes or wine. Nicholas prepares his with pennoni (large macaroni-like pasta, cut on diagonal). Allow 1 lb. pkg. to serve 4-6 people.

# Joey Heatherton

Joey Heatherton likes "creamy, rich things made with good gravy." Those include: stroganoff, roast beef with Yorkshire pudding, chicken in wine, lasagna, most any kind of *pasta*, steak seasoned with garlic, hot dogs, and "Oysters Rockefeller I can eat at the drop of a hat." In short, her food likes are as numerous as her growing list of credits.

Born into a show biz family, Joey loves to travel and eat the local fare. But it's the cooking of her London-born mother, Davenie Watson Heatherton, a retired hoofer, that draws rave notices from Joey. "We had our first chili in Chasens', in California," Joey said. "My mother kept the taste of it in her mouth and went home to duplicate it in her own kitchen."

I asked her how a girl with a size-5 figure can eat so much and stay so slim.

"There's no special secret," Joey said. "I don't have a special diet. My father always says, 'You have to eat to keep going.' Maybe it's psychosomatic, but I think if I eat well, I'll sing or dance well. If I have a really important audition, I'll make myself eat an egg. I'm not a health nut.

"Guys who know me take me places where they know I like the food. If we're going to the theater, we go to 21. I love the steak and their sauce. And I love to go to a good deli and have a hot pastrami sandwich or roast beef with hot red peppers."

Few people can afford to indulge in all of Joey's food loves. But if eating peanut butter sandwiches and drinking lots of milk ("My brother and I split a quart in one sitting") has given Joey Heatherton her all-American good looks, we suggest others try it.

# Joey Heatherton's Pray Thee Pie

Serves 6

## For topping

4 large potatoes, peeled
¾ cup milk
½ stick sweet butter

1 tsp. salt
1/16 tsp. freshly ground
  pepper

## For meat layer

3 small yellow onions, chopped
1 tbsp. beef drippings from
  roast beef, or sweet butter
1 large clove garlic, minced
1 ½ lbs. chopped, lean
  sirloin

2 tsps. beef extract or
  1 tbsp. undiluted consommé
1 tsp. salt
¼ tsp. freshly ground
  pepper
5 tbsps. water

1. *Cook peeled potatoes until tender. Drain well.*
2. *Mash until very light; add milk, butter and seasonings.*
3. *Beat again until light. Add more milk if necessary.*
4. *Sauté onion in melted beef drippings until golden.*
5. *Add garlic and cook 1 minute over low heat, stirring.*
6. *Stir in meat; brown lightly.*
7. *Add beef extract, seasonings, and water. Stir lightly to mix.*
8. *Cover loosely with lid and steam slowly 7 minutes.*
9. *Turn meat mixture into a well-buttered pyrex pie plate. Top with layer of hot mashed potatoes. Dot top with butter and sprinkle lightly with freshly ground pepper.*
10. *Bake uncovered in 400° F. oven 30-35 minutes, or until light brown.*
11. *Brown top by running under the broiler.*

# Charlton Heston

"I would describe myself as a dropout from the social scene," said Charlton Heston. "I would think gatherings of actors are more interesting than gatherings of haberdashers or senators, but I'm just not that keen on gatherings. For me, it's a difficult process to get to know someone. I'm not that selective; it's just that I have a few friends that seem to satisfy my needs." (Billy Wilder and George Stevens are among them.)

Married since 1944, Heston describes his wife, Lydia, as more socially inclined. "My wife enjoys talking to people she meets. I don't doubt it is a rewarding experience, but it involves an effort I find difficult to make.

"I don't cook, but I can do steak tartar. I use olive oil because it seems to make the various items mix in a little better, a few capers for decoration, and sometimes a little brandy to give it a nice flavor. My wife often makes another family favorite: roast leg of lamb with a mint sauce, English style."

Home to the Hestons is a modern, nine-room hilltop house in Beverly Hills, with walls that are either all rock, glass or bricks. He calls it "medieval modern." Heston spends a lot of his time in his paneled study, and he and Lydia entertain at small home dinner parties for old friends – an interesting mix of directors, actors, stock brokers, psychiatrists and professional tennis players.

# Charlton Heston's Roast Leg of Lamb with Fresh Mint Sauce

Serves 6-8

## For the sauce

½ cup fresh mint leaves
2 tbsps. sugar

½ cup distilled vinegar, heated
4 tbsps. boiling water

1. *Wash and dry mint leaves; cut into tiny strips.*
2. *Place mint in glass dish with sugar. Pour hot vinegar and water over leaves, stirring to dissolve sugar and crushing mint leaves to draw out the aroma.*
3. *Cool; let sauce marinate several hours before using. Makes about ⅔ cup.*

## For the meat

1 leg of lamb, weighing about
  6 lbs., "frenched"

1 clove garlic
salt to taste

freshly ground pepper to taste

1. *Have butcher prepare "frenched" leg of lamb by trimming fat from bone. Leave outside skin intact.*
2. *Rub outside with cut garlic; sprinkle liberally with salt and pepper.*
3. *Place on rack in roasting pan. Roast, uncovered, in preheated 300° F. oven, allowing 20-25 minutes per lb., or until meat thermometer inserted in fleshy part of roast, but not touching bone, registers 170-175° F. for medium-rare.*
4. *Transfer lamb to heated platter; allow 20 minutes for roast to firm up before carving.*
5. *Decorate bone with paper frill before serving. Serve alone with mint sauce or garden fresh peas or brussels sprouts and new potatoes in lemon-parsley butter.*

NOTE: *The Hestons prefer their lamb "English" style, plain and "pink." Garlic cloves can be inserted in small slivers in roast using a sharp knife or ice pick to flavor during cooking. Onion rings, cut in thin rounds, attached to roast with toothpicks, add more flavor. Avoid using too generous amounts of garlic or onion, as natural flavor of lamb is delicate. For a delightful alternate: insert garlic in roast as described; combine 1 tsp. fresh chopped rosemary, ½ tsp. finely grated lemon peel, 3 tbsps. fresh lemon juice, and 3 tbsps. softened butter. Spread "herbed" butter mixture over surface of lamb. Cook as directed.*

# Dustin Hoffman

"Every time I finish a film, I say, 'Now, I'm going to study the piano again, take up a foreign language and learn how to cook,'" Dustin Hoffman said in his trailer parked on a movie lot. "I even went so far as to buy a wok and several Oriental cookbooks, but I never used them," the brown-eyed actor added as he finished a luncheon of celery tonic, salami, cheese and fruit.

"I love junk food: French fries, cheese dips, food from incredibly bad diners – terrible gravy, mashed potatoes, leathery meat. I love the hot dogs you buy at a baseball game, the ones that come wrapped in tin foil. Open it up and there's this damp rag of a bun with this semi-cereal hot dog. I love it! I could eat five of them right now," he said, his eyes beginning to sparkle.

"I love food loaded with spice, tons of garlic and fiery hot with pepper. In fact, I have yet to find food that's too hot for me. I enjoy going to Mexican or Pakistani restaurants. I've never understood why some people have resistance against certain foods. I'll eat anything if it tastes good – ants, snails, whatever! It's probably fear of the unknown that puts some people off unusual foods."

A Hoffman favorite is an eggplant casserole loaded with gooey mozzarella cheese and tomato sauce – a dish originally fashioned by his wife, Anne.

# Eggplant Mozzarella Bake, House of Dustin Hoffman

Serves 6-8

3-4 tbsps. safflower oil
1 lb. lean ground beef
1 large Bermuda onion,
  peeled and chopped
½ cup green pepper,
  finely chopped
¼ tsp. garlic salt
1 tsp. oregano
½ tsp. basil
salt to taste
freshly ground black
  pepper to taste

1 bay leaf
2 cans (1 lb. 4 ozs.)
  tomatoes, undrained
1 can (6 ozs.) tomato paste
1 large eggplant
water
1 egg beaten with 2 tbsps.
  water or milk
seasoned flour
½ lb. mozzarella
  cheese, cut in
  small pieces

¾ cup Parmesan cheese, grated

1. *Heat 1 tbsp. oil in large Dutch oven or skillet. Add beef, onion, green pepper, garlic salt, oregano, basil, bay leaf, and salt and pepper to taste.*
2. *Cook over medium heat, stirring, until meat is lightly browned and crumbly, and vegetables soften.*
3. *Add tomatoes and tomato paste; cook gently, uncovered, about 1¼ hours, or until thickened and seasonings are well blended.*
4. *Meanwhile, wash and peel eggplant; cut in ½-inch slices.*
5. *Soak slices in water 20 minutes. Drain well on absorbent paper.*
6. *Dip slices in egg; coat in seasoned flour.*
7. *Heat remaining oil in skillet; sauté eggplant on both sides until golden brown. Drain well on absorbent paper.*
8. *Spread some of the tomato sauce in bottom of a well-greased 13 x 9 x 2-inch baking pan.*
9. *Top with a layer of eggplant, a layer of mozzarella cheese, and a sprinkling of Parmesan cheese. Repeat layers, finishing with sauce and cheeses.*
10. *Bake in preheated 375° F. oven 30 minutes, or until cheese is bubbly and golden brown.*
11. *Serve alone or with mixed green salad, Italian bread sticks and your favorite chilled wine.*

NOTE: *If desired, omit beef and use more cheese to increase the protein. Anne advises, "Eggplant and sauce can be prepared in the morning. All you have to do is to assemble the dish and pop it into the oven at the last minute."*

# Bob Hope

"I'm always thankful for memories of dining with our boys, particularly at Christmas," veteran entertainer Bob Hope said, recalling his many Christmases spent entertaining the troops in far-flung places. "Christmas is a very emotional time; I always go to midnight mass, which is a sentimental thing when you're up in Alaska or in Africa or, like when we were in Spain. I couldn't get in the church; I had to stand outside, it was so crowded.

"I always eat with the men. In some places they want to do a big thing for you, so they make a big, special cake and put some kind of a little caricature of you on top! I get a big kick out of that!"

The Hope traditional family dinner is served on New Year's Eve. "I have a meal that I like very much — roast leg of lamb with mint sauce, mashed potatoes, peas and lemon pie. That's probably my favorite all-time meal. The lemon pie is famous. It goes back a few years to when my mother used to make it with that lattice thing on top. It's kind of a soup, but it's sensational!

"My favorite breakfast has always been lamb chops with lamb kidneys, scrambled eggs and toasted crumpets. You know, it's funny," he said, frowning a bit, "I've always said if I weren't in show business, I'd like to run a restaurant. I think running a restaurant is a little like being in my business! You are appealing to people's tastes, and I've never let anybody put anything on the table that I wouldn't eat myself. I've been very lucky with my stomach after all these years of being all over the world. I think it's because I always look for tearooms to eat in. I find that women's cooking is so good. I sort of ferret out great places like the Silver Dollar in Minneapolis. It's a great tearoom!"

# Bob Hope's Kidney Lamb Chops

Serves 2-4

4 lamb kidneys
4 lamb rib chops, cut ¾
   to 1-inch thick

1 clove garlic, cut
lemon rind
salt to taste

ground pepper to taste

1. Split kidneys almost in 2; remove white tubes and fat. Cover with cold water and let stand for 30 minutes.
2. Attach kidneys to lamb chops by wrapping a kidney around the extended tail of each chop; secure with a toothpick.
3. Rub each chop with cut garlic, then with lemon rind.
4. Heat heavy skillet over low heat. Rub skillet with a piece of trimmed fat; discard fat.
5. Increase heat to medium; add chops to skillet. Cook for about 6-7 minutes on each side, until well browned.
6. Remove chops and season to taste with salt and pepper.
7. Serve immediately alone or with scrambled eggs, hot crumpets or toast.

# Lena Horne

"My sign is Cancer," said beautiful Lena Horne. "Cancer people love food: they not only love to eat it, they like to smell, look, think and talk about it."

Only minutes before, Lena had used the same sensual approach to music that she has to food in wooing an audience packed into New York's Minskoff Theater. Wrapped in a huge towel and seated in her light, airy-looking dressing room between acts, surrounded by pictures of her grandchildren, Lena lived up to all of her Cancerian attributes.

"Becoming a cook wasn't easy," Lena said, laughing. "I only started learning how to cook during my first marriage. I'll never forget the first morning after the wedding. My husband got up very early. I didn't know where he had gone. He came back with a bag of flour, milk and other ingredients I knew nothing about. He said, 'I'd like to have some pancakes this morning' – and then he had to show me how to cook them!"

Gradually, Lena acquired the rudiments of cooking. "I learned how to cook with fatback (fat from the back of a hog, dried and salted) and how to cook and wash greens, which is a tiresome job! I think one of the reasons I've stayed in show business as long as I have is that I can always order room service," she said, teasing.

Lena's cooking reflects some Latin use of staples and spices. (Her mother was married to a Cuban for a long time.) "I'm crazy about black beans, but they are so fattening. Isn't that awful! Everywhere you go in the world you can find some variation of black beans – like the *frijoles* in Brazil or hoppin' John, made with black-eyed peas and rice in the South. I cook ordinary things like chicken fricassee by feel and smell, but I don't know how to make a soufflé. My daughter Gail is very good at that!"

# Lena Horne's Cancerian Beans

### Serves 6

2 cups (1 lb.) large
  black beans
about 5 cups water
1 tsp. salt
½ cup olive oil
2 large garlic cloves,
  pressed

1 onion, peeled and sliced
8 small, fresh tomatoes, peeled
  and chopped
freshly ground black pepper
  to taste
smoked ham hocks (cooked in
  water until tender)

1. *Pick over beans carefully and soak overnight.*
2. *Drain. Place beans in large saucepan with water. Water should cover beans by about 1½ inches.*
3. *Add salt; cover and cook until beans are "bitey" (about 1½ hours).*
4. *Meanwhile, prepare sauce: heat 2 tbsps. olive oil in skillet. Sauté garlic and onion until tender. Add tomatoes. Cook slowly over low fire to form thick, soft sauce.*
5. *Place cooked, drained beans in a casserole. Spoon sauce over top and heat until piping hot.*
6. *Drizzle remaining olive oil over top and sprinkle with pepper to taste.*
7. *Serve with sliced cooked ham hocks to complete meal.*

NOTE: *Salt pork or ham bone gives an excellent smokey flavor to beans. For a meatless version, use herbs like coriander, bay leaf, thyme or sage to flavor beans. Govern seasonings according to the use of ingredients. Ham or hocks will give a natural saltiness to the beans without adding excess amounts of salt and pepper. Cook by "feel" and "taste"!*

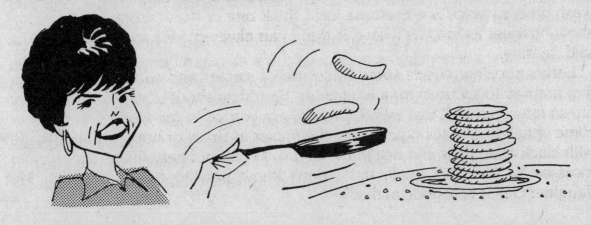

# Jacob Javits

America's 1966 Father of the Year and a then fast-moving United States Senator, Jacob K. Javits (R., N. Y.), took time out to talk about his family and the role food plays in family living. "How does it feel to be the Father of the Year?" I asked.

"It feels just great," he said, as he told how the auspicious occasion was marked with a family dinner at home. "We celebrated with champagne, lobster *en croute* (creamed lobster in puff pastry) for an appetizer, followed by veal scallops, creamed spinach (gently flavored with a hint of nutmeg and hard-cooked eggs), and my favorite dessert — fruit compote and sponge cake."

The setting for the dinner was the 12-room Upper Park Avenue apartment the senator shares with his wife, Marion, and their three children. The senator strongly adheres to the practice of serving domestic foods and drinks. A true native son (he was born in a Lower East Side ghetto and was reared in Brooklyn), Jack has a chauvinistic preference for the products of the Empire State. "We had New York champagne and white wine, and some of that wonderful Dunkirk cheddar cheese to finish our celebration dinner," he said with a straight face.

The senator admits to being an infrequent cook. "But when I'm home or on holiday, I can fix scrambled eggs, broiled tomatoes, hamburgers or steaks." The senator's lady, however, excels as a hostess. Marion is noted for her smallish dinner parties and lavish Sunday brunches attended by the elite of New York's transient society of writers, painters, actors and blue bloods.

Food has played a monetary if not a memorable role in the Javits success story, which reads like an updated version of Horatio Alger. He once helped support his mother by selling crockery from a pushcart and running errands for a candy store.

# Marion Javits's Veal Scallopini

### Serves 6

1½ lbs. veal scallops,
   cut ¼-inch thick
2 tbsps. olive oil
¼ cup fresh lemon juice
1 tsp. dried oregano,
   crushed

seasoned flour
1½ tbsps. each olive
   oil and sweet
   butter
anchovies
cut parsley

1. *Pound scallops between pieces of wax paper.*
2. *Combine 2 tbsps. olive oil, lemon juice, and oregano in a flat glass dish for marinade.*
3. *Refrigerate meat in marinade overnight, turning several times.*
4. *Drain veal well between paper towels; dust lightly with seasoned flour.*
5. *Heat olive oil and butter in large skillet until sizzling.*
6. *Brown veal quickly, about 3-4 minutes per side.*
7. *Serve immediately, garnished with anchovies and cut parsley.*

NOTE: *Select top quality veal, pound well (or tenderize briefly with unseasoned tenderizer) and cook quickly to insure best results.*

# Madeline Kahn

"I'm famous for my sweet and sour meatballs," said pretty Madeline Kahn as she devoured a huge croissant at New York's Brasserie. "My word, this thing is as big as a ham!" she added between bites.

Few Madeline Kahn fans would be surprised at anything this talented lady can do! Not only is she an accomplished actress, but she has a crazy quilt of interests that range from studying the social behavior of insects and orangutans to learning how to live a healthier, happier life by studying homeopathic medicine, herbs and organic foods!

"I only cook for fun!" she explained. "I used to cook a lot while I was living at home, while my mother was working. I did the shopping, planned the menus and prepared the meals much of the time. So, I've had that, and it doesn't turn me on. It's fun to cook for a man for a while, but when it's not fun, I'd rather go out or send out for food."

# Madeline Kahn's Sweet and Sour Meatballs

## For the sauce

Makes about 1¼ cups

1 cup tomato sauce
2 tbsps. fresh lemon juice
2 tbsps. dark brown sugar
1 tbsp. instant minced onion
1 tbsp. salad oil

1 tsp. powdered mustard
1 tsp. salt
½ tsp. garlic powder
¼ tsp. ground red pepper
1 chicken or beef bouillon cube

*Combine all ingredients. Bring to boil, stirring constantly. Set aside.*

## For the meatballs

Makes about 3 dozen

2 tbsps. instant minced onion
3 tbsps. water
1½ tbsps. butter
1 cup soft breadcrumbs
½ cup light cream
1½ lbs. lean ground beef

½ lb. lean ground veal
1 egg, beaten
1½ tsps. salt
⅛ tsp. ground white pepper
⅛ tsp. ground cinnamon
  or curry

⅛ tsp. ground nutmeg

1. *Rehydrate onion in water; let stand 10 minutes.*
2. *In large skillet, melt butter and sauté onion 5 minutes.*
3. *Soak breadcrumbs in cream.*
4. *In large mixing bowl, combine onion, breadcrumb mixture, meats, egg, salt, pepper, cinnamon and nutmeg. Mix well, but do not overmix.*
5. *Shape into 1½-inch meatballs. Let meatballs stand in refrigerator 30 minutes before cooking.*
6. *Line baking sheet or broiler tray with aluminum foil. Broil meatballs in preheated broiler until lightly browned.*
7. *Turn to brown on other side. Watch carefully so meatballs do not overcook.*
8. *Serve meatballs in heated sauce.*

NOTE: *Madeline's meatballs are terrific for a make-ahead, late-night supper, and great to serve with cocktails because they're hearty and not too sweet!*

# Gene Kelly

"A lot of people think acting is a piece of cake. It's long, hard hours of work," said Gene Kelly in one of the dressing room trailers. The sound of "Roll it!" was eclipsed by the panting of an ancient train about to take its rehearsal turn prior to a "take." An open attaché case stood on a nearby table, neatly filled with his scripts and notes. The versatile gentleman who has spent years high-stepping through some of Hollywood's greatest musicals was directing his first western, *The Cheyenne Social Club*, starring Jimmy Stewart and Hank Fonda.

"At home, I occasionally invade the kitchen," said Gene. The Kellys live in Beverly Hills, in what was the original farmhouse in the area. The spacious house has a swimming pool, volleyball court and nearly always a perpetual touch football game in progress. "When I want a very simple meal, I'll just make an Irish stew, but without gravy," explained Gene. "It's just potatoes, turnips, onions and carrots, but no peas. I just boil and boil that. And then the next day, reboil it and that's an Irish stew."

Gene prefers lamb, saying, "The beef you get for stew is much stringier. Besides, the lamb is tastier. The thing that really gives the stew its flavor is the onion."

It seemed an interesting coincidence that earlier on the set, Jimmy Stewart had mentioned stew as *his* favorite dish also. Gene said, "I just love it and all I do is put a hunk of horse radish on the plate and cut that. But I must confess, I eat bread and butter along with the meat and potatoes."

# Gene Kelly's Real Irish Stew

### Serves 6-8

3 lbs. lean boneless lamb
   (shoulder or leg), cut in
   1½-inch cubes
1 tbsp. vegetable oil
about 3 cups water
2 onions, sliced
2 tsps. salt

¼ tsp. freshly ground pepper
bay leaf
2 turnips, peeled and cut in
   large pieces
6 carrots, peeled and cut
   in chunks
3 cups Irish potatoes, diced

2 tbsps. fresh parsley, minced

1. Sprinkle lamb cubes with salt and pepper.
2. Brown meat on all sides in oil in large skillet.
3. Remove skillet from heat; add water to cover meat.
4. Add onion, salt, pepper and bay leaf; cover and simmer until meat is tender, about 1½ hours.
5. Add remaining vegetables; cover and cook until vegetables are tender, about 35 minutes. Remove cover during last 15 minutes of cooking time to reduce the stock.
6. Taste to correct seasonings.
7. Spoon lamb and vegetables into deep serving dish. Spoon juice over lamb and vegetables. For a touch of the "green," garnish with parsley.
8. Serve piping hot, alone, or with prepared horseradish and slabs of dark or crusty white bread and butter.

NOTE: Some cooks from the Emerald Isle prefer a "lighter" stew (meat is not browned before adding the liquid). For variations: substitute beef for lamb, add peas and/or green snap beans, cauliflower, tomatoes, lima beans or corn; flavor with favorite herbs (tarragon, thyme, parsley, oregano or rosemary). The flavor of the stew improves if prepared in advance. Refrigerate, discard layer of lamb fat that congeals on surface before reheating. For the "casserole treatment," top off stew with biscuits or prepare dumplings in the stock pot.

# Dorothy Kirsten

Opera star Dorothy Kirsten is as magnetic in person as she is on stage. The lovely, blue-eyed blonde lives with her husband, Dr. John French, in an elegant, formal townhouse in Brentwood. "Life in Los Angeles is a little strenuous," said Dorothy. "However, the minute we get into our car and head for our weekend home not far from San Diego, we start yawning. Relaxation begins in the mind, and just starting on that little trip does it, because we know we're going somewhere where we can let it all out!"

Husband John is director of the Brain Research Institute at UCLA. The Frenches like to cook as a team. "John's an excellent cook," said Dorothy enthusiastically. "I got him a Char-broiler and he's absolutely mastered the technique of barbecuing steak and chicken. His rosemary chicken is so beautiful, with a wonderful crust on the outside. I usually make him a butter-wine basting sauce, and I do the salads and vegetables."

The busy pair likes to serve pre-dinner cocktails in the atrium at the low coffee table made from a gold-leaf paneled door that once hung in the Rothschilds' mansion in Paris. "I love this table because the gold design looks exactly like the ceiling of the San Francisco Opera House," Dorothy said, flashing her famous smile.

# Dorothy Kirsten's Osso Bucco
# (Italian Veal Stew)

Serves 4

2-3 lbs. knuckle of veal
3-4 carrots
1-2 stalks celery
2 tbsps. butter
salt to taste
freshly ground black
    pepper to taste
1 cup tomato pulp: sauce,
    or chopped, peeled
    tomatoes

1 tbsp. flour
1 cup dry white wine
veal stock or canned
    beef broth or water
1 sprig thyme or pinch
    of dried
1 bay leaf
strip of lemon peel
handful of minced
    fresh parsley

1. *Have butcher saw veal in 2-inch lengths so marrow remains inside the bone.*
2. *Chop vegetables very fine.*
3. *Brown meat and vegetables in saucepan with butter; season well with salt and pepper.*
4. *Stir flour into vegetables and meat; stir in tomato pulp, wine and enough veal stock to barely cover meat. Add thyme and bay leaf.*
5. *Cover and simmer gently 1½ to 2 hours.*
6. *Ten minutes before serving, remove meat from saucepan and place on heated serving platter.*
7. *Strain sauce and pour over meat.*
8. *Garnish with lemon peel and minced parsley.*
9. *Serve at once. Terrific with crisp green salad and wine.*

# Judith Krantz

*Scruples* author Judith Krantz told us that her husband had been after her to write a novel for years. When she asked, "What makes you think I could?" his reply was: "Because you remember every meal you've ever eaten. You say things like 'Remember the tiny asparagus we ate in the local restaurant when our car broke down on the way from Rome to Venice? They were as skinny as pieces of spaghetti.' "

"That was 24 years ago," said Judy. "Somehow he thought having a memory for food meant I could write a novel. I'm a very good cook, but I didn't learn how until more than two years after I was married. My mother is a lawyer and always worked and had a cook. We were never allowed in the kitchen. When I was married, I had a woman who came in five nights a week to do the cooking and the laundry. One night a week, I did my triumph: broiled steak and baked potato. That's all I knew."

Judy and her husband went to cooking school at night in Greenwich Village. "Our instructor used his apartment," she recalled. "He bought all the groceries and we brought the liquor. By the time he'd cooked up an elaborate menu, including a soufflé, it was 11 o'clock and we'd all be smashed.

"I had my most fun cooking at our summer house in Westport, Connecticut. The fish was so fresh. We could go down to the dock, get lobsters, mussels and incredible bluefish. I would broil them and julienne six or seven different kinds of vegetables."

Judy likes to entertain with small dinners and do the cooking herself. She keeps her favorite recipes in an organized fashion in a notebook. One of her favorite summer menus includes *Vitello Tonnato*, an adaptation of a classic Italian veal dish. "It's a two-day recipe," she said. "A wonderful dish for brunch or buffet lunch or dinner."

# Judith Krantz's Vitello Tonnato

Serves 6

### For the veal

3-4 lbs. boneless veal, in
 one piece, securely tied
 with cord
cold water
1½ quarts chicken stock,
 homemade or canned
2 cups dry California
 white wine

4 carrots, peeled and sliced
2 stalks celery, sliced
2 medium onions, peeled and halved
handful parsley
1 leek, white part only
2 bay leaves
12 peppercorns
salt to taste

1. Place veal in stock pot; cover with water. Bring to boil and cook 2 minutes.
2. Discard water and accumulated scum. Rinse meat; wash stock pot.
3. Return veal to stock pot with remaining ingredients. Add water to cover.
4. Simmer, uncovered, about 1 hour and 40 minutes, or until meat is tender.
5. Cool to room temperature. Refrigerate veal overnight in stock.

### For the sauce

1 cup olive oil
2 cans (3½ ozs.) tuna
 fish packed in oil
6 flat anchovies, minced
2 egg yolks

2 tbsps. fresh lemon juice
¼ tsp. cayenne
6 tbsps. heavy cream
6 tbsps. stock liquid from braised
 veal or chicken stock

3 tbsps. capers, washed, drained and dried

1. In blender, combine olive oil, tuna fish, anchovies, egg yolks, lemon juice and cayenne. Blend only long enough to reduce to a smooth purée.
2. Transfer mixture to a small bowl and slowly stir in cream.
3. Thin by adding stock, a couple of tablespoons at a time, mixing well after each addition. Add capers.
4. Remove veal from stock; dry. Trim fat. Slice ¼" thick.
5. Spread thin layer of sauce in bottom of a long glass or china or stoneware serving platter. (Silver will tarnish.) Arrange veal slices side by side, overlapping only slightly. Pour rest of sauce over top to cover.
6. Cover platter tightly with plastic wrap. Refrigerate 24 hours or overnight.
7. Remove from refrigerator several hours before serving. Garnish with thin radish slices, cherry tomatoes, hard-cooked eggs, lemon slices, black olives, scallions, and sprigs of parsley.

# Burt Lancaster

Oscar winner Burt Lancaster, with the Oscar-shaped body, talked about the relationship of good health to diet and exercise. "I've always felt obesity is a deterrent to physical well-being. Many people diet properly, but the mistake they make is neglecting physical exercise."

Though the former acrobat-circus strongman declines to impose his own brand of diet and exercise on others, his thoughts are in accord with the findings of the National Academy of the Sciences and National Research Council. "It's the combination of proper diet and regular exercise that's essential," Burt said. "I don't pretend to have the last word on diets. Most people have their own formula.

"I eat lots of vegetables and substantial amounts of protein. I try to balance my diet with a great deal of fish and meat, but I eat moderately and at regular intervals. When I'm working, I always eat a good breakfast: orange or grapefruit juice, cereal or eggs, and a half slice of whole wheat toast. A typical lunch is cottage cheese and sliced tomatoes." He often skips lunch, however, in favor of a nap before resuming the afternoon filming. "At night I have a substantial meal, but I avoid the obvious bread, butter and desserts."

Lancaster is a moderate drinker. "It's best not to drink at all," he said, "but I might have a martini before dinner, or, better still, a glass of wine with dinner. Wine helps digestion."

Talking about his children, Burt explained, "My kids had weight problems at one time or another. But when my girls became interested in boys, we didn't have the problem anymore. They went on their own diets." He laughed.

# Burt Lancaster's Beef Curry

### Serves 6-8

1 tbsp. ginger root finely minced

1½ tbsps. green onion, minced (white part only)

1 clove garlic, mashed

½ cup butter

⅓ cup flour

2 cups coconut cream (available in supermarkets)

3 cups beef stock or diluted canned beef broth

1 cup heavy cream

2 tsps. salt

1 tbsp. curry powder

4 cups cold cooked beef, cut into 1-inch cubes

3 tbsps. lemon juice or 1 tsp. finely grated lemon rind

1. *Sauté ginger, onion and garlic in butter until onion is golden.*
2. *Add flour, stirring; cook 2 minutes over low flame.*
3. *Slowly add coconut cream, beef stock, cream, salt, and curry powder. Let the sauce cook until smooth and creamy.*
4. *Add meat. Cook, stirring often, for 10 minutes.*
5. *Add lemon juice to a little of the sauce, then stir it into remaining sauce.*
6. *Serve immediately, alone, or with cooked rice and top with any of the following condiments: chutney, grated coconut, crisp bacon crumbles, toasted almonds, peanuts, cashews, minced candied ginger, fried onion rings or chopped onions, mandarin orange sections, sieved hard-cooked egg or raisins plumped in rum or brandy.*

*NOTE: Ginger root is available in Oriental food shops. Ginger can be stored for future use by scraping the skin, cutting into large pieces and immersing in sherry before refrigerating.*

# Cleavon Little

Actor Cleavon Little says he learns a lot about people just by watching them eat or cook. "For example, I love oysters and clams," he explained. "It amazes me when I ask a girl to try some oysters and she says, 'No! They don't look good to me!' When someone absolutely refuses to try something new, I know her attitude is merely a reflection of her outlook on life, and that her focus falls somewhere within the 9-to-5 range."

Cleavon likes to cook two simple, delicious dishes. "I've never been able to find good tacos in New York, so I always make my own. I love to prepare chili, too. For tacos, I use good chopped meat mixed with salt, pepper, chili powder, oregano, garlic, onion and spices. I cook mine loose and really let it soak up all the flavors. I fry the tortillas so they are between hard and soft. My mother makes her tacos with mashed potato. They come out looking like meat patties and taste wonderful. Any way you fix them, tacos are delicious, served with cold beer or wine."

Leaning forward in his chair, Cleavon added, "Some people have a thing about the texture of food. For example, squash is something I've never liked. But that's changing. The older I get, the more I revise my feelings about food. I didn't used to like okra because of its texture, but now I love it, especially when it's mixed with black-eyed peas. Now, that's something really terrific!"

# Cleavon Little's Tacos Californian

Serves 6

## For the beef filling

1 tbsp. salad oil
1 medium onion, peeled and
   minced
1 clove garlic, pressed
1 lb. lean ground beef
salt to taste
freshly ground black pepper to taste

1 tbsp. chili powder
½ tsp. ground cumin
½ tsp. oregano
dash of paprika
1 ripe tomato, peeled and
   chopped, or ½ cup
   tomato sauce

1. *Heat oil in skillet. Sauté onion and garlic in it until onion is soft.*
2. *Add beef. Cook over medium heat until meat starts to turn light. Break up beef with fork as it cooks.*
3. *Reduce heat to low. Add salt, pepper, chili, and remaining ingredients.*
4. *Cook until mixture thickens, stirring often. Keep warm.*

## For the tacos

salad oil for frying
12 tortillas, fresh, frozen or canned

1. *Pour enough oil in skillet to reach ¼- to ½-inch depth. Heat until hot.*
2. *Put 1 tortilla at a time into hot oil. Cook a few seconds, or until soft.*
3. *Use tongs to remove tortilla from heat and fold into U-shape. Hold tacos with tongs until they harden, about 1 to 2 minutes.*
4. *Drain on absorbent paper. Keep warm. Repeat, using remaining tortillas.*

## To assemble

taco shells
beef filling
1 small onion, peeled and
   minced
½ head western iceberg
   lettuce, finely shredded

2 small tomatoes, cubed
fresh Parmesan cheese or
   Monterey Jack or
   cheddar, grated
taco sauce (canned) or
   Tabasco sauce

1. *Spoon 3 tbsps. beef filling in bottom of each taco shell.*
2. *Sprinkle with onion, lettuce, tomato, Parmesan cheese and taco or Tabasco sauce. Serve at once!*

# Keye Luke

"I'm an amateur cook. I have one or two Chinese dishes I prepare. I amaze myself and find I can eat it!" said veteran actor Keye Luke, over a sherry at the Brown Derby, famous watering spot for the stars. Still looking like the ageless number-one son of Charlie Chan and also like Dr. Wong, intern to Lionel Barrymore's Dr. Gillespie, Keye has long excelled as an artist, writer, linguist, philosopher and musician, as well as actor.

"I like to cook variations on one theme: beef and asparagus, beef and string beans or beef and *bok choy*," he said. "The beef is always flank steak because it's lean and tender. I call my dish 'Asparagus and Beef,' but I have a Chanogram in honor of the dish: 'Tough does not cook rice, but tough also does not cook asparagus and beef. It is artistry!' "

The Chinese-born actor used to create many of the Chanograms used in the Charlie Chan movies. "There is a general principle underlying the Chinese diet. All the strong, hot foods are the masculine *yang*, the cooler elements the feminine *yin*. Rice is feminine because it is grown in water and water is a feminine element; on the other hand, wheat, grown in the sun, is considered *yang*, or male. All of these foods have curative or herbal values, too. It's an elaborate state that goes on and on." His philosophy is an extension of his Zen Buddhist beliefs.

# Keye Luke's Asparagus and Beef

### Serves 4

1 lb. flank steak
1 lb. asparagus shoots
2 tbsps. peanut oil
3 spring onions
1 small yellow onion,
   peeled and thinly sliced
½ clove garlic, pressed

3 thin slices ginger, shredded,
   or ground ginger to taste
½ cake bean curd, diced
2-3 tbsps. soy sauce
water or beef broth
salt to taste
hot cooked rice or Chinese noodles

1. *Cut beef into very thin strips 1½-inches long.*
2. *Wash and clean tips of asparagus, discarding hard stems. French-cut tips into thin pieces with cleaver or sharp knife.*
3. *Heat 1 tbsp. peanut oil in wok or large skillet until hot.*
4. *Quickly brown beef on both sides. Lift out and place on warm platter.*
5. *Lightly brown spring onions and yellow onion in skillet, adding remaining oil.*
6. *Add garlic and ginger. Stir-fry over low heat a few minutes longer.*
7. *Make a paste with bean curd, soy sauce and enough water to make it thin. Pour paste over onions, adding asparagus and beef to wok. Cook until asparagus is crisp-tender.*
8. *Add salt to taste and serve at once over rice.*

*NOTE: Change vegetable by using bok choy, Chinese cabbage, spinach, red cabbage, string beans (cut French-style), green pepper, Chinese mushrooms (soak in warm water 30 minutes before chopping), Chinese pea pods, broccoli or bean sprouts. For sweet-sour effect: marinate beef strips in mixture of Chinese rice wine (or pale dry sherry), ground star anise and shredded ginger. Dry off meat before browning in wok. Sweeten sauce with sherry or brown sugar to taste. You can substitute thin strips of chicken breast, pork or ham for beef. Adjust seasonings to balance sauce.*

# Shirley MacLaine

"I dance better than I cook," said freckle-faced Shirley MacLaine, "but Steve (her husband at the time, Steve Parker) does all kinds of great gourmet cooking. I love Japanese food, especially *sushi* made with raw fish, flavored with *wasabi* (Japanese horseradish), and served on mounds of vinegared rice in individual rice bowls. I suppose I like Japanese food because my body needs the iodine from the fish. I always find myself eating things I think my body needs. I really prefer Chinese cooking, but – " Shirley left the sentence hanging as she went on.

"There are two things I need every day. I demand sweets and salads, and eat them all the time." When the role demands it, she will go on eating jags to gain weight. "I love ice cream, especially hot fudge sundaes, but I understand they can be habit-forming," she said somewhat regretfully. "They do give me great energy, though."

Shirley is an addict to chocolate. "The best chocolate I ever had was in Tunisia. It was a long bar imbedded with huge nuts that had been roasted and had a smoky flavor. I can cook, but I'd rather bake cookies, particularly Toll House cookies. Steve can make anything from a succulent roast goose to the most delicate Chinese dish. I do better on the pots and pans," the three-time Oscar nominee said.

# Shirley MacLaine's Gourmet Lamb Stew

### Serves 6-8

5-6 lbs. boneless leg of lamb,
    cut into 1½-inch cubes
1 tbsp. lard
2 tbsps. flour
1 clove garlic, minced
about 3 cups water
2 tbsps. tomato paste
¼ tsp. lamb herbs or oregano
1½ tsps. salt
⅛ tsp. freshly ground
    black pepper
10 cubes sugar

1 tbsp. hot water
3 tbsps. sweet butter
1 small yellow onion, peeled
    and chopped
6 pearl onions, peeled
    and left whole
2 small yellow turnips, peeled
    and diced
2 small carrots, peeled
    and chopped
1 tsp. sugar
1 tbsp. parsley, chopped

1. *Brown lamb in lard.*
2. *Spinkle flour over meat and cook a few minutes, stirring constantly.*
3. *Add garlic; cook over very low heat until garlic begins to smell.*
4. *Add water (enough to barely cover meat), tomato paste, lamb herbs, salt and pepper. Cover and simmer about 15 minutes.*
5. *Meanwhile, put sugar lumps and 1 tbsp. water in a small saucepan; heat over low heat until sugar carmelizes.*
6. *Add sugar mixture to meat, stirring to blend well. Cover and simmer 30 minutes, stirring occasionally.*
7. *Melt butter over low heat; add vegetables; sprinkle with sugar.*
8. *Add vegetables to lamb; cover and cook, simmering about 30 minutes, or until vegetables and lamb are tender.*
9. *Remove vegetables and lamb to a platter.*
10. *Skim off surface fat before pouring sauce over meat.*
11. *Garnish with parsley. Serve with crusty French bread and tossed green salad.*

FULL OF IODINE

# Ann Margret &
# Roger Smith

"I've got a thing about food!" said Ann-Margret, curling up cat-like in the den of the pretty hilltop house she shares with Roger Smith, her husband, manager, and, as she sees it, mentor and protector. "I start salivating just thinking about food – chocolate malts, hot dogs, caviar, pizza pie, steak tartar, you name it."

Roger said, with a broad grin, that one of his pleasures is "cooking for Ann-Margret, but I have to keep a close watch to see she doesn't eat too much!"

"My weight would go up and down like an elevator if I let it," she said, sipping a diet cola. "I'm a food freak, you see. Just give me two minutes in any city in any country in the world and I will find, without fail, the best food available."

Roger and Ann-Margret like to give small dinner parties for close friends. "We never have more than five or six people, and it's always informal," they explained. An invitation to dinner at the Smiths often involves athletic events as well – a friendly game of tennis, volleyball or badminton. The Smiths live on 10 wild acres, populated by cats, deer and rabbits.

# Ann-Margret's Steak Tartar

Serves 4

1½ lbs. freshly ground lean round or porterhouse steak (fat well trimmed)

1 small onion, peeled and minced

2-3 tbsps. capers

1 cup dill pickles, finely diced

1 can (2 ozs.) flat anchovy fillets, chopped

4 egg yolks

salt to taste

freshly ground black pepper to taste

Swedish limpa bread or rye bread rounds

1. *Divide meat into 4 portions and place on individual plates.*
2. *Surround meat with ¼ each of the onion, capers, pickles and anchovies.*
3. *With the back of a tablespoon, make hollow on top of each serving of meat and place 1 egg yolk in each hollow. Each serving will be mixed individually at the table and seasoned to taste with salt and pepper.*
4. *Serve with bread slices spread with softened sweet butter, if you're not dieting! Garnish with capers.*

NOTE: *The ingredients can be prepared and assembled in advance for delicious non-cook dining pleasure. But be sure to keep them chilled. Serve with fine vintage dry red wine, domestic or imported. For extra touches, garnish with smoked salmon or tiny canned shrimp and sliced hard-cooked egg. Top with minced pickle, minced white onion or freshly shredded horseradish. A real boon to dieters, too, because it's low in calories, high in protein!*

# Robert Merrill

Metropolitan Opera star Robert Merrill is a world traveler, baseball nut and food buff. Although he has a sophisticated palate from mingling with opera stars from nearly every country in the world, he still hankers for the peasant food prepared by his Polish mother during his childhood in Brooklyn. "I had to shop off the pushcarts for my mother," he recalled. "I remember buying milk when they ladled it out from a huge can. It was six cents a quart." He laughed. "We were always big herring eaters. It was cheap food in those days and so good tasting. I'm getting hungry just talking to you!"

Bob generates a tremendous amount of energy when he sings, but, as he says, "it's a mental thing. The enthusiasm, I feel. I become as strong as a bull during a performance without eating. I'll let you in on a little secret. The day of a performance at the opera, at three in the afternoon, I eat a huge bowl of oatmeal with honey. Honey gives me energy.

"I've done a lot of cooking in my day. I invent the darnedest concoctions," he said proudly. "I make delicious soups from leftover lamb, fish or chicken." Recalling an experience in an Italian restaurant in Elmira, New York, Bob ordered spaghetti *al dente*. "I told the chef how to make *ajo e ajo*, or garlic and oil sauce. It's so simple to fix. Peasants eat it in Italy. I told the chef how to make a fresh tomato sauce with herbs and onions too. I then mixed the two sauces together and poured them over the pasta. My dinner friends thought it was the most fabulous dish in the world. You can put the same sauce on veal parmesan."

# Robert Merrill's Veal Parmesan

### Serves 4

### For fresh tomato sauce

1 large yellow onion,
  peeled and chopped
2 small cloves garlic,
  peeled and pressed
¼ cup fine-grade olive
  oil or butter

4 large ripe tomatoes,
  peeled, chopped and drained
½ tsp. sugar
1 tsp. dried basil or oregano
3 large sprigs parsley,
  chopped

1. *Sauté onion and garlic in olive oil until onion is limp.*
2. *Add tomatoes, sugar, basil. Cook slowly 15 minutes, stirring often.*
3. *Add parsley; cook 10 minutes longer.*

### For veal cutlets

1½ lbs. veal cutlets
salt to taste
pepper to taste
¼ cup fine-grade olive oil

½ lb. mozzarella, sliced thin
tomato sauce
¼ cup Parmesan cheese,
  freshly grated

1. *Season veal liberally on both sides with salt and pepper.*
2. *Heat olive oil in large skillet; brown veal quickly on both sides.*
3. *Lift out; top each cutlet with mozzarella and tomato sauce.*
4. *Sprinkle top liberally with Parmesan cheese.*
5. *Broil until cheese melts and is bubbly and golden brown.*
6. *Serve at once with tossed green salad or finger foods of fresh vegetables: tomato, celery, radishes, cherry tomatoes, cucumber slices.*
7. *Pass remaining sauce.*

NOTE: *If desired, cutlets can be coated with egg and Italian-flavored bread crumbs, partially browned on each side, then topped with tomato sauce, mozzarella and Parmesan cheese and baked in moderate oven for 15 minutes until mozzarella turns golden brown and cutlets are cooked through. If desired, sauce can be served separately with cooked pasta. Vary seasoning of sauce by using rosemary, sage or mint. Gardeners will find Bob's sauce an excellent excuse for using fresh herbs.*

# Mary Tyler Moore

When Mary Tyler Moore takes to her tiny Malibu beach house, she does something she rarely does and that's cook. "I cook simple things, peasant dishes, casseroles, vegetables or toss a salad," Mary once told me. "Maybe I'm just too lazy to learn how to cook. There's a strange futility that comes from preparing a meal. You slave over something for hours only to have it consumed in minutes."

She never pretended to limit herself to being a housewife. "If I weren't an actress, I'd have to be doing something. I'd go to school, or I'd be a doctor, but I'd do something."

The TV and now Broadway star has always been careful about her food, particularly since she discovered she's diabetic. Insulin and correct diet have helped her control the disease.

Typically, Mary is reluctant to adopt any food fad or reducing diet. However, she was tempted to become a vegetarian until she discovered, "It demands a real commitment, almost a way of life."

Despite her disclaimers, Mary is a better cook than she admits. "There's a simple supper dish I fix. It's no struggle. It's so easy to prepare, it's shameful. It's poor man's stroganoff made with onions, mushrooms and sour cream. Lately, I've taken to pouring in a little dry sherry," she added, laughing.

# Mary Tyler Moore's Non-Fail Hamburger Stroganoff

### Serves 4

2 cans (3 oz.) mushrooms,
  drained and chopped
1 medium yellow onion,
  peeled and diced
2 tbsps. butter or
  margarine

1 lb. lean ground sirloin
1/2 tsp. salt
few gratings freshly
  ground pepper
1 cup dairy sour cream

1. *Sauté mushrooms and onion in butter. Cook until soft. Shake pan often for even cooking.*
2. *Add beef and seasonings to onion mixture. Cook over medium heat until meat begins to turn grey. Stir with a fork to prevent meat from lumping.*
3. *Remove from heat and pour in sour cream.*
4. *Replace skillet over low heat and cook until sauce begins to simmer. Do not boil!*
5. *Serve alone, or over hot cooked rice, buttered noodles tossed with poppy seeds, or toast points. Great with crisp green salad and hot garlic bread.*

*NOTE: Mary advises, "If you wish to delay serving the stroganoff, cover the skillet and reheat just before serving. It's a non-fail main dish that can sit as long as you want it to — within reason, that is — without the sauce curdling."*

# Wayne Newton

Skinny singer Wayne Newton has always had phenomenal success in show biz, but until recently, he also had a phenomenal problem. He was invariably described as "the pudgy, pink-faced singer with the big voice." The new Wayne Newton is 100 pounds slimmer and in better voice than ever. He attributes his dieting success to "a string of Caesar salads."

Wayne talked in the large Las Vegas house he shares with his wife, Elaine, a former airline stewardess. "I'm super-impatient and, therefore, can't take that losing-a-pound-a-week nonsense! And that's the usual approach of most doctors. Although their method may be healthier, I found that Dr. Newton's salad diet finally did it for me. What really happened was, I just quit eating. Once you've lost the weight, the challenge is to keep it off. I have totally changed my eating habits. I eat once a day, around five in the afternoon, and eat what I want, omitting sweets. On my salad diet, I had a big plate or two of Caesar salad. That's just straight greens with very little protein other than a little egg, a taste of grated cheese, anchovies, a few croutons and lemon-oil dressing. I didn't take vitamins at the time, and I found the salad gave me all the energy I needed. I'd have the salad every day for six days. On the seventh day, I'd eat nothing but protein — veal, broiled or baked fish, occasionally some chicken."

Wayne claims no credit for his abilities in the kitchen, but he has nothing but praise for the combined efforts of "our incredible cook, Julia, and my magnificent wife." He particularly likes the Japanese dishes Elaine prepares.

# Elaine Newton's Teriyaki

Serves 6

2 lbs. lean sirloin steak
½ cup soy sauce
dash of sugar

1-inch piece fresh
ginger root, minced
1 tbsp. salad oil

1 small clove garlic, pressed

1. *Cut beef into strips 1- x 2-inches long.*
2. *Combine remaining ingredients for marinade.*
3. *Put meat in marinade for 5 hours or overnight in refrigerator, keeping tightly covered.*
4. *String beef on metal skewers. Reserve marinade for future use. (Store it in a jar with tight-fitting lid. Can be used as a glaze for roast or broiled seafood or poultry.)*
5. *Grill teriyaki on hibachi for 3 minutes, turning once, or until meat is tender but rare.*
6. *Teriyaki is delicious with plain or "herbed" rice.*

*NOTE: Teriyaki is usually garnished with tiny cucumbers marinated in vinegar and soy sauce.*

# Kathleen Nolan

"I was tired of being without my things," said actress Kathleen Nolan, well known for her role as Richard Crenna's wife on TV's "The Real McCoys." Standing on her bed and holding a huge blue-and-white oil painting, the red-headed star explained, "This time I decided I'd bring along my most prized possessions." She and her son spend most of the time at their home in California, but she keeps an apartment in the Dakota, a famed New York landmark overlooking Central Park.

"When you spend your life traveling and you have a child, it's important to keep some semblance of home. So here I am with my overweight of 1600 pounds. The air freight only cost about 200 dollars. I couldn't store the things for that.

"Much of the weight was taken up by my oversized spaghetti pots. I brought them along because I can't find pots like them here. I also have my electric fry pans but only a few cookbooks, because I'm a throw-it-in-the-pot cook. I find meals-in-the-pot are very convenient for entertaining. If you make anything like an Irish stew or *Calienti* (similar to her chili stew but made with macaroni shells instead of noodles), people think you're absolutely brilliant."

Kathleen's fans often seem surprised at her fondness for cooking. "I don't know what people expect," she said. "They think I sleep under gold sheets and get up at noon and that someone does everything for me. I love cooking. I can't keep my hands out of things even when I'm trying to be the grand lady and playing hostess."

# Kathleen Nolan's Chili Stew for 25

1 lb. dried navy beans, soaked
   overnight in cold water
2 tbsps. salad oil
4 lbs. lean round steak, cubed
6 medium-sized yellow onions,
   peeled and chopped
2 large green peppers,
   coarsely chopped
2 cloves garlic, pressed
4 loin pork chops, about 1 lb.
3 lbs. coarsely ground chuck
½ lb. "hot" Italian pepperoni,
   skinned and sliced thin
1 tbsp. salt
½ tsp. freshly ground
   black pepper

1 heaping tsp. red pepper,
   crushed, or Tabasco sauce
   to taste
4 tbsps. chili powder
2½ tsps. oregano
1 tsp. basil
1 can (1 lb.) tomato purée
1 can (1 lb.) peeled Italian
   plum tomatoes
2 cans (8 ozs.) tomato sauce
4 cans (1 lb.) red kidney beans
2 cans (1 lb.) Mexican pinto beans
1 pkg. (10 ozs.) frozen lima beans
1 can (1 lb.) pearl onions,
   drained
1 pkg. (1 lb.) broad noodles

1 can (4 oz.) whole roasted green chiles, peeled and chopped,
or 6 chili peppers, crushed

1. Drain beans, place in large saucepan, and cover with water. Bring to boil and simmer about 1½ hours.
2. Heat 1 tbsp. oil in large cast iron skillet. Add cubed beef, ½ each of the onions, green peppers and garlic. Brown meat over high heat, stirring.
3. Heat remaining oil in another large skillet. Brown pork chops well on both sides; set aside.
4. Add ground chuck, remaining onion, green pepper and garlic to first skillet. Cook over medium heat, stirring occasionally so meat is lumpy.
5. Divide between both skillets: pepperoni, salt, freshly ground pepper, green chiles, crushed red pepper, chili powder, oregano, basil, tomato purée, plum tomatoes and tomato sauce. Cook about 30 minutes.
6. Transfer ingredients in both skillets to one large stock pot. Add cooked navy beans, plus about 1½ cups broth from cooking beans. Let simmer, uncovered, about 1 hour.
7. Add browned pork chops, kidney and pinto beans. Cook 1 hour longer, stirring often to keep stew from sticking.
8. Add lima beans, pearl onions and noodles, or cook noodles separately. Cook about 20 minutes, or until lima beans and noodles are tender. Keep tasting to correct seasonings.
9. To serve: ladle stew into individual soup bowls or spoon chili over hot cooked noodles. Makes approximately 2½ gallons. (Leftovers freeze well.)

# Henry Ringling North

"There are three English expressions that foreign circus performers always knew: 'pay day,' 'red wagon,' (where the paymaster presided) and 'flag's up.' When the food was ready in the big cookhouse, the flag was hoisted," said Henry Ringling North who, with his brother John, is the last of the Circus Kings.

"We did away with the cookhouse in 1956," he said. "Few people realize what a tremendous impediment it was to transport just the kitchen equipment. We used to feed 1200 personnel three times a day. We now have a pie wagon. That's circus parlance for dining car. It's mainly short-order service. But you can get anything from a piece of pie or steak sandwich to a complete meal. Actually, many of our people prefer to do their own cooking, particularly the married couples."

Describing the days of the cookhouse, North explained, "There was a certain protocol that went along with dining in the performers' quarters. Once I had to borrow a coat before they would seat me at the table. Dining was elegant, with white linen tablecloths and fine tableware.

"I love simple food like German food, particularly bratwurst and sauerkraut. My favorite meal is prepared in Rome (where North maintains a permanent residence with his beautiful wife, Gloria) by our Italian cook. I am a great beef lover and enjoy a hearty beef stew made with plenty of good marrow bones. Half the pleasure is digging out the marrow with a knife-like instrument with a scoop at one end. The Italians call the pick '*agente della tasse*' or 'tax collector.' I guess that's how you feel after you've paid all your taxes, as though you've been scraped to the bone," he said, smiling.

# Henry Ringling North's Marrow Beef Stew

Serves 8

12 marrow bones, sawed into
    2½-inch pieces
seasoned flour
2 tbsps. olive oil
3 lbs. stewing beef, cut
    in 2-inch cubes
1 small carrot, peeled and
    minced
1 small yellow onion,
    minced
1 leek (white part only),
    minced

1 stalk celery, minced
1 tbsp. parsley, minced
1½ tsps. salt
⅛ tsp. freshly ground
    pepper
1 cup dry white wine
1 can (10½ ozs.) beef
    consommé, diluted with
    2½ cups water
8 whole carrots, scraped
8 small potatoes, scraped
fresh parsley, chopped

1. *Roll bones in seasoned flour and brown slowly in olive oil in a large, deep skillet or cooking pot.*
2. *Lift out bones.*
3. *Brown meat and lift out.*
4. *Brown minced vegetables, excluding parsley, in same skillet for 1 minute.*
5. *Return browned meat to the skillet and add minced parsley, salt, pepper, wine and diluted consommé.*
6. *Cover and cook slowly 2 hours.*
7. *Add marrow bones, carrots and potatoes. Cook 45 minutes longer, or until vegetables are tender. Be careful not to overcook the bones, or marrow will fall out.*
8. *Serve meat, vegetables and bones on a heated platter. Garnish with chopped parsley. Pass gravy in side dish.*

# Cesar Romero

Seated in the quiet comfort of his Brentwood home, the perenially elegant Cesar Romero leaned back, smiled, and said, "Sure, I enjoy eating, but then, I seem to enjoy everything in life! I appreciate a good dinner, attractively served on a well-laid table, but I'd just as soon go to McDonald's and have a big Mac!" He laughed, then added, "I'm no wine connoisseur, either. The wine we drink in this house costs $1.98 a gallon."

Romero's rating as a social asset has always been high in the film domain, due to his exquisite manners and lack of the egocentric airs that so often characterize the traditional Hollywood actor. "My mother learned to cook out of necessity. She was a good cook, both of American-style meals and the family's Cuban favorites. I was always especially fond of her *picadillo*. It's a little like the American 'Sloppy Joe,' served over hamburger or hotdog buns. My mother also used to fix plain black beans and rice, and bananas fried in the Cuban manner. Another of our favorites was sliced avocado in clear soup. That's delicious!"

Cesar misses the panache of the old Hollywood. "Dinner in white tie and tails was an everyday event in those days. There was a motion picture colony and within that colony, there were definite societies. Everyone knew everyone. Now, all you read about are those huge benefit balls. Every star in this business used to give at least one big party every year, and then there were the grand social things given by people like Darryl Zanuck and Basil Rathbone. It's all gone now. Those were great years! I'm glad I had them — they were marvelous, glamorous and exciting, and they'll never return. What a shame!"

# Cesar Romero's Picadillo

Serves 4-6

1 medium-size onion, peeled
  and chopped
2 tbsps. olive oil
1½ lbs. lean ground round
½ tsp. salt
⅛ tsp. freshly ground
  black pepper

1 can (16 ozs.) tomatoes
½ cup Spanish pimento-
  stuffed green olives,
  sliced
½ cup raisins
hot cooked rice

1. *Sauté onion in oil until soft.*
2. *Season beef with salt and pepper; add to onion. Cook until meat begins to brown, stirring often with a fork to keep mixture soft and crumbly.*
3. *Add remaining ingredients except rice. Simmer, uncovered, 20 minutes, stirring often until most of the liquid has been absorbed.*
4. *Serve at once over hot cooked rice with carrots or peas, accompanied by crusty French bread, nice, crisp, green salad and dry red wine or your favorite libation!*

*NOTE: Cesar's favorite Cuban creation is deceptively easy to make and can be the beginning of a medley of flavorful, inexpensive dishes. Serve it "sandwich-style," over split hamburger or hot dog buns or casserole-style: fill an unbaked 9-inch pie shell with picadillo, top with shredded American or mozzarella cheese, and bake in a preheated 375° F. oven until crust is done and cheese is golden brown. Stuff picadillo into red or green pepper shells (parboiled), bake in moderate oven until pepper is soft. Adjust the amounts of olives and raisins to suit personal taste. For flavor nuances: use ½ cup chopped fresh parsley (add during last 5 minutes of cooking time) or a hint of garlic or ground cumin.*

# William Shatner

Actor William Shatner of "Star Trek" fame confesses, "I have a compulsive desire to try anything new." That may be why he is now very much into health foods.

He jokingly recalled some exotic food served during his travels. "I ordered something in a restaurant in Milwaukee, one that I'll never order again. The waiter told me it was lion steak. I sawed and sawed away on that piece of meat. It was like rubber bands, but the ridiculous thing was the meat came out tasting like house cat. Overall, I've found the food in this country to be excellent. I've had wonderful beef Wellington one place; in another, quail. I had superb salmon in Portland," he quipped. He rates the clams and steamed lobster in Boston "top drawer," and lauded the pompano of Miami. Interestingly enough, the best food he ever encountered was some scones he had at the Oregon State Fair.

"Good cooking demands care, even to the making of coffee," said Shatner. "There's an art to making coffee, grinding it fresh and adding chicory, just the right amount. But the best coffee is always on camping trips. Thanks to modern technology, it's the ash from the campfire and the hot tin cup that make it taste the best."

Asked about his role as a rocket skipper in "Star Trek," Shatner replied, "We were always concerned on the show about what people in the future will be eating or drinking. With food, we will have progressed beyond the little-packages-of-pills period and can indulge once again in the great gustatory pleasure in life. We'll have overcome the problem of radiation in food and will be able to stop off on an unknown planet and utilize the great plant and animal species that we find there. Food may exist in many different shapes or colors and be exotic in flavor."

# William Shatner's Steak Picado

Serves 6-8

2 green peppers
1 large Bermuda onion,
   peeled
4 ripe tomatoes, peeled
1 tbsp. olive oil
2 lbs. lean top sirloin steak

2 tsps. chili powder
pinch dried oregano
1 clove garlic, pressed
salt to taste
freshly ground black
   pepper to taste

1. Cut up peppers, onions and tomatoes into ½-inch pieces.
2. Sauté in olive oil until onions are transparent.
3. Cube steak into bite-size pieces.
4. In separate pan rubbed with olive oil, sear meat quickly until brown outside, but rare inside.
5. Add sautéed vegetables, chili powder, oregano and garlic.
6. Season to taste; mix well.
7. Cover and simmer for 10 minutes.
8. Serve at once, alone, or with side dishes of rice, tortillas and green salad tossed with vinegar-oil dressing, and dry red wine.

# Dinah Shore

"I've always liked to cook because you get instant results, and can savor the wonderful smells and tastes," said Dinah Shore, coming off the set of her TV show looking cool and chic in a comfortable beige, two-piece slack set with matching shirt. "I think loving and enjoying good food are the prime requisites of a good cook. I don't waste myself on bad food. You don't have to eat enormous amounts of food if it's well-prepared. When food is superb, then you savor it, eat less, more slowly, and enjoy it more.

"I've had several disasters on the show," recalled Dinah, describing, in particular, "a wonderful chicken dish" for which she did "everything right." Then she "got busy talking and the whole thing caught fire. I smiled desperately and tried to put out the fire while the camera kept grinding away. There was no way I could fake it — so I had *flambéed* (flaming) chicken in *buerre noir* (black butter). *Flambéed* fingers is what I really had!"

Dinah loves to try out new dishes on her tennis pals. "I'll have three or four different kinds of meat, an unusual meat loaf, brisket of beef, stew and three or four kinds of desserts. Afterwards, we all waddle out on the court and resume play.

"I really enjoy small informal dinner parties for six or eight people. I have a wonderful kitchen I spent four years planning; we eat in the kitchen and line up the whole thing, with the grill and hot-tray in the center. That way, people get up from the table and go serve themselves. The conversation is warm, the atmosphere congenial and the setting pretty. The candles are lit, the food nice and hot, and the wine good."

# Dinah Shore's Brisket of Beef
# with Puréed Vegetable Gravy

Serves 6-8

3-4 lbs. lean beef brisket
salt to taste
freshly ground pepper
  to taste
3 tbsps. vegetable oil or
  butter
4 stalks celery, coarsely
  chopped

½ green pepper,
  coarsely chopped
3 carrots, peeled and
  coarsely chopped
3 tomatoes, peeled
  and coarsely chopped
½ cup dry red wine
½ cup beef broth

1. *Season brisket generously with salt and pepper. Brown on both sides in vegetable oil in a Dutch oven or heavy skillet.*
2. *Add vegetables to form layer on bottom of pan; replace meat on top.*
3. *Cover and bake in preheated 300° F. oven about 2 hours, basting occasionally with meat juices.*
4. *Uncover; add wine and beef broth.*
5. *Continue baking, uncovered, until meat is tender.*
6. *Remove meat to a heated platter.*
7. *Skim and discard excess fat from pan.*
8. *Strain vegetables and remaining pan juices, pressing through a sieve or using a food mill to make the purée.*
9. *Return purée to pan and cook, stirring until smooth and thick.*
10. *Season to taste and return meat to pan to reheat.*
11. *Serve alone or with kasha or potato pancakes, or with potatoes, cut in half, roasted and basted with meat-vegetable juices during the last hour of cooking.*

# Robert Stack

"When I go home at night, I shut the door and spend the time with my family. Now I have time for my wife and my children. At night, I enjoy good food. I like to drink a little *vino*. I found out that by drinking wine, you aren't blotto," actor Robert Stack said, his steel-blue eyes crinkling into a ready smile.

"I grew up in Europe and love good food, good wines and excellent company. I don't really cook as much as I love to eat." Stack, a fifth generation Californian, grew up among motion picture and concert artists. "You can eat very well in Italy without indulging in the pasta. The veal is fantastic," he said, praising some veal he'd sampled on a skiing vacation in Cortina with his wife, Rosemarie, and their two children, Elizabeth and Robert.

"I'm in favor of outdoor cooking. I do the same thing every other California husband does: destroy good meat over charcoal. Seriously, though, we use soy sauce and marinate the meat. We have a Chinese oven we're very fond of," he added. "We've had great luck with wild game. I've cooked some wonderful ducks in the Chinese oven. It gives a wonderful flavor that goes through the meat. The most important thing is using aromatic wood, either orange or hickory chips, that gives the bird a wonderfully exotic flavor unlike anything you've ever eaten before.

"I take good care of myself and exercise a good deal," he said. "I play tennis, golf, water ski, whatever comes up if it's there. Rosemarie is an excellent athlete. When we go shooting or we do a lot of walking and hiking and even when I play golf, I try to jog about half of the 18 holes to get the heart going a bit. I love to feel well."

# Robert Stack's Barbecued Steak with Marinade

### Serves 8-10

1 cup onion, thinly sliced
¾ cup carrot, thinly
   sliced
1 tsp. garlic, finely chopped
2 bay leaves, crumbled
2 tbsps. parsley, finely
   chopped
1 tsp. thyme, crumbled
3 cups dry white wine

½ cup olive or vegetable
   oil
1 cup vinegar
1 tbsp. salt
¼ tsp. freshly ground
   black pepper
3 lbs. filet of steak,
   cut at least 2 inches
   thick

1. *Combine all ingredients except salt, pepper and steak. Mix well.*
2. *Rub salt and pepper into both sides of the steak and place in a shallow glass dish.*
3. *Pour marinade over meat until it is well moistened on all sides. The oil floating on the surface prevents the meat from discoloring and helps the marinade retain its flavor.*
4. *Cover and marinate at least 6 hours at room temperature, or 12-24 hours in the refrigerator, turning often.*
5. *When ready to cook, wipe the meat with a clean cloth. (Reserve marinade for basting.)*
6. *Cook meat in Chinese oven, using aromatic chips of orange or hickory according to manufacturer's directions, or on an outdoor barbecue, or place on broiler pan 3-4 inches from heat, cooking 8-10 minutes on each side for rare steak, slightly longer for better done. Baste several times with marinade.*

# Jean Stapleton

Jean Stapleton and her husband, William Putch, and their two children live in West Los Angeles when she does TV or movies. The rest of the time they live in Fayetteville, Pennsylvania, where Bill runs the Totem Pole Playhouse. The Putches do most of their "western" entertaining around the pool, and Jean often fixes simple make-ahead casseroles.

"Lately, I've been making *quiche Lorraine* (onion-egg tart)," said Jean. "It's simple and can be made ahead. I like the kind made with bacon or crabmeat. I try new dishes whenever I can. A nice crisp salad makes a wonderful accompaniment to the *quiche*."

Jean has a special chili recipe which, she said, "started with CBS. Our makeup man, Al Schultz, occasionally brings in some of his fabulous chili. I asked him for the recipe. He mailed it to me one summer, the week before the Playhouse opened. The whole company was invited to go out on a yacht on Chesapeake Bay the next Sunday afternoon. There were 40 of us, and Bill and I wanted to bring the food, so, of course, I thought, 'I've got the perfect answer – I'll make Al's chili.' It was the hit of Chesapeake Bay! We brought along two huge pots and heated it on a little stove in the galley. We brought Kentucky Fried Chicken too, but it was the chili that was the triumph of the day."

# Jean Stapleton's Chili

### Serves 8-10

1 lb. fresh mushrooms or
2 cans (6 - 8 oz. each),
sliced
6 tbsps. butter,
divided in half
¼ cup instant minced
onion
¼ tsp. instant minced
garlic
¼ cup water

2 lbs. lean ground beef
1 can (2 lb. 12 oz.) tomatoes,
broken up
1 can (1 lb. 4 oz.) red kidney
beans, drained
1 tbsp. chili powder
2 tsps. salt
1 tsp. ground cumin
2 cups cooked spaghetti,
cut up

1. Rinse, dry and slice fresh mushrooms, or drain canned mushrooms.
2. In a large skillet, melt 3 tbsps. of butter. Add mushrooms and sauté 5 minutes. Remove mushrooms and set aside.
3. Rehydrate onion and garlic in water about 10 minutes.
4. In same skillet used for mushrooms, melt remaining butter.
5. Add onion and garlic. Sauté for 2 minutes.
6. Add ground beef, a third at a time. Cook and stir until brown, about 5 minutes.
7. Add tomatoes, kidney beans, chili powder, salt and cumin. Stir well.
8. Bring to boiling; reduce heat; cover and simmer for 20 minutes.
9. Add reserved mushrooms and spaghetti. Cover and simmer for 2 minutes longer.
10. Serve with corn chips and shredded sharp cheese, if desired.

# Maureen Stapleton

"I love anything fat or fattening!" said movie-TV-Broadway star Maureen Stapleton. "My big hangup is Franco-American spaghetti — and I just can't have it. I just have to pull myself together and be passionately interested in something else. But it's irresistible, the way their spaghetti tastes. They must put dope in it!" She laughed.

"I like to cook to please my kids, but something decidedly unfancy, meat loaf or a roast. They both love it when I add corn niblets to frozen potato soup. But again, that's a trap for me. You have to be strong-willed to diet and when I do creative things in the kitchen, I'm a failure in that department."

# Maureen Stapleton's Veal Scallops with Ham

Serves 6-8

1½ lbs. veal scallops
salt to taste
freshly ground
   black pepper to taste
1 tsp. sage

toothpicks
2 tbsps. olive oil
1 tbsp. butter
about ½ cup
   Marsala wine

¼ lb. prosciutto or boiled ham, thinly sliced

1. *Flatten veal by pounding; cut into 5-inch rectangles.*
2. *Season each side with salt and pepper; sprinkle with sage.*
3. *Top with a slice of prosciutto ham; fasten with toothpick.*
4. *Heat olive oil in large skillet. Brown meat, veal side down.*
5. *Turn and brown reverse side.*
6. *Remove to heated serving platter.*
7. *Pour off excess fat from skillet. Add butter and wine; cook over low heat until most of wine evaporates.*
8. *Spoon sauce over meat, alone, or with rice.*

# Jimmy Stewart

"I normally only pass through the kitchen on my way to the garage," said Jimmy Stewart. "I've never been a huge eater. Early in my life, I used to try to find ways to keep from being skinny. Hank Fonda has always had much the same problem. We used to try everything to gain weight. One time somebody told us a wonderful way to put on weight was to drink a huge malted milk mixed with two eggs in the morning. To give us an appetite for it, we were told to spike it with a little brandy. But we noticed the malted milks kept getting darker. We didn't gain very much weight, but by midmorning we were in 'fine shape.' So we had to cut that out!

"Gloria (Jimmy's wife) and I are not big party-givers. We like small dinners for six or eight people, and then it's always something simple like barbecued spareribs. Everyone helps himself from the sideboard, and it's comfortable and relaxed."

# Jimmy Stewart's Spareribs with Barbecue Sauce

Serves 8-10

9-10 lbs. spareribs, cut
    into 2-rib pieces
salt to taste
ground pepper to taste

1 lemon, sliced
1 large onion,
    chopped
Barbecue Sauce

1. *Have butcher cut spareribs for you.*
2. *Preheat oven to 350° F.*
3. *Arrange spareribs in shallow baking pan and sprinkle liberally with salt and pepper.*
4. *Place a slice of lemon on each piece, then top with chopped onion.*
5. *Bake for about 45 minutes, basting occasionally with Barbecue Sauce. Turn meat several times so it cooks evenly.*

## Barbecue Sauce

1 yellow onion, grated
1 small clove garlic, pressed
2 tbsps. butter
1 tsp. salt
1 tsp. chili powder
1/2 tsp. celery seed

1/2 cup brown sugar
1/2 cup vinegar
1 cup chili sauce
1 cup catsup
2 cups water
few drops Tabasco Sauce

1. *Sauté onion and garlic in butter.*
2. *Add remaining ingredients and simmer slowly for 30 minutes, stirring often.*
3. *Serve along with spareribs.*

# Marlo Thomas

"I've gotten so I don't particularly like eating meat. I found it dull and boring and then I found myself leaning more and more towards French food. To me, any meat worth cooking is worth cooking with wine," said Marlo Thomas, looking pretty and impeccably groomed, as she contemplated her tastes in food. "I've found the best way for me, is to have special food, like French food. For instance, I could never stand veal before, but now veal cooked in wine is fine."

Marlo lives in Beverly Hills in a charming home – a lovely hill-top, old English stone house – she has decorated herself, with bright colors, mixed styles and an abundance of paintings. "I like sitting at my own dining room table rather than rented tables and chairs. I use my own cook and get extra men to help her husband serve. When I'm going to have 50 people to my home, whether it's for business or pleasure, to me they're in my home. I want to give them part of me: what I feel about food, service or hospitality. I'm totally involved with everything from planning the menu to how the plates are going to look and choosing and tasting the different sauces. I keep a record of all the parties I've given, listing the menus and the guests, so I won't repeat."

Despite her fondness for elegance, opulence and *haute cuisine*, Marlo has a hangup for chocolate: chocolate covered cherries or candy bars. During the filming of *Jenny* – her first movie – she earned the nickname of "Hersh." She explained, "I ate so many chocolate bars, they even printed the name on the back of my chair!"

# Marlo Thomas's Beef Tournedos Rossini

Serves 6

1 small can truffles
2 tbsps. sweet butter
¼ cup Madeira wine
1 tbsp. beef stock (canned)
1 tbsp. peanut or vegetable
　oil
6 fillets of beef, cut
　1-inch thick

1 tsp. salt
freshly ground black pepper
　to taste
6 slices French bread, sautéed
　in butter until lightly
　browned on both sides
6 slices *pâté de fois gras,*
　cut ¼-inch thick

1. *Drain and slice truffles, reserving juice.*
2. *Melt 1 tbsp. butter in saucepan. Add Madeira, beef broth, truffles and reserved liquid. Simmer gently until reduced in volume by one-third.*
3. *Heat remaining butter and peanut oil in large skillet until butter stops foaming.*
4. *Sear fillets on both sides, allowing 3 minutes per side for rare (longer for better-done).*
5. *Season with salt and freshly ground black pepper to taste.*
6. *Remove fillets to heated platter.*
7. *Discard fat in large skillet in which fillets were cooked. Add truffle sauce.*
8. *Serve fillets on individual plates, placing them on top of toasted bread rounds (reheated in moderate oven). Top with slices of pâté de fois gras and spoon heated truffle sauce over pâté.*
9. *Serve alone, or with cauliflower and hollandaise sauce and tomato halves filled with spinach soufflé.*

# Margaret Truman

"Dining at the White House was never memorable. It's very difficult to serve dinners for quantities of people and still have great food," said writer Margaret Truman. Her aversion to large dinners still persists. "We entertain surprisingly little," Margaret disclosed over lunch at the Polo Lounge.

The daughter of President Harry S. Truman is married to Clifton Daniel, former managing editor of the *New York Times*. Margaret, like her famous father, is a woman of definite opinions. "I think the woman who is a wife, homemaker and mother and who does not have an outside career is the real woman of courage, but I couldn't stand just staying home. In fact, finding myself, a few years ago, a housewife and a mother came as quite a shock! Fortunately, I have a very helpful and understanding husband. I am a cook, much against my better nature," she said with a laugh as she dug into her favorite Cobb salad.

"My husband is a very good cook. If I roast veal, the next day my husband will fix *vitello tonnato* (veal with tuna fish sauce) and we'll have it for lunch." However, the leftover veal never gets served for dinner the next night. "Clifton wouldn't like that. He always wants something different. Most men are like that, aren't they?"

What are Margaret's feelings about living in the White House?

"It was fascinating to meet people like Winston Churchill, but the 'Great White Jail' was not an easy place to get out of. Dad did get out to take his walks, but I couldn't just walk out and go downtown to shop in a department store. It wasn't much fun, really."

# Margaret Truman's Roast Veal

Serves 6

1 veal roast, weighing
   about 3 lbs.
salt to taste
white pepper to taste
1/3 cup butter
2 tbsps. peanut oil

2 large carrots, peeled
   and thinly sliced
2 onions, peeled and
   thinly sliced
3-4 sprigs parsley
1 bay leaf

good pinch dried thyme

1. Sprinkle roast with salt and pepper.
2. Heat half the butter and all the oil in Dutch oven. Brown veal until golden all over, turning frequently.
3. Remove veal; add remaining butter, carrots and onions. Sauté, stirring, about 5 minutes.
4. Return veal to Dutch oven; add remaining ingredients.
5. Cover meat with aluminum foil and bake in preheated 325°F. oven 1 to 1½ hours, or until meat is done. (If meat thermometer is used, it should register 175° F. when meat is done.)
6. Transfer veal to heated platter.
7. Strain juice and skim off most of the fat; reduce sauce by cooking it over a high heat.
8. Taste to correct seasonings.
9. Serve sauce separately.

NOTE: If desired, cook small baby carrots and small onions separately; use to garnish roast. Makes a delicious meal-in-one.

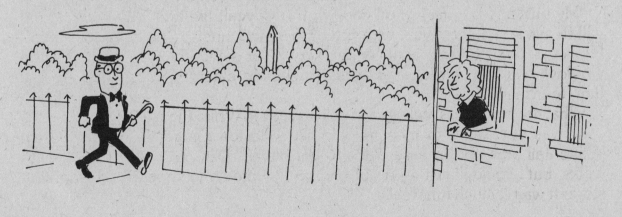

# Bobby Van

Actor-dancer Bobby Van agrees with his beautiful, blonde wife, Elaine Joyce, when she says, "Our life is like a Neil Simon comedy." Talking to this happy, nutty pair is like trying to balance on both sides of a seesaw simultaneously.

"Hey, do you like hors d'oeuvres?" asked Bobby. "I'm constantly looking for restaurants that serve great hors d'oeuvres. That's what I enjoy about Europe. When you go to the Savoy in London and order hors d'oeuvres, out comes this guy with a cart stacked with three tall trays of terrific stuff. When I eat that along with French bread and wine, I go crazy!"

"Bobby loves any kind of bread or rolls," added Elaine.

"If it weren't for dancing and for Elaine, I'd be playing roles like 'Cannon!' "

"Bobby likes his food at night," continued Elaine. "I wake up in the morning and head for the kitchen because I'm ravenous. I can't eat much at night because I have bizarre dreams, but Bobby can sit down with his Yankee Doodles and go through a quart of milk. It drives me nuts, so I go right to a gallon of ice cream! Often I sit in bed and munch on a head of lettuce or eat my ice cream. Nobody believes the way we live. It's insanity. I don't know who is nuttier. I think Bobby's more neurotic. He likes his pizza with a bottle of champagne."

"Elaine is a great cook." interjected Bobby. "I love her chicken paprikash. I make spicy beef and a thing called *Matzo Brie* (matzo meal scrambled with eggs), served with applesauce and sour cream. That, with some nice, sweet whipped cream cheese and good Scotch Salmon is my idea of a real treat!"

# Bobby Van's Spicy Beef

### Serves 4

1 lb. lean tender steak
4 tbsps. soy sauce
2 tbsps. sherry or rice wine
1 tsp. sugar
5 tbsps. peanut oil
2 large green peppers, diced
   in 1-inch cubes

4 scallions, cut in 1-inch
   pieces
1 tsp. salt
1 to 2 tsps. *lae mirchi* powder
   (available in Indian food
   shops)
2 cups celery, thinly sliced

1 tsp. cornstarch mixed with 2 tbsps. water

1. *Slice steak in thin strips across the grain, using Chinese meat cleaver or sharp knife.*
2. *Combine soy sauce, sherry and sugar; pour over beef.*
3. *Heat half the peanut oil in wok or large skillet over high heat.*
4. *Stir-fry green peppers and scallions a minute; lift out.*
5. *Add remaining oil and quickly stir-fry beef.*
6. *Return pepper-scallion mixture to wok, along with salt, lae mirchi and celery. Stir-fry 2 minutes.*
7. *Pour in remaining marinade and cornstarch mixture.*
8. *Cook, stirring over medium heat, until thick and smooth.*
9. *Serve alone, or over hot cooked rice or Chinese noodles.*

*NOTE: Lae mirchi is a pungent spice that gives the flavor to beef. If not available, substitute Five-Spice powder (a powdered blend of Chinese star anise, fennel, cinnamon, clove and Szechuan pepper).*

# Brenda Vaccaro

Brenda Vaccaro has been called "a beautiful kook," "terrific comedienne" and "a smoldering Mount Vesuvius." She's also a rabid eater and exceptional cook. From her late lawyer-restaurateur father, Brenda inherited four barrels of extraordinarily fine cookbooks, a great palate and an open admiration for non-conformist thinking; from her mother, valuable exposure to the finest Italian culinary arts and a yen to act.

Brenda is well into the food scene. "I'll have one of those tomato things (Virgin Marys)," she said, designating a diet lunch at Sardi's, "two poached eggs, dry on spinach, not Florentine."

The "beautiful kook's" two favorite scents are Madame Rochas and garlic (it's hard to tell in which order). "Sometimes when I'm mashing the garlic, I can't believe you can't eat it, it smells so good. I just love to eat," she continued, nibbling on the melba toast. "I was always around great food and my family particularly loved to cook a lot. We all got together on Sunday and they cooked different things and brought them over to the house. Naturally, unlike a lot of kids, I wasn't around plain food. It was more spicy tomato sauces and fantastic things like that.

"My mother used to make an omelet with onions, potatoes and mushrooms. *Frittata*, they called it in Italian. No plain scrambled eggs for me. I learned to love to eat, like European kids grow up with a love for wine. They love wine because they've been exposed to it. I was exposed to really great food."

# Brenda Vaccaro's Terrific Italian Sausages

Serves 4

1 lb. sweet Italian
   pork sausages
salt for skillet
2 tbsps. top-grade
   olive oil
1 yellow onion, peeled
   and chopped

3 large red or green
   peppers, diced
8-10 ripe Italian
   plum tomatoes
salt to taste
freshly ground pepper
   to taste

1 cut lemon

1. *Separate sausages into individual links.*
2. *Spread thin layer of salt evenly on bottom of large iron skillet; heat over high flame.*
3. *Add sausages, reduce heat, and cook slowly until sausages are brown and crisp on all sides.*
4. *In separate skillet, heat olive oil. Add onion and peppers; cook over low heat, stirring.*
5. *Cut and seed tomatoes; press through sieve. Add to skillet with peppers.*
6. *Cook over moderate heat, stirring until thickened and nicely colored.*
7. *Season to taste with salt and pepper.*
8. *Drain cooked hot sausages on absorbent paper, removing excess salt and grease.*
9. *Serve sausages on plate, squeeze lemon juice over sausages.*
10. *Serve sauce hot on the side, or spoon over sausages.*

NOTE: *Brenda's specialty can be more pungent if made with pressed garlic or herbs such as basil, oregano or Italian parsley. Sweet Italian sausages are available in supermarkets, but for optimal results, buy luganica (pork sausage) from a good Italian butcher or sausage maker.*

# Oskar Werner

"The last time I really cooked for any number of people was for my daughter's twenty-first birthday," Viennese actor Oskar Werner said in his Plaza Hotel suite. "Thanks to the lovely catered help that never showed up, I found myself cooking wiener schnitzel all day long for 56 people. I made three or four kinds of salads, too. I don't really like big affairs, but because it was my daughter's birthday and she was being married three weeks later, we made it an occasion."

Werner, who is blond and slender and could pass for a college sophomore, had held the party in the summer of 1965 for his daughter, Eleanor, known as "Noni" in Hollywood. "And now I'm already a grandfather twice," Oskar said with pride.

"I only cook for friends," he admitted. "Cooking for myself gives me no pleasure. I don't care to eat very much."

Oskar is more likely to indulge his appetite for reading; he has a library of some 4,000 volumes. He shuns Hollywood-type parties, he said, even though he likes Hollywood. "At one party for 160 people, I found myself standing in a corner with Rock Hudson and Glenn Ford, like three boys from the Vienna Boys' choir, just standing there watching."

# Oskar Werner's Weiner Schnitzel

Serves 4

1 lb. veal steaks, cut from
   leg, cut ¼-inch thick
1 egg
few drops water or milk
½ tsp. salt
¼ tsp. freshly ground
   pepper

½ cup fine breadcrumbs
3 tbsps. sweet butter
cooked beets
sliced lemon
8 anchovy filets
8 capers
mixed cooked vegetables

1. *Pound meat with wooden mallet to flatten.*
2. *Beat egg with water.*
3. *Season meat well; dip into the breadcrumbs. Shake off; then dip in egg. Let stand 10 minutes. Dip again in breadcrumbs.*
4. *Heat butter in heavy skillet; brown meat quickly on both sides.*
5. *Remove meat to heated platter.*
6. *Garnish with sliced small beets, slice of lemon over which cross 2 anchovy filets and sprinkle with capers.*
7. *Serve alone, or with mixed cooked vegetables: brussels sprouts, asparagus tips or green beans and boiled or mashed potatoes.*

*NOTE: For California touches, Oskar uses paprika, nutmeg and white pepper to season the veal. Add grated Parmesan or Swiss cheese to breadcrumbs. Deglaze pan, using white wine flavored with chopped fresh basil, rosemary or tarragon mixed with sour cream.*

# Nancy Wilson

"I've never been on a diet. In fact, it took me better than two years to get my weight up to 130 pounds," said pretty songstress Nancy Wilson, digging into a plate of fettuccine Alfredo with her fork.

Nancy is a well-turned size eight on a five-foot eight-inch frame. "I never cook by recipe, I just reach for things," she said, laughing. "I guess I've always known how to sing – and cook." Nancy made her kitchen debut, she said, preparing breakfast for her father while perched on a crate by the stove. She was six years old. "My mother was an excellent cook and I learned a lot from my stepmother, too, mostly Southern-styled meals, for example, how to turn out a smothered steak. I love good, fluffy mashed potatoes and fresh succotash made with string beans and corn seasoned with ham hocks."

Nancy likes to entertain, she said, but informally. "Since I have had to eat out so often and dress for dinner, I like strictly casual entertaining, with easy menus like spaghetti and a nice green salad, or veal cutlets with fettuccine. I really prefer home-prepared meals. I hate steaks, and roast beef on a plane irritates me. I don't really like to make sweets, but once I made a sour-cream fudge cake from a recipe I got off a box of cocoa. I was about 16 at the time. I've lost the recipe since, but I'm sure it was the best cake I ever made," she boasted.

# Nancy Wilson's Italian Veal Cutlets

Serves 4-6

1½ lbs. veal cutlets
seasoned flour (2 tbsps.
    flour mixed with ½ tsp.
    garlic salt, large pinch
    dried basil, few gratings
    freshly ground pepper)

3 tbsps. olive oil
¾ cup rosé wine
⅓ cup dairy sour cream
⅓ cup Parmesan cheese,
    freshly grated

1. Bone cutlets and pound meat to flatten slightly. Cut into bite-size pieces.
2. Dredge meat in seasoned flour.
3. Heat olive oil until sizzling in large skillet. Brown meat quickly on both sides.
3. Reduce heat; pour in wine.
4. Cover and simmer until meat is tender (about 35 minutes).
5. Add sour cream and Parmesan cheese until sauce begins to bubble. Do not boil.
6. Taste to correct seasonings.
7. Serve at once.

NOTE: If desired, wine may be omitted and diluted chicken stock substituted. For a slightly fruity flavor, add chicken stock with heaping tbsp. of melted currant jelly.

# Henry Winkler

"My mother was the worst cook," said The Fonz with a sigh over a chicken salad lunch at the Brown Derby. "She had this ambition – to make a great chocolate cake – but her cakes never had more than one layer because she always burned the other one. When I was a little kid, I kept hearing about 'snap, crackle, pop!' on TV, and one day at breakfast, my mother came in and found me with my ear in the Rice Krispies, trying to get the message. You should have seen her, a plump German lady, chasing me around the kitchen and yelling, 'What do you think you're doing? You EAT your breakfast, you don't LISTEN to it!' "

Henry says his mother was always very frugal. "If I told her the milk was sour, she would drink some and say, 'What's sour? It's not sour. Drink!' We had to have a housekeeper to survive!"

The Winklers ate very well, thanks to Rosalie, their housekeeper. "Rosalie could make roast beef that to this day is unequalled, no matter where I've eaten. Rosalie taught me two things: to say 'I'm sorry' and how to dance!

"I'm great with leftovers! My favorite creation is a purée made with leftover vegetables, sour cream, sometimes a little catsup and mayonnaise. Another thing I like to do is take a steak, serrate it and soak it in different things, such as beer. I've got to tell you what's really terrific: Hong Kong pot roast! You marinate it in black coffee."

Henry claims he's a champion tuna fish sandwich-maker. "I make it with cheese; it'll make your tongue fall out!"

# Henry Winkler's Steak in Beer

Serves 4

2 lbs. top sirloin, cut
   1½-inches thick
1 cup beer
12 dashes Tabasco sauce
2 tbsps. parsley, chopped
2 tbsps. chives, chopped

2 tbsps. soft butter or
   margarine
salt to taste
freshly ground
   pepper to taste

1. *Trim excess fat from steak.*
2. *Combine beer and Tabasco; marinate steak in beer-Tabasco combination in refrigerator 12-24 hours, turning several times.*
3. *Remove from refrigerator, allowing steak to warm to room temperature before cooking.*
4. *Combine parsley, chives, butter, salt and pepper to taste.*
5. *Smear steak on one side with half the parsley paste. Broil to desired doneness.*
6. *Reverse to cook on second side, coating with remaining paste. Serve at once.*

*NOTE: Terrific with red-wine butter sauce: combine 1 tsp. pressed garlic, 2 tbsps. chopped parsley, 2 tbsps. butter, ½ cup dry red wine. Heat and cook to reduce slightly in volume. Pour over steaks just before serving.*

# Fish & Seafood

# Jane Alexander

"You turn blue in the face when you see your son at the door with 50 bluefish begging to be cooked," said actress Jane Alexander, explaining one of the reasons she authored *The Bluefish Cookbook* with her friend, Greta Jacobs. "Our cookbook came about because for years Greta and I and our friends have amassed many different ways to prepare bluefish, which we kept eating all summer at Nantucket."

For the last 30 years, the actress, who is well known for her role as Eleanor Roosevelt in TV's "Eleanor and Franklin," has summered on Nantucket Island off Cape Cod, first with her parents, now with her husband, stage director Ed Sherin, and their four teen-age sons. Jane said, "When the bluefish are running off the Atlantic Ocean and if there are fisherpersons among your family and friends, bluefish can become a staple in your daily diet. It's hard to think in terms of substitutes for bluefish. There are a few recipes where salmon can be substituted, like the ones for grilling or baking, or bass for blox (cold cured bluefish, pickled in allspice and dill)."

The Sherins do most of their cooking and entertaining in their peaceful retreat, an elegant, burgundy-painted clapboard farmhouse on an eight-acre estate (including a trout stream) in Putnam County, New York. Jane says "I prefer entertaining little clusters of people or really large parties. With larger groups, I go in for casseroles or roasts. With smaller groups, I prepare something special."

# Jane Alexander's Bluefish and Scallions

Serves 8

2 fillets from
   2 six-pound bluefish
½ to ¾ cup soy sauce

¼ cup fresh ginger root,
   minced, or 3 tsps.
   ground ginger

½ cup scallions, chopped

1. *Marinate fillets in soy sauce for 10 minutes on each side.*
2. *Rub flesh with ginger and scallions.*
3. *Place fillets in greased baking dish.*
4. *Pour soy sauce over fillets and bake in preheated 350° F. oven 20 minutes, or until done.*

NOTE: *Jane advises, "You can substitute bass very nicely for bluefish. Use either ocean or lake bass." Her recipe is a boon to dieters!*

# Woody Allen

"I like food – in fact, I'm in favor of it. I like to eat lots of short meals, maybe 16 to 17 a day, because I hate to sit down," said Brooklyn-born actor, writer, director and master funnyman Woody Allen, seated in the quiet, understated elegance of his Manhattan penthouse.

"During filming of *What's New Pussycat?* I was cured of my great love of clams," he explained. "I used to eat them by the dozens. While dining with Capucine (his co-star) in a Paris bistro, she showed me the right way to eat clams. She opened, squeezed, killed and squirted the clams with sauce. After Cap's demonstration, I fled from the table in sections."

While directing and starring in *Annie Hall,* Woody had a strange encounter with a lobster. His leading lady, played by Diane Keaton, was scurrying around the kitchen in pursuit of a live lobster hiding behind the refrigerator, prompting Woody to quip, "Maybe if I put a little dish of butter sauce along here with a nutcracker, it will run out the other side."

To satisfy his "craving for certain things," Woody habitually eats jelly for breakfast, candy bars and cake for lunch and pie at dinner! The comedian has a fondness for homemade malts and makes one nightly when he's home.

"Some people like to languish over breakfast," said Woody, "but I like breakfast standing up or a sandwich on the telephone. When it comes to dining out, I try to beat it as often as possible." But he does prefer Chinese food for its infinite variety.

At home, Woody cooks steak and fettuccine for his girlfriends. "I only do that when I want to have dinner in with her and only to seduce her! I don't have the patience to make them otherwise!"

Asked if steak and fettuccine always work, Woody stated, "I don't cook unless I'm already home free. I won't cook on spec!"

# Woody Allen's Chinese Steamed Bass

### Serves 3-4

1 whole 2 lb. sea bass or
   porgy, trout, butterfish,
   sole or flounder
1 tsp. ginger root, shredded
2 tbsps. scallion, chopped

¾ tsp. fermented black beans
   or ½ tsp. salt
1½ tbsps. soy sauce
1½ tbsps. dry sherry
1½ tbsps. peanut or corn oil

2 quarts water

1. Clean fish; then wash, drain, dry and place whole fish in heatproof dish.
2. Mix together ginger, scallion, black beans, soy sauce, sherry and peanut oil. Pour over fish.
3. Heat 2 quarts of water in a large saucepan. Place rack in saucepan; put dish containing fish on rack. Be certain the fish is well above the water level. Cover and steam 15 minutes.
4. Serve whole fish, including the head.

NOTE: Serve with hot steamed rice. For optimal flavor and texture, use only fresh fish. For unusual touch, use small sprinkling of Szechuan pepper (available in Oriental food shops or through mail-order catalogs) over fish before it is steamed.

# Bernard Berkowitz & Mildred Newman

Bernard Berkowitz and his wife, Mildred Newman, are enthusiastic weekend cooks, both in their Manhattan flat and at their country house. You know this psychologist-psychoanalyst pair for their three national best sellers: *How to Be Your Own Best Friend, How to Be Awake and Alive,* and *How to Take Charge of Your Life.*

"Mildred insists I taught her how to cook," said Bernard. "Actually, all I did was to encourage her to take a few chances!"

"Bernie cooks better than I do," said Mildred. "But I do have a few special dishes that always seem to come out perfectly. I have a way of doing a chicken dish that's so simple and lovely. Everyone who's ever tasted it loves it."

Out of Bernie's vast cooking repertoire, his rendering of Sunday Shrimp is Mildred's favorite. "The only trouble with Bernie's cooking is he never makes the sauce the same way twice," she teased.

With their overweight patients, Mildred and Bernie have both noticed that "when their other problems get ironed out, the weight problem often takes care of itself. People who are severely overweight often had parents who used food to comfort or reward their children."

# Bernard Berkowitz's Sunday Shrimp

Serves 4

1½ lbs. raw shrimp,
   shelled and deveined
½ cup Chablis wine
½ cup Meursault (white
   Burgundy wine)

½ tsp. shallot, minced
⅓ cup sweet butter
¼ tsp. dry mustard
2 tbsps. fresh parsley,
   chopped

lemon wedges

1. Marinate shrimp in Chablis and Meursault about 30 minutes at room temperature.
2. Meanwhile, heat shallot in butter a few seconds over medium heat, stirring or shaking pan to be sure shallot does not burn.
3. Remove shrimp from marinade; add to shallot-butter mixture and toss over high heat for 2-3 minutes, or until shrimp are barely cooked.
4. Sprinkle in mustard and stir to coat evenly.
5. Remove shrimp from pan; keep warm.
6. Add the wine marinade to pan and reduce over high heat until liquid is a syrupy glaze.
7. Serve shrimp on thin, toasted triangles or spoon over saffron-flavored rice.
8. Pour wine glaze over all and garnish with minced parsley and lemon wedges. Serve piping hot.

NOTE: Bernie's shrimp makes an excellent first course or a delightful and different brunch dish. Recipe can be ad-libbed to suit your palate. If desired, add a few drops of soy sauce to hot butter sauce, or cook a small piece of lemon peel in the butter to give it a tangy flavor.

# Gary Burghoff

Gary Burghoff, Cpl. Radar of TV's "M*A*S*H," said, "I'm a fowl cook! I love roast duck, but I don't do anything fancy like orange sauce. That spoils it for me. I come from New England, where the food is generally bland. I love tapioca pudding and vanilla. When I cook duck, all I do is put salt and pepper on it, inside and out, and spice it up a little before throwing it in the oven."

Gary and his wife, Janet, live in Malibu near the beach. "We love having people over," he said, "but it's got to be very informal. I wouldn't know what to do at an at-home formal. Sure, it's fun to wear a tuxedo and go to something like the Emmy Awards, but to have a formal dinner at home would seem sacrilegious!"

Gary cooks mostly by intuition. "I don't have any fancy, out-of-the-ordinary recipes. I love broiled lobster. I get them fresh off the pier, split them and cook them right now! I'm not one for boiling them, because I think it interferes with the flavor. The main thing is, don't overcook lobster; it should be soft. You can even eat lobster rare," he said, laughing.

# Gary Burghoff's Broiled Lobster

### Serves 2

2 cleaned lobsters, each
weighing 1½ to 2 lbs.

lemon wedges

melted butter
paprika

1. *Have butcher clean and split lobster or do it yourself. To kill lobster, insert sharp knife deeply into back at point where head joins body to sever spinal cord. To split lobster, turn on back; split from head to tail, cutting through to back shell with very sharp knife. Discard intestinal vein at back of head. Leave the green liver and red roe. Crack claws.*
2. *Place lobster on buttered, preheated broiler and broil about 12 minutes, basting often with melted butter and sprinkling well with paprika.*
3. *Serve at once on a heated plate with additional melted butter and lemon wedges.*

NOTE: *Select only fresh lobster! If desired, lobster tails may be used. "Be careful not to overcook the lobster," Gary advises.*

# Diahann Carroll

"I can only tell you that I love to cook! And I consider myself not bad when I have time," said actress Diahann Carroll. She was dressed in a floor-length, cinnamon-colored bruised velvet hostess gown accented with a tiny row of rhinestone buttons down the front and looked like she'd never entered the kitchen.

"Fortunately, my daughter is a fan of my cooking—some of my cooking. I *like* that! I make the best steak you've ever tasted. It takes two days to marinate. The steak should be cooked so it's brown on the outside, but inside all nice and red. I try and eat as much steak as possible, because I don't really like to think I'm watching my weight all the time. That becomes kind of a bore.

"I'm a thrower-in-cook. And I come up with some goodies! Once in a while, I'll get very grand and sit down to dinner, but my preference is: put everything on the table—all the plates, silverware and the food—and everyone grab a plate and go sit where they're the most comfortable, by the pool or fireplace."

Diahann happily recalled a family feast prepared by her mother. "She had a big dinner out on the porch. And it was delicious. She made sweet potato pie, which is my favorite. Mother recently made a trip to North Carolina and carried back the sweet potatoes in the car. There's an enormous difference in the flavor. My parents grow their own greens in the back yard and they are delicious. So we had greens and then she made a big leg of lamb and some spareribs because she knows Susie (Diahann's daughter) loves them. I cannot make them. You see, I don't like spareribs and as many times as I've said, 'Now don't be greedy and let's try them,' I don't. I'm just not mad for her eating spareribs that often. I don't know where that comes from."

Happily, Diahann has discovered the joys of preparing delicious meals raw or with little cooking or adornment. Her salads are a splendid example or she prepares cracked crab with a lemon-butter sauce.

# Diahann Carroll's Cracked Crab with Lemon-Butter Sauce

### Serves 6

3 live Dungeness crabs,
  weighing 1½ lbs. each
8 quarts boiling water
1 tsp. salt
piece of cut lemon

½ tsp. bruised
  peppercorns
½ cup butter, melted
1½ tbsps. fresh lemon
  juice

2-3 tbsps. chopped parsley

1. Dress crabs by inserting a table knife under the back of the top shell and prying it off. Remove spongy parts under shell (gills, stomach and intestines).
2. Place in boiling salted water mixed with lemon and peppercorns. Cover and return to boiling point.
3. Simmer for 15 minutes. Drain.
4. Crack claws and legs with nutcracker. Serve hot with butter mixed with lemon juice and parsley, or chill and serve with mayonnaise.

NOTE: In season, Dungeness crabs can be purchased cooked from fish shops. To crack: get a firm hold on the front claws and twist off where joined to the body. Repeat with other claws and legs. If desired, remove viscera after cooking, leaving shell intact. Twist. Break front claws as directed. Pull off top shell with sharp knife. Remove gills, spongy part, save creamy crab butter. Hold legs and crack shell with mallet or hammer. Tap the back of knife with mallet to cut body cavity first in half, then each half into several chunks.

# Joan Crawford

"I never eat bread, butter, potatoes or desserts, because I learned a long time ago not to eat things that would put on weight," the late Joan Crawford said in a 1966 interview.

"I love to cook," the all-time glamour gal explained. "I earned my way through school by cooking for a family of eight and a school (Rockingham Academy in Kansas City) with 30 students, starting at the tender age of nine and cooking until I was 13, while my mother ran a laundry agency.

"I never measure, I cook to taste, and I prefer simple foods with a definite flavor, tart or bland. I always cook for my maid, even make her breakfast when I'm home. I favor American foods, minus rich sauces and heavy desserts. But I've come to love the local fish, especially in Jamaica and Mexico. It's too bad that Americans invariably say, 'I'll have a steak, medium rare.' They're missing out on a lot of good eating by not eating more fish.

"I love fillet of flounder or a poached salmon, fresh salmon, that is with a mayonnaise dressing. Cut a lemon, skin and all, and wrap it in the cheesecloth with the fish before poaching. That way, the oil of the skin, as well as the lemon juice, flavor the fish."

Joan's other specialities include broilers and pork chops.

Returning to her fondness for fish, Joan recalled, a magazine article in which she mentioned covering a smoked trout with a tinned meat gelée (an imported gelatin product). "I got a letter from Alfred Hitchcock, who is a great cook. He asked me 'What are you doing covering a smoked trout with a meat gelée, and where do you get it?' I replied by sending him two dozen tins. He graciously answered with three dozen red roses and note saying, 'But I didn't want enough to cover my whole body!'"

# Joan Crawford's Poached Salmon with Mayonnaise-Mustard Dressing

### Serves 8

3 lbs. fresh salmon (one piece)
3 lemons
6 cups water
10 pearl onions, peeled
½ stalk celery with leaves

2 sprigs parsley
3 small bay leaves
12 peppercorns, crushed
2 tsps. salt
2 cups mayonnaise
4 tsps. prepared mustard

¼ cup fresh lemon juice

1. Wipe cleaned fish with damp cloth.
2. Cut lemons in thin slices. Place slices inside cavity and on both sides of fish.
3. Wrap fish with double thickness of cheesecloth and secure with string.
4. Put water, onions, celery, parsley, bay leaves, peppercorns and salt in a fish kettle (or deep saucepan with rack). Cover and simmer 30 minutes.
5. Place fish on rack in poaching kettle. The fish should be halfway out of hot water when placed on rack. Cover and slowly simmer 40 minutes, or until fish is barely done.
6. Remove fish to heated platter; carefully remove cloth and lemon slices.
7. Combine mayonnaise, prepared mustard and lemon juice. Mix well and serve as side dish for fish.
8. Garnish fish with lemon wedges and cut parsley.
9. To serve fish cold, chill and arrange on a bed of field salad or watercress. Garnish with quartered hard-cooked eggs and thin lemon slices. Serve with chilled dressing.

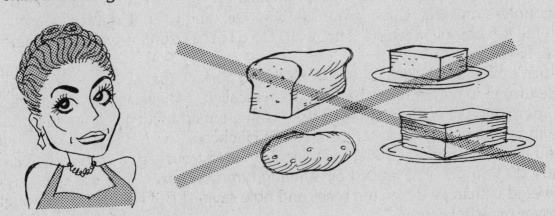

# Geraldine Fitzgerald

"There's always been a great similarity between French and Irish food," claims Dublin-born actress Geraldine Fitzgerald. "In the United States, where German, Italian and Dutch influences are very strong, the French influence is very weak. But French influence did permeate the Irish food culture, but in the Irish manner!"

Gerry, as she is known to her friends, was pouring afternoon tea, prepared in the Chinese style (steeped only until amber-colored and served with sugar and lemon). She sat in the pretty, airy living room of her Upper East Side apartment that overlooks the art galleries on New York's Madison Avenue. "In France, if an ingredient is good, they don't do anything to it but add a little parsley, lemon and butter," she explained. "The French never cover up good ingredients with herbs or sauces. Their food is pure, simple and elegant. And, that's what we do, using Irish ingredients but treating them in the French manner! French mayonnaise is made the same way as Irish mayonnaise, but I make "green mayonnaise" by adding chopped watercress. Wouldn't that be smashing for St. Patrick's Day?" she said gleefully.

Gerry and husband Stuart Scheftel treasure the "cottage dishes" her mother used to prepare. The first, a classic St. Patrick's Day treat, is Shepherd's Pie made with roast beef or lamb. Gerry calls it "simple but lovely!" Her other cottage favorites are two versions of bread pudding. "The first kind you make in the summer with fresh fruit, and serve very cold. The second version is made with vanilla custard and loads of raisins, topped off with brown sugar, dotted with butter and oven-broiled after baking to give it a *crème brûlée* effect. It's great now, when food is so expensive! It's very nourishing, and children love it!"

# Geraldine Fitzgerald's "Green" Mayonnaise for Fish

2 egg yolks
1 tsp. prepared French
   mustard or dry mustard
½ tsp. salt
pinch freshly ground
   black pepper

1½ cups salad oil
1 tbsp. tarragon vinegar
3 tbsps. watercress, finely
   chopped
3 tbsps. parsley, finely
   chopped

1 tbsp. dairy sour cream

1. *Put egg yolks, mustard, salt and pepper in small deep bowl. Stir with wire whisk, beating yolk mixture until smooth.*
2. *Add salad oil, a few drops at a time, beating well after each addition; then add a few drops vinegar. Keep adding oil to the mixture, then a few drops vinegar, beating after each addition until the sauce is smooth and thick.*
3. *Stir finely chopped herbs into the mayonnaise (oil-vinegar-egg mixture), or put through an electric blender.*
4. *Lastly, add sour cream; stir to blend.*
5. *Serve very cold on poached fish or grilled salmon.*

*NOTE: If mayonnaise should curdle, break another egg yolk into a clean bowl, gradually beat in the curdled mayonnaise, stirring until smooth and thick. If desired, more salt and pepper may be added to flavor sauce.*

# Chief Dan George

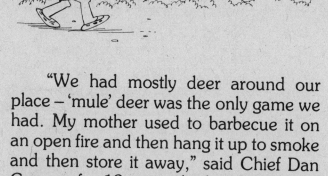

"We had mostly deer around our place – 'mule' deer was the only game we had. My mother used to barbecue it on an open fire and then hang it up to smoke and then store it away," said Chief Dan George, for 12 years chief of the Tse-lal-watt tribe, as he recalled his childhood, when he really hunted with a bow and arrow.

The chief lives in a two-room frame house with his wife, Amy, his daughter and her three children. He spoke softly, but with authority. I had to ask if he takes to the kitchen. "No, my wife, does that!" he said, laughing easily.

To this day the chief still likes his fish cooked in the tribal manner of his people by spearing a stick with chunks of fish and "barbecuing" it over the fire. "It's over 60 years since I've seen my people eat in the authentic way. I'll try and explain it in a short way. Different tribes around here – the Squamish tribe here – invite people from different tribes to one of their big smoke houses and they have tribal songs and dances and feast on Indian food. Generally it was duck soup or dried salmon, potatoes and bread. But one funny thing I found attending their smoke house dances, they never used any butter or salt!"

I was interested in the duck soup. "It's made from wild duck cut up into small pieces and put in a pot," explained Dan. " Generally, they use a big pot because sometimes there's over a 100 people at the smoke house. They cook or dice up about 4 or 5 wild ducks and add just potatoes or a little rice!"

# Chief Dan George's Barbecued Fish, Indian Style

*"The best way I like my fish is barbecued. It's done in an open fire, made in an open pit with good-sized rocks. When the fire is built, the rocks get hot and barbecue the fish. Take salmon — any kind will do — remove backbone first, cut in small pieces and thread it on a thin, long stick, shish-kebab fashion. Lean it against a long piece of wood across the fire. It cooks very quickly that way."*

NOTE: *If you select a small whole fish, string it on a forked stick (use green wood soaked in water to keep the wood from burning), hold it over an open fire. It takes longer, but the fish acquires a marvelous smoked flavor.*

# Florence Henderson

"I grew up on a farm in Dale, Indiana. That's close enough to be part of the Kentucky hillbilly country," singer-actress Florence Henderson said in her suite at the Plaza Hotel. "Cooking then was such a chore, but my mother is one of a disappearing breed blessed with great will and incredible strength. She had 10 kids in that little farm house; she even delivered my sister by herself. I'll never know how she managed to live without electricity or running water. Mother canned everything we had to eat for the year — jars and jars of vegetables and fruits. When we butchered, there was meat to be hung, smoked or made into sausage and that was it.

"I grew up on real hillbilly fare: cornbread or fried corn meal mush, fried chicken or rabbit and lots of pork in our part of the country. The food came in king-size portions."

Florence still loves the foods of her childhood, but maintains her size-five figure by having smaller meals at more frequent intervals. She favors salads and cheeses to the fried foods of her childhood. When she's working, she foregoes completely the large meals which tend to make her logy.

Florence and her husband (Ira Bernstein) favor Italian fare. "Ira taught me to prepare a marvelous marinara sauce," she said. "He created his own recipe after rejecting the canned variety we get in the supermarket. It's so easy. It can be used on spaghetti and linguini and other pasta dishes, or spooned over meat and poultry for quick versions of veal Parmesan or chicken cacciatore, or used to poach sole or flounder."

# Florence Henderson's Marinara Sauce with Fish or Spaghetti

Serves 4

¼ cup olive oil
1 small clove garlic, minced
1 small onion, peeled and
  chopped
1 can (6 oz.) Italian tomato paste
1 can (1 lb.) Italian plum
  tomatoes, strained and chopped

1 bay leaf
½ tbsp. lemon juice
¾ tsp. oregano
1 tsp. light brown sugar
salt to taste
freshly ground black
  pepper to taste

1. *Heat olive oil in large skillet; cook garlic and onion until transparent.*
2. *Add remaining ingredients and simmer slowly, uncovered, about 1½ hours, or until thick; stir often to prevent burning.*
3. *Taste to correct seasonings.*

## To serve with spaghetti and shrimp

1 lb. cleaned, raw shrimp
1 cup dry white wine

handful parsley, chopped
1 lb. spaghetti or linguini

1. *Cook shrimp (chop, if large) with wine and parsley until they begin to turn pink.*
2. *Drain immediately.*
3. *Meanwhile, cook spaghetti in boiling salted water until al dente; drain.*
4. *Add shrimp, top with liberal amounts of heated marinara sauce, and garnish with a generous snipping of fresh parsley.*

## To serve with fillet of sole or flounder

salt and pepper to taste
1½ lbs. fillet of sole
  or flounder

few drops lemon juice
fresh parsley

1. *Season and arrange fillets in well-greased baking dish.*
2. *Squeeze lemon juice over fish.*
3. *Spoon marinara sauce over fish, covering well.*
4. *Cover and bake in preheated 375° F. oven about 25 minutes, or until fish is fork tender. Garnish with parsley.*

# Burl Ives

"Boats and food are my favorite talking subjects," Burl Ives said, polishing off a steak-and-grapefruit mid-afternoon lunch. "I'd rather talk to a Bahamian lobster fisherman than to most people I know. Anyone who goes out on the sea is an interesting person because he knows something most people don't know. There's something that keeps your ego to a proper size when you have to deal with the ocean!

"I love fish and could live happily on boiled grouper and conch," he added, chuckling. "When I was on the boat for periods of time, I had a stew on the stove and I never washed the soup pot. It got a little lower and I'd add a little something everyday to keep that fermentation going. It has to have been going for two weeks before it begins to get character."

Given time, Burl can turn out excellent casseroles. "I make one with mushroom soup for a change on the boat. I get a big can of tuna and start putting in peas and anything you want in the way of condiments – or a little herbs. I tell you what I think would go well – some dill or thyme with salmon or tuna. Just bake it so all the flavors are intermixed. I don't have a boat now. I swallowed the anchor about five years ago, but I'm getting the old feeling again. I was just looking . . .," he said, pointing to a newspaper ad for a 36-foot schooner.

# Burl Ives's Salmon Bake

### Serves 4

1 can (10¾ ozs.) condensed
  cream of mushroom soup
½ soup can water
1 tsp. dried dill leaves,
  crushed
4 tsps. lemon juice
2 cups rice, cooked

1 cup peas, cooked (fresh,
  frozen or canned)
1 can (16 ozs.) salmon,
  drained and flaked
½ cup almonds, sliced
lemon slices
paprika

1. *In a lightly buttered 1½-quart baking dish, blend soup and water.*
2. *Add remaining ingredients except almonds, lemon slices and paprika.*
3. *Bake in preheated 350° F. oven for 30 minutes, or until hot.*
4. *Stir in almonds. Garnish with lemon and paprika.*

NOTE: *Substitute tuna fish for salmon and season with ¼ tsp. thyme instead of dill. For "cheesy" version of fish bake: 1 can mushroom soup, ½ can water or skim milk, 1 cup grated American cheese, 2 cups rice, 1 cup cooked peas, 1 can salmon or tuna, 1 tbsp. grated onion, ½ tbsp. melted butter, ½ tsp. salt, ⅛ tsp. pepper and strips of sliced pimento for garnish. Bake as directed above.*

# Danny Kaye

"I cook or taste food with the same concentration I give an instrument approach in an airplane," said Danny Kaye. "There is no way you can do one thing well if you have three things occupying your mind. There has to be total concentration."

Danny gives the same effort to performing, flying his plane, working for UNICEF or playing golf as he does to whipping up an eight-course Chinese feast! As we talked, Danny quickly prepared a stir-fry oyster-shrimp feast. He obviously knew to the split second the precise moment to drop the seafood into the sizzling oil.

In addition to Chinese cooking, Danny's repertoire of cuisines includes Japanese, Italian and French. He operates in two kitchens, one conventional and one Chinese. The Chinese kitchen consists of a 10-foot stainless steel, professional battery of stoves. The range has three giant woks fired by gas jets that are controlled by a knee lever. Easily accessible refrigerator drawers are located across from the woks. Danny keeps an array of Chinese cooking ingredients at hand, including a special 11-year-old, licorice-flavored sauce he constantly replenishes and reboils to keep in top condition.

"Producing a dinner can be as creative as making a picture," said Danny. "It's the same kind of self-expression as playing a musical instrument or writing or painting. If someone can express himself in the kitchen, even if it's as simple as taking three shrimp and cooking them in a skillet so that they look, smell and taste beautiful, that's a creative process."

# Danny Kaye's Chinese Stir-Fry Oysters and Shrimps

### Serves 8

1 cup raw oysters
¼ cup flour
water
½ lb. raw shrimp, shelled
   and deveined
2 tbsps. peanut or vegetable oil
1 two-inch piece fresh ginger
   root, peeled and cut into
   fine shreds

5 scallions, trimmed and
   cut in 2-inch lengths
1 tsp. light soy sauce
1 tsp. sesame oil
salt to taste
freshly ground black pepper
1½ tbsps. cornstarch
2 tbsps. cold water
   (more if needed)

1. *Place oysters in mixing bowl; add flour and enough water to cover. (Flour will cleanse and plump oysters.)*
2. *Stir oysters in the liquid. Drain well; then run under several changes of cold water. Drain well again.*
3. *Prepare shrimp; set aside.*
4. *Drop oysters into barely simmering water. Turn off heat and let stand 1 minute. Drain and set aside.*
5. *Repeat with shrimp.*
6. *Heat oil in wok or skillet over high heat.*
7. *Add ginger and scallions. Cook, stirring, 5 seconds.*
8. *Add oysters and shrimp, stirring rapidly. Cook 15 seconds.*
9. *Add soy sauce, sesame oil, salt and pepper to taste, stirring constantly.*
10. *Blend cornstarch into cold water and stir into the wok or skillet. Cook 12 seconds. Serve at once.*

*NOTE: The success of Danny's dish depends on the skill and speed of the chef! Do not overcook oysters or shrimp.*

# Guy Lombardo

Versatile music man, restauranteur and boatman Guy Lombardo never meddled with the style of his Royal Canadians' "sweetest music this side of heaven" for four decades, and the late band leader exercised the same respect for tradition in food. "We have a recipe for a salad that's been handed down from generation to generation in our family. It's like a prized heirloom and it's different from any salad you've ever eaten. It's so easy to prepare, it's laughable," Guy said, waving his hand as he might his baton.

"Cut four tomatoes into bite-size pieces; slice one cucumber thinly and place in a salad bowl. Add about a cup of red Italian onion rings, three good pinches of chopped fresh basil and two generous pinches of minced oregano. Lavish it with salt and chill about a half hour. Then add about three-quarters of a cup of olive oil, toss lightly, and let stand 15 minutes. Grind in a bit of black pepper if you wish, but don't add one speck of vinegar or you'll ruin it. There's a chemical reaction between the tomatoes and salt that draws out enough juice. Just dunk hunks of crusty Italian bread in the juice and you have the most delicious salad I know."

Asked what led him into the restaurant business, Guy explained, "A local (Long Island) man wanted to retire, so I bought him out. I built a restaurant on the waterfront and fashioned it after a boat. We soon found our image was lobster and seafood, as 65 percent of our customers preferred seafood. On one Sunday alone we served over 700 pounds of fresh lobster, either broiled or in Lobster Lombardo. That's a recipe that was willed to me by a chef."

# Guy Lombardo's Lobster Lombardo

Serves 6

1 pkg. (8 oz.) green noodles
5 tbsps. butter
1 cup light cream
2 egg yolks, beaten
1 tsp. salt
1/16 tsp. white pepper

1/2 cup sherry
1/2 cup Romano cheese, grated
2 cups cooked lobster meat, cut
in large pieces
2 tbsps. breadcrumbs
3 tbsps. Parmesan cheese,
grated

1. Cook noodles according to package instructions; drain.
2. Butter a 2-quart casserole; cover bottom with cooked green noodles.
3. Melt 4 tbsps. butter in saucepan over medium heat; gradually stir in cream and heat through, stirring.
4. Cool 5 minutes.
5. Gradually stir in egg yolks, salt, white pepper, sherry and Romano cheese.
6. Cook over low heat to reduce sauce one-fourth, stirring constantly.
7. Add lobster meat, mix well and pour over green noodles.
8. Top with breadcrumbs, Parmesan cheese and dot with remaining butter.
9. Bake, uncovered, in a preheated 400° F. oven 20-25 minutes, or until top is brown.

NOTE: Use frozen lobster, raw shrimp or cooked crab. Or prepare in individual ramekins, baking 5-7 minutes at 400° F.

# George Maharis

"I eat like I live," said the highly original, non-conformist George Maharis. "I operate on eight cylinders, live out of every pore. I've always got them going and I ain't gonna change that for one second. I devour life! As I see my lifestyle, my body is my vehicle in life and my brain I've always felt is something that will go on indefinitely. Now, how can I keep the body running? You do it with food in one way, with exercise in another.

"I'm an earth person really. I'm never suave; it doesn't fit me. There are no aspirin in my medicine cabinet. I squeeze my own juice. There's no ice cream in the freezer and no coffee and no cigarettes. I forbid smoking in my house and if people don't like it, they shouldn't come there because it is my house."

The actor's concern for his body and good food is a carry-over from a bout of hepatitis that caused him to bow out of the highly successful television series, "Route 66."

George has always enjoyed good food and likes to create Greek, or what he calls "goofy," dishes. His father was a professional cook. "My parents are both good cooks. My mother used to do a lot of Greek as well as American dishes." George loves to entertain. He lives in the Santa Monica hills of California and treasures his privacy. "I like to do off-beat things, rather than the usual bottle of gin. I like to entertain people with new tastes. If, for example, I find people who have never had Filipino food, I'd have that brought in, or if they've never had health foods, I prepare that. They say I'm a vegetarian, but I'm not really. I cook simply because I can't stand the chore of washing dishes."

# George Maharis's Poached Fish, Greek Style

Serves 6-8

3 yellow onions, peeled
  and chopped
1½ tbsps. salad oil
about ⅓ cup dry white wine
  or clam juice
about ⅓ cup water

2 lbs. fresh fish fillets: red
  snapper, sole or flounder
3-4 ripe tomatoes, peeled
  and chopped
2 tbsps. parsley, minced
salt to taste

freshly ground pepper to taste

1. Sauté onions in salad oil until golden.
2. Add wine and water. Heat to boiling point; lower heat.
3. Add fillets to skillet with wine-onion mixture. Top each fillet with tomatoes, parsley, and salt and pepper to taste.
4. Add more liquid (wine or water) if needed.
5. Cover and let simmer 15 minutes, or until fish begins to flake.
6. Serve at once, alone, or with Greek salad made with lettuce, tomato, onion, green pepper, cucumber, feta cheese and vinegar-oil dressing, and garnished with anchovy fillets or herring.

# Gavin MacLeod

Gavin MacLeod's worst vice may be food. The handsome captain of TV's "Love Boat" admits that his tendency to "live life to its fullest" nearly did him in six years ago, when his weight ballooned to 260 pounds. "I woke up one morning with a terrible pain," he said. "I was scared to death. Patti (his second wife) said, 'You'd better see a doctor.'" The actor claims that Patti changed his life. "I abused myself, eating spaghetti dinners late at night, drinking too much, not getting enough sleep," he said, digging lustily into Chinese chicken salad at the Twentieth Century-Fox Commissary.

After an eight-day fast, a diet doctor put the actor on a regimen of no sugars, salts or red meats, and advised a diet rich in vegetable proteins, nuts, fruits and cheese. "I wanted to live. I had a woman who believed in me," he said happily. Since then, he's shed more than 50 pounds, and quit drinking and smoking.

"I'm not a cook, but I adore good food," said Gavin, who recently gave Patti a helping hand in preparing Peasant Quiche when they entertained three other couples. "Patti had never made quiche before. She didn't have a bread board big enough to roll out the dough. She ended up rolling out dough on a little board inscribed with the words, 'God Save This Home.' When she baked the crusts and poured in the custard, the crust wasn't high enough and the filling started to run over the sides. Suddenly I got an inspiration and grabbed some big casseroles. We threw the crust in those and poured in the filling. I told her, 'It looks like peasant quiche. Don't tell anyone. The funny part was, everyone loved it. One friend, an expert quiche maker, said, 'It's the best quiche I ever had.'"

# Stuffed Fillets of Sole, House of Gavin MacLeod

Serves 6

6 large fillets of sole
2 cups seasoned dressing mix
4 tbsps. butter, divided
4 tbsps. celery, minced
2-3 tbsps. onion, minced
½ cup mushrooms or water
  chestnuts, sliced

2 tbsps. fresh parsley,
  minced
1 egg, beaten
7-8 tbsps. water or
  milk
1 tbsp. fresh lemon juice
½ tsp. paprika

1. Lay fillets flat on large sheet of waxed paper or aluminum foil.
2. Place dressing mix in large mixing bowl.
3. Melt half the butter in skillet and sauté celery, onion and mushrooms until softened.
4. Add sauté mix to dressing, along with 1 tbsp. parsley, egg and liquid. Toss lightly.
5. Spread stuffing evenly on fillets and roll up jellyroll fashion. Secure with toothpicks and arrange in greased, shallow baking dish.
6. Melt remaining butter, mix with lemon juice. Pour butter-lemon sauce over fish. Sprinkle with paprika.
7. Bake, uncovered, in preheated 350° F. oven about 30 minutes, or until fish flakes easily with a fork.
8. Serve at once, garnished with remaining parsley. Delicious alone, or with crisp romaine lettuce salad with oil and vinegar dressing.

NOTE: Seasoned dressing mix is made from wholewheat or wholegrain bread and seasoned with sage, onion, black pepper, thyme, other spices and herbs. No shortening or preservatives are added. Vary flavorings according to personal preference. This dieter's delight can be made many ways: top fillets with chopped fresh tomatoes spiked with fresh herbs and seasonings, or slather with dollop of sour cream and wrap fillets in squares of aluminum foil; seal like a package. Bake on cookie sheet as directed.

# Dr. Jean Mayer

Nutritionist Dr. Jean Mayer's daily food regimen is simple: orange juice, bran cereal or hot oatmeal, whole wheat toast, and tea for breakfast. "I used to eat eggs and I'm very fond of them, but now I don't." (Because of their high chloresterol content.) Mayer eats a light lunch: a sandwich and a glass of orange juice at his desk or fish if he eats lunch out with friends.

Dinners at the Mayers' are happy, relaxed occasions. "We have a soup course, a main course of meat, fish or poultry, three vegetables, usually boiled potatoes, carrots and broccoli, and salad." Dr Mayer is not one for desserts, but he does enjoy fruit and cheeses. "Often in lieu of meat, we have cheese. I am fond of all sorts of cheese: brie, pont l'Eveque, Camembert. All those are fairly high in fat so I go easy on them. I like Gruyere and cottage cheese. We eat fish several times a week, firm white fish – real fish, not processed or frozen. Often, we have fried chicken or, on occasion, *coq au vin*. New England boiled dinner is probably our favorite family dinner, and we have it once a week."

Dr. Mayer cooks when the family goes on camping trips or when he fishes at their seashore summer home. The Mayers limit their use of salt, using wine or lemon to season food. Their preference is for fresh fruits and vegetables in season, but do supplement them with frozen or canned varieties. "In the winter, we often use canned and frozen fruits and vegetables because they are usually better nutritionally than out-of-season food that has traveled 3,000 miles."

# Dr. Jean Mayer's Mackerel
# Poached in White Wine

Serves 6

3 cups dry white wine
½ tsp. salt
½ tsp. peppercorns
2 whole cloves
2 onions, peeled and sliced
  very thin

2 lemons, sliced very thin
⅛ tsp. thyme
1 bay leaf
6 medium-sized mackerel,
  very firm and
  very fresh

## For the court bouillon

1. *Combine wine, salt, peppercorns, cloves, onions, 1 lemon sliced, thyme and bay leaf.*
2. *Bring to boil and simmer 20 minutes.*
3. *Cool.*

## For the fish

1. *Clean and rinse mackerel; put in deep oven dish.*
2. *Pour bouillon over mackerel. Liquid should reach to ½ the depth of the dish. If not, add more wine.*
3. *Cover and bring to a very slow simmer.*
4. *Place casserole in preheated 350° F. oven for 10 minutes.*
5. *Remove and let cool.*
6. *Remove bay leaf; cover and refrigerate overnight.*
7. *Remove from refrigerator, let stand few minutes to take the chill off. Place fish on serving platter or individual dishes. Garnish with sliced lemon.*

*NOTE: This dish is only 200 calories per serving.*

# Dina Merrill

"I'm a sometime cook," confessed Dina Merrill, the blue-eyed, blonde and beautiful actress. "To be more specific, when the urge hits, I turn into a throw-in-and-taste cook." Dressed smartly in an oatmeal-colored shift, Dina talked with me in the green and white "snuggery" that she uses as an office at home – home being a large River House apartment overlooking New York's East River.

Dina Merrill is a continental cook, tempered slightly by her own American palate. "When I made a trip to Italy, I started making fettuccine with green noodles, prosciutto ham and Parmigiano cheese. From France, I started making a mussel soup with white wine. In fact, I often go in for 'fishy dinners' by following the soup with a fillet of sole." She uses domestic wines in cooking. "But hard liquor is good in cooking, too. I make a different and delicious lobster Newburg with bourbon."

The New York-born actress, the only child of the late E.P. Hutton and Mrs. Herbert May (Marjorie Merriweather Post), recalled that her first attempts at cooking were as a child making brownies. "My real cooking (as an adult) began while we were living in Washington, D.C. The help situation was somewhat sketchy. One morning, when I found myself without a cook, I said to my son, 'I'm it. Now tell me what you want me to prepare.' He chose a cheese soufflé. I told him, 'I'm game. If you'll eat it, I'll try making it.' "

# Dina Merrill's Mussels Marinière

### Serves 4-6

4 pints mussels
1 cup dry white wine
1 tbsp. scallion, chopped
1 sprig parsley
½ clove garlic
1 small bay leaf

$\frac{1}{16}$ tsp. thyme
several gratings freshly
   ground pepper
3 tbsps. butter
salt to taste
1 tbsp. parsley, chopped

1. *Scrub mussel shells thoroughly with a stiff brush, wash in several waters.*
2. *Place shells in a kettle with the wine, scallion, parsley, garlic, bay leaf, thyme and pepper. Cover kettle tightly and cook over high heat until the shells open, about 5 minutes.*
3. *Remove the mussels from the kettle, take off the top shell and place mussels in a deep heated dish or tureen.*
4. *Strain the stock and cook it over high flame until it is reduced by ⅓ its original quantity.*
5. *Add butter and salt to taste; heat through.*
6. *Pour over the mussels in tureen. Add chopped parsley for garnish. Serve in deep soup plates or small casseroles and eat the mussels directly from the shell.*
7. *Serve with thick slices of crusty French bread.*

# Agnes Moorehead

"Do you cast any spells in the kitchen?" I asked Agnes Moorehead, the actress of a thousand voices who many television-watchers knew as the witty, sophistocated Endora, the mother-witch on "Bewitched." We talked in Salem, Massachusetts, the historic setting of the famed witches' trials during "on-location" shooting just prior to her death.

"I hope I cast a spell on other people in the kitchen. I like to experiment," replied Aggie, who did most of her cooking on the family farm near Zanesville, Ohio. "My mother's mother came from Dublin and was an extremely fine cook, but we didn't learn; we just admired what she did. My mother taught me how to make Boston baked beans. She always said they're filling and when you can't get anything else, this will last for quite a while and she was right."

Aggie described her farm's kitchen as having "beautiful storage space, everything you can possibly think of: all the cooking accessories, blenders, broilers, self-cleaning stoves that make cooking easier." However, most of her entertaining was done in her 14-room Mediterranean villa in Beverly Hills (formerly owned by Sigmund Romberg). "I give big brunches with great cheese soufflés or a lobster or shellfish mousse, with a light sweet or fruit and cheese for dessert. And although I don't drink very much, some people like a very light wine with their lunch."

The actress nostalgically recalled the old-fashioned taffy pulls and toboggan parties of her youth, then added that "children today don't know the fun of a great sleigh ride with three or four progressive dinners where you stopped off at one house for soup, then you went to another house. And you'd be laughing and singing and get out of the sleigh and have the entrée or dessert at the last house."

# Agnes Moorehead's Lobster Mousse

Serves 4-6

1 lb. fresh lobster meat  
few drops fresh lemon juice  
salt to taste  
white pepper to taste  
pinch of nutmeg  

¾ cup heavy cream  
2 tbsps. dry sherry  
3 egg whites  
parsley sprigs  
lemon wedges  

shrimp or truffles to garnish (optional)

1. *Chop lobster meat finely. Put through fine blade of chopper; then pound in a mortar until smooth.*
2. *Sprinkle lightly with few drops of lemon juice, then place in sieve to strain off lemon juice.*
3. *Season to taste with salt, white pepper and nutmeg.*
4. *Gradually beat in cream and sherry with wire whisk.*
5. *Beat egg whites until stiff but not dry; gently fold in egg whites.*
6. *Butter a large deep mold. Turn lobster mixture into mold and place in pan filled with hot water.*
7. *Garnish with whole shrimp or bits of truffles.*
8. *Bake in preheated 350° F. oven 20 minutes or until firm. Or poach over hot water 35 minutes.*
9. *Wait a few minutes before turning out on a large heated platter.*
10. *Garnish with parsley and lemon wedges.*

NOTE: *Agnes Moorehead's elegant mousse can be served with a variety of sauces: lobster, Hollandaise or sherry-flavored Bechamel sauce. If desired, use finely minced lemon rind in lieu of lemon juice.*

# Zero Mostel

"I'm no cookbook fella, not a recipe man, but I cook simple things very well," said rotund, friendly, multi-talented Zero Mostel. We were in his studio, deep in the Chelsea district, on Manhattan's Lower West Side. "I like to read cookbooks, but I think you've got to cook in your own way." The late actor's kitchen philosophy dovetailed completely with his theory: "Who says you have to sign paintings, or date them for that matter?"

Zero was appropriately dressed for cooking in a white chef's jacket and white cotton pants, but he had been painting. (He worked on 10 to 20 paintings simultaneously, alternating canvasses until one dried or another caught his fancy.) We sat at a round card table (he's had a continuous card game going here with his cronies, sculptors, poets and painters with the same stakes for 35 years), next to a fully equipped kitchen. "We don't cook down here. This is cottage cheese land," Zero joked.

Aside from his fondness for lobsters and clams, Zero also had a great passion for herring, broiled or pickled. "Broiled, it's the most delicious piece of fish you ever had, but it must be fresh. I wouldn't refer to something you eat as an art. The only thing art has is its own life. But, I must tell you. My wife, Katy, made bread for the first time and something happened. It didn't rise, but she baked it anyway. It weighed about 30 pounds, this little loaf of bread. My sculptor friend downstairs lacquered Katy's bread and it was a great piece of pop art. It was beautiful! We put it on an old scale we had and it was fantastic to behold!" Katy's now a first-class baker, especially of rye bread. "And she turns out glorious coffee cakes," Zero added.

# Zero Mostel's Poached Salmon with Green Mayonnaise

Serves 4-6

## For the fish

1½ cups dry white wine
1½ cups water
bouquet garni: 1 small bay leaf,
 2 sprigs parsley, 1 sprig
 fresh thyme or ½ tsp. dried,
 tied in cheesecloth bag
1 small onion, stuck with 2
 cloves

8 peppercorns, bruised
1 small carrot, cut in chunks
1½ tsps. salt
juice of ½ lemon
5-6 lbs. whole fresh salmon,
 dressed
1 stalk celery with tops,
 chopped

1. *Place all ingredients, except fish, in fish kettle or pan deep enough and long enough to cook whole fish.*
2. *Bring to boiling point and simmer, uncovered, 45 minutes to reduce volume slightly. Strain and set aside.*
3. *Prepare fish by drawing, leave head and tail on, remove eyes. Wipe fish with clean, damp cloth; wrap in double thickness of cheesecloth.*
4. *Bring liquid again to boiling point; lower fish slowly and carefully into pot.*
5. *Bring back to boiling, then lower heat; let simmer only 3 minutes, then remove pot from heat. Let fish cool in stock.*
6. *Carefully lift fish from pot; place on long, narrow plate. Chill; carefully remove skin, keeping fish intact.*
7. *Decorate with parsley and lemon slices. Fashion a realistic "eye" with end slice of hard-cooked egg white, centered with speck of black olive. Serve with green mayonnaise for main dish or buffet offering.*

## For the green mayonnaise

1 large egg yolk
¼ tsp. salt
sprinkling of white pepper
1 tsp. fresh lemon juice or
 vinegar
1 cup salad oil

1 tbsp. boiling water
few drops oil from pressed garlic
1 tbsp. capers
2 tbsps. fresh basil or
 watercress or parsley,
 finely chopped

1. *Mix egg yolk, salt, pepper and few drops lemon juice in small deep bowl.*
2. *Add oil, drop by drop, beating constantly with whisk or electric blender. Sauce should be thick and creamy. Thin down with remaining lemon juice.*
3. *To "set" mayonnaise sauce and prevent curdling, add boiling water at end, beating vigorously. Add garlic, capers, basil; mix well. Chill before serving.*

# Jean Nidetch

Jean Nidetch, high priestess and innovator of *Weight Watchers International*, is an avid fish lover. She was preparing a beautiful striped bass for a family meal in her sunny, "outdoorsy-looking" kitchen, at home in Queens and explained how cake and a love of sweet things were her great downfall in what she calls the "old days," when she weighed in at 214 (she's now a slim 145).

"When we lived in Warrenton, Pennsylvania, there were no bakery shops, only supermarket pastries," said Jean. "I used to make my own chocolate eclairs. I even got one of those things that shoot the whipped cream into the eclairs. Then I would sit down and eat 20 of them!" Now Jean settles for a pineapple upside-down cake creation a dieting Texas friend sent her recently when she was down with a broken leg.

Jean's thoughts on diet are very positive and are based largely on the advice of the late Dr. Norman Joliffe, long-time diet specialist and New York City Board of Health advisor. "I'd tried everything from prayers to diets to appetite depressants to hypnosis to doctors with injections. The health clinic was the last stop," said Jean, who is greatly enthused about the new changes in the Weight Watchers' diet: the addition of potatoes, spaghetti and rice. "In the old days, if you told a compulsive eater you can have spaghetti, the word would signify a bowl. Now to say you can have half a cup, they're in control. They've released the shovel, they've picked up the fork. And to have a half-cup of spaghetti is a joy. When I know I'm going to have a half-cup of spaghetti, I'll taste it for hours, because to me, it was forbidden for so long."

# Jean Nidetch's Baked Striped Bass Harborside with Gourmet Rice

Serves 4

1 striped bass or bluefish
  (2½ lbs. dressed
  weight)
2 tsps. salt
½ tsp. pepper
*Gourmet rice
1 tsp. paprika

4 tsps. fresh parsley, minced
1 tbsp. lemon juice or wine
  vinegar
2 tsps. capers
6 tbsps. imitation (or diet)
  margarine, at room
  temperature

1. Wash, dry and split the underside of fish. Remove backbone, but do not cut through the fine bone.
2. Season fish inside and out with salt and pepper.
3. Stuff fish loosely with gourmet rice. Close openings with skewers or string.
4. Place stuffed fish on baking pan. Dust outside with paprika. Bake in preheated 425° F. oven 30-40 minutes, or until fish flakes easily when tested with a fork.
5. While fish bakes, blend parsley, lemon juice, capers and margarine. Divide into 4 equal portions and serve in lemon cups, or spread on each individual portion at serving time.

## *Gourmet Rice

2 cups hot cooked enriched
  rice
2 tbsps. imitation (or diet)
  margarine
2 tsps. dehydrated onion
  flakes

4 tsps. chives, minced
1 envelope or 1 cube
  vegetable bouillon
1 tsp. original
  Worcestershire sauce

Combine all ingredients and toss lightly. If vegetable cube is used, dissolve in a small amount of water.

# Louis Nizer

"We meet for conversation and fellowship. We converse on anything from current affairs to sports and the theater," said lawyer Louis Nizer, as he discussed food and his favorite "institution" in a niche at the famous old Algonquin Hotel in the middle of Manhattan. He was describing the Algonquin Round Table, that celebrated American tradition of lunch and conversation started in 1919.

Today, Nizer and interesting people of our day maintain the tradition of easy, unrehearsed and informed conversation. "Food plays a minor role, conversation dominates. We go in for a healthy diet. You might call it pragmatic and restrained eating. I've believed for a long time: You are what you eat. If you eat correctly, you don't have to deprive yourself."

Learning to eat correctly requires self discipline, Nizer implied. His thinking is influenced somewhat by a doctor friend of his in Florida who, Nizer said, "shows you a picture of bread and tells you the bread is made from flour and water, the same as the paste you used as a child. Then he asks, 'What do you need with flour and water?' Soon you reject bread. If you develop this philosophy, you can easily by-pass apple pie. I never use a salt shaker and I avoid foods high in salt such as celery. My lunches at the Round Table frequently are fish. Today I had broiled bay scallops and decaffeinated coffee sweetened with honey. I eat even less when I'm in court, perhaps a bowl of soup or cottage cheese."

Though generally Spartan in his food tastes, Nizer likes broiled swordfish topped with anchovies, Boston scrod (young codfish) poached in a wine-herb-butter sauce, and pancakes with chicken hash. Algonquin chefs bow to his palate and omit salt; they lean heavily on lemon and honey to prepare his food.

# Louis Nizer's Broiled Bay Scallops

### Serves 2-3

1 lb. bay scallops
1 tbsp. safflower oil
3 tbsps. sweet butter, melted
2 tbsps. lemon juice

1 tbsp. leek, minced
½ tsp. powdered thyme
1 lemon, cut in
 thin slices

fresh parsley, chopped

1. *Wash scallops and dry between paper towels.*
2. *Brush scallops with safflower oil and place in broiler pan.*
3. *Mix together melted butter, lemon juice, leeks and thyme; spoon liberally over scallops in pan.*
4. *Broil 5 minutes, basting twice with butter sauce.*
5. *Serve on heated platter, covering with lemon slices and parsley.*

# Robert Shaw

The late English actor Robert Shaw, a charming rogue, was not only a successful actor and writer, but an accomplished cook as well. "I'm very good at cooking, but not in the sense that I can bake cakes," he said over a mushroom omelet breakfast in his suite at the Beverly Hills Hotel shortly before he died.

"I'm good at anything that has to do with fish or meat," he explained. "I'm certain the simplest cooking is the greatest and I do precisely that kind of cooking. We have wonderful fish in Ireland — Irish salmon is the best in the world. We get trout from the lake near our house."

The salty sea captain of *Jaws* fame lived in a large stone house built in 1814, in Tourmakeady in County Mayo, on the West Coast. "One of my favorite dishes is pickled herring," he said. "That's a very English dish, and it's a very inexpensive one. We get them every Friday in the village, and I gut them and cook them in vinegar sauce."

# Robert Shaw's Fresh Pickled Herring

### Serves 4

8 fresh sea herring, about
  10-inches long
salt
1 cup malt vinegar
3 bay leaves, crumbled
1 tsp. pickling spices

12 peppercorns
1 large white onion,
  peeled and cut in
  thin rings
chopped fresh dill or chives
8 small whole potatoes, boiled

1. *Wash herring; pat dry.*
2. *Cut off heads and clean them.*
3. *Put herring in an ovenproof dish, and between each layer, sprinkle with salt.*
4. *Cover fish with vinegar. Sprinkle bay leaves, pickling spice, peppercorns and onions over fish.*
5. *Cover dish with aluminum foil and bake in preheated 300° F. about 35 minutes.*
6. *Allow fish to cool in liquid and serve very cold with a little of the tangy liquid poured over the fish. Garnish with fresh dill or chives. Or serve hot, with hot boiled potatoes.*

NOTE: *This delicious and inexpensive dish is a boon for summer fishermen! If selecting herring in a shop, choose those that have a bright, silvery look. Herring in the British Isles are found in great abundance in June or July. In America, sea herring are available on the Pacific Coast from San Francisco to Canada, and on the East Coast from Long Island Sound north. Jack mackerel is an inexpensive substitute. If desired, substitute salt herring: Wash fish well. Soak in water to remove salt. Drain well. Bone, fillet fish. Cut into thin strips and marinate in vinegar-spice mixture several hours in refrigerator in covered dish.*

# Carrie Snodgress

Actress Carrie Snodgress said, "My mother's a great cook. That's why I lived at home so much because she cooked all those good things. She has an amazing way of making things work for little money because we had to do that growing up." Carrie lived at home and commuted while she was a drama student at the Goodman Theater in Chicago.

"I was never interested in cooking as a kid," she recalled. "I was very athletic and very physically coordinated. I mean I was very active and had that energy that gives me that drive and I just moved! But as for food, I don't eat very much but try to make sure it's something kind of interesting and exciting. For example, I eat a lot of fish. I'm a vegetarian mostly, by accident. It's just no fun to cook meat and eat it by yourself. Anyway, I just eat on the run, very casually. The easiest thing is making salads and eating fruit. Then I got into vegetables. I really dig spinach and cauliflower. Suddenly, I'd just cook that and found myself just eating vegetables and fruits.

"I drink a lot of spring water, eight or ten glasses a day, because in California you can buy it every two blocks. Everyone is sort of into that, a health food trip. But hey! I have a red snapper recipe! I put onions in the bottom of the pan and lay the fish on the top with tomatoes, celery and general seasonings – anything you happen to have in the ice box. That's kind of groovy and with a mixture of white wine poured over the fish, I mean, it's incredible!"

# Carrie Snodgress' Hearty Red Snapper

Serves 4

2 lbs. fresh red snapper
 filets
⅔ cup sweet white onion,
 thinly sliced
2 stalks celery, minced
3 small ripe tomatoes,
 peeled and chopped
½ green pepper,
 chopped

½ cup dry white wine or
 clam juice
2 tbsps. fresh lemon juice
pinch dried basil
1 tsp. salt
freshly ground black
 or white pepper
 to taste
lemon wedges

¼ cup fresh parsley, chopped

1. *Wipe snapper with damp cloth; pat dry.*
2. *Line baking pan with aluminum foil; arrange onion in bottom of pan; place fish on top of onion.*
3. *Combine remaining vegetables and spread over top of fish.*
4. *Combine wine, lemon juice and seasonings, and pour over fish.*
5. *Bake in preheated 350° F. oven for 25-30 minutes, or until fish flakes easily when tested with a fork.*
6. *Garnish with lemon wedges and minced parsley. Serve alone, or with side dish of fresh garden spinach or cauliflower, green salad and chilled white wine.*

NOTE: *Carrie's delicious fish offering can be made with striped bass or freshwater trout or bass. Change vegetables, using fresh mushrooms, water chestnuts or slivered carrots and seasonings of a crumbled bay leaf, thyme or oregano. For a baked chowder effect, substitute cod fish for snapper; use clam juice instead of wine; omit green pepper and use paper-thin sliced potatoes and bacon bits in the bottom of the pan. Adjust cooking time, adding fish 20 minutes later to prevent overcooking.*

# Jack Warner

"I like plain food, not garnishy things loaded down with mushrooms or sauces. I like good, and I wouldn't call it American, but just good food," the late pioneer movie producer Jack Warner said over his favorite libation, a "blutty Mary." Jack looked tanned and trim in a pin-striped suit, remarkably spry for a man who worked for better than half a century in the movie business. "By good food, I mean quality meat, New York cut steaks, lamb chops, fish and seafood like lobsters, shrimp and oysters.

"Listen, I'm strictly a spectator cook. The only things I cook up are good scripts and good movies," he said, in a typical example of the corny sides interspersed into his rambling, ad lib dialogue.

Jack was renowned for feuding with his stars during his reign as head of Warner Brothers. He always claimed that his favorite movie star was Rin Tin Tin. "He was the only leading man, or woman if you prefer, who never gave a bad performance. He'd face each hazard one after another and was always grateful for an extra hamburger. He never asked for a raise or a new press agent or leading lady. Finally, however, I had to let him go though, because we gave him a bone and then he wanted two, so I had to can him!"

One of Warner's corniest jokes happened during a luncheon honoring Madame Chiang Kai-shek. He had just bought the movie rights to Col. Robert Scott's book, God Is My Co-Pilot. "Bob had been with the Flying Tigers and kept telling all these incredible things about Madame Chiang Kai-shek to the point I was disbelieving. I arrived at the luncheon late and when I saw this sea of inscrutable Oriental faces, I was immediately overcome by a fiendish impulse. When I met her I said, 'Holy Cow! I forgot to pick up my laundry!' "

# Jack Warner's Broiled Salmon – Vegetable Medley

Serves 1

1 salmon steak, cut 1-inch
  thick
3 tbsps. sweet butter
1 lemon

1 cup fresh peas, cooked
1 cup baby carrots, cooked
1 cup green beans, cooked
  and cut in julienne strips

1. *Place salmon steak on broiler pan lined with aluminum foil.*
2. *Melt 2 tbsps. butter and add juice of half a lemon. Brush salmon with lemon-butter.*
3. *Broil fish on one side 8 minutes, or until fish flakes easily when tested with fork; turn, again brush with butter, broil about 5 minutes, or until it begins to flake easily when tested with fork.*
4. *Arrange fish on hot serving platter with vegetable garniture of hot cooked peas, carrots and green beans.*
5. *Melt remaining butter with rest of lemon juice and pour over fish and vegetables.*

# Flip Wilson

"My face," says comedian Flip Wilson, "has made my living! So every day, I throw a party for my face! My party is dinner, because when I eat well, it makes my face happy."

Flip made me smile, as he happily dug into escargots over lunch at the elegant French establishment called simply Le Restaurant. "I like to eat all kinds of food: Italian, German, Japanese – but fish is my real thing!" he said enthusiastically. "If you call up the Bahamas, you'll probably find there's a shortage of fish because I've eaten so much of it!"

In the eight years since I first met Flip, he has become a cook. "I am learning how to make seven different dishes," he said. "This is how I am liberating myself. I'll eat some of what I cook and put the rest away. I eat out every other night; the other nights, I eat the leftovers. This way, my seven dishes will last me a month!"

Flip's palate is now much more sophisticated than it once was. For example, the day we lunched, his first choice on the extensive menu was duck. Eight years ago, he detested duck!

"I spend a lot of time in the Bahamas," said fish-lover Flip. "Grouper and yellow jack are what I eat. I've got to tell you, I really have the lock on their way of frying grouper. Linquini with white clam sauce used to be number one until I got on to cooking grouper. I've been working on the linquini for quite some time. I practiced it on my gang, but they're getting older now and they like my fish better!" Flip's "gang" includes two sons and two daughters.

# Fried Grouper à La Flip Wilson

### Serves 6

6 large slices filleted
  grouper or yellow jack
dried hot pepper (available
  in Spanish groceries)

vinegar
fresh lime juice
bacon fat

1. *Wash and dry fillets carefully.*
2. *Slash skin in several places.*
3. *Cut red pepper in small pieces; marinate in vinegar.*
4. *Remove from vinegar and rub slits of fish with pepper pieces and squeeze lime juice over all sides.*
5. *Heat generous amount of bacon fat in large, deep iron skillet until sizzling.*
6. *Plunge fish in hot grease; cook quickly but do not overcook. Turn to cook on reverse side.*
7. *Drain fish on absorbent paper.*
8. *Serve at once. Tremendous alone, or with hot corn bread!*

# fowl & Game

# John Banner

"As you can see, I've brought along my chef," said Viennese actor John Banner, as he introduced his French wife, Christine, in an interview before his death. "She's only a magician in the kitchen!" said the former comic Sergeant Schultz in the television series, "Hogan's Heroes." John's love for food was obvious any way you looked at it. He weighed in at 280 lbs., but looked lighter in person, neatly dressed in a dark blue suit.

Asked what he liked most about his wife's cooking, John said, "I love everything she makes. There's positively nothing she fixes that I don't like. Her cooking is so superb, we have a six-month waiting list of people who want to come to our house for dinner. She cooks only with the best of ingredients and then she says to me, 'You're too fat!' "

John explained the eating habits he acquired in his native Vienna. "Austrians eat all day long, beginning with a breakfast of Kaiser rolls, sweet butter, marmalade and coffee. At one o'clock it's goulash and beer. At two they close their shops and go home for dessert. And at four everyone meets in the coffee houses for pastry and coffee. Then it's a light supper and after the theater, into the coffee houses again. It's impossible to diet in Vienna!" Then he added, "The French enjoy eating, too. With them, eating, like cooking, is a real art. Being married to a French wife – oh, la, la – is only pleasurable. I gave up cooking after I met Christine."

Banner disapproved of American food habits. "Eating steak every day is so boring, but steak with some of Chris's *buerre maître d'hotel* (butter sauce flavored with shallots, lemon and parsley) is another story."

# Christine Banner's Flambéed Chicken

### Serves 3-4

11 tbsps. butter
1 broiler-fryer chicken,
    quartered
salt to taste
freshly ground black pepper
    to taste
4-5 cooking apples, peeled,
    cored and cut in thin slices

1 tbsp. sugar (optional)
½ lb. mushrooms, cleaned
    and chopped
3 oz. calvados or
    apple brandy
½ cup heavy cream
2 egg yolks

1. *Melt 4 tbsps. butter in skillet. Brown chicken quickly on all sides; season with salt and pepper. Set aside.*
2. *Melt 4 tbsps. butter in separate skillet. Sauté apple slices until soft but not mushy. Set aside. (If apples are tart, add about 1 tbsp. sugar.)*
3. *Melt 3 tbsps. butter in large saucepan. Sauté mushrooms in butter; cover and simmer 5 minutes.*
4. *Pour calvados or brandy over chicken; touch with a lighted match.*
5. *When flaming stops, transfer chicken to saucepan containing mushrooms, but reserve skillet and its drippings. Continue cooking chicken in saucepan over low fire.*
6. *Add cream, beaten slightly with egg yolks, to skillet that chicken was cooked in. Stir over low heat until thickened. Do not boil.*
7. *Remove chicken and mushrooms to heated serving plate.*
8. *Pour sauce over chicken. Serve with sautéed apple slices.*

# Jack Benny

Over breakfast in New York, the late Jack Benny talked about the high cost of being a tightwad, the reputation he cultivated so brilliantly for so many years on radio and TV. "I always worry about tipping, so I overcompensate," said Jack. "Everyone hollers at me: 'You're overdoing it.' Actually, my wife (Mary Livingstone) and I are big spenders. If I were stingy – really stingy – I don't think I could have made my penurious 'character' pay off."

Jack was a lover of parties. He recalled, "The best publicity gag we ever staged was in New York. Before a TV season or a special, we invited people, most of them pretty rich, to the Automat. They came in Rolls-Royces and other beautiful cars with chauffeurs. I gave them $2 worth of nickels to get food. It was a great stunt."

Jack and Mary entertained lavishly in their Beverly Hills mansion. One of his favorite foods was steak tartar. "I like it when it's not gummy. Mary makes it very well," he said. As for his own culinary skills, Jack added, "I couldn't prepare a cup of coffee, if you want to know. I never tried in my life. I would have to go into our kitchen and ask our cook, 'Will you show me how to make a cup of coffee, because I might want some tonight when I come home?' "

Jack's favorite food was Chinese, and his recipe for Chicken Chop Suey is an excellent offering for . . . who else? Penny-pinching cooks!

# Jack Benny's Chicken Chop Suey

Serves 4

1 bunch Chinese cabbage
1 can (10 ozs.) bean sprouts
6 scallions
3 large celery stalks
3 tbsps. vegetable oil
1½ cups cooked chicken
   (or turkey, veal, beef or ham)
   cut in strips
1 tsp. salt

few gratings freshly ground
   black pepper
1 cup green peas, fresh or
   frozen, or ½ pkg.
   frozen Chinese peapods
2½ tbsps. soy sauce
1 tbsp. corn starch
1 tbsp. sugar
½ cup clear chicken broth

cooked rice or Chinese noodles

1. Chop cabbage coarsely. Drain bean sprouts and rinse well under running water; dry with paper towel. Chop scallions coarsely. Cut celery in ¼-inch slices diagonally.
2. Sauté scallions and celery in vegetable oil in a Chinese wok or heavy skillet about 2 minutes.
3. Add chicken (or other meat), salt and pepper.
4. Stir-fry over medium heat, adding chopped vegetables and peas, one at a time. Set aside.
5. In a small bowl, mix soy sauce with corn starch, sugar, and 2 tbsps. chicken broth. Blend well.
6. Pour into a saucepan and slowly add remaining chicken broth. Bring to a quick boil. Cook a few minutes, stirring constantly.
7. Serve at once over hot cooked rice or Chinese noodles.

NOTE: Never overcook chop suey. Actual preparation should take no longer than 5-7 minutes. If desired, start with paper-thin sliced red meat, cooking quickly in vegetable oil until it begins to turn color. Then proceed as directed, sautéeing vegetables. For a change of pace, vary vegetables, substituting Chinese vegetables, water chestnut slivers or Chinese mushrooms. An excellent choice for weight-watchers!

# David Birney &
# Meredith Baxter

"I will give you a recipe for peanut butter and jelly on zweiback," said actor David Birney, as I lunched on crab salad with him and his wife, actress Meredith Baxter, in his dressing room. "I'm very plain about food for the most part," David said. "I like fish, steak and eggs. That's my lower middle-class background coming out!" David is the son of an FBI agent, and was born in Washington, D.C. and raised in Cleveland, Ohio.

"I cook some eggs — omelettes and stuff like that — and I broil lamb chops and steak. Other than that, I'm pretty much of a disaster in the kitchen. But, hey, I *do* make waffles!" he said.

"And terrific waffles!" Meredith chimed in.

"Meredith gave me a waffle iron which I had to learn how to use," he said. "No, it wasn't a wedding gift. On a Sunday morning in New York, I really enjoy doing that: cooking bacon and making waffles, and stretching it out through the day over the *New York Times*."

"Waffles are great with scrambled eggs and bacon on top," Meredith suggested. "I cook a lot of chicken, but I've never been able to cook steaks too well. I always cook them too long. I cook other things, too, like milkshakes — you know, hard stuff," she said with a serious face. Her other "hard stuff" includes chicken cacciatore or chicken with a wine-lemon sauce.

Meredith, who grew up in Los Angeles and attended Hollywood High before studying music and acting, is the daughter of TV actress Whitney Blake. "My mother is a fantastic cook," said Meredith. "She makes wonderful meat dishes, cooking lamb in pastry. She'd shape little flowers in the pastry and stuff it. Incredible! She's always doing something great."

"Listen, can't you make up a camp recipe for me: peanut butter and cyclamates, Spanish rice and lemon juice?" David said, his eyes glinting!

# Meredith Baxter's Chicken Tarragon

### Serves 2-3

seasoned flour
1 cleaned broiler-fryer
   chicken, cut into
   serving pieces
¼ cup olive oil
1 cup fresh mushrooms, sliced
½ cup onion, sliced

½ clove garlic, pressed
½ tsp. tarragon leaves
¼ cup Rhine wine
¼ cup chicken broth
half lemon, squeezed
1 tbsp. flour
hot cooked rice

1. *Place seasoned flour in a paper bag. Place chicken pieces in bag, twist top tightly, and shake vigorously to coat.*
2. *Brown coated chicken in olive oil in flame-proof casserole.*
3. *Remove chicken.*
4. *Lightly sauté mushrooms, onion and garlic in pan drippings.*
5. *Add tarragon, wine, chicken broth and lemon juice to casserole; heat over low flame, stirring.*
6. *Return chicken pieces to casserole, spooning sauce over chicken. Cover and bake in preheated 350° F. oven about 45 minutes, or until chicken is tender.*
7. *Remove chicken to warm platter.*
8. *Mix broth with flour until smooth; stir into drippings. (Fat may be skimmed from drippings first, if desired.)*
9. *Cook, stirring, over medium heat, until thickened.*
10. *Serve with chicken and gravy over hot cooked rice.*

# Raymond Burr

"The most important thing, in talking about Fijian food and American cooking, in terms of recipes, is that one simply cannot get the ingredients in the U.S.," said Raymond Burr. The huge man, with the dramatic eyes and the infectious smile, joked, teased and presided over a Bahamian feast of broiled lobsters, his favorite rosé wine and good conversation at the famed Pink Sands on Harbour Island, Bahamas. With Burr, who has been coming here for a score of years, was a group of old friends who predate his Perry Mason days.

Thoughts of Fiji were not so incongruous, for Burr is as at home at Pink Sands as he is at Fiji's Naitauba plantation. His face is well known to the islanders as a friend and benefactor, and even his production company is named for the island.

Burr's gourmet cooking talents rival his acting ability. Typically, he approaches both with dedication, tolerating no short cuts or substitutes. But then, that's the way it is with any project he undertakes in life, whether it's supporting some two dozen foster children, entertaining front-line troops, or lending himself to some other good cause.

"Probably the most interesting Fiji custom," Burr said, "is when they entertain, they bring out tinned foods instead of their wonderful tropical fruits. It's kind of a status thing!"

Burr is so interested in preserving authentic recipes, he is doing an island cookbook. He has an encyclopedic knowledge of Fijian farming: "There are eight kinds of limes that grow there, five kinds of papaya, nine kinds of bananas, large wild lemons that turn green when they are ripe, and pomelo, which originated in Haiti and is like a wonderful green grapefruit, deliciously sweet."

# Raymond Burr's Chicken Lolo

Serves 4-6

1 cup fresh coconut, grated
1 cup water
1 lemon, peeled and sliced
½ cup chopped onion
2 tbsps. butter

3 whole chicken breasts, boned,
   skinned and cut into chunks
½ tsp. ground ginger
1 tsp. salt
1 tbsp. flour

1 canned green chili pepper, sliced

1. *In a saucepan, combine coconut, water, lemon and onion. Bring to boil.*
2. *Remove from heat and strain.*
3. *Melt butter in a large skillet and add chicken breasts. Cook until meat turns white.*
4. *Add ginger, salt and chili pepper.*
5. *Pour in strained coconut liquid, cover, and simmer for 10 minutes.*
6. *Mix flour with a small amount of cold water to make a paste. Stir into sauce, bring to a boil, and simmer 2 minutes.*

*NOTE: Lolo, or coconut cream, can be prepared from fresh coconuts. Pierce eyes of coconut with ice pick. Pour out coconut milk and reserve. Bake coconut 20 minutes in preheated 350° F. oven, or until shell cracks. Break open shell, remove coconut meat, and grate. Burr's favorite is a popular Fiji school lunch: Dinner in a Nutshell! In the Fijian manner, the top of coconut is removed, then most of the coconut flesh removed and grated, mixed with fish or fowl, vegetables, lolo and condiments, popped back into coconut shell, topped with cover, and steamed or baked for 1 hour. American cooks who own wood or electric saws can halve coconut shells, brown chicken separately in butter, then combine with other ingredients. Shells are then filled, wrapped with aluminum foil, and baked in oven until bubbly. Shells can be reserved for future use, then the dish prepared as directed above and heated in shells to serve!*

# Zoe Caldwell

Zoe Caldwell, of the smokey voice and enormous brown eyes and a talent to match – has an uncanny resemblance to a much younger Sarah Bernhardt. It seemed incredible that she had ever worked in a pickle factory in her native Australia.

Her tastes in food? "I like to cook roasts and chickens," she said. "I do chicken in some fancy ways. I'm a saucier," saying the last word gleefully as if it sounded a little wicked. "The only thing my husband (Robert Whitehead) absolutely insists is that it (chicken) falls from the bone: I mean literally falls from the bone. So if you picked up a bone, the chicken all falls down. Anything less than that with any bird won't do. And we have pheasants. But I do smothered chicken. I put it in a pot, brown it, put in some garlic and some wine – any old leftover wine will do – and I leave it all night long on simmer. So that literally in the morning, it falls from the bone. Then from the butter and juices from the chicken, I just mix in some sour cream. Or I do a boiled chicken which I love with carrots. Chicken's kinda good because it's cheap."

Zoe's mother is a good cook, but as she explained it, "a different kind of cook, an Australian cook, an old-fashioned cook: beef and kidney pie and dumplings. I'm not big on that, but then Robert isn't either. I like to cook to my taste – and Robert's. The only trouble is he likes all his meat very well done and I don't, and that's difficult with a roast to make sufficient enough outside cuts that are good for Robert and still have some nice, red inside meat for me."

The Whiteheads, who love salads, plan to have an herb garden in the new house they're building at Pound Ridge (New York) on a wooded, 125-acre retreat overlooking a 15-acre lake.

# Zoe Caldwell's Smothered Chicken

### Serves 4

1 cleaned broiler-fryer
  chicken, cut into
  serving pieces
seasoned flour
4 tbsps. butter
2 tbsps. olive oil
2 tbsps. onion, chopped

1 small clove garlic,
  pressed
good pinch fresh herbs
  (optional): parsley,
  thyme, bayleaf
½ bottle good dry
  white wine

½ cup dairy sour cream

1. *Shake chicken pieces in paper bag with seasoned flour.*
2. *Heat butter and oil in large Dutch oven until hot; sauté onion until golden; lift out.*
3. *Brown chicken lightly on all sides.*
4. *Add cooked onion, garlic, herbs and enough wine to cover chicken.*
5. *Cover and cook over low flame, simmering until chicken is tender.*
6. *Remove chicken to heated platter.*
7. *Skim off excess fat and strain stock. Cook to reduce stock in volume.*
8. *Add chicken and taste to correct seasonings.*
9. *Add sour cream and barely heat through. Do not boil. Serve alone, or over hot cooked rice.*

NOTE: *If desired, chicken can be cooked in a crock pot or oven. Precook baby carrots and cauliflowerets, and add to smothered chicken just before serving, making certain vegetables are hot.*

# Vikki Carr

Songstress Vikki Carr is an enthusiastic cook. Her figure is bone-thin because she sticks to a Spartan diet: broiled fish and chicken, skimmed milk, soft boiled eggs, cheese, steamed vegetables and fruit. Although her own intake is sparing, she cooks very well in almost any language, and is known as one of California's greatest Mexican cooks!

"Cooking gives me some of my greatest pleasures in life," Vikki said enthusiastically. "I love it." For a special meal, Vikki creates a pungent chicken dish called *arroz a la catalana*, a dish reminiscent of *paella*. Chicken plus squid, tomatoes and vegetables, are delicately flavored with saffron and a whiff of garlic!

Vikki still treasures memories of Christmas food celebrations with her family. "We always went to Christmas Eve midnight mass and came home to my mother's hot corn tamales, steamed in the corn husks," she recalled. "They were so good, we even had them for breakfast Christmas morning!" Vikki spends simple Christmases with family and very close friends. She loves to prepare Christmas dinner, using Vincent Price's cookbook, *A Treasury of Great Recipes.* "I like the menu Vincent got from the Wayside Inn, in South Sudsbury, Massachusetts, right down to the turkey stuffed with sausage and Boston brown bread. The directions say that you should never use a knife to cut the brown bread – you should use string! Mine always comes out so moist and nice that I cut it with a thread. And the Yorkshire pudding tastes like popovers – it's delicious!"

# Vikki Carr's Arroz a la Catalana
# (Chicken Catalana)

Serves 4-6

1 cleaned broiler-fryer
  chicken, cut into
  serving pieces
⅓ cup vegetable oil
½ tsp. thyme
½ cup dry white wine,
  more if needed
3 tbsps. olive oil
1 lb. squid
1 cup onion, finely chopped
1 cup ripe tomatoes, peeled
  and chopped

18 mussels, well scrubbed
  to remove sand
  and seaweed
2 cups uncooked
  long-grain rice
4 cups boiling
  salted water
1 cup frozen green peas
½ tsp. salt
3 cloves garlic
pinch of saffron
1 pimento, cut in strips

1. Sauté chicken in vegetable oil until golden. Add thyme and wine.
2. Cover and continue cooking until almost done; then remove chicken.
3. Heat 2 tbsps. olive oil in separate pan. Clean and cut up squid; add to heated olive oil.
4. Cover and cook over low heat until soft.
5. Add onion; cook slightly. Add tomatoes, then mussels.
6. Cover pan and continue cooking, shaking the pan from time to time, until mussels open.
7. In pan in which chicken was cooked, fry rice a few minutes in remaining olive oil, stirring constantly.
8. Add 4 cups boiling salted water and stir.
9. Combine chicken and squid-onion-tomato-mussel mixture with rice and water. Cook until rice is almost tender.
10. Add peas to mixture. Season with salt.
11. Pound garlic with saffron in a mortar and add to pan. Cook 20 minutes longer.
12. Decorate with pimento strips. Serve at once.

NOTE: Vikki's dish is a form of paella. If desired, substitute shrimp or crab for squid. If desired, use chicken broth in lieu of water.

# Billy Casper

"I feel great. My diet's made a big difference in my golf game, and the rewards are clearly evident," said well-tanned Billy Casper. If the way to success in professional golf is through the stomach, then Casper, many times the PGA Golfer of the Year, has a unique answer to the big pay-off. "My whole eating procedure has given me stamina, helped me lose weight and avoid illness (referring to his many allergies)," he declared while sitting in the living room of his spacious 22-room California mansion.

Although Billy gets a lot of ribbing about his exotic diet and is often accused of being a kind of food nut – he eats such off-beat meats as mooseburger or bear pot roast – he said, "I'm not really offended. It's only a scientifically proven method to improve your health." He was referring to the non-allergy diet prescribed by a Chicago allergist and internist. Billy learned that most allergies are caused by the foods you eat or the clothing you wear, the furniture you sit on or the air you breathe. His allergies included eggs, wheat, citrus, beans, lamb, chocolate, chicken, butter, apples and a long list of other foods. He later discovered he was sensitive to certain chemical and petroleum products, a problem which he shares with his wife and children.

Therefore, the Caspers have no foam rubber, plastics or gas heat in their house. Billy's wizard chef wife, Shirley, explained, "We do primary cooking, using three or four foods per meal. Each week we receive crated boxes of frozen meat (elk, buffalo, bear, venison and rabbit) from Chicago. We've often read about our fondness for hippopotamus in the newspaper. Actually, we've only had it once!"

# Billy Casper's Fried Rabbit

Serves 4-6

2 cleaned young rabbits,
weighing about
1½ to 2 lbs. each
arrowroot flour

salt
freshly ground black pepper
safflower oil or
sesame seed oil

*fines herbes*

1. *Cut rabbits into serving pieces; place in paper bag with arrowroot flour, fines herbes, salt and pepper.*
2. *Close bag; shake vigorously until pieces are well coated.*
3. *Pour oil into stainless steel skillet or electric frying pan to ½-inch depth. Heat oil until sizzling.*
4. *Cook rabbit in oil, browning on all sides.*
5. *Finish by roasting to crispen in preheated 325° F. oven 20 minutes, or until tender.*

NOTE: *Fines herbes are finely chopped herbs, such as parsley, chives, tarragon, and thyme.*

# Tina Cristiani

"We were famous for our cook house!" said Tina Cristiani of the famed circus family. "In fact, if the pay was the same and it came to an act's making a decision between our circus or another show, we often got the act after they'd checked out our cook house. Our family, being Italian, set a really great table! My grandmother cooked every day and always had special olives and hors d'oeuvres on the table."

Originally, the Ringling Brothers Circus brought the Cristianis to the U.S. Later, the family owned and operated its own circus and toured the country. At that time, dinner under the big top was surprisingly formal: the tables covered with sparkling linens and the men required to wear jackets at dinner.

"We always had soup every day: minestrone, lentil or bean," recalled Tina. "My mother prepared a lot of chicken and veal dishes. When I was growing up in Sarasota, I remember my father going hunting and bringing home pigeon and quail. Mother would spread the cavities of the quail with butter and rosemary, and roast them. I cooked quail the same way recently. I spent $20 for four little birds I got in a small shop on Madison Avenue. But they were so delicious, it was worth it!"

# Tina Cristiani's Wine-Smothered Quail

Serves 2

2 large quail, picked,
  drawn and cleaned
salt to taste
freshly ground black
  pepper to taste

dried rosemary
2-3 tbsps. sweet butter,
  melted
2-3 tbsps. top-grade
  olive oil

about ½ cup dry red wine

1. *Wash and dry birds; truss by tying them with string.*
2. *Rub cavities with salt, pepper and rosemary. Rub inside and outside liberally with butter and olive oil.*
3. *Brown quickly in heavy skillet.*
4. *Add wine, reduce heat, and cook until birds are tender.*
5. *Serve with Tina's green salad (Romaine, bacon bits and Roquefort dressing) and good red wine.*

NOTE: *Allow 1 bird per person, more if birds are small. Squab may be substituted if quail is not available. Quail can also be oven-roasted: place in preheated 450° F. oven 5 minutes, reduce oven temperature to 325° F., roast 15-20 minutes longer, depending on size of the bird. Baste frequently with a wine-butter-olive oil sauce.*

# Perry Como

Perry Como and his wife, Roselle, enjoy good food at home with friends or family. "My wife is always messing around in the kitchen, trying out new dishes," said the affable singer. "She is particularly fond of Chinese food. She has a wok and even put in gas because she prefers to cook with gas.

"I'm not much of a cook. I can burn a steak like the next guy. I used to think about those people who cooked steaks to order and put little flags in the steak saying, 'rare,' 'medium,' or 'well-done.' Mine always came out the same way!

"I'm particularly fond of Roselle's way with Chinese vegetables. We get a lot of wonderful home-grown vegetables in Florida, like celery and scallions. She cooks them in a wonderful Chinese dish called Moo Goo Gai Pan. It's terrific!"

# Moo Goo Gai Pan, House of Perry Como

Serves 4

½ lb. fresh mushrooms
1 partially frozen chicken
   breast, skinned, split
   and boned
1 egg white, lightly beaten
1 tbsp. cornstarch
1 tbsp. dry sherry
1 tsp. salt
⅛ tsp. ground white pepper
4 tbsps. vegetable oil

2½ cups celery,
   thinly sliced
1 can (8½ oz.) water
   chestnuts, drained
   and thinly sliced
1 pkg. (6 oz.) frozen snow peas
   or ½ lb. fresh snow peas
½ cup scallions, sliced
½ tsp. garlic, finely minced
2 tsps. soy sauce

½ tsp. sugar (optional)

1. Rinse, pat dry and slice fresh mushrooms; set aside.
2. With Chinese meat cleaver or sharp knife, thinly slice chicken into ¼-inch strips.
3. In a small bowl, combine egg white, cornstarch, sherry, ¼ tsp. of salt and white pepper; blend well.
4. Add chicken, coating well.
5. In a wok or large skillet, heat 2 tbsps. of vegetable oil. Add mushrooms, celery, water chestnuts, snow peas and remaining salt; sauté 5 minutes.
6. Remove vegetables from wok; reserve.
7. Heat remaining 2 tbsps. vegetable oil in wok. Add scallions, garlic and chicken; cook over high heat, stir-frying constantly.
8. Stir in soy sauce, sugar and vegetable mixture; cook 2 minutes longer, stirring often.
9. Remove to a heated platter. Serve at once over hot cooked rice.

# Peter Duchin

Pianist Peter Duchin, who hoards old White House menus and mementoes of Russian state dinners in the Stalin era, was tutored in the culinary arts as a boy by Averell Harriman's French chef. Peter then polished off his cookery and piano virtuosity as a student living on a barge in post-war Paris.

The White House menus were collected by his father, the immortal Eddie Duchin. "There are a bunch from dinners that he played," explained Peter. "Mainly, he liked the idea of having them autographed for me by people who were there. My father was a very close friend of Harry Hopkins, who was FDR's Kissinger. Another of his best friends was Averell Harriman, who was in those days working for President Roosevelt. The menus from Moscow, of course, were collected for me by Averell Harriman from dinners he had there with Stalin, Molotov, and other Russian leaders."

The Harrimans raised Peter when his father died and it was in their home that he got the French cooking lessons. The cooking à la barge came when he was studying music at the conservatory in Paris. "Cooking-wise on the barge," Peter said, "we would mostly stew away in large pots, bouillabaisse, pot au feu, coq au vin, the sort of stuff you could just leave there all day while people helped themselves. We didn't have a phone. Friends just came out whether we were docked or floating. I had a piano on the boat and we'd have jam sessions. It was fun. When it rained, we went below and tried to plug up the leaks. I cooked on a little pot-bellied stove. It was a gas! Here in town (New York), I cook less, but I do like cooking game, quail, dove, duck and wild duck very much. I do a wild duck in about eight to ten minutes in a very, very hot oven. My wife, Cheray, is an excellent cook. She can do anything."

# Peter Duchin's Kraut & Pheasant

### Serves 4-6

### For the vegetable mixture

½ tart apple, chopped
1 small onion, chopped
1 tbsp. parsley, chopped

1 rib celery, diced
½ green pepper, diced
1 small clove garlic, crushed

*Combine all ingredients in bowl; set aside as stuffing for pheasant.*

### For the pheasants

3 cleaned pheasants, 1½
   to 2 lbs. each
brandy
salt, freshly ground pepper
   and paprika
6 slices bacon
4 juniper berries
6 whole cloves

12 peppercorns
7½ cups undrained
   sauerkraut
2 carrots, peeled and chopped
1 medium onion, peeled
   and sliced
2 tsps. caraway seed
1 cup dairy sour cream

guava jelly

1. *Brush pheasants with brandy; sprinkle with salt, pepper and paprika.*
2. *Stuff pheasants with vegetable mixture and truss birds with heavy thread or skewers.*
3. *Arrange birds, breast-side up, in shallow roasting pan; place 2 strips of bacon lengthwise on each bird.*
4. *Bake in preheated 350° F. oven 25 minutes, or until birds test done, basting occasionally with pan drippings.*
5. *Enclose juniper berries, cloves and peppercorns in a cheesecloth bag. Toss with kraut, carrots, onion and caraway seed together.*
6. *Add kraut mixture with cheesecloth bag to roasting pan about 30 minutes before birds are done.*
7. *Remove pheasants from oven and discard vegetable mixture. Keep warm on serving platter.*
8. *Stir sour cream into kraut mixture; add salt and pepper to taste.*
9. *Return pan to oven; cook about 10 minutes more, or until kraut mixture is hot. Discard cheesecloth bag.*
10. *Serve pheasants and kraut mixture with guava jelly.*

# Gil Gerard

"When I first went to New York, it was a real luxury when my roomate and I could afford to buy a package of hot dogs. I know more ways to cook a hot dog than you can shake a stick at to make them taste better. I broiled, boiled, baked and fried 'em," said TV's Buck Rogers, actor Gil Gerard, as we talked in the posh outdoor setting of the Toluca Lake Tennis Club.

Gil started cooking as a youngster after he had visited a friend in his hometown of Little Rock, Arkansas. "I must have been in the fourth grade," he recalled. "I thought it was just great my friend could cook for himself. My father urged me to try my hand at the stove, but insisted that I had to eat everything I cooked whether I liked it or not. I started with scrambled eggs and then began to experiment by adding different ingredients. I learned all about different seasonings. Some things were awfully hard to eat, but I soon learned how to cook.

"I got into *haute cuisine* when I started collecting wines. I suddenly realized that you can't eat hamburgers with fine wines." As he began to learn more about the intricacies of gourmet cooking, Gil became quite adept at making something as elaborate as *Supremes de Volaille* (breasts of chicken with brown sauce) or Fillet of Sole with White Sauce.

"I've even tried baking bread," said Gil. "When I came to California, my whole diet changed. I've gone from *haute cuisine* and drinking wines to a diet of seafood and stir-fry vegetables."

# Gil Gerard's Chicken Breasts with Brown Sauce

Serves 4

## For the chicken breasts

4 boneless chicken breasts
few drops lemon juice
¼ tsp. salt

freshly ground black pepper
flour
½ cup clarified butter*

1. Sprinkle breasts with lemon juice, then salt and pepper. Roll them in flour; shake off excess flour.
2. Pour clarified butter into large skillet to ¹⁄₁₆-inch depth. Heat butter over medium heat until it begins to turn color slightly.
3. Add chicken breasts and sauté about 3 minutes on each side, regulating heat so butter never turns more than a deep yellow.
4. Press tops of breasts with fingers to see if they are done (springy to the touch).
5. Remove to heated platter, leaving butter in the skillet.

## For the brown sauce

¼ cup clarified butter*
3-4 tbsps. parsley, minced
1 tbsp. fresh lemon juice

salt to taste
freshly ground pepper
to taste

1. Add additional clarified butter to chicken skillet; heat over moderate heat until butter turns light golden brown.
2. Remove skillet from heat; stir in parsley, lemon juice, salt and pepper to taste.
3. Pour over hot chicken breasts. Serve at once. Delicious with butter-browned mushrooms, asparagus tips, artichoke hearts or creamed spinach.

NOTE: *Clarified butter is made by heating butter in a saucepan over moderate heat. When butter has melted, skim off the foam and strain off the clear yellow liquid, leaving milky residue in bottom of pan. Use residue to season soups and sauces.

# Lee Grant

"My old man, (Joe Feury) gets more turned on by food than women! In fact, when he sees eggplant Parmesan or artichokes vinaigrette, his eyes glaze over, his pulse quickens in the same way I've seen men look at beautiful women!" laughed actress extraordinaire Lee Grant.

"I must say Joey has a relationship to food. He always worries, no matter how much I cook, there won't be enough to go around. He was brought up by an Italian mother (Rachel Fioretti) who made 24 pork chops for breakfast. It's amazing he's not five-by-five! When I cook, it's usually a family affair. Joey and I often prepare a chicken dish together. He chops the vegetables; I sauté the chicken so it won't have to cook all day long. You see, I'm really a great pretender. I'll go along so far and start tossing in things. People think I know how to cook. What they don't know is, if I get in a jam, I simply call in one or two of my friends who come to my rescue. Somehow, it always turns out all right!"

# Lee Grant's Chicken Malibu

### Serves 12

2 broiler-fryer chickens,
  each cut in 8 pieces
8 chicken wings
about ½ cup olive oil
2 onions, peeled and chopped
2 large green peppers,
  chopped
1 large clove garlic,
  pressed
2 carrots, peeled and grated
½ lb. mushrooms, sliced

2-3 tbsps. butter
about 2 tsps. salt
¼ tsp. white pepper
2-3 tsps. curry powder
2-3 tbsps. parsley, chopped
2 cans (10½ ozs. each) undiluted
  chicken stock
2 bay leaves
pinch of thyme
flour to thicken
hot cooked rice

1. *Wash chicken parts, pat dry with paper towels.*
2. *Heat oil in large skillet or Dutch oven; brown chicken quickly on both sides; remove to drain on paper towels.*
3. *Add onion, green pepper, garlic and carrot to pan drippings; sauté vegetables until limp, stirring over low heat.*
4. *Cook mushrooms slowly in butter in another skillet, adding salt, white pepper and curry, until mushrooms are brown and seasonings are well blended.*
5. *Add mushroom-curry mixture to skillet along with chicken. Add parsley and chicken stock, enough to cover vegetables and chicken pieces, adding bay leaves and thyme, more water if necessary.*
6. *Cover; cook in preheated 350° F. oven 40 minutes, or until chicken is tender.*
7. *Remove from oven; cool to room temperature.*
8. *Refrigerate until fat congeals on top. Remove and discard fat.*
9. *Make gravy, using flour dissolved in a little chicken stock to form smooth paste before adding to main pot.*
10. *Reheat chicken, stirring to smooth and thicken gravy. Taste to correct seasonings. Serve over hot cooked rice.*

*NOTE: Lee advises, "For a frivolous touch, serve over hot cooked brown and white rice! Garnish with butter-browned slivered almonds or pine nuts and candied kumquats. Your guests will think you've been cooking all day!"*

# Germaine Greer

"Cooking should be spontaneous, not just an activity to feed people. You should be able to offer people things that you've made with pride and imagination. There's no dignity in serving up a TV dinner," said Germaine Greer, an amazon-sized girl, stretched out on her bed, barely able to talk after a gross reaction to American food and a horrendous publicity tour in behalf of her best selling book, *The Female Eunuch*.

"At home, my diet's more or less microbiotic (the Oriental philosophy for true health and happiness calls for a balance between the Yin – all food in the primary sense – and the Yang – man). I eat fish. I can't eat chicken. In any case, the meat's less contaminated there (England) than here. I simply can't eat American meat. In fact, I think that's why I'm ill. Last night I ate some veal. Your meats have so many steroids. I'm probably more of a cook than the average American housewife, because, to me, cooking's not using packaged foods or contaminated ones. Organic foods, yes, which means I have to buy expensive brown rice and cook that for hours on end."

Germaine often feeds, as well as teaches, her students. "I prepare things like pigeons simply because that's all I could afford on my $50-a-week salary! Or sometimes a friend brings me a rabbit to cook." She noted there are probably 600 ways to cook the tiny pigeon. Germaine's recipe – as interesting as the lady herself – follows with one minor change: squab (young pigeons) have been substituted for pigeons, which were not available to test due to the mating season!

# Germaine Greer's Potted Squabs with Olives

Serves 6

6 squabs or pigeons
⅓ cup olive oil
½ cup onion, chopped
1 can (14 oz.) Italian tomatoes or 5-6 plum tomatoes, crushed

¾ tsp. salt
⅛ tsp. freshly ground black pepper
⅓ cup green pepper, diced
1 cup whole pimento-stuffed olives

rice Pilaf

1. Brown squabs in olive oil in Dutch oven.
2. Pour off all but 2 tbsps. of the drippings; reserve drippings.
3. Add onion and cook until tender, stirring often.
4. Stir in tomatoes, salt and pepper; spoon mixture over squabs.
5. Cover and simmer about 1 hour and 10 minutes, or until birds are tender. Spoon tomato mixture over squabs occasionally during cooking.
6. About 15 minutes before end of cooking time, add green pepper and olives to Dutch oven.
7. Serve squabs with rice Pilaf.

## Rice Pilaf

¾ cup onion
1 clove garlic, pressed
¼ cup pan drippings or margarine

1¼ cups rice, uncooked
2½ cups chicken broth (or wine)
salt to taste

freshly ground black pepper to taste

1. Sauté onion and garlic in pan drippings until onion is limp.
2. Add rice; cook until rice turns golden, stirring often.
3. Add chicken broth. Cover and simmer until rice is tender, stirring occasionally.
4. Add salt and pepper to taste.

NOTE: Pigeons are more easily available in England, but can be found in limited supply in the United States. Squabs require shorter cooking time than pigeons.

# Edith Head

"I don't think I'm the greatest designer in the world, but I AM one of the greatest cooks," said Academy Award winner costume designer Edith Head. Edith approaches food with flair and gaiety. She likes to show off at home, cooking up a storm in the pretty kitchen of her ranch-style Beverly Hills home.

Dressed in a lemon-bright hostess gown of her own design, Edith was in the throes of preparing a buffet dinner for six. She "designs" food the same way she designs clothes or furnishes her home. "I know how to make clothes look any way I want by the way I trim them. I can do the same thing with food." She has continued to adjust her menus to keep pace with her changing lifestyle. "I can't make rules for other people. Your menus are influenced by your budget, your family size and your husband's interests. I happen to think food is one of the most important things in the world. Eating attractively served meals is not only good for you physically, it's good for you mentally too! As a designer, I suppose I am more interested in the visual effect of food than most people. I love to decorate food. Even when we have something as simple as scrambled eggs, I always add a garnish of chopped parsley or chives. The only person who doesn't get any is the cat, who doesn't care for parsley!"

# Edith Head's Chicken Casa Ladera

### Serves 6-8

2 broiler-fryers, cut in
  serving pieces
1 tsp. salt
1/4 tsp. freshly ground black
  pepper
1/4 tsp. paprika
about 1/2 cup butter
  or margarine

1/2 lb. fresh mushrooms,
  chopped
about 1/3 cup flour
2 cups chicken stock (homemade or canned)
1/2 cup pitted black olives
3 tbsps. dry sherry
1 tbsp. chives, chopped

1. Season chicken pieces well with salt, pepper and paprika, and sauté in melted butter until golden brown on all sides.
2. Cover and cook until tender.
3. When chicken is done, remove from pan to heated platter.
4. Sauté mushrooms in pan drippings; then lift mushrooms out.
5. Stir flour into pan drippings and cook, stirring, over low heat, about 2 minutes.
6. Gradually stir in chicken stock, stirring and cooking over high heat until sauce is thickened and smooth.
7. Add olives, sherry and mushrooms; cook, stirring, 5 minutes.
8. Taste to correct seasonings.
9. Pour sauce over hot chicken and garnish with chives. Wonderful alone, or served with rice.

# Barbara Howar

"Cooking is my passion! I do it instead of boozing or beating children. It relaxes me and gives vent to my frustrations, ego and undisciplined gluttony," confided Barbara Howar, a Southern lady with many labels: "President Johnson's super social hostess" (until he fired her), "intimate of Washington's most powerful cliques," "erstwhile television personality," and "Peck's bad girl."

Barbara is brutally honest, funny, and remarkably perceptive, particularly in what she reveals about herself. "I don't cook by recipes, and I find it more fun to fool around with ingredients than to play culinary chemist with the fruits of someone else's imagination."

When Barbara invites people, usually eight, to dinner, she explained, "We always eat in the kitchen. I stick everything in the middle of the table and everyone helps himself. I never have any help so I do all the cooking, something that's easy. It's always on one platter and if I'm really lazy, I'll spring for steaks, but I can almost take someone out to dinner cheaper than I can buy steak. I love big wine glasses, candles and good Bordeaux wine. So entertaining is easy.

"All I care about in this world are my two children, the dog and myself. And that's to see that we don't starve or have to go on public relief." The success of Barbara's books (her first was *Laughing All the Way*) indicates she'll have no trouble staying off the relief rolls for some time to come.

# Barbara Howar's Chicken and Pasta

Serves 6-8

1 lb. small link sausages
6 chicken thighs and 6 boned
  chicken breasts, split
  (or about 5 lbs. chicken
  parts)
1 large onion, peeled
  and cut into rings
2 large green peppers,
  cut into strips
½ lb. fresh mushrooms,
  sliced

1 can (8½ ozs.)
  water chestnuts,
  drained and sliced
1 clove garlic, minced
about 2 tbsps. salt
¼ tsp. freshly ground
  black pepper
2-3 drops Tabasco sauce
12 ozs. linguini
4-5 quarts boiling water
¼ cup butter

1. Brown sausages in very large skillet or Dutch oven.
2. Remove sausages with slotted spoon and set aside.
3. Fry chicken in sausage drippings until browned on all sides. Cover skillet; cook chicken for about 25 minutes, or until tender.
4. Pour off and discard all but about 2 tbsps. of the pan drippings.
5. Move chicken to side of skillet; add onion, green peppers, mushrooms, water chestnuts, garlic, 1 tsp. salt, pepper and Tabasco. Toss vegetables to mix.
6. Fry about 5 minutes, uncovered, or until vegetables are tender, stirring occasionally.
7. Add reserved sausages; cook until ingredients are hot.
8. About 15 minutes before chicken-vegetable mixture is done, bring the 4-5 quarts of water to a rapid boil. Gradually add linguini and about 1½ tbsps. salt to water. Cook, uncovered, stirring occasionally, until tender.
9. Drain linguini in colander; toss with butter; add salt and pepper to taste.
10. Place linguini on serving platter; top with chicken-vegetable mixture.

# Rock Hudson

"Years ago, whenever I was interviewed, people would ask me if I cooked," said actor Rock Hudson. "I'd always just say, 'Yes.' Back then, I didn't really know how to do an interview. I didn't know I was expected to expound on a given question! I was expected to be rather shy about it, too! The truth is, I really did used to cook! But now I'm out of practice. Last week, I cooked a steak and corn on the cob. The steak was charred and the corn was underdone!"

Rock is easygoing, charming and casually comfortable in blue jeans. "I have a very good houseman, Peter," he explained. "Boy, can he cook!" Recently, Rock honored Nancy Walker at a special birthday dinner. "Peter made a birthday cake of pâté. He wrote 'Happy Birthday, Nancy,' in mayonnaise!"

Rock enjoys nothing more than a evening of bridge with his friends. He likes to serve a simple menu, including a hearty stew or delicious beef stroganoff. Over the years, his formula for a successful party has not changed: "Lots of good food, music and plenty of good booze. A lot of people hide their good liquor when they entertain and bring on the supermarket special Scotch. Frankly, I find that offensive. It's an insult to your guests. Most people don't know the difference, and generally I can't tell either. It's the idea that offends me!"

# Rock Hudson's Chicken Casserole Dinner

### Serves 4-6

¼ cup butter
1½ tbsps. flour
1 cup chicken broth
1 cup milk
½ tsp. paprika
salt to taste
freshly ground pepper
  to taste
1 cup mushroom caps,
  sliced

2½ cups cooked chicken,
  diced
½ pkg. (10 oz.) frozen
  petit pois,
  lightly cooked
1 cup cooked noodles
1 tbsp. sherry
⅓ cup breadcrumbs
1 tsp. sweet butter, softened

1. *Melt half the butter in skillet; gradually stir in flour. Cook over low heat, stirring.*
2. *Gradually stir in chicken broth, milk, paprika, salt and pepper; cook over low heat about 10 minutes until thickened.*
3. *Sauté mushrooms lightly in remaining butter in separate skillet.*
4. *Add to cream sauce with chicken, drained petit pois, noodles and sherry.*
5. *Place in well-greased casserole; top with breadcrumbs and dot with butter.*
6. *Bake 30 minutes in preheated 350° F. oven.*
7. *Serve at once, alone, or with tossed green or wilted lettuce salad.*

# Brian Keith

"We love good food and we're always dieting!" said burly 6-footer Brian Keith in his New York hotel suite. "Why, I can walk by a good restaurant and gain two pounds. We starve ourselves all week and gorge on the weekends. We try to stick to meat and fish. But when we make spaghetti, it's literally a two-day deal. In fact, we wallow in spaghetti!" Keith's colorful talk is in keeping with the rugged outdoorsman he so frequently portrays on the screen.

"For years, we've fixed a roast suckling pig for New Year's Eve," Brian said. "We cook up some corn bread for the stuffing and let it stale up. It takes a lot of stuffing because that's a hell of a cavern to fill. We like to serve the pig with a few side dishes, applesauce, a relish platter and some pine nuts. We rarely have any meat left, and the skin goes first, it's so crisp, it's great!" he said, smacking his lips.

The actor's fondness for food began during his service days as a Marine gunner in the Pacific. "If there was any food to be found on the islands, especially meat, I'd find it," he said. "Once I found a sheep. I can remember running through the jungle carrying an axe in one hand with the hind quarters draped over my shoulders. I didn't know what to do with the meat, but I built a fire and cut the mutton into hunks and strung it over a bayonet. I devised a makeshift spit to roast the meat. I broke into a tent and stole a gallon of catsup and mixed it with some dehydrated onion to make the sauce. When I'd lathered the meat with it, the smell began to waft into the air. Pretty soon the guys came out of a deep sleep."

# Brian Keith's Good Chicken Gus

### Serves 2-3

1 cleaned small chicken,
  weighing about 3 lbs.
salt to taste
freshly ground pepper
  to taste

2 tbsps. sweet butter
2 tbsps. olive oil
1 clove garlic, pressed
¾ cup parsley, chopped
¾ cup dry sauterne

1. *Cut chicken into 8 serving pieces. Season liberally with salt and pepper.*
2. *Melt butter and olive oil in a heavy skillet over low heat.*
3. *Add garlic and seasoned chicken pieces. Cook, uncovered, over low heat, turning chicken pieces with tongs until chicken is fork tender.*
4. *Remove pieces to a heated casserole.*
5. *Add chopped parsley and sauterne to the skillet. Cover and boil 1 minute.*
6. *Pour pan drippings over chicken in casserole. Serve alone or with crusty garlic bread and a crisp mixed green salad.*

# Cheryl Ladd

Cheryl Ladd, one of "Charlie's Angels," was seated in her pretty living room, dressed in blue jeans and a tank top. She's married to actor David Ladd, son of the late Alan Ladd. They have a young daughter named Jordan, a tiny blonde duplicate of her mother.

Cheryl's hung up on chocolate, especially candy bars. "It's terrible, but I can't help it!" she exclaimed. "I had so few when I was a child. Kate (Jackson) and Jackie (Smith) are very much into health foods, and every now and then I promise I'm going to be good to myself and eat healthily, too.

"I always thought my mother was a wonderful cook — not that I don't think she is now, but in South Dakota, the most exotic thing around is French fried shrimp! We had the traditional Midwestern diet of meat, potatoes and vegetables — but it was awfully good!"

Cheryl's father is a hunter, and he always brought home wild pheasants in the fall. "If you want to eat something wonderful, you must have wild pheasant burgers! They're fantastic!" she exclaimed.

Cheryl led the way to her backyard pool and barbecue area. "This old stove," she said, "is my pride and joy. It came out of Sue's store." Susan Ladd, David's mother, operates the Alan Ladd Hardware and Gift Store in Palm Springs. "She has hammers and nails, but also beautiful china and silver. She got some stoves from the Antique Guild and this is one of them. I use it for barbecuing."

# Cheryl Ladd's Pheasant Burgers

Serves 6

1 small onion, peeled and minced
1½ lbs. ground pheasant

½ lb. pork sausage
salt to taste

freshly ground black pepper to taste

1. *Combine all ingredients. Mix well and shape with fingers into 6 patties.*
2. *Broil over coals in outdoor barbecue or broil indoors, turning once. Cook until meat is no longer pink, but do not overcook.*
3. *Serve piping hot, alone, or with mashed potatoes, a green vegetable, applesauce or apple butter.*

NOTE: *If you don't have a hunter in your family, subsitute ground turkey for pheasant. If desired, add more seasoning, such as a hint of ground sage, to suit your palate. Normally, however, the seasoning in the sausage is enough to flavor the burgers.*

# Linda Lavin &
# Ron Leibman

Actress Linda Lavin of CBS's "Alice" and her actor husband Ron Leibman have eclectic, if not "liberated," food styles. They both like dining very privately at home à deux or en masse whenever the place, mood or occasion moves them.

"Sure, I can cook – pork chops and onions," said Ron. "But do you call that cooking? Linda's a very good cook. Last night she was working, so I didn't bother to go out. Instead of eating ice cream, like I usually do when I feel like a bachelor, I made some swordfish steak. I just threw the fish in a pan with some butter and lemon and had swordfish steak with corn on the cob!" Ron is proud of Linda's talent, as well as her flair in the kitchen.

The dark-eyed actress talked about how her husband's feelings tie in with their entertaining. "I really love to entertain, and I love to cook, so it's really no big deal. But Ron doesn't expect it from me. He's genuinely pleased when I do it because he's a delightful person to live with. If I say, 'Let's have a party,' and if he wants to, we do. But if it's his idea and I just can't cut it, we work things out. We've done a different kind of entertaining in California than we did in New York, because, obviously, we have more room. That is, after we moved into a lovely big house in Beverly Hills from the beach house. It started a whole new life for me: I got a caterer who was a butler and a bartender. I really began to employ people to do a party for me, and we both love that!"

# Linda Lavin's Hoo-Ha Chicken

### Serves 2-3

broiler-fryer chicken,
   cut into 8 pieces
1 cup Rose's lime juice
½ tsp. grated lime rind

1 cup dry vermouth
3 cloves garlic, crushed
salt to taste
freshly ground black pepper
   to taste

1. Combine lime juice, lime rind, vermouth, garlic, salt and pepper for marinade. Marinate chicken in it for several hours or overnight, turning often.
2. Grill over charcoal, or oven-fry by placing chicken pieces in shallow baking dish lined with aluminum foil and bake in preheated 350° F. oven 35 minutes, or until tender. Baste several times while chicken is baking.
3. Serve with huge tossed salad made with as many garden-fresh vegetables as you can find. Make a dressing with freshly-squeezed lime, cracked pepper and salt.

# Johnny Mathis

Singer Johnny Mathis likes to cook so much, he even does his own cooking when he's on tour. "Virginia ham and grits are staples in my house," he said.

When Johnny goes to the kitchen for a bite to eat, he doesn't just fix a sandwich or heat up whatever's around. "I usually end up making sukiyaki, chili or wild duck and rice, always enough for any friends who might drop by!" He enjoys entertaining at home since he has finally settled down in a place of his own in the Hollywood Hills. His one-bedroom house, which was built by Howard Hughes for Jean Harlow, is one of the few in Hollywood with an inside swimming pool. The kitchen has been enlarged, modernized to Johnny's exact specifications, and filled with all the latest cooking gadgets.

"Since I love to cook and entertain at home, I needed a kitchen designed to make the cooking part as easy as possible – and also large enough to accommodate my guests so I wouldn't be stuck in the kitchen by myself," he said with a laugh.

One of Johnny's standby menus includes roast duck and wild rice, mustard greens and an elegant apricot dessert.

# Johnny Mathis's Wild Duck

Serves 2-3

2½-3 lbs. wild duck
salt to taste
freshly ground black
  pepper to taste

1 sweet green pepper, sliced
2 stalks celery, chopped
3 cups water

½ cup yellow onion, chopped

1. *Rinse and pat-dry duck.*
2. *Rub inside and out with salt and pepper.*
3. *Place breast-side up on rack in roasting pan. Add remaining ingredients to pan.*
4. *Cover and bake in preheated 375° F. oven for about 45 minutes, or until duck is tender. Baste occasionally with pan juice.*
5. *Serve alone or on bed of hot, cooked wild rice.*

NOTE: *If desired, duck can be filled with chopped apple or onion, celery and carrot mixed with poultry seasoning to reduce the "wild" flavor.*

# Paula Prentiss & Dick Benjamin

"Paula has an insane interest in food and excels in the kitchen. Her biggest failing, though, is not having any dinner left for me. She eats up everything as soon as she cooks it. And then she says, 'I had some wonderful carrots, but – ,'" deadpan actor Dick Benjamin said, kidding his actress wife, Paula Prentiss.

"After I've eaten Dick's dinner, I either have to go out and shop for more food or I spread the food out thinly on the plate," leggy, lovely Paula said, settling in a sofa. "I haunt specialty shops selling imported cookware; I collect cookbooks and food catalogues. I started cooking when Dick was touring in 'The Odd Couple.' We had a kitchenette apartment in Chicago."

"But you first cooked for me when we were in school," Dick interjected. The pair met when both were students at Northwestern University and they married in 1961. "Whatever happened to that thing-a-ma-jig, what do you call it?"

"You mean the electric cooker that belonged to my mother. It must have been over 50 years old. It was like a hot plate, but there was a place to cook a waffle and broil a steak underneath," Paula said.

"If anyone made something like that now, it would be fabulous," said Dick.

Dick's favorite tuna fish salad sandwiches are "the kind you make with chopped apples, celery, sweet pickles, you know, the works. Shortly after we were married, I asked Paula to fix me one. She threw everything into a blender. What she brought me was unbelievable: two slices of bread floating on something grey! If you let that gadget go a couple of seconds too long, it completely wipes out the food," he said, laughing.

But Paula is a talented cook now and dreams up everything from cassoulets that take her two days to her favorite chicken dishes. "I don't like red meats particularly," she said, "but I thrive on chicken and fish dishes."

# Paula Prentiss's Chicken Sweet and Sour

## Serves 3-4

3½ lb. broiler-fryer
  chicken, cut in 8 pieces
salt to taste
freshly ground pepper
  to taste
2 tbsps. sweet butter
2 tbsps. olive oil
2 tbsps. Grand Marnier or
  Cointreau

1½ cups fresh
  orange juice
  (strained)
½ cup water
pinch ground cinnamon
pinch ground cloves
14 drops Tabasco sauce
½ tsp. salt
cooked rice

3 tbsps. toasted slivered almonds or pine nuts

1. *Wash chicken parts and dry carefully; sprinkle sparingly with salt and pepper.*
2. *Heat butter and olive oil in large skillet or electric frying pan until sizzling.*
3. *Place chicken, skin-side down, in skillet; cook over medium heat until chicken is golden on all sides.*
4. *Remove chicken to another pan; pour warmed Grand Marnier over chicken; ignite.*
5. *Discard half the fat in skillet, then brown the almonds over low heat, shaking pan to prevent burning; remove almonds.*
6. *Add orange juice, stirring to clean pan.*
7. *Add water, cinnamon, cloves, Tabasco and salt, stirring.*
8. *Add chicken and nuts to sauce; cover and cook over low heat until chicken is fork-tender.*
9. *Uncover and remove chicken to heated platter.*
10. *Reduce sauce slightly, cooking over low heat, stirring.*
11. *Taste to correct seasonings.*
12. *Serve with fluffy cooked white rice; spoon sauce over chicken and rice. Serve alone or with broccoli spears flavored with lemon-butter, endive salad, and chilled white wine (Chablis, Pouilly Fumé or California Pinot Blanc).*

# Vincent Price & Coral Browne

Movie badman Vincent Price and his wife, Australian actress Coral Browne, are avid gourmets with diverse views about food preparation. "I detest cooking," Coral admitted. "It makes me very nervous because I'm a perfectionist, whereas Vinnie does it so easily. He has a beautiful time in the kitchen."

In person, the tall actor is so charming and witty, it's hard to believe he's the same man who's earned the nickname, "Merchant of Menace" for his stunning performances in horror pictures. "The kitchen is the heart of the home," he said. "The room should be 100 percent useful. A friend of mine recently spent $20,000 on his kitchen, and he's never in it!"

The Prices' kitchen is a pretty room with a bright handwoven rug on the floor, stainless steel counters, and both gas and electric white enamel appliances. Both like gadgets. Vince is particularly fond of using his Cuisinart; Coral prefers to chop by hand with a knife or scissors.

Coral said, "I gave him a spaghetti-making machine and a wok. He must have 575 chicken recipes," she said, laughing.

"People who come to our house for dinner joke about always getting chicken," Vince said. "We adore roast chicken stuffed with rosemary."

The Prices have herbs growing in pots, indoors and in a small herb garden outdoors. "What was that marvelous thing you cooked several weeks ago with seafood?" Coral asked Vince. "It was divine!"

"Gumbo made with scallops and shrimp," Vince answered. "I also use chicken breasts. I sauté each component of the gumbo in a different flavor. For example, I cook chicken in shallot-butter; shrimps in butter and garlic. Sometimes I add some thyme."

# Vincent Price's Chicken and Seafood Gumbo

### Serves 6-8

2 medium white onions,
  peeled
1 large stalk celery
  with leaves
½ cup fresh parsley
2 cloves garlic, peeled
1 stick sweet butter
  (more if needed)
2 shallots, peeled
  and minced
3 lbs. boneless chicken
  breasts
½ tsp. thyme

1½ lbs. medium-size frozen
  shrimp, thawed
1 lb. scallops
1 can (16 ozs.) tomatoes
1 can (7½ ozs.) salsa
2 cups chicken stock,
  canned or homemade
1 pkg. frozen whole okra,
  thawed, or 2 cups fresh
  diced okra
salt to taste
freshly ground black
  pepper to taste

1.  *Put onion, celery, parsley and 1 clove garlic through Cuisinart or chop.*
2.  *Cook onion, celery, parsley and garlic together in 4 tbsps. butter until vegetables are tender; set aside.*
3.  *Sauté shallots lightly in 2 tbsps. butter in separate skillet; lift out shallots and reserve.*
4.  *Brown chicken breasts on both sides in shallot butter. Cool chicken and cut into fairly large pieces, preferably same size as scallops.*
5.  *Melt 2-3 tbsps. butter in separate skillet; press remaining garlic in melted butter; add thyme.*
6.  *Sauté shrimp lightly in garlic butter until they begin to turn pink; lift out.*
7.  *Lightly brown scallops in remaining butter; set aside.*
8.  *Combine onion-parsley mixture with tomatoes, salsa and chicken stock; simmer over low heat, uncovered, until flavors "marry" and volume is slightly reduced.*
9.  *Thirty minutes before serving, reheat tomato-vegetable stock with chicken. Add okra and seafood; cook 5 to 8 minutes before serving, making certain gumbo is piping hot.*
10. *Season to taste with salt and pepper. Delicious over hot, steaming rice!*

*NOTE: Vincent advises, "The secret to making a great gumbo is cooking each component separately. I flavor each separately. The dish can be made ahead, then assembled just before serving."*

# Joan Rivers

"My boners in the kitchen become part of my act. Everything, even my cooking, like my whole life, is trouble," says blonde comedienne Joan Rivers. She was seated in the living room of her Beverly Hills home. Joan jokes about the traumas and trials of cooking which harassed her when she first married her movie producer husband, Edgar Rosenberg.

"I cook to please my husband," she started out seriously, but then added, "Somehow, his tastes don't always jibe with mine. For example, after we'd had chicken 14 times, I finally found out he doesn't like it after he put his head down on the table and cried. Now, if God had really intended a girl to cook, he'd have given her aluminum hands.

"My real problem is trying to cook unfamiliar foods. Take cheese fondue, for instance. I never knew what a fondue was. I took it off the flame. And that was a tragic mistake. It congealed and I couldn't get it out of the pan.

"Preparing duckling requires the addition of booze. You have two choices. You can either buy a duck and get it drunk, or give it a good rubdown after it's gone. To make the duck look pretty, I put a rose in its mouth and drape some grapes around it. It literally knocks people out, it looks so pretty," the zany lady said. The fast-chef who doesn't pretend to be a scientific cook finished her list of instructions with, "I turn the dial on the oven to the middle, throw in the duck and pray!"

# Joan Rivers's Roast Flaming Duck

### Serves 4

1 4½-5 lb. duckling,
  fresh or frozen
cut garlic
salt to taste
freshly ground black
  pepper to taste

2 tbsps. honey
1½ tsps. bottled
  browning sauce or
  soy sauce
2 tbsps. lemon juice
⅓ cup Grand Marnier

⅓ cup strained orange marmalade

1. *Quarter the duckling, using poultry shears or a sharp knife. Cut bird lengthwise through breastbone and 1 side of backbone. Divide halves just above thighs.*
2. *Rub both sides with garlic, salt and pepper; let stand ½ hour.*
3. *Place pieces, skin side down, on a rack in a roasting pan.*
4. *Spoon over marinade made by mixing together orange marmalade, honey, browning sauce and lemon juice.*
5. *Roast 45 minutes in preheated 325° F. oven, basting once.*
6. *Turn pieces, skin side up. Baste twice with marinade mixed with pan drippings.*
7. *Roast about 45 minutes longer, or until drumstick meat is done.*
8. *Run under broiler to crispen skin.*
9. *Remove duck to a heated platter. Put pieces together with toothpicks to form whole duck.*
10. *Heat Grand Marnier, pour over duck and ignite.*
11. *Mound steamed rice around duck. Garnish with a rose for the head and grapes on the side. Serve at once.*
12. *A delicious sauce can be made from pan drippings. Skim off excess fat before adding flour and water mixture to thicken. Cook over low heat, stirring until thick and smooth. Season with salt and pepper to taste.*

*NOTE: If desired, duck can be roasted whole. Marinate longer at room temperature, then roast in slow oven, 325° F., for 3 hours, or until drumstick meat is tender. It's important to drain off excess fat before making gravy or sauce. Do not overcook bird or duckling will be tough and dry. A pair of ducklings served in a bed of hot rice and garnished with pineapple rings and watercress will provide great company fare!*

# Isabel Sanford

"When I watched myself on the tube, I saw my behind following me about 10 minutes later," actress Isabel Sanford said with a roar of laughter. Isabel is a charming and glarmorous woman, quite unlike Louise Jefferson, the homey, lady-of-the-house character she portrays in the CBS-TV series, "The Jeffersons."

"I was unhappy about myself because I was just plain too fat," she explained. "Then, I found myself with a four-month hiatus away from my work and nothing to do. I thought, 'Why not try to improve myself?' I'd been to reducing salons, but it never worked. Imagine being part of a group of big, fat women sitting around on the floor and trying to pull their big toes up to their faces, just like the tiny little thing who's instructing them! I'd just break out in a sweat and think, 'What am I doing here?'

"As for dieting, I used to manage to drop a few pounds whenever I took a good look in the mirror and realized there was nothing there but fat, fat, fat! I'd cut down for a while and eat salads, but I'd always gain right back whatever weight I lost. I've tried different diets. One called for grapefruit three times a day. That made my face break out and I ended up running to the dermatologist. Now I'm on my own diet. I don't eat unless I'm hungry and I try to eat only one meal a day, with plenty of vegetables and fruit and protein."

The results of Isabel's concentrated efforts have been gratifying. "I've learned how to cook chicken in a crock pot. I'm not the greatest cook in the world, but I manage."

# Isabel Sanford's "Crocked" Chicken

Serves 3-4

1 whole broiler-fryer chicken,
  cleaned and dressed,
  weighing about 3½ lbs.
salt to taste
freshly ground black
  pepper to taste
2-3 carrots, peeled and cut in
  large pieces

2 stalks celery, chopped
1 medium onion, chopped
2-3 tbsps. parsley, chopped
1 bay leaf
½ cup liquid: water or
  white wine or
  water flavored with
  1 chicken bouillon cube

1½ tbsps. salad oil

1. Tie and truss chicken with string or metal skewers.
2. Season outside well with salt and pepper.
3. Heat oil in large skillet; brown chicken on all sides.
4. Place vegetables, herbs and liquid in crock pot; top with chicken.
5. Cover and cook on low heat for 6-8 hours.
6. Remove chicken carefully to carve. Serve with vegetables.

NOTE: Dieters thrive on chicken cooked in the crock pot! Skim extra fat that forms on the top. Remove and discard outside skin (it traps hidden fat under the skin as well as containing highly saturated fats). For the "slim" crowd, add a potato or two, or a handful of rice or egg noodles to the crock pot. Leftover chicken cooked in this manner makes a delightful, well-flavored basis for a protein-rich salad supper.

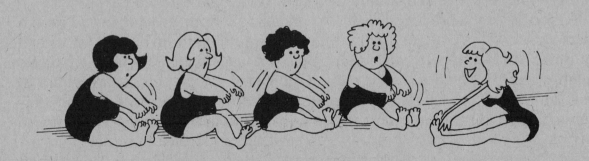

# George Segal

"I'm a lusty eater, but only when the food is good," said actor George Segal. "More than anything in the world, I love clams – Little Neck clams, that is, and baby steamed female lobsters with drawn butter. My father hails from Boston and he taught me to like broiled kippers, scrambled eggs, boiled potatoes, rye bread and sweet butter. And another of his Boston specialties, it's so good it'll make you cry: hot baked beans mixed with bits of salt pork, vinegar, salt and pepper."

George boasts, "I'm very good with eggs." In bartender's lingo, he prepares scrambled eggs by "beating up the eggs, adding a shot of milk, salt and pepper. Serve it with day-old bread. And that's about the extent of my cooking repertoire," he admitted.

His wife, Marion, a former editor with CBS, does most of the cooking. "She does great things with sour cream," said George. "Her specialty is chicken paprika."

The actor, who eats almost anything, "hates spinach, rice and tapioca pudding. I loathe the texture of all those little things in your mouth," he said. "I avoid stews, because most of them are made with gristly meat."

# Marion Segal's Chicken Paprika

Serves 4

1 medium yellow onion, peeled
and cut in large pieces
4 tbsps. olive oil
3½ lb. broiler-fryer
chicken, cut in serving
pieces
2 cups tomato juice

1 pinch oregano
1 large bay leaf
1 pinch marjoram
1½ tsps. paprika
1¼ tsps. salt
½ tsp. freshly
ground pepper

2 cups dairy sour cream

1. Sauté onion in heated oil in a heavy skillet; brown slightly; remove and reserve onion.
2. Brown chicken quickly on all sides in onion-flavored oil.
3. Add onion, tomato juice (enough to cover chicken), oregano, bay leaf, marjoram, paprika, salt and pepper.
4. Cover and simmer 45 minutes, or until chicken is fork-tender.
5. Remove chicken to a heated platter. Reduce sauce ¼ over medium heat, stirring often.
6. Using a wire whisk, add sauce slowly to sour cream in a large mixing bowl; blend until smooth.
7. Return sauce to skillet; add chicken and reheat gently to serve. Do not boil.
8. Serve alone, or with steamed rice.

NOTE: Marion Segal, the creator of her husband's favorite dish, suggests, "Add the sauce to the sour cream carefully to prevent lumping." The Segals team the pièce de resistance with a green vegetable, chilled green salad, crisp Italian bread and fruit for dessert. Their choice of wine: Valpolicella.

# Karen Valentine

"I like to cook a lot. Before I was married, I cooked great lasagna. That was my best dish," said Karen Valentine. ("Everyone thinks Valentine is really a fake name, but it's real.")

"On Thanksgiving – you see I lived on a chicken ranch and I hate poultry because I had so much of it as a child – I made lasagna for Thanksgiving dinner. Now I like to experiment with spices and all that jazz. I just make up things as I go along and never follow a recipe. I just add a little of this, a little of that and it comes out! I cook very simple things because I'm usually dieting, you know – trying to watch my weight.

"I like to cook, especially when I'm having company. Sometimes, I cook when I'm working, but we only have four chairs, so if it's company, it's a sit-down dinner for another couple. I like to eat by candlelight because I look better!" she said impishly. "And I like to fix it. I love to go marketing and pick out great meats. It's crazy that way, but I like doing things myself because it gives me a sense of having done something! Someday I would love to have a house with a brick kitchen with copper pots hanging around."

# Karen Valentine's Marinated Chicken

### Serves 6

2 cleaned broiler-fryer
  chickens, cut into
  serving pieces
1 cup dry sherry
¼ cup salad oil
2 tbsps. parsley flakes
2½ tsps. salt

2 tsps. paprika
1½ tsps. thyme leaves
1½ tsps. basil leaves
1 tsp. tarragon leaves
½ tsp. curry powder
½ tsp. garlic powder
⅛ tsp. ground black pepper

1. *Place chicken in a tight-fitting container or plastic bag; set aside.*
2. *Combine remaining ingredients; pour over chicken.*
3. *Cover and refrigerate 12 hours or longer.*
4. *Remove chicken from marinade; place on grill over hot charcoal.*
5. *Broil 45-60 minutes, turning and basting often. Or place skin-side up on rack in roasting pan and bake in preheated 350° F. oven 1 hour, or until chicken is tender, basting often with marinade.*

# Dick Van Patten

Actor Dick Van Patten attacked his ham-and-eggs luncheon with enthusiasm and reminisced about the days when he toured with the late Alfred Lunt and Lynn Fontanne in "Oh Mistress Mine."

"Between performances, I used to grab a hot dog and go to a double feature, then dash back to my dressing room," Dick recalled. "Mr. Lunt had an ulcer and couldn't eat anything interesting, but he was a wonderful cook and he loved to talk about food. He'd send his valet for me so I could describe the latest dinner to him, and I'd say things like, 'Oh, I had a little pheasant under glass, Mr. Lunt.' I just couldn't tell him about the hot dogs at the movies!

"I'm not a cook," the affable gentleman said, "but I sure love to eat." Among great cooks, Dick ranks his wife "the greatest. In fact, Pat is a great girl all around. She's a terrific Italian cook. I'm half-Dutch and half-Italian. My mother was born in Italy and she was a great cook, *but* her mother was, if possibie, even better. When we got married, my grandmother taught Pat how to cook Italian, so she knows how to make marvelous lasagna and eggplant, and the best breaded veal cutlets you ever tasted."

Dick turned his smile on the waitress. "What about some dessert? What kind of ice cream do you have? I've got a real sweet tooth, as you can see. Eating as much as I do, it's a good thing I run around a lot!"

Pat's not making lasagna quite so often for Dick these days and is concentrating on less fattening dishes, explaining, "I've been doing a lot of boneless chicken dishes, similar to the way Dickie's grandmother used to make them."

# Dick Van Patten's Low-Calorie
# Orange Broiled Chicken

Serves 6

3 large chicken breasts,
   split and skinned
¼ cup orange juice
1 tsp. orange peel, grated

2 tbsps. soy sauce
½ tsp. ground cinnamon,
   ginger or curry powder
freshly ground black pepper

1. *Wash and dry chicken breasts; place in 13 x 9 x 2-inch baking dish.*
2. *Combine remaining ingredients; pour over chicken.*
3. *Cover and refrigerate about 2 hours, occasionally tilting dish and spooning orange mixture over chicken.*
4. *Drain, reserving liquid.*
5. *Broil chicken until crisp and brown; turn to brown on other side.*
6. *Meanwhile, cook down marinade to serve piping hot over broiled chicken, alone, or with hot, cooked rice.*

NOTE: *This simple recipe is extremely satisfying for dieters. For slightly sweeter touch, add a tablespoon of honey to marinade.*

# Betty White

Actress Betty White has made a career out of projecting "the happy housewife" image on the tube. She's exactly that in private life – she's married to TV personality Allen Ludden – but she claims, "Allen's really the cook in our family, I'm sorry to say." She said it with such a belly laugh, I knew it was a put-on!

The couple, who have been married 17 years, live in a pretty Brentwood house where they share the cooking chores on weekends. "It's fun cooking together," Betty said with her warm smile. "Allen performs masterfully at the barbecue. He's really an outdoor cook, and even likes to ad-lib recipes indoors, whereas I'm down to about four basic, quick and easy recipes. It isn't that I don't like to cook, but I don't have much time. I have to laugh about playing the happy homemaker who can do anything and cook everything.

"We're having a party a week from Friday. Allen loves to entertain, but poor baby, he's married to the wrong lady! Since several of our guests are from the East, we're going to do a California-style menu: barbecued chicken à la Ludden, corn-on-the-cob and beans Pacific. I like to do something I can prepare ahead, like the beans. If I cook in advance, then all I have to do is to pop something into the oven and I can sit down and relax with my guests."

Betty's standbys are "something as simple as a good veal scaloppini when I can find good veal, and my favorite chicken dish is an inexpensive one – it's made with wings, marinated all day in a sweet-sour sauce."

# Betty White's Chicken Wings Bake

## Serves 6-8

4 lbs. chicken wings,
    cleaned
1 cup soy sauce

1 stick butter, melted
1 scant cup brown sugar
1 tsp. dry mustard.

1. *Arrange chicken wings in deep bowl.*
2. *Prepare marinade by combining the rest of the ingredients.*
3. *Pour marinade over chicken wings in bowl. Cover and leave at room temperature several hours.*
4. *Turn chicken in marinade several times.*
5. *Line shallow baking dish with aluminum foil. Arrange chicken wings in dish.*
6. *Spoon enough sauce over wings to dampen them well.*
7. *Bake, uncovered, in 375° F. oven about 1 hour, or until chicken is tender. Great as an appetizer or entrée!*

# Darryl F. Zanuck

"I've always been a gourmet, going back to my early trips to Europe when I was still at Warner Bros. I knew every restaurant, its quality and specialties. Paris had always had the finest food in the world," proclaimed the late film giant, Darryl F. Zanuck in a 1971 interview. "Now I usually eat downstairs at Trader Vic's – they make a special Mai Tai cooler there for me, without rum – and, at least once a week, I go to 21. Mario knows my habits well. (Mario listed his favorites as: terrapin Maryland, turtle stew cooked in light cream sauce; hamburgers; lyonnaise potatoes; chicken hash; and Dungeness crab with a mustard-mayonnaise sauce.) I usually go for exotic dishes. When it is on the menu, I love pheasant, cooked in its natural sauce, or *poule au pot.*"

Zanuck's sunny corner suite at the Plaza overlooked Central Park and was full of momentos of a lifetime of making movies. Around the room were Aztec artifacts, what looked like a swashbuckling sword that in reality was the Scottish equivalent of the coveted "Oscar," a sheathed hunter's gun and a much treasured photo inscribed by the British war hero, "Dickie Montbatten." Also, the original ad for a movie made by his studio and obviously dear to his heart, 20th Century Fox's *The Longest Day.*

"I'm still a gourmet," he said, "but I gave up wine ten years ago to rid myself of that drowsy feeling. I drink only beer, Piels beer, because it's the lightest and yet has the same alcohol content as top foreign beers. (He used to drink only Danish beer.) I have two glasses if I take a rest in the afternoon and sometimes before I go to bed. I eat only two meals a day: breakfast, when I get up, and dinner at about nine o'clock."

# Darryl F. Zanuck's Chicken Hash

### Serves 4

¼ cup butter
2 tbsps. shallots, chopped
3 tbsps. flour
2 cups hot milk
1 oz. veal, chopped
½ stalk celery, minced
pinch powdered thyme

¼ tsp. ground nutmeg
salt to taste
white pepper to taste
1 tbsp. sherry or Madeira
2 cups cooked (roasted or poached) breast of chicken, finely chopped

½ cup buttered breadcrumbs

1. *Heat 3 tbsps. butter and chopped shallots in pan until shallots become transparent.*
2. *Stir in flour; cook, stirring, over low fire a few minutes until smooth and flour begins to turn light brown.*
3. *Gradually stir in hot milk; cook over low heat, stirring constantly until sauce is thick and smooth.*
4. *In separate pan, cook veal and celery in remaining butter until meat begins to turn white.*
5. *Add to shallot sauce with thyme, nutmeg, salt and pepper. Cook slowly over low heat about 45 minutes, stirring until thick and smooth.*
6. *Strain sauce, spike with sherry and blend.*
7. *Add sauce to chicken; mix well.*
8. *Turn into 4 individual well-greased ramekins; top with buttered crumbs.*
9. *Bake in preheated 400° F. oven until heated through, or until breadcrumbs brown. Serve alone or with crisp green salad.*

# Pasta & Rice

# Lucie Arnaz

Lucie Arnaz is an accomplished cook. These days she whips up such gastronomic wonders as befits a Bacchanalian feast – chocolate mousse, tomatoes gervais. Her mother, Lucille Ball, is even urging her to do her own culinary compendium. Lucie's been fooling around in the kitchen in earnest since she got her own digs.

"I guess I've always liked to make things and mix ingredients together to see if they taste good," said Lucie. "But when I got my own apartment, then I had the time and my own equipment and kitchen. That's when I really got serious about it. The biggest thing I've ever done is a regular roast chicken or a large roast. The chicken amazed me because it looked so big in the oven. I kept thinking, 'What's goin' on in there?' I mean, you don't want to slice him up to find out if it's cooked. You just have to guess.

"What I love is how they tell you in cookbooks, step-by-step, to cook 'em: 'Tie the little legs together,' right? I mean, this one cookbook said, 'Tie the legs together at the bottoms securely so they don't move around' – or fall off, right? And you do the whole thing, all through the basting processes and the other things that are supposed to be done. Now, how do you test to see if the bird is ready? Well, you see if the drumstick moves easily. How can you see if the drumstick moves easily if it is tied together? It says press your finger to the bird and see if it feels soft. It doesn't say, however, that if you press your finger to the bird, you'll get a burnt finger! And you get nowhere because you scream 'Ouch!' and run and put your finger on an ice cube."

One of Lucie's favorite recipes is for a layered shrimp-rice concoction which combines the elements of a *paella* and a seafood *risotto*.

# Lucie Arnaz's Shrimp & Yellow Rice

Serves 8

## For the shrimp

2 lbs. green shrimp, washed
   under cold, running water
4 quarts boiling water
2 tbsps. salt

2 tbsps. pickling spices (tied
   in cheesecloth bag)
piece lemon rind
slice of onion

1. *Add pickling spices, lemon rind and onion to boiling salted water.*
2. *Drop in shrimp and bring to a boil. Lower heat and simmer 2-5 minutes.*
3. *Remove at once. Drain, cool, shell and devein shrimp. Set aside.*

## For the yellow rice

1/8 tsp. powdered saffron,
   steeped in 3 tbsps. hot water
4 tbsps. butter

1 small onion, minced
2 cups rice
1 tsp. salt

3 cups water or chicken broth

1. *Melt butter in large pan. Add onion; cook until golden.*
2. *Add rice; toss with fork, letting it cook over very low heat 2-3 minutes.*
3. *Add liquid and dissolved saffron and salt. Bring to boiling point; cover, reduce heat and cook until rice is tender.*

## To assemble

1 lb. crabmeat or lobster
   meat, cooked and cleaned
1/2 lb. mushrooms caps,
   cleaned and sautéed with
   3 tbsps. butter and 2
   tbsps. white onion or
   minced scallions
1 pkg. (10 oz.) frozen petit
   pois or peas, barely cooked

2 tbsps. pimento, chopped
1/2 tsp. lemon rind, finely
   grated
juice of 1/2 lemon
salt to taste
pepper to taste
1/2 cup slivered almonds (slowly
   browned in 250° F. oven or
   in 1 tbsp. clarified butter)

enough liquid to moisten (chicken stock or Moselle wine)

1. *Add all ingredients to rice and shrimp, except lemon juice, liquid, salt, pepper, and almonds.*
2. *Squeeze lemon juice all over; moisten with liquid; add salt and pepper.*
3. *Mix well. Place in well-buttered baking dish; cover and cook in preheated 350° F. oven about 25-30 minutes. Top with toasted almonds.*

# Burt Bacharach

Composer Burt Bacharach, a friendly but modest and quiet man, speaks best through his music. When he's inspired, he works untiringly — sometimes as long as 32 straight hours. But he loves unwinding by "dining at a barbecue at home or at my manager's house, eating properly aged sirloin with Caesar salad accompanied by a good Bordeaux wine and fresh fruit for dessert. I enjoy the relaxed atmosphere, with very few people.

"When we dine out in Los Angeles, we look for small Mexican restaurants where we are not recognized so we can concentrate on just enjoying our meal. My tastes in food range from barbecued steak to spicy Mexican and curry dishes. I love plentiful and simple foods."

Burt's recipe for Curry of Shrimp came from his restaurant, the Dover House, located in Westbury, New York.

# Burt Bacharach's Curry of Shrimp Madras with Rice Pilau

Serves 6-8

### For the shrimp

2 lbs. medium shrimp
½ lemon, cut in pieces

½ tsp. salt
boiling water

1. Put shrimp, lemon and salt in enough water to cover in saucepan.
2. Bring to boil; simmer about 1 minute, or until shrimp begins to turn pink.
3. Remove from heat; run under cold water; shell and devein. Set aside.

### For the sauce

½ cup onions, chopped
¼ cup butter
1 tbsp. curry powder
2½ cups chicken stock

⅓ cup raisins
¼ cup brown sugar
⅓ cup chopped chutney
½ cup applesauce

¾ cup heavy cream

1. Sauté onion in butter until soft. Stir in curry powder and cook over low heat about 3 minutes, stirring.
2. Slowly stir in chicken stock; cook 30 minutes, stirring often (sauce should reduce in volume by ⅓).
3. Add raisins, brown sugar, chutney and applesauce. Simmer few minutes.
4. Add heavy cream and shrimp; heat through.
5. Serve at once over rice pilau alone or with side dishes of chutney, shredded coconut, raisins and onion rings.

### For the rice pilau

½ cup onions, chopped
¼ cup butter
3 cups chicken stock
1 tsp. salt

1 bay leaf
1½ cups uncooked rice
freshly ground pepper to taste

1. Sauté onion in butter until limp.
2. Add chicken stock, salt, bay leaf; heat to boiling.
3. Arrange rice in bottom of greased baking dish and pour seasoned chicken stock over it.
4. Cover and cook in preheated 350° F. oven 25 minutes, or until rice is fluffy.
5. Grate lightly with pepper before serving.

# Truman Capote

The perceptive Truman Capote believes you get a good insight into people by what they eat, and how they eat it. We were seated at the "most desirable" table in the Colony, a restaurant now gone, but one where celebrities once found privacy and superb food. Looking around, Truman commented, "I notice that all these marvelous-looking women, who know a tremendous amount about food, consume enormous amounts. They must exercise a lot; they're so trim."

Truman often lunched at the Colony with many of the world's most elegant women: the Bouvier sisters — Lee Radziwill and Jacqueline Onassis, the late Babe Paley, Gloria Steinem, Eunice Shriver and Pat Lawford, among others. "Take Gloria Guinness, for instance," he said. "She's pencil-thin and eats like there's no tomorrow. Maybe these women only eat once a day or just a tiny breakfast."

He dug lustily into his fettuccine and continued on about breakfast, "I've got to tell you my favorite grits story: One time I was driving a new Jag to California, taking the southern route. I stopped in a Mississippi motel and ordered some eggs and bacon. The waitress said, 'Sorry, honey, no bacon and eggs.' I said, 'You mean you don't have any eggs?' 'Yas, honey, we have eggs.' 'Do you have any bacon?' 'Yas, honey!' 'Then why can't I have eggs and bacon?' 'Cause we ain't got no grits, honey!' "

Truman still loves his grits and those big breakfasts he enjoyed during his Alabama childhood: hot cakes, chicken, squirrel, sausages and little steaks.

In 1966, the captivating Mr. Capote gave the most exquisite and well-planned party of the century. He called it his "little masked ball for (Washington Post owner) Kay Graham and all my friends," but there were 540 guests — as spectacular a group as has ever been assembled for a private party in New York! "I don't really like to give parties at all. I don't," Truman said. "But if I'm going to do it, I *really* do it!"

# Truman Capote's (The Colony's) Fettuccine

### Serves 6

1 lb. fettuccine noodles
boiling salted water
few drops vegetable oil
½ cup prosciutto ham, cut in 1-inch
   squares
½ cup lean bacon, cut in small pieces

2 egg yolks
½ cup hot heavy cream
salt to taste
freshly ground pepper to taste
½ cup Gruyere or Parmesan
   cheese, finely grated

1. *Place noodles in boiling salted water with a few drops of oil to prevent noodles from sticking. Cover and cook al dente, 8-9 minutes.*
2. *Drain in colander and keep warm.*
3. *Meanwhile, cook prosciutto and bacon over low heat until crisp and brown. Pour off half the fat.*
4. *Put noodles in lightly-buttered chafing dish; add prosciutto ham mixture; toss lightly and quickly.*
5. *Add egg yolks, one at a time, and toss quickly. Add hot cream, salt and pepper to taste, and toss quickly.*
6. *Serve at once on heated plates. Serve au natural or let guests add grated Gruyere or Parmesan at the table. Serve alone or with crisp arugula (Italian salad greens), dressed with lemon-oil dressing, and well-chilled white wine.*

*NOTE: Success with this recipe is in having all the ingredients ready and to serve within seconds after they are cooked. For a delightful variation, the Colony suggests omitting eggs and substituting a large, garden-ripe tomato, peeled and crushed.*

# Jimmy Coco

"If I had to plan my last meal in this world, I would include linguini with red clam sauce," said Jimmy Coco. "I start to think about what I'm going to eat for dinner right after breakfast! If I knew it would be my last dinner, I would start off with some of your wonderful cheese soup," he said to Nancy Walker, seated next to him in a director's chair.

"Nancy's soup is great! She serves it in a dug-out Gouda cheese shell. As you dip the soup, you scrape the edges of the shell and dig out some of the melted cheese. It's just gorgeous! Then I'd have some Japanese shrimp, broiled with butter and lemon. With that I'd drink some cheap Italian Chianti. I'll have dessert, expresso coffee and then, for an extra dessert, some lasagna or maybe a dumpling!" Jimmy laughed happily.

In his New York digs, a beautifully furnished apartment in Greenwich Village, he frequently has friends in for one of his splendid, home-cooked dinners followed by late-night card games. Jimmy is reconciled to "just being happy and not quite so thin. I've never really trusted people who are indifferent to food anyway! Food is one of the great pleasures left in life. Besides, food is a terribly sensual experience. Listen, I'm starving!" he said plaintively.

# Jimmy Coco's Linguini with Red Clam Sauce

Serves 4

3 dozen littleneck clams
3 tbsps. olive oil
3 large cloves garlic, peeled and minced
1 can (28 ozs.) Italian plum tomatoes, drained
1 tsp. salt

½ cup red wine
½ cup clam juice
large pinch red pepper, crushed
1 tsp. dried oregano leaves, crumbled
2 tsps. dried basil, crumbled
1 lb. linguini

¼ cup fresh parsley, chopped

1. Scrub clams thoroughly; shuck, measure juice; reserve.
2. Heat olive oil in large skillet. Sauté garlic in hot oil until golden.
3. Add tomatoes and salt; simmer 10 minutes.
4. Add remaining ingredients except linguini, parsley and clams. Simmer ½ hour, adding more liquid (wine or clam juice) as needed.
5. Cook linguini in 4 quarts boiling salted water, only until pasta is al dente (barely tender).
6. Drain; spoon into heated serving bowl.
7. A few minutes before pasta is cooked, add clams and parsley to sauce. Toss hot clam sauce with linguini.
8. Consume at once! Wonderful alone or with hot, crusty, garlic-buttered Italian bread and Chianti!

# Francis Ford Coppola

Writer-director-producer Francis Ford Coppola works at such a feverish pitch on his movies that he admittedly becomes "catatonic while I work."

When he's at home in his beautiful big house in San Francisco, cooking is one of his favorite ways to relax. Baking pizza for his friends and family is an act of love. "I'm not a great cook," he said, "but if I made something for you, I'm sure you would like it. I make all kinds of stuff."

Francis is easy to like. This giant of a man is gentle, unpretentious and interesting. He comes from an Italian family that enjoys the tradition of beautiful music and great food. His grandfather once accompanied Caruso; his father, Carmine Coppola, was solo flutist with the N.B.C. Symphony under the baton of Arturo Toscanini.

"I'm good with pasta," Francis said proudly. "I make some unusual dishes not well known in this country. Spaghetti *primavira* ('spring' in Italian) is a nice dish to make. Nobody makes it here. I heard about it in Naples. It's really fantastic. The trick to making pizza is using good ingredients."

# Francis Ford Coppola's Pizza

Makes two 12-inch pizzas

## For the dough

1 cup warm water (105° F. to 115° F.)

1 pkg. active dry yeast

2 tsps. sugar

1½ tsps. salt

2 tbsps. olive oil

2¾ to 3¼ cups unsifted all-purpose flour

1. *Measure water into large mixing bowl. Sprinkle in yeast, stirring until dissolved.*
2. *Stir in sugar, salt, olive oil and 1½ cups flour; beat until smooth. Add enough additional flour to make a stiff dough.*
3. *Turn out onto lightly floured board. Cover; let rise in warm place, free from draft, until doubled in bulk, about 45 minutes.*
4. *Punch dough down; divide in half. Roll and stretch each half into a 13-inch round.*
5. *Place in 2 ungreased 12-inch pizza pans, pressing around edge to form a standing rim of dough. Bake in preheated 350° F. oven 15 minutes.*

## For the topping

olive oil

1 can (1 lb.) Italian plum tomatoes

1 tsp. oregano, crushed

½ tsp. basil, crushed

⅓ cup Parmesan cheese, freshly grated

½ tsp. salt

freshly ground pepper to taste

2 cups mozzarella cheese, shredded

1. *Spread thin layer of olive oil on surface of baked crusts.*
2. *Drain tomatoes and squeeze with hands. (Reserve juice for flavoring soups.)*
3. *Spread tomatoes evenly over both crusts.*
4. *Combine oregano, basil, Parmesan cheese and salt, and sprinkle evenly over tomatoes.*
5. *Season lightly with pepper to taste; top with shredded mozzarella; drizzle olive oil sparingly over the top.*
6. *Bake 15 minutes, or until mozzarella cheese is melted but not browned. Cut into wedges to serve.*

# Eileen Farrell

"I love to cook," said super soprano Eileen Farrell in the electric kitchen of her Manhattan apartment. "The whole family loves to cook." She takes turns in the kitchen with her husband, retired policeman Robert Reagan Sr., and their daughter, Kathleen. Her son, Robert, Jr., holds his own in the eating department.

"Cooking takes my mind off everything." the singer said. "It's relaxing and creative. I completely forget the words of an opera."

Eileen came by the tradition of family cookery in New England, where she was born and raised. "My father was in vaudeville, so they made him a cook in the Army during World War I. I can never remember my mother preparing a turkey. My father roasted the bird, and he even prepared the stuffing and gravy. I like to experiment, but I especially adore baking bread. I started making it because most bread you buy is unbelievably awful. And I make a delicious roast loin of pork with sauerkraut. But my favorite dish to prepare is soup. I buy neck bones with lots of good meat, marrow bones, and chicken wings to flavor the stock."

"Have you any special tonic for your throat?" I asked.

"You'll laugh at this probably," Eileen said, "but I take sips of warm Coca Cola between numbers. Some singers drink tea or chew lemon lozenges. Lily Pons always used to put a cube of sugar in a glass of water when she was performing.

"I do most of my cooking in our summer home in Maine. Each summer we give a big party and prepare an Italian meal, because those New Englanders don't know real Italian food. My daughter makes the pasta and my husband, the sauce. It takes 2 days to prepare the sauce, but the meal is easy, as everything can be made ahead except the salad. For dessert I make small cream puffs filled with an Italian vanilla custard."

# Eileen Farrell's Lasagna with Beef, Ham and Chicken

Serves 8

### Sauce

2 cans (1 lb. 12 ozs.) Italian
   plum tomatoes
2 cans (12 ozs.) tomato
   paste
2 cups water
4 large garlic cloves
2 large yellow onions, chopped
4 tbsps. dried parsley
½ tsp. oregano

½ tsp. rosemary
1 tsp. basil
2 large bay leaves
2 tbsps. sugar
1 tsp. salt
⅛ tsp. freshly ground pepper
½ lb. lean ground beef (or
   cooked, diced pork, lamb
   or lobster)

1. *Combine all ingredients (excluding meat) in large stew pan.*
2. *Cover and barely simmer 6 hours. Stir occasionally, adding more water if needed. Add meat during last 20 minutes.*

### Meat layer

¼ cup prosciutto ham or
   cooked bacon crumbles or
   Smithfield ham
1 cup cooked chicken, minced

1½ tsps. fresh parsley,
   minced
⅛ tsp. mint flakes
dash pepper

*Combine all ingredients.*

### Lasagna

½ lb. lasagna noodles
1 lb. mozzarella, thinly
   sliced

15 ozs. ricotta cheese
½ cup Parmesan cheese,
   grated

1. *While sauce simmers, cook lasagna according to package directions.*
2. *Drain well: arrange lasagna in the casserole in layers, alternating with layers of sauce, mozzarella, ricotta, and meat mixture until lasagna is all used.*
3. *Sprinkle each layer with grated cheese.*
4. *End with ricotta layer, topped with grated cheese.*
5. *Bake at 375° F. about 30 minutes, or until the cheese melts.*

# Sophia Loren

"I always think of people in terms of food, because food, like people I love, is so essential to life. Food is a symbol of security, especially to those who have suffered hunger," Sophia Loren exclaimed, between sips of coffee expresso. To illustrate her point, she said, "I call Chipi (Carlo Ponti, Jr.) 'Spaghetti' all the time, because he adores it – fixed any way. Carlo, my husband, is either 'Eggplant Parmesan,' or 'Involtini' (beef birds in sauce), because it's my favorite dish and he is my favorite man!"

What about the sultry actress who once said, "Everything I am, I owe to spaghetti!"?

"I may have said so, but at that moment I was in a trance. It's not true! I think everything I have I owe to my husband, my sons and myself, not spaghetti," she said, a great bubble of laughter bursting forth. "How do I really think of myself? It depends on the mood I'm in. I think of myself as a pizza – which I like very much – something quite common. I like myself and I am Neapolitan so I would see myself as the classic pizza, with tomato and mozzarella."

Sophia Loren, a tomato yes, but a pizza? *Mamma Mia!* She more closely resembles the Mona Lisa – high cheek bones, flawless teeth, green-gold flecked cat eyes, crinkling into a smile as enigmatic as the Sphinx. She also thinks of herself as very much a Neapolitan housewife. "Why? Because I think I am a very common housewife in the traditional sense of the word. Every woman should have a husband to love, a baby to hold and a meal to cook! My grandmother, Luisa, taught me to cook. She was like a second mother to me. We were so poor, but she taught me the most indispensible ingredient of all good home cooking is love for those you are cooking for."

# Sophia Loren's Pizza Alla Napoletana

Serves 4

## Dough

2 cups flour
1 tsp. salt
1 tsp. olive oil

1 pkg. active dry yeast,
   dissolved in 1¼ cups
   lukewarm water

## Garniture

tomato sauce or canned marinara
   sauce, or peeled, chopped
   tomatoes
small tin filleted anchovies or
   sliced sweet Italian sausage,
   salami or thin strips prosciutto
   ham

dried sweet basil
freshly grated Parmesan cheese
freshly ground pepper
   to taste
2-3 tbsps. olive oil
mozzarella cheese

1. *Place flour and salt on board. Add dissolved yeast. Knead thoroughly, add oil, continue kneading until smooth.*
2. *Place in lightly greased bowl and cover. Set in warm place about 3 hours, or until dough doubles in bulk.*
3. *Flatten, roll out dough into a 10-inch disc about ¼-inch thick. Spread surface with your choice of garniture.*
4. *Heat olive oil in large, cast-iron skillet. When oil is sizzling, add pizza. Cook over medium flame about 10 minutes, or until golden and topping is bubbly. Serve immediately.*

NOTE: *Neapolitans prepare a closed-style pizza using half the above dough. Roll out to ¼-inch thickness. Spread lightly with ⅓ cup ricotta cheese, 4 ozs. minced prosciutto ham, light grating of freshly ground pepper and 1 tbsp. Parmesan cheese. Cut dough into 2-inch squares, fold in half, sealing edges. Plunge envelopes into sizzling deep fat, brown quickly on both sides. Drain on absorbent paper. Serve immediately. Makes 20 small pizzas.*

# Peter Max

" 'God is the greatest cook! He prepares the fruit in the right temperature, taste and texture. When the fruit falls off the tree, it means it's ripe, it's ready and that's it' – that's what a friend said to me recently in San Francisco," said artist Peter Max, stroking his Fu Manchu moustache, seated on a yellow inflatable chair (one of his own design, natch) in his airy-white studio overlooking Riverside Drive and the Hudson River. Peter was describing his friend, who's a fruitarian. "That's the next step after vegetarian." Peter's a vegetarian by choice and conviction.

I asked if his childhood, spent in the Orient, might have stimulated his interest in vegetarianism. (The Berlin-born, 30-year-old artist fled Germany with his parents to Shanghai during his early infancy. Later, he became an astronomy scholar at Haifa University in Israel at age 13.)

"It happened much later, when I matured, in a sense – when I started understanding certain other values in life," he asserted. "I was never particularly fond of meat. It tasted good, but now that I really understand *what* I'm eating, I can't eat it! Let me give you my list of good foods for a day: For breakfast, I would have a glass of orange juice with a few spoonfuls of one of those protein-supplement powders. Three oranges and a banana would be fantastic and that could be lunch! I would love not to have to have dinner at this point. I should rather like to just have another orange. But sometimes I go and have Chinese food: unpolished rice or rice noodles with Chinese vegetables. Snow peas or bean sprouts, that's something I enjoyed as a child."

"Is the world your canvas?" I asked.

"Absolutely! Everything is a canvas and has a potential."

# Peter Max's Rice with Chinese Vegetables

Serves 2-3

## For the rice

½ cup hand polished (or long-
　grained) rice, washed in
　2 cups cold water

½ tsp. salt
1 tbsp. butter

1. Add rice to water in deep saucepan. When water begins to boil, add salt and butter.
2. Stir once; cook 15-20 minutes, or until rice is tender.
3. Remove from heat; drain in colander; serve at once.

NOTE: Natural brown rice may be used. Rinse rice very well (3 times) in cold water. Use ½ cup rice plus 2½ times as much water.

## To prepare the vegetables

½ cup blanched almonds,
　slivered
2-3 tbsps. corn oil
½ small onion, peeled
　and chopped
½-inch piece ginger root,
　minced
6 white mushrooms, cleaned
　and sliced
2 stalks celery, cut in thin
　slices diagonally
4 water chestnuts (canned),
　thinly sliced

1 cup bamboo shoots, chopped
　in large pieces
½ green pepper, cut in
　½-inch pieces
12 Chinese snow pea pods,
　sliced in 2-inch pieces
1 vegetable cube,
　dissolved in 3 tbsps. hot water
good pinch sugar
2-3 tbsps. soy sauce
salt to taste
freshly ground pepper
　to taste

1½ tsps. cornstarch, dissolved in 2 tbsps. hot water

1. Sauté almonds in heated corn oil in large skillet or wok; lift out.
2. Add onion and ginger root to skillet; stir-fry 1½ minutes.
3. Add remaining vegetables except green pepper and pea pods; stir-fry 1 minute.
4. Add rest of ingredients; cook over low heat 2 minutes, or until sauce is smooth and shiny, stirring occasionally.
6. Serve at once on hot cooked rice. Garnish with almonds.

# Robert Wagner

Robert Wagner is an enthusiastic cook, a market freak and a madman about the sea. He and his mate, Natalie Wood, do most of their cooking when they make their favorite get-away trips out on blue water. "I've always been a cook!" said Bob. "I know a lot of other guys who get a real boot out of cooking too. In fact, I just read a survey that said that most of the world's great chefs are men!

"I like to make marinara sauce. I do the garlic thing, letting it brown in good olive oil, then I break up the tomatoes and add them. It's great served with pasta, preferably vermicelli, cooked *al dente,* or spooned over veal scallops. Be sure and get the very tender veal; pound it slightly. Cook it quickly in a little olive oil.

"I'll tell you what else I like," he said affably. "Roasted peppers! Just hold them over the gas stove, peel off the skin and serve with olive oil and a little garlic.

"What I like best about cooking is shopping! I love to go to markets. The whole trick to great cooking, of course, is in buying and using fresh, high quality ingredients. We know a little shop that has the greatest sausages in the world. I'm mad about sausages and fine cheeses! We do most of our shopping for staples at the supermarket, but we go to special little places to buy meat and out-of-the-ordinary foods."

The Wagners live in a large, rambling, six-bedroom house in Beverly Hills with their daughters. "We entertain a lot," he said. "Natalie is a very flexible and a very super lady. Life is terrific. I don't feel one bit guilty enjoying every minute of it!"

# Robert Wagner's Marinara Sauce with Vermicelli

Serves 4

2 cloves garlic, crushed
1 tbsp. olive oil
4 cups (about 2 lbs.) Italian
    plum tomatoes, peeled and diced,
    or 1 can (35 ozs.) Italian
    plum tomatoes
¼ cup parsley, chopped
1 tsp. sugar
½ tsp. oregano, crushed

½ tsp. sweet basil,
    crushed
½ bay leaf
⅛ tsp. freshly ground
    black pepper
4 tsps. salt
8 ozs. vermicelli (thin
    spaghetti)
3 quarts boiling water

Parmesan cheese, freshly grated

1. *Sauté garlic in olive oil until golden.*
2. *Stir in tomatoes, parsley, sugar, oregano, basil, bay leaf, pepper and 1 tsp. salt. Cover and simmer 45 minutes. (If you use canned tomatoes, double simmering time.)*
3. *Uncover and cook 30 minutes longer, stirring occasionally.*
4. *Meanwhile, gradually add vermicelli and remaining salt to rapidly boiling water. Cook, uncovered, stirring occassionally, until pasta is tender.*
5. *Drain in colander.*
6. *Combine vermicelli with marinara sauce and serve with Parmesan cheese, if desired.*

NOTE: *For a delightful variation, quickly brown 1½ lbs. veal scallops (cut thin and slightly pounded to flatten), lightly dusted with seasoned flour, in 2 tbsps. hot olive oil. Brown quickly on other side; add to heatproof casserole. Spoon Bob's marinara sauce over veal. Heat in 350° F. oven until bubbly. Or top with freshly grated Parmesan or Romano cheese and strips of mozzarella cheese. Run under broiler until sauce is hot and cheese is brown and bubbly. Delicious, and a breeze to prepare!*

# Nancy Walker

"I'm worried about my garden because I water it a lot. I'm a crazy lady because I'm a waterer, but it hasn't proven me wrong so far!" said comedienne Nancy Walker in a very serious tone.

Nancy lives with her husband, David Craig, in a pretty house in Studio City, California, where "everything grows like crazy on our mountain top!"

Nancy is an experimental cook, often changing the proportion of ingredients once she has tried a recipe. "For instance," she explained, "I make chicken in the pot, and someone once told me to put a clove in it. Well, that's just to die, and I'd never known about that before! It's just wonderful. All you add is one teeny tiny little clove in the whole big pot! But, you know, you can't get soup out of chicken! I mean I don't know how they do it. I can never make chicken soup from a chicken. I use the chicken base (canned). What can you expect from a poor chicken? It's ridiculous! I mean the chicken is boiling away and it's trying to give you chicken soup, but you've got to help it along.

"When I'm not working, we entertain about twice a week. That can be for anywhere from three to no more than eight people. I get a little testy when it's more than eight. We love having brunches. We might have the lobster thing or *vitello tonnato* (veal with tuna fish), a large roast or chicken and cheese. I have also learned how to oven-poach a fish (striped bass, red snapper or swordfish) in white wine, water, butter, salt and pepper. At the last minute, I put sour cream on it. Everyone thinks I've been cooking for days!"

# Nancy Walker's Linguini with Lobster

Serves 6

2 medium onions, chopped
2 garlic cloves, pressed
¼ cup olive oil
1 can (35 oz.) Italian
    plum tomatoes
1 can (6 oz.) tomato paste
¼ cup parsley, chopped
2 sprigs fresh mint
2 tsps. salt
1 tsp. sugar

¾ tsp. basil
½ tsp. red pepper,
    crushed
¼ tsp. oregano leaves
8 ozs. linguini
1 tbsp. salt
3 quarts boiling water
½ cup dry red wine
Parmesan or Romano cheese,
    freshly grated

6 frozen lobster tails (8 ozs. each), slightly thawed

1. Sauté onion and garlic in hot oil in 4-quart Dutch oven until tender.
2. Stir in undrained tomatoes, tomato paste, parsley, mint, salt, sugar, basil, red pepper and oregano. Heat to boiling.
3. Reduce heat to low and simmer, uncovered, for 35 minutes, stirring occasionally.
4. Meanwhile, gradually add linguini and salt to rapidly boiling water so water continues to boil. Cook, uncovered, stirring occasionally, until tender.
5. Drain in colander; keep warm.
6. Cut each lobster in half lengthwise with a sharp knife.
7. Add lobster and wine to tomato mixture. Cover and continue cooking, spooning sauce over lobster occasionally, 10-15 minutes, or until shells turn pink and lobster meat is fork-tender.
8. To serve: place linguini in 6 individual soup bowls or ramekins; keep warm. Cook sauce, stirring frequently, 5 more minutes, or until slightly thickened. Ladle sauce over linguini and lobster. Sprinkle with grated Parmesan cheese as desired.

# Eggs & Cheese

# Bill Cullen

"I started fooling around with cooking for the fun of it when I left home. In fact, I used to invite girls up to dinner. It was better than saying, 'Come up and see my etchings.' " Bill Cullen, one of television's most familiar personalities, talked with us at an East Side restaurant while drinking his diet lunch of black coffee.

"I'm hard to cook for. In fact, I'm terrible," he said. "The trouble is, I hate pork, veal, fish or seafood of any kind. As a kid, I ate a meat-and-potato diet. I grew up in Pittsburgh during the height of the depression. People couldn't afford steak then. I liked plain food, especially stuffed cabbage, a staple in our Polish neighborhood.

"My cooking these days mostly consists of barbecuing steak, preparing a spaghetti sauce or a cheese soufflé."

# Bill Cullen's Cheese Soufflé

Serves 4

3 tbsps. butter
3 tbsps. flour
1 cup milk
½ tsp. salt

pinch of cayenne

4 egg yolks
½ cup each, Swiss and
   sharp Cheddar, crumbled
5 egg whites

1. *Melt butter in top of double boiler over direct heat.*
2. *Blend in flour.*
3. *Stir in milk and seasonings; remove from fire.*
4. *Beat in egg yolks, one at a time, alternately with cheese.*
5. *Place top of double boiler over hot water; stir until cheese has melted.*
6. *Blend well; remove from hot water; cool slightly.*
7. *Fold in stiffly beaten egg whites.*
8. *Pour into a buttered 1½-quart soufflé dish. Bake at 375° F. for 30 minutes, or until top is lightly browned.*
9. *Fold a wax paper collar around the soufflé dish about 2 inches over the top of the dish during baking. Secure with string around collar to hold in place. Remove before serving.*
10. *Serve immediately. Good topped with medium white sauce flavored with Dijon mustard.*

# Eileen Fulton

Eileen Fulton bears little resemblance to Lisa, the character she portrays on the CBS-TV daytime series, "As the World Turns." She was dressed in a two-piece, bandana print, bare midriff, floor-length dress, as she picked up a Chinese cleaver and began attacking a chicken. "I always like to buy a fresh chicken and cut it up myself," she said. "I always skin the chicken because of the fat on the skin.

"Even though I grew up in the South, my cooking is not typically southern. I love to eat and I love to cook, especially since I have discovered what different herbs and spices do to food. For instance, herbs are delightful tossed in a crisp green salad! And I've found out what a splash of wine can do to a sauce to get that special flavor!"

The chicken Eileen was preparing for dinner is a Chinese-Italian concoction, if you can imagine the combination. Another Fulton specialty is "wild" grits. She makes a casserole using grits with layers of cheese and breadcrumbs. "They taste better than *gnocchi!*" she exclaimed.

# Eileen Fulton's "Wild" Grits

Serves 4

1 cup white hominy grits
5 cups boiling water
1½ tsps. salt
½ tsp. baking powder
1 cup Parmesan cheese,
  freshly grated

freshly ground black pepper
1 egg, beaten
1 tbsp. milk
½ cup Italian-flavored
  breadcrumbs
2 tbsps. butter

1 scant tsp. instant onion flakes

1. Add grits to boiling salted water. Reduce heat, simmer 25 to 30 minutes, stirring occasionally.
2. Cool 30 minutes.
3. Add baking powder, ¾ cup cheese, onion and pepper. Mix well.
4. Combine egg and milk; add to cooked grits.
5. Pour mixture into well-greased 2-quart baking dish.
6. Top with breadcrumbs and remaining cheese. Dot with butter.
7. Bake in preheated 350° F. oven 25 minutes, or until browned on top. Great with chicken or meat dishes!

# Lynda Day George

When you visit actress Lynda Day George at home, you'll probably find her in her kitchen cooking up something special just for you! We found Lynda by calling through the open window in the back. She was in her kitchen getting ready to complete a peach omelet.

"I love to be in here," she said of her 15-foot square, white, tile-lined kitchen. "I find that people congregate in the kitchen first because they want a drink. So while they stand here, I'd just as soon be doing something!"

Lynda was informally dressed in white slacks, an open-necked blouse and bare feet. As she deftly beat the egg yolks, the air was pungent with the fresh peaches marinating in lemon juice and the mysterious, seductive smell of a Greek pastry baking in the oven. Presiding over an ancient English stove of white enamel trimmed in cornflower blue, Lynda melted butter before pouring in the eggs. Her cookbook was lying open on a Chinese lacquer table; a portrait of George Washington was hanging over the stove and a lithograph of Abraham Lincoln was in the dining room. Tin-lined copper cooking pots were hung above the kitchen sink and Lynda worked with her sleek black cat sprawled at her feet.

# Lynda Day George's Fresh Peach Omelet

Serves 4

8 ripe fresh peaches
juice of 1 large lemon
1 tsp. lemon rind,
  finely grated
pinch ground nutmeg
3 tbsps. peach brandy

few dashes brandy or
  almond extract
6 tbsps. butter, divided
6 eggs, separated
2 tbsps. heavy cream
2 tbsps. sugar

pinch salt

1. *Peel peaches and cut in quarters; arrange in bottom of aluminum-foil-lined skillet.*
2. *Sprinkle lemon juice and lemon rind evenly over peaches; top with nutmeg, peach brandy and brandy extract.*
3. *Let peaches marinate about 15 minutes at room temperature.*
4. *Then drizzle 3 tbsps. melted butter over peaches in skillet; cook slowly over very low heat about 5 minutes, or until marinade forms a thin syrup in pan. Set aside.*
5. *Meanwhile, prepare omelet. Beat egg yolks in small bowl with cream, sugar and salt until frothy.*
6. *Beat egg whites until stiff but not dry; fold into egg yolk mixture until well blended.*
7. *Heat remaining butter in 12-inch omelet pan, rotating butter in pan to spread evenly.*
8. *Pour in beaten egg mixture; cook omelet slowly until light brown on bottom.*
9. *Run under broiler a few minutes until top is golden.*
10. *Carefully remove omelet from pan. Spread peach mixture on ½ of omelet and roll up jelly-roll fashion. If desired, divide peaches, using half inside and the other half spread on top to form a glaze. Serve at once!*

NOTE: *Apricots may be substituted for peaches. Taste is tart and fruity. Sugar may be added to fruit during heating, if desired.*

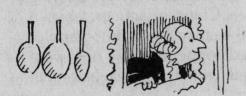

# Eydie Gorme

"I'm a *help* cook with a big staff," said Eydie Gorme, the prettier half of the star singing team of Steve Lawrence and Eydie Gorme. "Actually, I'm a good cook," the Bronx-born singer went on to explain. "I've always cooked on the road, even if it's only a hot plate. So far I've escaped the house detectives! Obviously, I don't make my mother's sweet and sour cabbage."

Steve said, "She's a lucky cook, because I eat out a lot."

Most of Eydie's cooking takes place in the roomy kitchen that took a solid year of revamping before it suited her. "Most gourmet cookbooks are bunk," she said. "They always call for a cow hanging up in the kitchen. I make many dishes that are the end, such as spaghetti sauce with meatballs, pepperoni and sweet Italian sausages or peppers fried in olive oil." She explained her preference for Italian cuisine. "I suppose because there's so much variety. Day in and day out, the food is healthy and satisfying."

Steve's kitchen talents are limited to egg cookery and occasionally barbecuing steaks or chickens. "He'll never starve on his own cooking," Eydie reported.

"We're headed for Vegas next, where everyone likes to cook for you, especially Italian food," said Eydie. "I'm getting very spoiled. When I'm out there, there's an Italian grocery store where the owner makes things to order, from pasta (lasagna or rigatoni) to sauces. You name it, and she makes it. Her spaghetti sauces are superb, so why should I make them when I can buy them ready made!"

# Eydie Gorme's Spinach Frittata

### Serves 4

⅓ cup salad oil
1 cup matzoh meal
2 pkgs. (10½ ozs.) frozen
 chopped spinach, thawed
8 ozs. pot cheese or large
 curd, cream-style cottage
6 large eggs

¼ cup freshly grated Parmesan
 or Romano cheese
1½ tsps. salt
1/16 tsp. freshly ground
 pepper
1 cup feta cheese, crumbled
plain yogurt

1. *Oil an 8 x 12 x 2-inch layer pan generously with some of the oil; sprinkle matzoh meal evenly over the bottom of the pan.*
2. *Squeeze excess water from frozen thawed spinach and place in mixing bowl with pot cheese.*
3. *In separate bowl, beat 5 eggs until lemon colored; stir into spinach-cheese mixture.*
4. *Add Parmesan cheese, remaining vegetable oil, salt and pepper. Stir lightly to blend.*
5. *Pour over matzoh crust, distributing evenly throughout.*
6. *Add feta cheese to spinach-egg layer, distributing evenly.*
7. *Beat remaining egg until light; pour in a thin stream over the entire surface, forming top custard crust.*
8. *Bake in preheated 425° F. oven, cooking about 30 minutes, or until top is golden brown and filling is puffy.*
9. *Remove from oven, cut in squares. Serve at once with side dish of chilled yogurt. Serve with mixed green salad.*

NOTE: *The Gorme creation, which is closely related to an Italian frittata (omelet), is also similar to the traditional Turkish borek (pastry). The Middle Eastern version is made by preparing an egg-butter pastry to line a pie plate and filling with a spinach-onion-feta cheese mixture, sealed with pastry and baked in a hot oven. The daily dish is thought to have been brought to Turkey by the Sephardic (Spanish) Jews during the time of the Inquisition.*

# Elliott Gould

Actor Elliott Gould is quixotic, quiet, hilariously funny by turns, but constant in his unfulfilled fantasy of being a short-order chef! In real life, he likes to live out that fantasy in his Malibu beach house in California when the mood strikes him and his friends gather. "I have always had a vision of myself cooking in a trolley-car diner." said Elliott. "I would cook anything – hamburgers, hot dogs, eggs, westerns, B.L.T.'s with mayo (counterman lingo for bacon, lettuce and tomato with mayonnaise) and whole wheat toast! I did once work on the boardwalk at Far Rockaway Beach selling hot dogs. It was probably the first legitimate job I ever had. I was about 14 years old.

"Listen," he said, leaning forward, "I often cook. The last thing I cooked was knockwurst and beans. Sometimes, I think all of us are like knockwursts – the skin keeps us together and we're all linked. I can cook delicious broiled chicken, nothing fancy, but good.

"I had lunch the other day on the beach for Timothy Bottoms, who sailed down from Santa Barbara. The menu? Hamburgers and corn on the cob!"

Elliott is also great with eggs. "Westerns are great!" he exclaimed enthusiastically. "I start with scallions and chopped-up ham. I use a lot of tomatoes sometimes, but save the tomatoes for when you're making a Spanish omelet!"

# Elliott Gould's Western Omelet Supreme

## Serves 4

½ cup scallion, chopped
½ cup green pepper, chopped
5 tbsps. butter
1 cup canned corn, drained
¾ cup ham, diced
8 eggs

½ cup milk
½ tsp. salt
¼ tsp. freshly ground black pepper
2 large beefsteak tomatoes
French bread loaf, cut in thick slices

1. Brown scallion and green pepper in butter: add corn and ham. Keep turning with a spatula; browning lightly.
2. Remove to warm place.
3. Beat together eggs, milk, salt and pepper.
4. Heat large skillet; pour in egg mixture.
5. As soon as eggs start to set, spread the ham-vegetable mixture on top.
6. Loosen edge of eggs with spatula and carefully fold omelet in half. Slide onto a serving platter.
7. Serve at once with thick slices of beefsteak tomatoes and French bread. Eat at once. It's delicious!

NOTE: If skillet is not large enough for 8 eggs, divide egg and vegetable mixtures in half and use two skillets. Also, if desired, soft cheese (mozzarella or American) can be added on top of omelet and run under broiler to brown. Vegetables can also be varied, adding chopped tomatoes, diced boiled potatoes or peas.

# Alfred Hitchcock

"I'm not talking about food. It's a miserable subject, since I'm on a diet," said Alfred Hitchcock, the portly master of cinematic suspense. Despite his prelude, Hitchcock is as fond of talking about food as he is about homicide.

"Most people think a gourmet is a food lover who tucks in his napkin and starts in eating fine food. I'm a theoretical gourmet. I'm really more interested in the acquisition of hard-to-find foods than in eating them. We have oysters flown in from England each September and we savor *pauillac*. That's milk-fed lamb that's never fed on grass," he explained. "We roast it lightly to keep it moist and tender."

About food he intensely dislikes, he said, "One of the lowest forms of food is catsup. It's so awful, it's an insult to any food. The worst sound in the world is the hand smacking the bottom of a catsup bottle. What happens? A horrible red goo emerges and spreads over a plate of inoffensive looking French fried potatoes. There they were minding their own business and what did they do to deserve this?" he demanded.

"I've never eaten an egg in my entire life, an egg cooked by itself, that is. And I can't stand the smell of a hard-boiled egg.

"And I hate to see quantities of food on a plate. It's so vulgar. They put fish and meat all on the same plate at those Hollywood-type buffets. When I put one piece of meat on a dish, people just can't believe that's all I want," he said indignantly. "But it's only a matter of taste. It's the home influence. Like speech, food tastes are acquired."

Hitchcock admits an aversion to beer. "It's so coarse and offensive. I have delicate tastes and drink wine." He keeps an impressive store of domestic and imported vintages in the basement wine cellar of his Bel Air mansion.

# Alfred Hitchcock's Quiche Lorraine

"Make your favorite dough for a one-crust, 10-inch pie. If you have never made this vital choice, use this recipe, which is enough for two tarts."

### Tart Pastry

2 cups pastry flour
½ cup butter
1 egg yolk
salt
about ¼ cup cold water

### Filling

2 or 3 slices cooked, diced ham
2 onions, sliced
4 eggs
a grain or two cayenne
light grating nutmeg
2 cups hot milk

1. *Work lightly together pastry flour, butter, egg yolk, a pinch of salt and cold water.*
2. *Chill the dough 1 hour, or until it is needed.*
3. *Roll out half the dough to line the pie pan. Prick here and there with the point of a knife and crimp the edge with the tines of a fork. (Save the rest of the pastry for another pie.)*
4. *Scatter diced ham on the crust.*
5. *Sauté sliced onions in butter until they are soft, but not brown; spread over ham.*
6. *In a saucepan beat 4 eggs with a good pinch of salt, a grain or two of cayenne and a light grating of nutmeg.*
7. *Gradually add 2 cups of hot milk, beating continually with a wire whisk.*
8. *Continue to beat the mixture over a low fire until the custard begins to thicken.*
9. *Pour it into the tart shell and bake in a moderate oven 375° F. for 30 minutes, or until custard is set and the top is golden. Serve hot, directly from the pan.*

# John Houseman

"I can make a superb omelet," said John Houseman over lunch at the pastoral Bel Air Hotel. "I fill it with ham or bacon, or for a dessert omelet, with wild sweet strawberries."

The legendary actor, director and writer is one of the few genuine Renaissance men in the arts today and has incredible energy. He seems to thrive on having a number of projects going at the same time. When he produced movies for major studios in California, he was also producing one or two plays a year in New York. Currently, he is a professor of drama at the University of Southern California, but is best known to mass audiences as Professor Kingsfield on "Paper Chase."

Houseman and his wife, Joan, live in Malibu, but have kept their modern, Mediterranean-style house near New York City. However, the California lifestyle appeals to them, with its many outdoor activities, especially barbecuing. "I grill meat with great audacity," said John. "Flank steak, chops or butterflied leg of lamb."

However, the gentleman leaves the marinating to his French wife. "John cooks some things very well," said Joan. "For example, I never make the omelets."

The Housemans like to entertain their guests informally at noon with a lunch. One of John's favorites is roast chicken, which Joan prepares, stuffing it with cream cheese and spiking it with fresh herbs.

# John Houseman's Classic French Omelet

Serves 1

1 tbsp. sweet butter
2 eggs
2 tbsps. water or milk
¼ tsp. salt

dash pepper
¼ cup cooked ham,
  chopped, or crisp
  bacon bits

1. *Melt butter in an omelet pan or skillet until it is hot enough for a drop of water to sizzle on skillet.*
2. *Mix eggs, water and seasonings with fork; pour into hot pan. (The edges should set immediately.)*
3. *With a pancake turner, draw the cooked edges toward the center. Tip pan to allow the uncooked portion to run to outer edge of pan.*
4. *While the top is still moist, put ham on left side of the omelet (on right side if left-handed).*
5. *Fold one side over filling with pancake turner.*
6. *Tip pan over serving platter and turn omelet onto it. Serve at once. Great with toast points and sliced tomatoes.*

*NOTE: John Houseman advises, "Lately, I've been omitting the liquid. It works just as well." For a dessert omelet, he uses a little sugar in place of salt and pepper, and fills egg mixture with fresh, sweetened strawberries. Once you've mastered the art of making omelets, there's no end to the wondrous creations you can whip up. Omelets are an excellent excuse to use up leftovers – bits of cooked meat, canned fish or vegetables. For example, for a Reuben omelet, fill with corned beef, sauerkraut and Swiss cheese.*

# Harry Reasoner

Veteran newsman Harry Reasoner gets into the kitchen occasionally. "I used to wash dishes." he said, "but I don't do that very much anymore. I make good martinis and I sit in the kitchen a lot because, out of long practice, I like to sit and talk to my wife as she's preparing the food, rather than sit in the living room where there is no conversation. I suppose we spend most of the time in the kitchen.

"I burn meat like any good American man, but I don't do much else. I can get along and make breakfasts. I can make a meal if I'm left to my devices, and have on many occasions. My girls are all capable cooks; a couple of them are actually pretty good. My son, Stuart, is a first-class cook, and I don't know how that came about. We have always liked to eat good food and have paid a lot of attention to the quality of food, but how he got into preparing food I don't know.

"I'm suspicious of people who claim they never bother about food. It's sort of like denying that you spend any time at all on love. You would be suspicious of anyone like that in their human relationships. And I'm suspicious of someone who does not fuss about their food. Food is very important to me.

"We go to a fair amount of effort when we entertain — generally sit-down dinners. I make a good bouillabaisse, but I have to follow recipes. We live in a big old house with many nooks and crannies, where we often entertain old friends. I make eggs Benedict for breakfast with Hollandaise sauce and a good soy sauce with fish."

# Harry Reasoner's Eggs Benedict

Serves 4

### For the Hollandaise sauce

½ cup butter, divided into
   three portions
2 egg yolks

1½ tbsps. lemon juice
   or vinegar
¼ tsp. salt

few grains cayenne

1. *Place 1 portion of butter in heavy bowl with egg yolks and lemon juice. Cook over hot (never boiling) water, stirring constantly with wire whisk or wooden spoon until butter melts.*
2. *Add second portion of butter; stir.*
3. *When mixture thickens, add last portion of butter, stirring constantly until thick and smooth.*
4. *Season with salt and cayenne.*
5. *If mixture separates, stir in 2 tbsps. cream or boiling water, drop by drop.*
   *(Mixture can be made in advance and reheated over warm water, stirring. If sauce is too thick, a few additional drops of cream or boiling water may be added.)*

### For the eggs

4 slices boiled ham or
   Canadian bacon
4 eggs, poached

4 English muffins, split
   and toasted
Hollandaise sauce

1. *Sauté ham slightly; arrange on toasted English muffin halves.*
2. *Place poached eggs on top of ham.*
3. *Pour Hollandaise sauce on top. Serve as hearty breakfast, brunch or supper offering.*

# Natalie Wood

"I cook only occasionally, but, curiously enough, I seem to do most of my cooking on boats," said diminutive Natalie Wood as we sat on a bench in New York's Central Park. "Mostly, I go for breakfasts. It's all I have time to do. I'm especially fond of eggs. On board, I often whip up eggs ranchero.

"Oh, I fix a brunch thing, too, with Nova Scotia salmon and cream cheese," she added. "Or I might barbecue a steak over a hibachi. But more often, my friends insist on cooking for me."

Entertaining ashore in her Bel Air mansion, however, is strictly a Wood production, though she delegates the actual cooking to her English housekeeper. "When I entertain formally, it's a place-card affair for from 10 to 25 people." Natalie's sit-down dinners are splendid repasts, planned in minute detail and served in her spacious dining room. "When I have more than 25 guests, I tent over the terrace and serve there. With cocktails, I favor tiny quiche Lorraine and caviar. For the first course, cracked crab, followed by baked capon, wild rice, a medley of garden vegetables, small potato puffs, limestone lettuce salad with cheese dressing. The dessert is always something simple, like fresh strawberries and ice cream."

When she feels thin — the dark-eyed beauty weighs in at 100 pounds — her menu is hefty: prosciutto ham and melon, lasagna, green salad and garbanzo beans dressed with olive oil and lemon. "Actually, I like all kinds of food from Polynesian to Chinese, especially egg roll and barbecued beef. I like Japanese and Russian, too." Natalie's preference for the latter comes from her Franco-Russian parents.

Natalie likes wine with everything. "My favorites are Chateau Margaux, Chateau Haut-Brion, Chateauneuf-du-Pape, Pouilly Fuissé and Valpolicella with Italian food."

# Natalie Wood's Eggs Ranchero

Serves 2-4

4 tortillas (fresh, frozen
   or canned)
2 tbsps. oil
1 large clove garlic, mashed
½ tsp. marjoram
1 small Serrano or any hot
   chili pepper, chopped, or
   2 tsps. red chili powder

1 cup fresh tomatoes, peeled
   and chopped, or 1 cup
   canned tomato sauce
salt to taste
freshly ground black pepper
   to taste
4 eggs
butter

1. *Fry tortillas quickly in hot oil; drain on absorbent paper.*
2. *Keep oil hot; add garlic, marjoram, chopped chili, tomatoes, salt and pepper to taste.*
3. *Simmer tomato mixture for a few minutes until flavors are well blended and sauce has thickened slightly.*
4. *Fry eggs in small amount of butter in separate pan, or poach in the hot tomato sauce.*
5. *To serve, place 1 egg on each tortilla, cover with sauce. Serve at once.*

NOTE: *If desired, eggs can be made into omelet, wrapped with tortillas and topped with tomato sauce. Avocado or chorizo (Spanish sausage) are often served with this hearty dish. Very tasty any way you serve it!*

# Vegetables

# Joey Bishop

"I eat steak, salad, a hunk of melon and that's it," comedian Joey Bishop said poolside at the Sands Hotel. Joey was soaking up a bit of sun after his Las Vegas opening the night before in the Copa Room. "I'm really not a cook, but I am an expert eater," he commented, turning over in the deck chair to bake his other side.

"Now let's talk about my wife, Sylvia. Besides coming from Chicago and being 6 foot 7 inches tall, she's a terrific cook!" he said.

"I've got to tell you about my only real experience as a cook," Bishop said. "It was on television a few years ago. I was doing a series with Abby Dalton and I had to cook up some loosely scrambled eggs. The over-zealous prop man wanted to be sure the eggs wouldn't stick to the pan so he put half a pound of butter in the skillet. It could have been disastrous but, as it turned out, the effect was only funnier. When I poured the eggs out of the pan, I had made truly unscrambled eggs. They were better done in the shell."

Although Joey would be the last star to claim that he can cook, he did offer his favorite recipe passed along to his wife by his mother, the late Anna Gottlieb of Philadelphia. "My mother was some cook. She thought I didn't eat enough when I was on the road, so she used to bring some *pirogen* (a food resembling ravioli) in a jar for me. My favorite, however, is easy and quick but so delicious. Just mash some potatoes and throw in some hard-cooked egg, browned onion, season with salt and pepper. That's all, except you gotta add some *schmaltz* (rendered chicken fat)."

"And what do you call your concoction, Joey?" I asked.

"Why it's that 'Make-Me-That-Potato-Jazz.' We always have it when Sylvia doesn't want to cook and I don't want to go out."

# Joey Bishop's Make-Me-That-Potato-Jazz

Irish potatoes, peeled
hard-boiled eggs, diced
yellow onion, sliced and
   browned in schmaltz

salt to taste
freshly ground pepper
   to taste
schmaltz (rendered chicken fat)

1. *Boil potatoes in salted water until tender.*
2. *Drain; mash until light, adding a little hot water if necessary.*
3. *Add eggs, browned onion, and salt and pepper to taste. Mix well.*
4. *Heat schmaltz in a cast-iron skillet and add potato; or place in casserole lightly rubbed with schmaltz and heat in a moderate oven.*
5. *Cook over low flame about 5 minutes.*
6. *Serve as a main course for luncheon or supper dish, or as side dish for roast breast of beef.*

NOTE: *Ready-made schmaltz can be purchased from a kosher butcher or prepared in the following manner: cut chicken skin and fat into 1-inch squares. Place in a heavy saucepan with a small amount of diced yellow onion and a little water. Simmer very gently until all the fat has been rendered and the chicken skin is crisp and brown. Strain schmaltz. Reserve grebenes (cracklings) and use to season chopped liver or eat plain.*

# Jim Brady

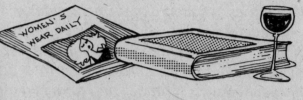

Jim Brady, magazine editor, novelist, raconteur and Francophile, is also a confirmed food appreciator. "You can tell a lot about a person by his taste in food and wine, as well as by his taste in clothes and other things. I appreciate a man or woman who really knows good wine and how to select it properly."

Brady is a bachelor who dines out continually. He frequents both the famous and elegant places and the less grand eateries, where the food is great and the ambiance in abundance. During his days as publisher of *Women's Wear Daily,* he was surrounded by the giants and the "Beautiful People" of the fashion world.

He recalled a memorable meal at Manhattan's The Palace, billed as the most expensive restaurant in the world. "I was there as the guest of Elaine Kauffman, the great saloon keeper. After a tremendous meal and many wines, we got to the stage where we should be having brandy. Instead, Elaine had the *sommelier* bring something from the wine cellar I'd never seen before, a 1922 port. I'm not a port drinker and hadn't had any since I'd lived in England, 15 years earlier. The port was served in little pony glasses and it was like velvet going down. It unzipped my tonsils! It was a wonderful experience and just the taste to put the cap on the meal! It took someone like Elaine, who knows her stuff, and the *sommelier,* who knew his cellar, to put that experience together."

# Jim Brady's Pommes Frites
## (French Fried Potatoes)

Serves 6-8

6 large potatoes (baking potatoes preferably)

about 2½ quarts peanut oil
salt

1. *Peel potatoes; wash and pat dry.*
2. *Cut potatoes into strips approximately ½-inch thick.*
3. *Heat peanut oil in deep-fat fryer to 370° F. Fry small batches of potatoes 2-3 minutes, keeping temperature as constant as possible. (An electric deep-fat fryer eliminates guesswork.)*
4. *Drain potatoes on paper towels and keep in warm place.*
5. *When all the potatoes have been fried, increase the temperature to 385° F. and return potatoes in larger batches to the oil; fry 2 minutes more or until golden brown.*
6. *Drain; sprinkle with salt. Serve immediately.*

*NOTE: Select potatoes that are uniform in size and slice uniformly for best results. Peanut oil is the best to use for frying. If your pocketbook permits, fry each batch of potatoes in a new batch of peanut oil for maximum flavor.*

# Eileen Brennan

"If I had to plan my last supper, I'd drink booze and eat potatoes in as many forms as I could find, including vichysoisse, mashed, scalloped, O'Brien (cottage fried potatoes seasoned with onion, pimento and green pepper), baked, fried, stuffed and souffléed," said actress Eileen Brennan. "I adore potatoes. That probably comes from my Irish background!"

Judging by her reed-slender figure, Eileen eats few potatoes these days. "But," she said, her blue eyes dancing, "I still enjoy a baked potato served with butter, or with nothing at all. To eat a baked potato with chives and sour cream is so lovely, it's sinful! I also love scalloped potatoes. I'd have popcorn at my last supper, too, because I'm a real popcorn freak."

Eileen loves to cook, particularly for her two sons, Patrick and Sam. "I like to bake whole wheat bread. It's delicious! We eat very well: plenty of nice garden vegetables, simply cooked, and as little meat as possible. However, I do make one hell of an Irish stew!"

After living in New York for nearly 10 years, where she worked primarily on the stage, the actress now makes her home in California.

# Eileen Brennan's Scalloped Potatoes

### Serves 6

1½ lbs. potatoes
1½ cups milk
2 tbsps. butter
1 tsp. salt

freshly ground pepper
to taste
1 clove garlic, pressed
¼ tsp. thyme

1 cup Monterey Jack cheese, grated

1. *Peel and pare potatoes into thin slices lengthwise, ⅛-inch thick.*
2. *Combine all the ingredients except cheese in a saucepan.*
3. *Bring to boil; simmer 15 minutes, stirring often.*
4. *Transfer to a well-greased 1½-quart baking dish.*
5. *Sprinkle with cheese.*
6. *Bake in preheated 350° F. oven about 30 minutes, or until potatoes are tender and cheese is bubbly and brown.*

NOTE: *If desired, omit cheese and herbs. Place a ½-inch thick slice of ham steak on top of the potatoes and bake in slower oven (about 300° F.) until ham is cooked. If desired, add about 1½ tsps. minced white onion to potatoes in lieu of garlic.*

# Ellen Burstyn

"I'm an on-again, off-again vegetarian," said actress Ellen Burstyn. "Right now, though, I seem to be in a high protein period. I don't know why. It just seems to be what my body wants."

Ellen shares a house with her son, Jefferson, in the Hollywood Hills overlooking Grauman's Chinese Theatre, and she often cooks for him. "Most of our friends are vegetarians (I'm one sometimes for as long as two years at a time), and for them I usually cook brown rice and vegetable dishes, most often vegetable curries."

On camping trips, Ellen and her son take along sleeping bags and lots of food, but occasionally "we fast and take along no food, just some juice. Usually, if I'm eating meat," she said, "I throw in steaks you can cook over flame. Sometimes I just buy local food and only bring along the pepper mill and some good, cold-packed olive oil I get in the health store. I'm fussy about oil since I lived in Italy and got used to wonderful Italian olive oil. And I could never go camping without my pepper mill!"

# Ellen Burstyn's Eggplant Curry

### Serves 6

3 tbsps. olive oil
pinch cumin seed
1 tsp. turmeric
½ tsp. cayenne
1 large eggplant, chopped
   with skin
1 large yellow onion,
   peeled and chopped

1 sweet green pepper, chopped
½ cup chicken stock
2 large ripe fresh tomatoes,
   peeled and chopped
1 cup yogurt
sea salt to taste
freshly ground black
   pepper to taste

1. *Heat olive oil in skillet; add cumin, turmeric and cayenne, and cook 1 minute.*
2. *Add eggplant, onion and pepper; stir until well blended.*
3. *Add chicken stock and tomatoes; cook over low flame about 15 minutes, stirring often.*
4. *Add yogurt, and salt and pepper to taste. (Do not boil mixture or the yogurt will curdle.)*
5. *Serve curry at once, alone, or spooned over steaming bowls of hot cooked brown rice.*

*NOTE: Ellen's favorite curry accompaniments: chopped raisins, carrots, cucumber and celery served as side dish with garnishes of cashews or sunflower seeds.*

# Bob Newhart

"I've never been a great fancier of food." said Bob Newhart. "When I was growing up in the Oak Park section of Chicago, I was raised on Midwestern fare. . . . My mother was a compulsive baker of brownies. Nobody ever ate them. We just let them stack up until they got so stale she had to throw them away." He laughed softly. "I used to take pills to put on weight because I couldn't have cared less about food. Now, however, I have a taste for it."

Bob lives in Bel Air with his wife, Ginnie, and their four children: Robert, Timothy, Jennifer and Courtney. "I'll never forget the first meal Ginnie ever prepared for me," Bob recalled. "It was a thing called 'baked steak' – the kind you put in the bottom of the boiler rack and 'bake' instead of broil. Since we were still on our honeymoon, I didn't dare tell her how tough or how awful it was."

Happily, Ginnie has become a great cook.

"There are still many things I don't like," continued Bob. "I still enjoy meat loaf. I'm particularly fond of Ginnie's Italian dishes like spaghetti, lasagna or manicotti. We entertain informally at home. Luckily, we have a small dining room because I hate large parties. (Don Rickles and his wife are Bob and Ginnie's closest friends.) You can never talk to anyone. Somebody is always pulling on your sleeve saying, 'The icemaker broke down.' What's the point of having people over unless you can talk to them?"

# Ginnie Newhart's Carrot Mold

Serves 6

1½ cups carrot, grated  
1 cup brown sugar  
½ cup soft margarine  

½ tsp. baking powder  
½ tsp. salt  
1 egg, beaten  

1 cup all-purpose flour

1. *Combine all ingredients; mix well.*
2. *Place in greased 5½-cup ring mold. Bake in preheated 350° F. oven about 45 minutes.*
3. *Unmold. Serve on platter with cooked green peas in the center.*

*NOTE: Ginnie comments, "I usually make 3 or 4 of these, one to use and the others to freeze. My family loves it. The ring looks so pretty with a green vegetable. Great with poultry, beef or fish."*

# Elizabeth Post

"Today entertaining is much more informal than it was when Emily Post was alive," said Elizabeth Post, the grand-daughter-in-law of Emily Post. "Now we offer streamlined menus for streamlined figures."

Elizabeth, known to friends as Libby, recalled her first nervous meeting with Emily Post. "Five minutes after meeting her, I found her so charming and gracious, I soon forgot that she was the First Lady of Etiquette. Manners, after all, are simply the easiest, most gracious way of doing things.

"While the glittering array of servants, the skilled butler, formal meals of banquet dimensions, 'shaded' candlesticks are now relics of Emily Post's day, certain anachronisms still remain," Libby said. "In Grandmama's day, two servants were necessary to wait on as few as two people. Grandmama's original book read almost like a novel. I always love the story of the leader of Newport society who made a world-wide reputation for the speed with which she served a formal dinner. She had a footman for every two guests, and anyone dining with her had to cling to the edge of his plate or it would be whisked away. Today we have servantless meals and our hostess might be bare-footed if she's one of the younger generation," Libby said gaily.

The tradition of gracious and relaxed dining is very much a part of the Post household. The informal practice of summer outdoor cooking is carried into the house as autumn days advance. "We like to cook in the fireplace. Bill cooks steaks with an electric rotisserie, but you can use your own andirons as support for an ordinary oven grill over the coals."

# Elizabeth Post's Artichoke Hearts and Spinach au Gratin

Serves 6-8

1 can (8 oz.) artichoke hearts, drained, or 1 pkg. (10 oz.) frozen, cooked and drained

1 tbsp. sweet butter

3 pkgs. (10 ozs.) chopped spinach

boiling salted water

salt to taste

freshly ground black pepper to taste

¾ cup heavy cream

1 cup Swiss cheese, grated

1. *Sauté artichoke hearts slowly in butter; set aside.*
2. *Cook spinach in boiling salted water according to package instructions; drain well.*
3. *Season to taste with salt and pepper.*
4. *Pour cream over cooked spinach; mix well.*
5. *Place artichoke hearts in bottom of fireproof dish; top with creamed spinach and sprinkle cheese over the top.*
6. *Cook, uncovered, in a preheated 350° F. oven 15 minutes. If necessary, run under broiler to brown cheese.*

NOTE: *Elizabeth's version is quick and eliminates the classic cheese sauce.*

# Anthony Quinn

"Most of the foods that I love, I love with passion. And the only passion I feel is for Mexican and Italian food," said Anthony Quinn. Tony was perched in a director's chair on a New York City rooftop overlooking an expanse of TV antennas, lines of wash, and chimney stacks. The veteran actor, making his 106th film, *Across 110th Street,* looked more like a bum than the off-beat detective he plays, in a shabby sports jacket, gray slacks with a small rip and an ill-fitting checked hat cocked on his head.

"I love Mexican food and I can eat it for hours. I love what Italians do to their vegetables. Outside of that, I don't care what the hell I eat!" he said, laughing the distinctive laugh that has stamped his many characterizations: his grizzled bandito, his exuberant Greek, his bumbling Italian.

Tony went on to reveal another of his talents. "I happen to be a very good cook! Listen, the interesting thing about Mexican food is that you can ad lib. It's all very personal; there aren't any staid recipes. Everybody adds his own little artistic touch, putting in more oregano or more cheese, flour or whatever it is, making it to his own taste. So it's not like a steak, which is just a steak and involves only three minutes of cooking.

"Listen, once I invented a dish when I was living on a little farm in Connecticut. Once, 30 people dropped in on us for dinner and we didn't have enough food to feed them. There were a lot of potatoes around and some hamburger, so I made the most fantastic dish of baked potatoes, refilling the shells with mashed potatoes, hamburger, seasonings and cheese. It was the greatest dish I ever invented."

# Anthony Quinn's Viva Stuffed Potatoes

Serves 4

4 large baking potatoes
½ lb. ground lean chuck
⅓ cup onion, chopped
1 tsp. salt

dash freshly ground
   black pepper
½ tsp. oregano
½ tsp. chili powder

cheddar cheese, shredded

1. Wrap scrubbed, dried, pricked potatoes in aluminum foil and bake in preheated 400° F. oven 1 hour, or until well done.
2. While potatoes are baking, brown beef and onions lightly.
3. When potatoes are done, cut in halves lengthwise right through foil. Scoop out insides, mash well, and add seasonings.
4. Drain off excess fat from meat; discard.
5. Combine meat and potato mixtures; return to the shells. Top with shredded cheese.
6. Bake at 400° F. for 20 minutes, or until cheese is nicely browned.

# Gena Rowlands

Actress Gena Rowlands admits to being an enthusiastic cook but a "cop-out when it comes to the routine of day-to-day cooking. That's boring. I like to prepare unusual dishes. My mother always said: 'When you get interested in cooking, you can cook if you can read.'

"Cooking is not mysterious," she said. "John (Cassavetes, her husband) taught me how to cook the basic Greek things, like their tomato sauce and their wonderful salad. I prepare some Greek dishes, like *spanika,* made with fresh spinach and rice. My mother-in-law is a great cook. Her *kourabiedes* are so fabulous, they not only melt, they practically explode in your mouth! There's pure magic in the way she combines brandy and butter."

Entertaining *chez* Cassavetes can vary from "20 for lunch to nobody!" said Gena. "We have friends who are vegetarians and friends who have ulcers. Everyone is quite free. They know that whatever I have is what they will get! If anyone has a special dietary problem, I let them go into the kitchen and fix for themselves. By the way, I don't want to give the impression that I take care of everyone all by myself. We have a housekeeper and a nurse. Strangely enough, I enjoy marketing. I like to know what goes into my family's stomachs. We live up in the hills, so getting to stores is difficult. I have a great, old-fashioned guy who grows his own fruits and vegetables and delivers them to the house in his own truck twice a week. That makes a tremendous difference. I wouldn't say it is less expensive, but we do get quality food."

# Gena Rowlands's Spinach and Rice

Serves 6

2 lbs. fresh spinach
2 medium-size onions, peeled
  and minced
1 small clove garlic, peeled
  and minced
1 cup uncooked rice

⅓ cup olive oil
2 tbsps. tomato sauce
2 bay leaves
salt to taste
ground white pepper
  to taste

2 cups beef broth

1. Wash and dry spinach. Tear leaves into pieces.
2. Sauté onion, garlic and rice in olive oil until onion is soft and golden-colored.
3. Add tomato sauce and stir.
4. Add spinach, bay leaves, salt and pepper to taste.
5. Add beef broth; cover and simmer over low heat about 20 minutes, or until rice is cooked.
6. Serve hot or cold. Terrific with cold roast chicken!

# Ann Rutherford

Ann Rutherford is a crazy lady, a latter-day "Auntie Mame" who is a gadget nut. She loves life, dotes on giving big parties celebrating things, and does her share of the cooking and planning. Her favorite "at-beach" dish is a mixed vegetable casserole she first called "Sludge," but graduated to "Jazz in a Basket!"

"When I started making it at our beach house," said Ann, "I put it in a casserole but changed to a lined basket as it got larger and larger. Finally, I bought one of those miniature wash baskets to hold it because our dinners had become so big. I never knew how many people were coming!"

Ann's beach dinners take place off the Pacific coast highway, in a wonderful house perched on stilts so when the tide is in, guests can fish from the deck or dive off for a swim. "Our favorite kind of entertaining is comfortable clothes and everybody participates. Our favorite party of the year has always been on Groundhog Day. It's the only untaken vacation day in the year. It's an ideal day to entertain because everyone else has glommed on Thanksgiving, Christmas, Easter and April Fool's Day. Food is served constantly, starting with the first guest's arrival. Hot coffee is always available. We have three or four kinds of meat: beef, corned beef, a whole ham — always something for everybody, always food that will hold. I'm very large on braziers and electric hot trays because I think it's an imposition to drag people out of their homes for dinner or luncheon and give them food that's less appetizing than they would get at home."

# Ann Rutherford's Vegetable Jazz in a Basket

### Serves 6-8

½ lb. fresh mushrooms or
   1 can (6-8 ozs.) sliced
6 ribs celery
3 ears corn
⅓ cup onion flakes
3 tbsps. water
6 tbsps. butter

2 cups zucchini, sliced
2 cups tomatoes, chopped
1 tbsp. parsley, snipped
2 tsps. salt
2 tsps. basil leaves
½ tsp. thyme leaves
¼ tsp. ground black pepper

¼ cup dry red wine

1. Rinse, pat dry, and slice fresh mushrooms, or drain canned mushrooms.
2. Rinse and trim celery ribs; cut into 1-inch chunks.
3. Cut kernels from corn (makes about 2½ cups). Set vegetables aside.
4. Rehydrate onion flakes in water for 10 minutes.
5. In a large saucepan or Dutch oven, melt butter. Add onion and sauté 2 minutes.
6. Add mushrooms and sauté 2 minutes longer.
7. Stir in celery and zucchini; sauté 2 minutes more.
8. Stir in corn, tomatoes, parsley, salt, basil, thyme and black pepper.
9. Cover and simmer 5 minutes, or until vegetables are crisp-tender.
10. Stir in red wine. Heat only until piping hot.
11. Arrange vegetables in basket lined with aluminum foil. Makes a terrific side dish to serve with barbecued chicken or steak cooked over the coals.

# Alexis Smith

Alexis Smith is a compulsive recipe collector. She even carries a rubber-banded parcel of her favorite recipes when she travels to movie locations. "Sometimes, though, the rubber band breaks and the recipes come tumbling out," she said, laughing merrily. Her husband, actor Craig Stevens, once remarked that her laugh "bears a haunting resemblance to Woody Woodpecker's."

The ageless actress was in the heart of Cajun food country, playing the role of a stylishly Southern millionaire horse breeder in the flick, *Casey's Shadow*. One of her favorite meals was prepared by the film's producer, Ray Stark. "Ray threw a party for the cast and crew, cooking up a storm. He served a whole smorgasbord, including ham, turkey and baked squash. Ray's a great cook," Alexis said, adding that she has acquired his recipe for baked squash, which he, in turn, got from Beatrice Lee, his cook back home in Beverly Hills.

Alexis's food styles reflect the state of her career. "If my career is sailing, it's limousine time, room service at the hotel or dining out. Then, if things are not going so swimmingly, and I'm back playing in stock, as Craig says, 'We're back on the bus again!' – and boom, I'm back in my own kitchen. It's wonderful to have life both ways!"

# Alexis Smith's Corn Pudding

### Serves 6

2 cups canned whole kernel
  corn, drained

1 can (4 ozs.) green chili
  peppers, drained and cubed

¼ lb. cheddar cheese,
  grated

1 cup milk

½ tsp. salt

3 eggs, beaten

1. *Mix ingredients in the order given.*
2. *Turn into a greased 1½-quart baking dish and set in a shallow pan of hot water.*
3. *Bake in preheated 350° F. oven about 1 hour, or until set.*
4. *Serve hot or cold. Great with barbecued chicken or spare ribs or steak.*

# Jon Voight

Actor Jon Voight finds food scenes a "very revealing way to say something to the audience about the character you're playing." Yet, when Jon is off camera, at home in California, he often skips meals or leaves in the middle of them, just because he's a daydreamer! "I think about all behavior in terms of my own craft. In a film, it's an opportunity to tell something about the character. For example, does he smoke or doesn't he smoke? If he's eating, I want to know what the prop man's going to bring. And, then, just by the way he eats something, you can reveal something about his character."

Voight might have been talking about himself. "I'm a non-cook. If I have to eat anything, I will go buy something already prepared or I will make a sandwich or hamburger. I'm a generous sandwich maker, lavish with butter, tomatoes, and lettuce heaped on the bread. I like ice cold milk. Left to my own devices, I'm really in quite a lot of trouble because I'm such a daydreamer. I like very simple food, but occasionally, I like to break that and have a French meal with sauces and wines. If I find something I particularly like, I feel wonderful. It's a very funny feeling, almost sexual! I had a martini one time. I don't drink very much. In fact, I've probably had four martinis in my life. When I finished this martini I said, 'This is the best martini I ever had.' It was a normal martini, but I went crazy. This happened again the other night, when I had artichokes vinaigrette. When the food is good, it drives me crazy! I was so happy with that food! Whole meals have done that to me, too," Jon said, laughing.

# Jon Voight's Artichokes, California Style

Serves 4

## For the artichokes

| | |
|---|---|
| 4 artichokes | boiling water |
| 1 tsp. salt | 1 tbsp. lemon juice |

1. *Wash artichokes; cut off stems at base and remove small bottom leaves. If desired, trim tips of leaves and cut off about 1 inch from top of artichokes.*
2. *Stand artichokes upright in deep saucepan large enough to hold snugly.*
3. *Add salt and enough boiling water to reach a depth of from 2-3 inches in saucepan. Add lemon juice.*
4. *Cover. Boil gently 30-45 minutes, or until base can be pierced easily with fork. Add a little more water if needed.*
5. *Gently spread leaves and remove "choke" (thistle portion) from center of artichoke with metal spoon. Turn artichokes upside down to drain.*

## For the marinade

| | |
|---|---|
| 1 tsps. salt | 1 tbsp. green onion, finely minced |
| ¼ tsp. pepper | 1 clove garlic, crushed |
| ½ tsp. dry mustard | 2 tbsps. vinegar |
| ½ tsp. oregano leaves, crushed | ⅓ cup salad oil |

1. *Combine all ingredients; beat well and spoon over artichokes.*
2. *Chill 6 hours or overnight, occasionally spooning marinade over artichokes.*
3. *Serve marinade as dip for leaves, if desired.*

# Dennis Weaver

Dennis Weaver and wife, Gerry, and their three grown sons, Rick, Bob and Rusty, celebrate a country Christmas each year with an enormous spread reminiscent of the huge Christmas feasts Dennis's mother used to prepare when he was growing up in Missouri.

"We have many good things to eat," said vegetarian Dennis. "Everything from yams to Waldorf salad, vegetarian dressing and corn. Most of our food comes from our own garden. We have some of the traditional foods, too, like cranberry sauce and pumpkin pie." Their country Christmas vegetarian-style always includes eggplant.

"Of course, not everyone in the family is a vegetarian," explained Dennis, "so Gerry roasts a turkey for Christmas dinner. Rusty is not a vegetarian and my two older sons eat turkey, chicken and fish."

The Weavers live in a charming, two-story Spanish structure that rises gracefully from the summit of a mountain ridge in Calabasas, California. Sharing has always been part of the Weaver family tradition. "I lived on a farm from the time I was five until I was 10 years old," said Dennis. "My mother prepared immense feasts to feed all my aunts, uncles and cousins. Eating was our only real indulgence. We didn't have electricity, so my mother cooked on a wood-burning stove. Cutting the wood and building the fire was my chore. We didn't have turkey because we didn't raise them. We ate only what we raised. Mother was forever canning. That's the reason we moved to the farm — to have enough food to survive." He recalled hiking into the woods to pick wild raspberries and blueberries. "Our hands were blue for weeks afterwards."

# Dennis Weaver's Vegetarian Top-of-the-Stove Special

### Serves 4-5

⅓ cup butter
2 ribs celery, including
    leaves, chopped
⅔ cups scallions, sliced
    (white part only)
large green pepper, diced in
    large pieces
salt to taste

freshly ground pepper
    to taste
2 cups aged Cheddar cheese,
    diced in large pieces
4 cups cooked unpolished
    brown (or wild) rice
2 large peeled tomatoes,
    cut in eighths

about 2 tbsps. water
1 tsp. "spiked"* herbs (available at health food stores) or your
favorite herbs (parsley flakes, fines herbes, thyme,
oregano, etc.)

1. Melt butter in large skillet or Dutch oven; add celery, scallions, green pepper, herbs and seasonings.
2. Toss with fork over low heat about 1 minute.
3. Add cheese and rice and mix well.
4. Arrange tomatoes on top; add water; and cover tightly.
5. Cook over low heat only until cheese is partially melted and vegetables are crisp and retain their color. Serve at once.

NOTE: Dennis says, "I use unpolished brown rice (available in health food stores) as it has more body and flavor and is better for you. This dish serves five hungry Weavers with a delicious cold portion left over for my lunch the next day! I serve the skillet right at the table along with unleavened Armenian bread and home-made organic applesauce (made with organically grown apples and slightly sweetened with raw brown sugar)."

*"Spiked" herbs is a seasoned salt flavored with sea salt, yeast concentrates and an assortment of dried, pulverized vegetables including spinach, celery root, pumpkin, watercress, carrots, etc.

# Joanne Woodward

Joanne Woodward attributes her abundant energy to "becoming a vegetarian, taking lots of vitamins and not eating too much." Seated in the airy, comfortable living room of her New England-style Beverly Hills house, she looked happy, healthy and serene as she busily knit a sweater.

"I grew up in the South where we ate big Sunday dinners in the middle of the day. I was raised on fried chicken, lots of rice and gravy and pecan pie," Joanne told me. "I don't think the body needs red meat. Besides, there are too many chemicals put into meat. I eat chicken, not much, and fish, prepared as simply as possible. Paul (husband Paul Newman), who is famous for his hamburgers, is getting to be a great fish cook.

"Our Thanksgiving is not as traditional, unlike Christmas, which is very traditional every year. We often have Thanksgiving dinner at the Ranch House Restaurant at Ojai, near Los Angeles. It's so charming. They make their own bread there, and some of my best recipes come from Alan Hooker who started the Ranch House. His recipes for sesame soya or honey whole-wheat bread are superb. I have to fast for a week beforehand to survive a meal up there because the food's so delicious."

Joanne showed me into her all-white kitchen with natural wood cabinets and pegboard floor. "I'm making organic applesauce," she said, handing me a glass. "Since I don't eat any sugar, I cut up green apples and simmer them in organic juice. You don't need to add anything else. Sometimes I add a little nutmeg and honey."

Discovering a crock pot has simplified much of her cooking. "You can make applesauce in one," she said. "I cook everything in it. I'd like to try cooking in clay pots."

# Joanne Woodward's Never-Fail Hollandaise Sauce for Vegetables

Makes about 1 cup

3 large egg yolks
3 wooden spoonfuls cold
   water (about 5 tbsps.)
¼ tsp. salt

pepper to taste
⅔ lb. salted butter,
   cut in small bits,
   at room temperature

fresh lemon juice to taste, about 1 tbsp.

1. *Place egg yolks and cold water in small crock or top of a double boiler, beating with wire whisk or wooden spoon.*
2. *Place bowl or upper half of double boiler over lower half of double boiler filled with hot, not boiling water.*
3. *Lower heat, then add salt and pepper to yolk-water mixture.*
4. *Cook, stirring constantly until mixture begins to coat the spoon.*
5. *Remove from heat, still keeping bowl over hot water.*
6. *Bit by bit, add butter to sauce, stirring constantly after each addition to make a thickened, smooth sauce.*
7. *Lastly, beat in lemon juice. (Sauce can be made in advance by placing in pan of lukewarm water or near the faint heat from a gas pilot light.) Serve warm with artichokes or asparagus.*

NOTE: *Joanne's Hollandaise Sauce particularly deserves your careful attention and patience! She advises, "Never, never melt butter before adding to the sauce — that would be total disaster. I had a failure only one time when I used sweet (unsalted) butter. Remember, the water must never be boiling, and while it seems to take forever to make, stirring for an eternity, the sauce comes out absolutely divine and never separates. Sauce can be reheated by placing over a bowl of warm water, stirring constantly." Weight watchers may want to reduce the quantity of butter slightly. But in any case, butter must be added to the yolk mixture very slowly to prevent curdling or separating.*

# Efrem Zimbalist, Jr.

"I became a vegetarian, mainly out of curiosity. I remain one, simply because I feel so marvelous," Efrem Zimbalist, Jr. said. "I have so much buoyancy, energy and stamina now. Our mania for a high protein diet is nonsense. We eat like stevedores, then sit around in an office all day long. I simply can't eat like that. Besides, by nature, man is not suited to be a carnivore. His teeth are better suited to an herbivorous diet!"

Efrem cited Pythagoras and G.B. Shaw among famous vegetarians. "The healthiest people in the world are the Hunzas who live in the Himalayas. They live to the incredible age of 160 and often play polo in their 'old age.' The Hunzas seldom overindulge and, for health reasons, fast for three to six days at a time. This practice came about quite accidently, however, since despite a rich soil, they run out of food about once a year.

"I eat twice a day. Breakfast is orange juice, eggs, cereal or pancakes without the usual sausage, and coffee or English tea. I depend a lot on vegetable protein foods available in the can which can be cooked alone or cooked into casseroles, or 'meatloaves' in much the same manner as meat. I get their meatless hotdogs, 'meat' cuts or patties cooked like chops or cutlets." The products are made from soybeans and peanuts.

"One of my favorite dishes is curry. I remember all the pomp and ceremony when I was a boy and traveled to Ceylon with my parents. It took 17 boys to carry in the curry and all the side-dishes."

# Efrem Zimbalist Jr.'s Meatless Casserole

Serves 4-6

1 can (4 ozs.) mushrooms
  (sliced or caps)
1 can (30 ozs.) vegetable
  protein dinner cuts
flavored breadcrumbs

4 tbsps. vegetable oil,
  divided
1 medium-sized onion,
  peeled and chopped
1 cup dairy sour cream

1. *Drain juices from mushrooms and vegetable protein; reserve juices.*
2. *Roll dinner cuts in breadcrumbs; brown quickly on both sides in 2 tbsps. vegetable oil. Set aside.*
3. *Sauté onion and mushrooms in remaining oil.*
4. *Arrange half the browned cuts in bottom of ovenproof casserole.*
5. *Top with half the onion-mushroom mixture.*
6. *Repeat both layers.*
7. *Mix reserved juices with sour cream. Pour over all.*
8. *Cover and bake in preheated 375° F. oven 45 minutes.*

# Breads & Batters

# Bill Bixby

"I used to be a meat-and-potatoes man. But now I'll eat anything that's put in front of me, willingly and with great anticipation. Food has become an art form to me now." This is the way actor Bill Bixby reacts to the cooking of his wife, actress Brenda Benet.

The Bixbys built a home they both helped to design when they married. The house, located in West Los Angeles, is filled with "only our furniture," Bill said. "We sold everything when we got married. We didn't want any remanants left over from our bachelor days!" They also lease a house at the beach and spend as much time as possible on their 110-acre ranch in Oregon, where they plan to build their permanent home.

"One of the nicest things about us both is, we're not extremists about anything," explained Bill. "And I think that's very important. Brenda eats four or five tiny meals a day. And while she's eating fettuccine Alfredo for breakfast, I'm enjoying my eggs and bacon!"

Both Bixbys are mad about Chinese Mandarin food. "I've got a great restaurant for you called the Chinese Dumpling House in Chicago! Their spicy beef with cellophane noodles are dynamite!" Bill said.

"I particularly love the way the Chinese cook their vegetables," added Brenda. "I love our home-grown vegetables on the ranch in Oregon. Say, have you ever eaten a carrot pulled right out of the ground? Isn't that something wonderful? It's already been chilled by the earth to just the right temperature!"

The Bixbys entertain "rarely and almost always on a one-to-one basis," said Brenda. "We had six people over to the house the other night. It almost seemed like a gang." Their beach fare is fun and off-beat. "We're zucchini buffs because we had a bumper crop up at the ranch."

# Bill Bixby's Zucchini Bread

Makes one 9-inch loaf

1½ cups all-purpose flour
2 tsps. ground cinnamon
2 tsps. baking powder
1 tsp. salt
2 eggs
1 cup sugar
1 cup salad oil

2 cups zucchini,
  coarsely grated
1 tsps. pure vanilla
  extract
1 cup English walnuts,
  coarsely chopped

1. Combine flour, cinnamon, baking powder and salt: set aside.
2. Beat eggs and sugar until foamy in large mixing bowl, using an electric mixer.
3. At low speed, blend in zucchini, oil and vanilla extract.
4. Add the reserved flour mixture, ⅓ at a time. Beat just until blended.
8. Stir in nuts.
9. Spoon batter into a greased 9 x 5 x 3-inch loaf pan. Bake in a preheated 350° F. oven for 1 hour, or until cake tester inserted into center comes out clean.
10. Cool in pan for 10 minutes. Remove to wire rack and cool completely.

NOTE: The bread is nice and spicy; a nice complement to the zucchini. Serve with coffee for an unusual dessert or for a coffee break, slicing bread into thin slices; spread lightly with softened sweet butter.

# Angie Dickinson

Angie Dickinson had come to our home for morning coffee. In private life she is the wife of composer-conductor Burt Bacharach Jr. and the mother of a daughter, Nikki. Although Angie believes it's a man's world, she explained, "Being a woman in a man's world is just great. As for cooking, it's important for a woman to satisfy a man's needs. In my case, my husband is a gourmet. He comes from an elegant family. He grew up in New York and has been exposed to the finest restaurants. He knows the best food and wines. After you've watched a ball game from a box, you don't want to sit in the bleachers anymore."

Her cocoa brown eyes smiled as she said, "I guess I'm a boiler-broiler. By boiling, I don't mean stews, with all that mixing and dunking."

"But how does a steak-and-salad girl satisfy a gourmet husband?" we asked.

"I let him take me out a lot," she answered, laughing.

Home-style cooking by Angie is simple and unadorned. "I broil lamb chops, but I always rub them with oregano. When I cook fresh vegetables, I always undercook them. Once when I was sick, Marlene Dietrich brought me some of her home-made soup and it was fantastic. It was a rich broth filled with carrots and peas, all undercooked just as I like them. She's such a wonderfully generous and kind person who's always interested in helping other people . . . . I just thought of something we (she and Burt) both love, called 'honeymoon sandwich.' We had it for our first brunch when we stayed at the Tennis Club in Palm Springs."

# Angie Dickinson's Honeymoon Sandwich

Serves 2

2 slices rye bread or one English muffin split

soft sweet butter

4 generous slices baked or boiled ham, or lightly broiled Canadian bacon

prepared or Dijon mustard

4 thick slices beefsteak tomato

1 dill pickle, sliced lengthwise

3-4 slices Cheddar or American cheese

1. *Lightly toast bread; spread lightly with butter.*
2. *Top each slice with ham; spread ham lightly with mustard.*
3. *Top with tomato, pickles, ending with cheese on top.*
4. *Run under broiler until cheese is melted and lightly browned.*
5. *Serve open-face style with good vintage brut champagne. Great for brunch or supper.*

# Jeane Dixon

"We Capricorns have to work hard to get ahead. Life is never easy for us," Jeane Dixon said. The lady, who is famous for her predictions, including the deaths of the Kennedy brothers and the national trauma of Watergate, lives in a large house in a quiet section of Washington, D.C., with Jimmy Dixon, her realtor husband.

"I believe in eating sensibly," said Jeane. "Through the years I've found I must eat the foods that suit me personally, foods that are in concert with my temperament and body chemistry." Jeane's greatest dietary concern is selecting foods that will not interfere with her psychic powers. "I have learned to avoid certain foods, including chocolate, coffee, tea and large quantities of meat. Otherwise, I loose my powers of concentration."

Jeane grew up in a strict German household where she learned naturally to eat nutritionally sound meals. "I'm certain my mother knew nothing about vitamins or minerals, but we had wonderful meals, big roasts, plenty of vegetables and fruits. I still hunger for the great bowls of vegetable soup my mother used to make and the aroma of her homemade bread wafting through the kitchen! I cook more often now that we're alone and no longer have a housekeeper. When we're rushed, I sometimes fix Jimmy buttermilk pancakes and sausages for supper. He loves my pancakes!"

She even cooks for "Mike, the Magi-Cat," who, Jeane says, also possesses psychic powers. Mike lives out in Jeane's backyard in an elegant house that resembles a miniature Chinese red pagoda!

Dinners chez Dixon are intimate and elegant. "I enjoy formal sit-down dinners. I love beautiful crystal, highly polished silver, gorgeous china and sparkling table linens, and I love to set off the table with a centerpiece of red roses!" There are times when Jeane prefers to eat lightly — or not at all. "When I'm very tired, something like a bowl of blueberries and milk can make the perfect meal for me!"

# Jeane Dixon's Favorite Buttermilk Pancakes

### Makes 8 pancakes

1 cup all-purpose flour
2 tsps. sugar
¾ tsp. baking powder
dash of salt

1¼ cups buttermilk
½ tsp. baking soda
2 egg yolks, slightly beaten
2 egg whites, stiffly beaten

2 tbsps. melted butter, at room temperature

1. In a mixing bowl, sift together flour, sugar, baking powder and salt.
2. Combine buttermilk, baking soda and egg yolks. Mix lightly and add to dry ingredients. Mix until batter is barely smooth.
3. Stir in melted butter and fold in egg whites.
4. Cook on hot greased pancake griddle, turning once, until pancakes are browned on both sides. Serve with crisp bacon curls or grilled ham.

NOTE: Jeane advises, "These pancakes are hearty enough for supper or brunch."

# Kirk Douglas

Kirk and Anne Douglas believe in mixing guests from all walks of life. That's probably why their parties are considered among the most successful in Hollywood. "I could think of nothing more disastrous than to have a dinner party with just a bunch of movie stars," said Kirk. "I mean, after a while, they'd have nothing to say to one another. "We had a party not very long ago, for example. We had Burt Lancaster and Gregory Peck, UCLA Chancellor Young and former Chancellor Franklin M. Murphy. Al Casey of American Airlines was there too. We also had Don Rickles. At first my wife said, 'My God, what a strange mixture!' It was funny because the university group were fascinated with the people in the entertainment world. So there was an exchange. And, Don Rickles, of course, he was fantastic. He started off with, 'By the way, Chancellor Young, the only reason you're here is because Kirk's having trouble getting his kid in your college.' This was new to them and they loved it."

We were talking over a leisurely blueberry muffin breakfast in the sun-filled solarium of the functional and attractive Douglas home. There were plants all around us, a bronze modern statue, and an ancient vase rescued from a wrecked Israeli ship. A monkey, part of his son Peter's collection of animals, was going back into his cage on the other side of the glass-paneled sliding door.

"Please have some muffins," said Kirk, "but be careful, they're nice and hot, but fattening. Great for building character role." He roared.

"People think movie people come here and every night are out on the town," he continued. "They're surprised when they find we can just sit around in the evening, have dinner and talk to people."

Kirk loves to eat, but admits he's no chef. "Peter can barbecue well, but when I do it, it's disastrous! I make a great fire though," he said.

# Kirk Douglas's Blueberry Buttermilk Muffins

Makes 24 small muffins

2½ cups all-purpose flour
2 tsps. baking powder
½ tsp. baking soda
¼ cup sugar

¼ tsp. salt
1 cup buttermilk
2 eggs, beaten
⅔ cup butter, melted

1½ cups blueberries

1. *Sift together dry ingredients in large bowl.*
2. *Make a well; add buttermilk, eggs and butter which has been melted and browned slightly. Mix well.*
3. *Fold in blueberries.*
4. *Drop batter by tablespoons into greased muffin tins.*
5. *Bake 25 minutes in preheated 400° F. oven.*
6. *Serve warm with sweet butter.*

NOTE: For delightful aromatic touches, "scent" the batter with freshly ground nutmeg or mace.

PUT THE KID IN YOUR SCHOOL, DUMMY!

# Katherine Helmond

"I strongly believe that what you put in your body results in your entire spiritual and mental outlook because the brain cells are affected by what you feed the body," said beautiful actress Katherine Helmond.

On a cold rainy day, she talked with me in the small house where she was sitting with a canine friend, a loving black dachshund, who snuggled in her lap. Fans know the Texas-born Helmond best as Jessica Tate, the bubble-brained character she portrays on ABC-TV's prime-time spoof, "Soap."

Katherine is a vegetarian and enthusiastic follower of Zen Buddhism. Since giving up meat some years ago, the slender, auburn-haired lady has never felt better. She credits her husband, sculptor David Christian, for her switch in diet. When David suffered from hypoglycemia, a condition caused by an abnormally high level of glucose in the blood, Katherine became interested in finding foods without sugar or preservatives.

"Vegetarianism need not be kooky, nutty or freaky. For example, we eat many lovely breads," she said, showing me recipes for delicious wheat germ corn bread and banana bread. "We like whole-grain bread, bran muffins and *chappati* (Indian bread)."

# Katherine Helmond's Wheat Germ Corn Bread

Makes 1 loaf

1 cup whole wheat flour
1 cup wheat germ
1 cup stone ground corn meal
⅓ cup brown sugar or honey
5 tsps. baking powder

1 tsp. salt
3 large eggs
1½ cups raw milk
⅓ cup margarine, melted
sesame seeds

1. *Mix all the dry ingredients together.*
2. *Beat eggs; combine with the rest of the wet ingredients, just until they are mixed.*
3. *Pour batter into greased 9 x 13-inch baking pan.*
4. *Sprinkle with sesame seeds.*
5. *Bake in preheated 350° F. oven about 45 minutes, or until a toothpick comes out clean when inserted into loaf.*
6. *Cool slightly on wire rack before cutting. Great with margarine or sweet butter.*

*NICE ADDITIONS: For flavor and texture, add sunflower seeds, raisins, dried fruit (dates, apricots). Or for an accompaniment to fish or fowl, use thyme or sage. Add grated cheddar for protein.*

# Peggy Lee

"I have a ridiculous memory of falling down the cellar steps with a huge pot of chicken and dumplings, and winding up in the coal bin with it all over me. It really was pretty funny," said singer Peggy Lee, bursting forth with a crescendo of laughter as she recalled with wonderful, dry, gentle humor her childhood on a Jamestown, North Dakota, farm.

Peggy has been cooking almost as long as she's been singing. "My manager tells me I make a great spaghetti sauce," she said. "He wants me to go into the flash-freeze business, but I never measure anything. I love to cook, but it's a little off-limits now! I did something I'm very proud of, I cooked a whole pot of shells and didn't eat any. I did put a little of the sauce on some cottage cheese."

The songstress is a careful hostess and chooses her music to match her guests as carefully as she selects a menu. "I think entertaining friends is like something Emerson said, 'Bring out all the best things.' For cocktails, I'd choose something light, a quiet soft jazz that will encourage people to get together and talk, not listen to the music. I'd say something like Sergio Mendes or the Carpenters, something to get things bubbling. And for dinner music, something soft. Johnny Mandel is one of my favorites, particularly his "The Shadow of Your Smile" or that whole score from *The Sandpiper*. Later, you play something to listen to. I love Brahms's "Third Symphony" (in F Major). There's a beautiful theme to it, something very comforting and soothing to me."

Peggy's not much for recipes, but she did mention that among the favorites in her repertoire are buttermilk pancakes with boysenberry topping, reminiscent of huge country breakfasts typical of the Midwest.

# Peggy Lee's Buttermilk Pancakes with Boysenberry Topping

Serves 6

2 cups packaged pancake mix
½ tsp. baking soda
2 tbsps. sugar

2 large eggs
2 cups buttermilk
2 tbsps. butter, melted

1. *Sift together pancake mix, baking soda and sugar.*
2. *Beat eggs and mix with buttermilk; add to pancake mixture, stirring only until barely smooth.*
3. *Stir in melted butter.*
4. *Rub griddle with melted butter. Heat until a drop of water sizzles when dropped on griddle.*
5. *Pour pancake batter by spoonfuls on hot griddle. Fry until browned on both sides.*
6. *Serve at once with boysenberry topping, whipped or melted butter, hot maple or brown-sugar syrup, cold applesauce sprinkled with cinnamon, or molasses. Serve alone, or with fried ham, crisp bacon, or sausage.*

## Boysenberry topping

2 cups fresh boysenberries
1 scant cup sugar

few drops fresh lemon juice

1. *Wash, dry, and pick over berries.*
2. *Crush slightly; add sugar and fresh lemon juice.*
3. *Chill well before serving over hot pancakes.*

NOTE: For convenience, an excellent frozen buttermilk pancake batter is now available in many supermarkets across the country. Boysenberry syrup is available in some food specialty or health food shops. Fresh blueberries, black raspberries or fresh strawberries make tasteful variations.

# Pat O'Brien

Pat O'Brien is a man with many heroes and many stories. Over bacon and eggs at midday in a corner of Danny's Hideaway, this beloved Irish actor, humanitarian, *bon vivant,* leprechaun and master raconteur ranged from football to living with Spencer Tracy in Ireland to movies and even to the lion who ate ice cream at the bar in this very *boîte* 21 years ago. "We were doing a show ('Masquerade Party') and had a lion . . . it was no gimmick . . . it was a real lion. Somebody had the bright idea to take him over to Danny's. It was 11 at night, the lion comes over, he loves ice cream so they brought some vanilla ice cream into the bar. The lion puts both paws on the bar while he gulped down the confection. I've got news for you! This must have put at least 150 guys on the wagon that night. Guys ran outta here like pickpockets, thieves and wounded buffaloes. I had to go home and say 'Mom, (referring to his wife, Eloise), the lion was eating that ice cream! I'll never take a drink as long as I live' . . ."

I asked about the days when he was a chorus boy with Jimmy Cagney and lived with Spencer Tracy in a twelve-dollar-a-week room in New York.

Pat related how the two existed on a near-starvation diet, filling up on beans lavishly doused with catsup and mustard, grabbing the largest hunks of bread they would find or freeloading. An occasional splurge for a party meant a platter of cold cuts, salami and ham sandwiches, cakes, wine and the local booze. "At the time Spence said, 'If they outlawed steak and onions, we didn't know it,'" Pat recalled.

# Eloise O'Brien's Irish Brown Bread

Makes 1 loaf

4 cups whole wheat flour                            1 tsp. baking soda
2 cups all-purpose flour                              1 tsps. salt
about 1¼ cups buttermilk

1. *Mix together all the dry ingredients; add enough buttermilk to form a soft dough.*
2. *Turn out on lightly floured board; knead lightly.*
3. *Form dough into a circle; place in greased 9-inch baking pan or greased baking sheet. The dough should be about 1½ to 2 inches high. Cut a cross ½-inch deep over the top with a floured knife. This helps bread cook more evenly.*
4. *Bake in preheated 400° F. oven 40 minutes, or until loaf sounds hollow when rapped lightly on the base with the knuckles.*
5. *Remove bread from pan; cool on a wire cake rack. Bread should not be cut until it firms up. Toast it for breakfast or tea; spread lavishly with butter.*

*NOTE: When properly baked, the bread has a rough texture, a "tweedy," brown and white appearance, and comes out about 3 inches high.*

# Hildy Parks & Alex Cohen

"My husband militantly prefers to eat out, so it's been a very difficult 22 years gastronomically!" says Hildy Parks. She was speaking in the presence of her famous theatrical producer husband, Alex Cohen. "It's the idea of having someone else decide what he wants for dinner."

"I never know what I want to eat until I pick up the menu, so how in the hell would you know?" Alex answered.

"I love to cook. I have all kinds of beautiful kitchen equipment," Hildy said sadly. "Now and then Alex does me the enormous favor of staying home for dinner. He never lets me know until the last minute. I find that infuriating! Eating in our house is never a regular occurrence as it is with normal people who dine together. The rare times when we do eat at home I like to do something special. Sometimes I have a salmon mousse made in advance. I love to smell bread baking in the oven! I bake mostly whole-wheat bread. I'll invent recipes, adding things as I go along: honey, molasses, wheat germ."

Alex is a gracious host and is famous for his lavish, beautifully executed parties. "I never invite six people to dinner if 20 are available. I don't know small gestures," he said.

"That's true," Hildy admitted.

Cohen, who regards himself as "the last of the big-time spenders," has become a show business legend through such extravagances as his 1960 midnight block party in Manhattan's Shubert Alley on opening night of "An Evening with Mike Nichols and Elaine May." He transported a ferris wheel from the Bronx, served hot dogs and cotton candy, and supplied water coolers filled with champagne.

# Hildy Parks's Country Whole Wheat Bread

Makes 2 loaves

4 cups all-purpose flour
2 pkgs. active dry yeast
1 tbsp. salt
2½ tbsps. molasses
3 tbsps. butter,
  softened

2½ tbsps. honey
1½ cups milk
½ cup water
1 egg, optional
1 cup wheat germ
cooking oil

2-3 cups stone ground whole wheat flour or equal
amounts whole wheat and graham flour

1. Combine 2 cups all-purpose flour, yeast, and salt in large mixing bowl. Stir to blend.
2. Add molasses, butter and honey.
3. Heat together milk and water until warm but not scalding. Beat with electric mixer on medium speed 2 minutes, scraping bowl.
4. Add egg and wheat germ; beat at high speed 1 minute longer.
5. Stir in remaining all-purpose flour and 2 cups whole wheat flour; beat with wooden spoon until dough leaves side of bowl. Add more whole wheat flour if needed.
6. Turn out on lightly floured board. Knead lightly 5 to 10 minutes, or until dough is smooth and elastic. Divide dough into 2 balls. Shape into 2 loaves.
7. Place seam side down into 2 well-greased 8½ x 4 x 2½-inch pans. Brush tops with cooking oil.
8. Place in warm place, free from drafts, to rise 1 inch above tops of pans.
9. Bake on lower rack in preheated 375° F. oven 30 to 40 minutes, or until bread gives hollow sound when thumped with fingers. For best results, cover crusts with aluminum foil during last 10 minutes to prevent crusts from getting too brown.
10. Remove from pans; cool on wire racks. Delicious served with warm sweet butter and applesauce.

NOTE: Hildy's recipe is streamlined for quick baking, eliminating double raising of dough. Egg is optional, but improves texture of bread.

# Dolly Parton

"You can't outcook my mama and me or my sisters! It's hard to taste anything better'n what we all cook," said singer-composer Dolly Parton with a ringing laugh. "I'm truly a country cook," Dolly added, hugging her body with her arms. "But I have a few specialties that aren't country. Spaghetti's a big treat for everyone back home if I'm there long enough to cook it."

"Home" is Nashville, where she lives with her husband, Carl Dean, in a rented house. She and Carl built a 23-room mansion, "Tara," on 200 acres located 20 miles outside the country-music mecca. "We go there all the time, but the house is too big to live in. It's like a warehouse, and it's not homey enough for us." Various members of Dolly's family live on the farm, along with 25 Herefords, two peacocks and two hounds.

"I fix things like pork chops, corn bread and fried potatoes, made my special way with green pepper, onions and hamburger. I cook with a lot of grease! I don't like cooking with oil because it gives food a funny taste. We made our own lard back in the country — that's how I acquired a taste for it. I know that sounds terrible, because I have enough lard on me!" she said, convulsed with laughter. The Parton dimensions are indeed impressive. She kiddingly suggests her celebrated measurements approach something like "80-80-80!"

# Dolly Parton's Banana Loaf Bread

### Makes 2 loaves

2 pkgs. dry active yeast
5½-6 cups whole wheat flour
1 tsp. salt
about 2½ cups hot water

3 tbsps. vegetable oil
½ cup honey
2-3 bananas, peeled
  and mashed

1. Mix together yeast, 2 cups flour, and salt in large mixing bowl.
2. Pour in hot water (not boiling), mixing well.
3. Add remaining ingredients; beat until well blended with wooden spoon. Add more flour while stirring until dough is stiff enough to knead.
4. Knead on lightly floured board, adding only enough flour to keep dough from sticking. Knead dough thoroughly for 10-15 minutes.
5. Place dough in lightly greased bowl; cover loosely with a cloth and let rise in a warm place, free of drafts, until doubled in bulk, about 1½ hours.
6. When dough has risen, punch down, divide in 2, and place halves in 2 well-greased 9 x 5 x 3-inch baking pans.
7. Cover loosely with cloth and let rise again.
8. When dough has risen, place pans in preheated 375° F. oven 45 minutes, or until tops of loaves are light brown.
9. Place a piece of aluminum foil over each loaf and bake 20 minutes longer, or until loaves sound hollow when tapped on the bottom.
10. Remove loaves from pans; cool on wire racks. Slice, spread with sweet butter while still warm.

NOTE: Dolly's bread is delicious and different. If desired, use ½ cup pineapple juice for part of the water.

# Desserts

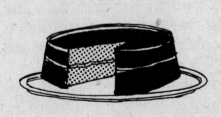

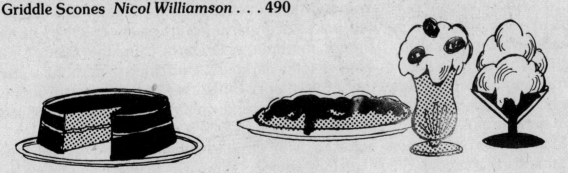

# Maxene Andrews

Maxene Andrews, of the legendary singing sisters, a live-wire lady who possesses a delicious, wacky sense of humor, is not an enthusiastic cook. "I'm better as a dishwasher than as a cook!" she exclaimed. "Mama never allowed us to cook—she always wanted us to practice."

Undoubtedly, her preference for plain fare is due to the regime of years of travel and eating simply to keep in top form to perform. Her food styles were reinforced by her experiences trouping with the USO during the war. "We were always very lucky and very well fed. We didn't look like Betty Grable, maybe that's why the fellas looked out for us and treated us like their sisters! For example, we always had a fresh egg apiece for breakfast. That was unheard of during wartime. And we always had a fresh sheet and pillow case, even if it meant sleeping three in a bed!"

The Andrews Sisters had a memorable bread and burger party in Verona. "There were Italian chefs who baked wonderful long loaves of crisp Italian bread," Maxene recalled. "We got the bread still warm from the oven. One night, we started to eat in almost total darkness, and then I thought I saw something move. The bread was full of ants! Since there was no other bread, the boys scooped out the inside of the loaves and we ate the outside crusts filled with hamburger!"

Maxene and her sisters adjusted with ease to the rigors of wartime entertaining. She credits Bing Crosby's advice. "Bing said, 'When you go over, don't expect anything. Just remember what you're doing and why you are there! Don't be disappointed in anything!' And, you know, we weren't!"

# Maxene Andrews's Norwegian Cold Fruit Soup

Serves 8

1½ cups California
    apricots, dried
handful of pears, dried
1½ cups water
¾ cup sugar
1 cinnamon stick

⅓ cup currants or
    seedless raisins
1 small lemon, cut in thin
    slices
¼ tsp. whole cloves
2 tbsps. cornstarch

handful of almonds, toasted

1. *Combine all ingredients in large saucepan except cornstarch and almonds. Heat to boiling; reduce heat.*
2. *Simmer, uncovered, 10 minutes; stir occasionally.*
3. *Combine cornstarch with a little cold water to form a smooth paste; gradually stir into fruit mixture.*
4. *Cook, stirring, until mixture thickens slightly.*
5. *Remove lemon, cinnamon and cloves if desired. Cool to room temperature.*
6. *Cover; chill well before serving. Ladle into individual glass serving bowls. Garnish with almonds.*

# Eddy Arnold

"I'm just like the average guy you meet on the street. On Saturday night, I'll have a little shot of Scotch, invite some friends in, and cook a steak. I can cook it pretty good, too," said affable Country and Western singer Eddy Arnold, moments before he was due to go on stage at the Palace. "I love to have my friends in. We tell a few corny stories and have a couple of laughs!" he said.

The performer's simple approach to life is probably the key to his durable success. He says he owes his philosophy to his mother. "She taught me to keep my life very simple and to always be very honest. My mother had a tough time just getting enough food together to feed us. When I went to school, she sent me off with a lunch of tiny little biscuits spread with butter and sugar, and that's all! Things are a hell of a lot different now!" he said, laughing.

"I'm a very private person. When I'm home, I'm a husband and a father. I don't like going out to nightclubs or big parties. If you invite me to a party where you're going to have 200 or 300 people, I will say, 'Thank you very much, but I won't be there.'

"At Christmas, we have a big turkey. My wife, Sally, loves to cook the dinner. She cooks enough food for two log rollings. I really love her desserts, especially upsidedown cake and banana pudding and of course, the coconut pie."

Later, I talked with Sally by phone from the Arnolds' 90-acre home in Nashville. She explained, "I make my dressing the day before with a little cornbread and white bread mixed together with seasonings, onion and celery. I usually use chicken broth instead of turkey broth to flavor the dressing and giblet gravy. I generally cook up a hen the day before to get the broth. It tastes real good."

# Eddy Arnold's Coconut Cream Pie

Makes one 9-inch pie

1 9-inch fluted pastry
  shell
1 cup sugar
½ tsp. salt
2½ tbsps. cornstarch
1 tbsp. flour

3 eggs, separated
3 cups milk
1¼ cups coconut, shredded
1 tbsp. butter
2 tsps. pure vanilla extract
½ tsp. cream of tartar

1. Bake pie shell in preheated 450° F. oven about 15 minutes, or until golden. Set aside.
2. Mix together ⅔ cup sugar, salt, cornstarch and flour.
3. Beat egg yolks in separate bowl; gradually add milk.
4. Gradually add egg-milk mixture to dry ingredients, beating well.
5. Cook and stir custard over boiling water or over very low heat. Stir custard constantly until it thickens.
6. Add 1 cup coconut, butter and 1½ tsps. vanilla extract. Cool.
7. Pour custard into baked pastry shell.
8. Meanwhile, prepare meringue by beating egg whites, remaining vanilla extract and cream of tartar until soft peaks form.
9. Gradually add remaining sugar, beating until egg whites are stiff and smooth.
10. Lightly pile meringue evenly over top of custard. Sprinkle top with remaining coconut.
11. Bake in preheated 400° F. oven about 10 minutes, or until meringue is golden brown. Cool. Serve at room temperature or well chilled.

NOTE: Sally Arnold cautions, "Watch your pie carefully or the meringue and coconut will burn!"

# Patty Duke Astin

"I learned the rudiments of cooking from books," Patty Duke Astin confided. "At first I was terrified making dinner for friends, but it's become much easier. I like to entertain casually – a quiet evening with friends, good food, good wines and good conversation. I've even tackled a whole Christmas dinner by myself for a dozen people, preparing the bird, creamed onions and all the trimmings. I wanted to include a Virginia baked ham, but I just couldn't find one," she said.

"I like collecting recipes, particularly from friends. I'm addicted to almost any kind of food, except perhaps Mexican, and I really adore Chinese fare. I've had my problems with cooking, but not with complicated things. Simple things, like rice. No matter how I try, my rice always comes out looking and tasting like a glue factory – even when I've measured carefully and read all the instructions. But it's my jello that's a joke. The last batch came out as runny as ever. Maybe you can tell what I'm doing wrong?"

Much of Patty's charisma stems from being as good a listener as she is an actress.

"As a child," Patty recalled, "I hated the lentil soup my mother used to make with ham bone. I suppose it was the combination of not liking it and the fact that it was all we had for dinner. Then I had some of my mother's soup about a year or so ago and loved it!"

# Patty Duke Astin's Deep Dish Apple Pie

### Serves 6-8

1 prepared double-crust pastry
tart green cooking apples, enough
   to make 7-7½ cups peeled
   and sliced apples
⅓ cup white sugar
⅓ cup light brown sugar
2 tbsps. flour
pinch salt
1 tsp. ground cinnamon or
  ½ tsp. ground mace

3 tbsps. sweet butter, cut
  in small pieces
juice and grated rind of 1 lemon
½ cup dairy sour cream
  or heavy cream
1 egg yolk mixed with 1 tbsp.
  water
whipped cream or ice cream or
  a good aged Cheddar cheese,
  sliced

1. *Roll out half the dough and line a deep, 9-inch pie plate; set aside.*
2. *Wrap remainder of dough in aluminum foil and refrigerate until ready to roll out.*
3. *Peel and slice apples.*
4. *Combine white sugar, brown sugar, flour, salt, spices. Coat apples with mixture.*
5. *Add butter, lemon juice and rind.*
6. *Fill lower crust with apple mixture. Spread sour cream over apples.*
7. *Roll out top crust; cut steam vent.*
8. *Attach top crust to lower crust, sealing edges. Brush top with egg yolk-water mixture.*
9. *Bake in preheated 375° F. oven for 50 minutes.*
10. *Serve warm with whipped cream, ice cream or a slice of Cheddar cheese per serving.*

NOTE: *The secret to Patty's pie is the selection of good, tart eating apples. If apples are not flavorful, sprinkle with lemon or lime juice to bring out natural flavor of the fruit.*

# Jill Clayburgh

"I can't believe I'm here at Mr. Chow's and not eating," said actress Jill Clayburgh. "Be sure and order some of the French fried seaweed."

It was hard to imagine that someone with such an obvious passion for food could refrain from ordering any of the tempting Chinese fare. But Jill had been living a Spartan life – eating simply once a day, daily visits to a health club for rigorous exercise – in order to prepare for her role of Carole Lombard. "I love to cook and I love to eat! Tonight, I'm going to Valentino's for some really good Italian food!"

Jill takes unrestrained pleasure in fine food, but she also has tremendous self-discipline. "My closest friends are wonderful actresses who have the greatest recipes!" she bubbled. Her friends, Jennifer Salk and Janet Margolin, are such successful cooks, they even run a business on the side called "Eat Your Heart Out," catering parties for their friends. "Jennifer and Janet make the most wonderful Moroccan dinners! Their pigeon pie and *cous-cous* are fantastic."

Jill's favorite quickie dessert is a delicious crunch made with blueberries and served with sour cream or ice cream. When Jill really feels like going on a cooking-eating binge, she turns out a luscious chocolate cheesecake. "This is what I call my Carole Lombard cake because the ingredients are unbelievably expensive, not to mention fattening! But the dessert will knock you out! It's the end!" she said, laughing.

# Jill Clayburgh's "Eat-Your-Heart-Out Chocolate Cheesecake"

Serves 16

1½ cups graham cracker
   crumbs
15 tbsps. butter
1 cup plus 3 tbsps. granulated sugar
13 ozs. semi-sweet chocolate

3 eggs
3 pkgs. (8 ozs.) cream cheese,
   softened
1 cup dairy sour cream
1 cup pecans, chopped
1 tsp. pure vanilla extract

1. Form crust by blending together graham cracker crumbs, 3 tbsps. melted butter, 3 tbsps. sugar and 1 oz. grated semi-sweet chocolate.
2. Press mixture evenly into bottom and sides of a greased 10-inch spring form pan.
3. Beat eggs and remaining sugar with electric mixer until thick.
4. In separate bowl, beat cream cheese until light and fluffy. Gradually add cream cheese to egg-sugar mixture, mixing well.
5. Meanwhile, melt remaining semi-sweet chocolate and butter in top of double boiler. Remove from heat; cool slightly.
6. Fold in sour cream, mixing well.
7. Gradually add chocolate mixture to cream cheese-egg mixture, using low speed on electric mixer.
8. Fold in pecans and vanilla.
9. Pour batter into spring form pan, completely covering graham cracker crust.
10. Bake cheesecake in preheated 325° F. oven 1½ to 2 hours, or until center is firm.
11. Cool on wire rack. Cover, chill completely 12 hours in refrigerator.
12. Remove from pan to serve. Slice in small portions. Top with whipped, sweetened cream and grated semi-sweet chocolate.

NOTE: The cheesecake tastes like baked fudge and is dense in texture, and very, very rich, so please offer very small portions! Serve on auspicious occasions. You'll have nothing left!

# Dom DeLuise

When actor Dom DeLuise talks about food or cooking, he invariably speaks in aesthetic terms. For example, he came to breakfast at the Beverly Hills Hotel armed with several recipes including one for a "gorgeous blueberry cheesecake."

This gentle giant of a man has been cooking since he was a small boy growing up in Brooklyn. He recalled his Italian family's tradition of "steak every Saturday. We didn't have an outdoor grill. We had a furnace. I used to go down to the basement and put the steak on the fire until it started to make a lot of noise, then I turned it over. It cooked quickly over this intense heat. There was no smoke. It was gorgeous – crunchy on the outside, moist inside. I've never tasted better meat!" His mother, Jenny, who still lives in the same house where Dom was born, inserted slits of garlic into the meat.

The actor has been on virtually every kind of diet. "I've lost thousands of pounds!" he claimed, looking trim and tanned. "Isn't it awful what we do to ourselves?" He smiled broadly.

The DeLuises entertain "very well" in their sprawling Pacific Palisades house. Dom often does the cooking. New Year's he did a buffet for 20, including a shrimperama – shrimp served five different ways. His guests, including Mel Brooks, Anne Bancroft and Gene Wilder, flipped over his cooking. He gets a kick out of cooking with his three sons. "The boys are great egg breakers," he said proudly. "They are good at toasting and frying. One Sunday I thought it would be fun to show them how to make ravioli. Someone gave me a ravioli machine. We made the dough, stuffed them, cooked and ate them."

Once, Dom made up enough homemade spaghetti to feed an army. The result? "We ran out of room and had to lay it out on the beds between layers of clean clothes."

# Dom DeLuise's Blueberry Cheesecake

Serves 10-12

### For the crust

1 baked 10-inch pie crust or prepare as follows:

1 small jar Macadamia nuts,
   crushed in blender or
   with rolling pin between
   waxed paper

1 cup flour
¼ cup brown sugar, firmly
   packed
¼ lb. sweet butter, softened

*Combine all ingredients; mix well. Press into a 10-inch spring form pan. Bake in preheated 400° F. oven 10-15 minutes.*

### For the filling

3 pkgs. (8 ozs.) cream cheese
1 cup sugar

4 eggs, room temperature
1 tsp. pure vanilla extract

1. *Crumble cheese in large mixing bowl. Add remaining ingredients.*
2. *Beat at high speed with portable mixer until well blended and smooth, about 5 minutes. Pour over crust.*
3. *Bake at 350° F. 40 minutes, or until set. Cool 10 minutes.*

### For the topping

1 carton (8 ozs.) dairy sour
   cream
2 tbsps. sugar
½ tsp. pure vanilla extract

1 tbsp. cornstarch
½ cup heavy cream,
   whipped and slightly
   sweetened

1 can (15 ozs.) blueberry pie filling or 2 cups dry-
packed frozen wild blueberries, thawed

1. *Combine sour cream, sugar and vanilla. Spread over top of cheesecake. Bake 5 minutes.*
2. *Let cool.*
3. *Spread blueberry pie filling over cheesecake. Or combine blueberries with cornstarch (mixed with few tbsps. cold water to form smooth paste). Stir and cook until thickened. Let cool and add to cake.*
4. *Cool 1 hour, then refrigerate.*
5. *Just before serving pie, top with whipped cream to form decorative pattern.*

# Mike Douglas

Over a lunch of steak and tomatoes, TV host Mike Douglas was recalling some of the more memorable culinary moments on his show. One incident, in particular, seemed a favorite of Mike's as he said, "We gathered up all the left-overs – tired old steak bones, remains of vegetables and all the scraps of salad we could find – and put it all together. That's how Phyllis Diller's famous garbage soup was invented, right here on the show. The audience could see we weren't serious, for we made up the recipe on the spot.

"Food's something everyone is interested in. The greatest amount of mail we get (averaging from 30,000 to 70,000 letters weekly) are requests for recipes we've shown on camera.

"After Barbara Rush showed how to prepare Rock Cornish hens, we presented her with the cooked birds in clay and gave her a mallet to open the shell. When she cracked it open, out flew a live dove that we had substituted. It was a fine finish to a Valentine show.

"When publisher Bennett Cerf was co-host, his recipe was quite brief," Mike recalled. " 'Here's my favorite recipe for making corn flakes with cream,' Bennett said. 'Open one package of cornflakes along the dotted line. Add the contents to a large bowl. Add cream and serve.' "

The guest who came up with the most popular recipe among his viewers was Betty Hughes, wife of the then governor of New Jersey. (Over 10,000 people wrote in for her Irish stew pie.)

Over the years, Mike has enjoyed cooking with his daughters, twins Michele and Cristine, and Kelly Anne. Cooking with Kelly is generally barbecuing a hot dog in the backyard, or baking a buttermilk chocolate cake from the recipe of Aunt Margene (Dowd) with chocolate butter cream icing.

# Mike Douglas's Buttermilk Chocolate Cake

Makes 1 cake

### For the cake

1 cup butter
2 cups sugar
5 eggs, separated and
  beaten
4 squares unsweetened
  chocolate (melted and
  cooled)

2½ cups cake flour,
  sifted
1 tsp. soda
¼ tsp. salt
1 cup buttermilk
1 tsp. vanilla

1. *Cream together butter and sugar. Add beaten yolks and melted chocolate. Beat well.*
2. *Sift together flour, soda and salt. Add alternately to creamed mixture with the buttermilk; add vanilla.*
3. *Fold in stiffly beaten egg whites.*
4. *Pour into a large oblong baking pan that has been greased and floured. Bake in preheated 350° F. oven until done (about 25 minutes).*
5. *Test with toothpick. When it comes out clean, cake is done.*

### For the icing

½ stick butter, melted
3 squares unsweetened
  chocolate (melted and
  cooled)

4 tbsps. half-and-half
1 tsp. vanilla
1 egg yolk, beaten
2 cups confectioner's sugar

1. *Combine butter and chocolate.*
2. *Add remaining ingredients, blending until smooth and of spreading consistency.*
3. *Spread on cake while still warm. Cut cake in squares to serve.*

# James Drury

"God knows I love blueberries!" exclaimed James Drury, the well-tanned, six-foot-plus star of TV's "The Virginian." "I can never get my fill: you can put them on breakfast cereal, in jam or jelly, or mix them into pancakes and waffles. I'll eat 'em all! . . . We used to have a commercial blueberry ranch during the early years of World War II, near Newport on the Oregon coast. At the time it was the only cultivated blueberry ranch on the West Coast. Now, there are many that bring in fifty to hundreds of acres."

"Did you ever bake a blueberry pie?" I asked.

"Oh, certainly! Just the way the book says and the way my mother taught me. Do you have any blueberries on you?" he jested. "We *never* use lemon with the berries, that's the way my mother schooled us. A lot of people use lemon in everything. I don't particularly care for the taste of it on fish. It's used too much with fruit and juices. Mind you, lemon's excellent in its place and lemonade's wonderful. But you ruin the true taste of blueberries or Johnnie Walker black label," he said, sipping his drink. We were talking at Shepherds, a posh Park Avenue bar.

One of Jim's favorite pursuits is deep sea or fresh water fishing. "That's a great way to relax. Basically I'm a fly fisherman, preferably trout." Like many anglers, Jim likes to cook his catch. He broils the trout, first making up a flour mixture seasoned with Worcestershire and Tabasco to rub on the fish. "People give me a baleful eye when I say I use Worcestershire on trout. The Indians made trout and salmon filets without any condiments. In fact, my father's favorite recipe for chinook salmon is a filet that you put in a sandwich board grill and bake over a Dutch oven until what he calls the 'milk' comes up. Then just turn it over and he'd put pepper and salt on it and that was it."

# James Drury's Blueberry Lattice Pie

### Serves 6

1 double crust 9-inch pre-
    pared pie pastry
4 cups blueberries
½ cup sugar
½ cup light brown sugar,
    firmly packed

scant ⅓ cup flour
½ tsp. salt
½ tsp. nutmeg
½ tsp. cinnamon or mace
¼ cup butter, melted

1. *Roll out ⅔ of the pastry on lightly floured board.*
2. *Line bottom and sides of an ungreased 9-inch pie pan.*
3. *Combine blueberries with remaining ingredients except pastry. Mix well; spoon into pie shell.*
4. *Roll out remaining pastry; cut into ten ½-inch wide strips. Arrange strips in a lattice over filling. Crimp or flute edges.*
5. *Bake in preheated 425° F. oven 35-45 minutes, or until brown and bubbly.*
6. *Cool slightly before serving.*
7. *Garnish spaces between "lattices" with additional uncooked fresh blueberries. Serve plain, or with cream or vanilla ice cream.*

NOTE: *Spices may be increased according to individual tastes. This recipe can be made with 4 cups frozen dry-pack blueberries or 2 cups blueberry pie filling.*

# Stephanie Faracy

When actress Stephanie Faracy was growing up in Chicago, she once turned in an award-winning home-made cherry pie "to make points with her home economics teacher." The real story behind the pie-baking incident is as zany as the character of Gail Collins, the inexperienced pastry chef the actress portrays on the CBS-TV series, "The Last Resort."

"Listen, the night before I was to bake the pie I told my teacher I was too busy to enter the contest. She got so upset, I went to my mother saying, 'How can I make this pie?' My mother called up a friend of hers who was a wonderful baker. She baked the pie and I won the contest. The awful thing was that once I had won the contest, I had to learn how to make the pie so I could enter the state contest. I spent weeks baking cherry pies and then I came in second because I didn't chill my pie!"

"Steph" won great critical acclaim for her dazzling performance as Angel, the obese young waitress in the movie, *When You Comin' Back, Red Ryder?* "I've always been slightly plump," she explained, "but I still wasn't heavy enough for the role, so I forced myself to eat as much as I could and gained 30 pounds. I was scared because I was afraid I might really BE that girl. Perhaps that's who I am in real life and I'm really fooling everyone. I didn't realize how heavy I was until everyone had gone home and they had taken away all the movie sets. I became so depressed. It became major panic time. Guys won't look at you. People think less of you. There is an awful lot of prejudice against obese people. Let's face it, fat is pain."

Two weeks at the famed "Golden Door" soon put her well on the way to becoming her svelte self again.

# Stephanie Faracy's Cherry Pie

Serves 6

## For the crust

2 cups all-purpose flour
½ tsp. baking powder
¾ tsp. salt

½ cup lard
½ cup butter
4-6 tbsps. cold milk

1. Mix together dry ingredients.
2. Cut lard and butter into flour with pastry blender or two knives until mixture resembles coarse crumbs.
3. Add milk slowly, tossing fat-particles lightly with fork to blend and mixture leaves side of bowl.
4. Divide dough in half and roll out on lightly floured board.
5. Line a 9-inch pie pan with pastry. Roll remaining pastry in waxed paper and refrigerate while you complete filling.

## For the filling

3 cups pitted sour pie
   cherries (canned)
1¼ cups cherry juice
2 tsps. fresh lemon juice

dash salt
1 scant cup sugar
3½ tbsps. cornstarch
red food coloring

½ tsp. almond extract

1. Reserve cherries; combine cherry juice, lemon juice, salt, sugar and cornstarch. Mix well.
2. Cook over low heat and stir until thick and transparent.
3. Heat cherries in sauce with red coloring and almond extract. Pour into pastry shell and cover with lattice top crust.
4. Bake in preheated 400° F. oven 45 minutes to 1 hour. Serve alone or with vanilla ice cream.

# Sally Field

Sally Field is a survivor, actress, nester and unusual cook. "If you know me for long, you'll get to know my Field specialties: they're all things that don't take much time but that look and taste great! I love to cook. I learned to cook for self-preservation," she said, smiling over coffee and confiding that her mother has never been "exactly a Cordon Bleu cook."

The Oscar winner for *Norma Rae* looks like your standard beautiful, outdoor California girl. She was wearing blue jeans and minimal makeup. Sally was born in California, the daughter of Maggie Field Mahoney and Dick Field, a pharmaceutical products salesman. She was raised by her mother and step-father, Jock Mahoney, who adopted her when she was three. Both Maggie and Jock were veteran performers.

"Having a home is a big part of me; I find pleasure in it," said Sally. "My mother is a nester and so am I. I love cooking, making jams and sewing. Until recently, this hasn't been able to mesh itself with the acting side of me at all. I cook for fun. I delight in preparing French dishes: quiches, strange soups, soufflés that aren't quite soufflés!"

Entertaining is usually simple, relaxed, and often family-style. Sally mentioned a dinner she fixed recently for her family, featuring roast pork and home-made applesauce. "I like to make jam and conserve to give my friends. I do it every year, usually at Christmas. This year, I made blackberry jam, rhubarb-raisin conserve and peanut-honey granola. The rhubarb conserve is fabulous with roast pork because it's nice and tart. I found the recipe in an old book my grandmother had."

# Sally Field's Peanut Butter-Honey Granola

Makes 8 cups

boiling hot water
1 cup raisins
⅔ cup creamy peanut butter
⅔ cup honey

½ tsp. ground cinnamon
1 tsp. pure vanilla extract
4 cups rolled oats
½ cup dried figs, snipped
1 cup peanuts

1. *Pour boiling water over raisins to plump them; let stand 10 minutes, drain, reserve.*
2. *In a saucepan, combine peanut butter, honey and cinnamon; heat thoroughly.*
3. *Remove from heat; stir in vanilla.*
4. *Scatter oats in bottom of a large baking dish or shallow roasting pan. Pour warm peanut mixture over oats, stirring gently to coat oats. Spread mixture with your hand.*
5. *Bake in preheated 300° F. oven 35-40 minutes, stirring occasionally.*
6. *Turn off oven. Stir in raisins, figs and nuts.*
7. *Let mixture dry in oven for 1½ hours.*
8. *Store in a cool dry place.*
9. *Great to serve as a snack or over ice cream.*

*NOTE: Sally advises, "The texture is both loose, and with some lumped together. Eat it by the handful. It's usually gone before I know it!" This granola is great served over mocha or almond ice cream, or used as a topping for fresh peach cobbler.*

# Paul Ford

"It was a great catering service. We started out doing box lunches and then went into the candy business," said the late comic actor Paul Ford. He was recalling the depression years when his candy-making talents enabled him to carry on his efforts to become an actor. "We used to make a fabulous peanut brittle. I'd go down to the Washington market and buy the peanuts wholesale. The nuts cooked right in the syrup. I wonder whatever happened to that recipe," he said, scratching his bald head and looking like a character out of a Thurber cartoon.

His maple fondant, he recalled, was a success because he used the right prop. "We poured the syrup onto a marble slab that we got off a second-hand man. We bought an old dresser with a marble top!"

"And now we can make the fondant on our six-hundred-dollar coffee table," interjected Paul's wife, Nell, who admits that she doesn't cook anything fancy. "I really hate the kitchen clean-up. All those pots and pans."

"I'd say I'm a gourmet," Paul continued. "I like French food particularly, and Oriental dishes. I believe in food separation. For example, I loathe seeing gravy spread all over food on a plate. I like to dip bread into the gravy. I like to see a little space between the different kinds of food. I just don't like to see it all mingled together on a plate. The meat and vegetables should stand alone. But I guess I have a few food quirks. I like to go into a restaurant and have a turkey sandwich with a coffee nut sundae. I like everything a little damp, particularly lobster, shad roe and lamb chops."

Paul's comment that Nell "fixes exceptional wilted lettuce" brought a laugh from Nell. "He calls it 'peculiar lettuce,'" she said.

# Paul Ford's English Toffee

¼ cup dark brown sugar
¼ cup white sugar
¼ cup light corn syrup
¼ tsp. salt
6 tbsps. heavy cream

1 tbsp. butter
½ tsp. pure vanilla extract
few drops oil of orange (available at drugstores)
¼ cup finely chopped English walnuts

1. *Combine brown and white sugar, corn syrup, salt and cream in a deep saucepan.*
2. *Stir over quick fire until sugar dissolves.*
3. *Cook over medium heat, stirring often to avoid scorching until temperature registers 240° F. on a candy thermometer, or until medium soft ball forms when a small amount of hot syrup is dropped into cup of cold water.*
4. *Add butter; stir; continue cooking to 250° F. for hard ball, or until a spoonful can just be molded when dropped into cold water for chewy toffee, or to 260° F. for extra hard toffee.*
5. *Stir occasionally to avoid burning.*
6. *Remove from fire. Flavorings and nuts may be added at this time. Pour into a buttered dish. When toffee has cooled, cut into squares.*

*NOTE: Paul says, "If you're making the candy during humid summer weather, cook the syrup to 265° F. for very hard toffee, or 250° F. for chewy candy." For making chocolate-coated toffee, do not add nuts with flavorings. Pour cooked toffee onto well-greased cookie sheet; cool. Melt 6 oz. bag semi-sweet chocolate bits; pour half the melted chocolate onto top of toffee; sprinkle with few tbsps. finely chopped walnuts; cool. Turn and repeat, using remaining chocolate and walnuts. Cool. Break toffee into pieces with wooden mallet.*

# David Frost

"My favorite American dishes are French toast, soft-shelled crab and cheesecake – Sardi's no-legged variety for starters, then the two-legged kind after dinner," quipped David Frost. "It's funny about French toast because that's an American dish you would never find in France any more than you'd find English muffins in England or Danish pastry in Denmark!"

David calls British Airways "home" even though he maintains an apartment at New York's Plaza Hotel and owns a townhouse in Knightsbridge, London. On his frequent flights, he sustains himself on large bags of potato chips and American beef sandwiches.

"I have a magnificent Spanish housekeeper in London," explained David. "If I have time, I like to choose the menu if I'm having a dinner party. I've never given big parties in the United States, but in London I once took over the Grand Hall at Alexandria Palace and installed a whole fun fair inside. I invited a thousand guests and organized fairground food for them: hot dogs, shrimps and candy floss (cotton candy)." That little mid-winter bash cost him $12,000.

Probably David Frost's most celebrated party was his 1966 breakfast staged at the Connaught Hotel for some of his "intimate friends in high places." Guests included then-Prime Minister Wilson, industrialists, journalists, earls, M.P.'s, the works. The menu was melon, grapefruit, eggs, bacon, kidney, toast and marmalade, followed by 1950 vintage champagne and caviar. "I just wanted to have an intimate private party," Frost said.

In his London townhouse, Frost likes sit-down dinners. "I choose a good strong meat course and may precede that with either something ornate like a soufflé and then a fruit course (he loves strawberries) or crème brûlée, my favorite dessert."

# David Frost's Crème Brûlée

Serves 6

2 cups heavy cream                    2½ tbsps. sugar
4 egg yolks                           1 tsp. pure vanilla extract
                    ¼ cup light brown sugar

1. Heat cream in double boiler.
2. Beat egg yolks, adding granulated sugar gradually.
3. Remove cream from heat and pour over egg mixture very slowly. Add vanilla; mix well.
4. Pour into a greased 1½-quart casserole; place casserole in pan of hot water. Bake uncovered in preheated 325° F. oven about 45 minutes, or until custard is set.
5. Sprinkle with brown sugar. Run under broiler for 1 minute or until sugar melts but does not burn.
6. Chill well.

NOTE: Serve alone or topped with fresh, hulled, sweetened strawberries.

# Shelley Hack

"I'm writing a cookbook about making preservatives, jams, jellies and chutneys," said model-turned-actress Shelley Hack. "I have a farm in upstate New York, where I grow my own vegetables and fruit."

"Charlie's" newest angel was consuming a gargantuan lunch at Le Serre. The lovely blue-eyed blonde is a lady of many talents. Growing her own vegetables, pressing her own cider, or baking bread or pies is a joyful pastime to Shelley. "I've collected some great recipes," she said. "I've been experimenting for several years to find out how much pectin to add to the fruit. Every fruit is different. I make my own pectin from green crab apples. It's actually apple jelly," she explained. "The pectin is what makes the fruit syrup jell. One year I made 50 gallons of my own apple cider. You've never tasted anything like it. It's the same difference as between fresh and canned peach."

Shelley's fond of baking apple pies. "The secret to good apple pies is in the selection of the fruit. I love real greenies or pippins. The crust can be anything I feel like. For example, if I've made a quiche, I use the same pastry for the apple pie."

# Shelley Hack's Apple Brown Betty

Serves 4

### For the apple layer

4 tart apples, pared and
   sliced

½ tsp. ground cinnamon

2-3 tbsps. brown or granulated sugar

¼ tsp. mace or cloves

1. *Arrange sliced apples in bottom of a buttered 9-inch pie plate.*
2. *Sprinkle with cinnamon, sugar and mace.*

### For the topping

1 stick butter

1 cup flour

1 cup brown sugar

1. *Cut butter into flour and brown sugar in mixing bowl to form fine crumbs.*
2. *Pile crumb topping evenly over sliced apples in pie plate.*
3. *Bake in preheated 350° F. oven 45 minutes until top is browned and apples are tender. Serve hot, alone, or with dollop of plain yogurt or whipped cream.*

# Glenda Jackson

Two-time Academy Award winner Glenda Jackson likes cooking (particularly for her son, Dan), talking to her plants, and working in the garden of her suburban London home. "I have a theory," she said, "that you're as good a cook as the people you cook for. I'm not what you'd call a Cordon Bleu cook, but my best friend married a man who's an absolute gourmet. I mean, he adores food and is a very good cook himself. When she married him, my friend couldn't boil an egg, but now she's a fantastic cook! I married a man (Roy Hodges, from who she is now divorced) who was happiest eating boiled eggs!"

The dishes Glenda most enjoys cooking are "simple ones – a nice stew, a casserole or a shepherd's pie. In summer, my menus run to things like roast chicken or beef." Cooking for friends, she says, "is fun, but I'm not one of those geniuses who can turn out a meal in forty-five minutes. I take all day to shop, cook and get ready!"

Glenda is fond of rich desserts. "I make the most delicious cheesecake! A Viennese lady gave me the recipe, and it's really quite lovely. I make mine with crumbled biscuits, but I suppose your graham crackers would work." (The English call all cookies "biscuits," not to be confused with the classic American short quick bread.)

Glenda likes to entertain, but only in small groups. "I'm not good at big parties. The people I see tend to be the ones I've known for a long time. To anyone who doesn't understand the business I'm in, I can appear very antisocial, but to old friends, I can say, 'I'm awfully sorry I can't come to dinner tonight because we're shooting late,' and they'll understand. American food is great but the portions are overwhelming! Dan is very fond of your hamburgers and ice cream."

# Glenda Jackson's Lemon Cheesecake

Makes one 8-inch cake

1½ cups graham cracker crumbs
¼ cup butter, melted
½ cup vanilla sugar*
3 large eggs, separated
1 pkg. (8 oz.) cream cheese,
  softened

3 tbsps. fresh lemon juice
finely grated rind of 1 lemon
½ cup raisins or currants
½ cup heavy cream, whipped, or
  comparable amount of dairy
  sour cream

1. *Combine graham cracker crumbs, butter and 2 tbsps. vanilla sugar.*
2. *Press into bottom and sides of a greased 8-inch spring form pan, reserving about ¼ cup of mixture for topping.*
3. *Beat egg yolks well; gradually beat in ¼ cup vanilla sugar, cream cheese, 2½ tbsps. lemon juice and lemon rind.*
4. *Beat egg whites until stiff but not dry; fold into cream mixture.*
5. *Stir in raisins.*
6. *Pile mixture into crust. Bake in preheated 300° F. oven 50 minutes, or until filling begins to brown on the top.*
7. *Whip cream, adding remaining lemon juice to sour it. Or use sour cream.*
8. *Add remaining vanilla sugar to cream. Spoon mixture over top and scatter remaining crumbs over that.*
9. *Bake 5-10 minutes longer (at same temperature).*
10. *Chill well until serving.*

NOTE: *Vanilla sugar is made by placing a piece of vanilla bean in a canister of sugar. Let it remain buried in sugar several days or until it perfumes and flavors the sugar. Also lovely to use over fresh fruit in season.*

GOOD MORNING!

# Norman Jewison

Director Norman Jewison, the soft-spoken Canadian with frosted, dark curly hair, sipped his morning tea as he explained that he cooks for pleasure, although he used to take out his hostilities by "spanking" bread dough.

An actor's director, Jewison goes to great lengths to empathize with his stars – even if it means fattening himself and adding pounds to the stars. "With Rod Steiger, I brought in frogs legs and everything else and got him up to 225. It took him a year and half to lose it and will take him even longer to forgive me! I gained nearly 15 pounds fattening and empathizing with Topol on *Fiddler On The Roof*. We fed him bread, potatoes, tons of *cevapcici*, the wonderful Yugoslavian sausages made from veal, lamb, onions, pepper and wonderful spices.

"If I weren't a director, I'd rather be a farmer. My family's always grown our own vegetables and flowers. I come from generations of farmers. And when I lived in England, I grew asparagus and tomatoes in a little green house."

The director and his family have taken to growing their own yogurt, too. "Our children love it. We just mix it with fresh fruit. All you do is get a few spoonfuls of yogurt and plant it in the bottom of an earthenware bowl and feed it with milk (first boiled, then cooled to room temperature) so the culture keeps renewing itself."

"I like to cook occasionally. It depends on how I feel. But I've made everything from bread to pies. I made bread a lot the year I spent in New York. I suppose it was kind of a release for me, because when I was the most frustrated – I was working in television then – and working the longest hours, I found myself making bread on my only day off. I'd pound the dough, releasing my hostilities. I highly recommend it to anyone, particularly people in television!" he said, laughing softly.

# Norman Jewison's Butter Tarts

Makes 12 tarts

1 prepared pastry (double
  crust)
1 egg
scant ½ cup brown sugar
⅓ cup light corn syrup

½ tsp. pure vanilla extract
½ cup currants or seedless
  raisins
¾ cup pecans, chopped, or
  almond slivers, toasted

1. *Line 12 small fluted tart shells with pastry; chill.*
2. *Beat egg; add rest of ingredients.*
3. *Divide mixture evenly, filling 12 tart shells.*
4. *Bake in preheated 375° F. oven about 20 minutes, or until filling has set, and crust is brown and crisp. Allow 2 tarts per person.*

*NOTE: Almonds can be oven-toasted by scattering them evenly in ungreased shallow baking dish, then baking them 1½ to 2 hours until they are evenly brown and crisp. Almonds can also be crispened and browned by slowly sautéeing them in clarified butter. If almonds are used instead of pecans, use almond extract in lieu of vanilla.*

# Van Johnson

Years ago, Spencer Tracy gave Van Johnson some sage advice, "Don't waste your time. Take up one new subject each year and see it through."

The famous redhead heeded Tracy's advice. His accomplishments are many, and include reading five or six books weekly, sculpting, painting, tennis, swimming, needlepoint, and even cooking. Van cooks as often as possible. "I'm a Virgo," he said with that famous smile, "so I've got to keep busy with my hands to stay out of the refrigerator! I cook almost anything. I like chili, clam chowder, Boston baked beans and one-pot dinners made with booze. I like to flavor food with booze, either red or white wine or vermouth. I enjoy cooking as a hobby on weekends. It's fun and great occupational therapy.

"I met Julia Child once and was so excited at meeting her that I got tongue-tied! I've never had any cooking lessons, damn it."

Van likes to collect cookbooks. Of all his cookbooks, he prefers Vincent Price's *A Treasury of Great Recipes*. "Cooking's an expensive hobby, but it's worth it. Tomorrow I'm going to try to prepare Lemon Chicken. Pearl gave me the 'recipt,' as my New England grandmother used to say. It's delicious." Pearl's is a famous Chinese restaurant in midtown Manhattan.

# Van Johnson's Orange Cake
# à la Vincent Price

Serves 10

### For the cake

1 cup soft butter
1 cup sugar
3 eggs, separated
2 cups sifted all-purpose
   flour

1 tsp. baking powder
1 tsp. baking soda
1¼ cups dairy sour cream
rind of 1 orange, grated
1 cup walnuts, chopped

1. *Cream together butter and sugar until fluffy.*
2. *Beat in egg yolks, one at a time.*
3. *Sift together flour, baking powder and baking soda.*
4. *Add dry ingredients to butter-egg mixture, alternating with sour cream, beginning and ending with dry ingredients. Mix until smooth.*
5. *Stir in orange rind and walnuts.*
6. *Beat egg whites until stiff but not dry; fold into cake batter.*
7. *Pour batter into a greased, 9-inch tube pan. Bake in preheated 350° F. oven 50-55 minutes, or until cake tests done.*

### For the topping

½ cup sugar
1 cup orange juice

⅓ cup Grand Marnier
   or Cointreau

½ cup blanched almonds, slivered

1. *Combine sugar, orange juice and Grand Marnier. Pour over hot cake while it is in pan.*
2. *Sprinkle with almonds.*
3. *Cool cake before removing from pan.*

NOTE: *If desired, flavor cake with ½ tsp. almond extract or 1 tsp. Grand Marnier. Cake is great served with tea or coffee.*

# Elia Kazan

"When I'm in the country writing, I cook for myself," said writer-director Elia Kazan. "I love it up there, especially when it's cold. I get up around 5:30, fix breakfast, start writing around 6:30 and work until one. Then I have a light lunch and go chop wood or clear brush or play tennis or swim or do all those things. Then I'll rest and shower, fix dinner. Actually, I like to dine alone. Sure, I'm eccentric! But, it's then that something happens: the book begins to come back to me. I begin to think what I'm going to write about the next day and I jot down some notes. Then I'll watch the news, drop off to sleep."

The Oscar winning writer-director, whose writing is his consuming interest in life, was comfortably sprawled on the couch of his paneled office located over a Times Square movie house, but he spends most of his time on the family homestead, a 113-acre farm in Newton, Connecticut, run by his son Chris, also a writer of novels and screenplays. On the farm, Elia lives alone in a studio-type house. In New York, he and his actress wife Barbara Loden share a rambling brownstone off Central Park with their two youngest sons.

"When I'm by myself, I'll make a sauté of spinach with garlic, Italian style. Or, I'll cook spaghetti sauce using pepperoni, ground meat, onions and tomatoes. I love cold tuna fish, too, with mayonnaise and onions. I eat the same thing all the time."

Elia, who was born to Greek parents in Turkey, came to the U.S. when he was four. Later, when he was at Harvard, the story goes that he made a big tin of baklava (a Turkish dessert delight) and was selling it to fellow students to make money.

# Baklava by Elia Kazan

Serves 12

1 lb. frozen filo pastry
  or strudel leaves
1 lb. butter
1 lb. walnut meats, finely
  chopped

¾ tsp. ground cinnamon
1 cup strained honey
1 cup water
about ⅔ cup sugar

1. *Buy filo from Middle Eastern bakery or food specialty shop; keep pastry wrapped in wax paper while it thaws. Keep covered with damp cloth as you work with it so pastry will not dry out.*
2. *Heat butter to clarify it; use only the clarified part of the butter, reserving remainder for other cooking.*
3. *Line shallow 13 x 15-inch pan with aluminum foil. Brush foil liner well with melted butter.*
4. *Lay down half the pastry sheets, one at a time, in bottom of buttered pan. Brush each well with melted butter; top with next sheet. Continue until half the sheets are used.*
5. *Combine walnuts and cinnamon; place on top of buttered sheets in pan.*
6. *Continue laying remaining sheets, buttering each layer well with melted butter. If there is any butter left, pour over top of pastry.*
7. *Cut through pastry to bottom of lower sheet, being careful not to puncture foil liner, cutting 2-inch diamond shapes.*
8. *Bake in preheated 325° F. oven about 45 minutes, or until pastry is brown and crisp.*
9. *Meanwhile, prepare syrup from honey, water and sugar. Cook until syrup comes to a good boil; remove from fire.*
10. *Syrup should be cooled to room temperature and poured over pastry while pastry is still quite warm.*
11. *Serve at room temperature. Pastry improves after standing 1 day; requires no refrigeration.*

NOTE: *There are many ways to prepare baklava. Many cooks contend pastry works better if it is hot before cold syrup is poured over, or pastry cooled before adding hot syrup. Some cook syrup with few drops of lemon juice to flavor it or just use honey. Any way it's consumed, it's a delicious, caloric delight!*

# Abbe Lane

"I cook all kinds of dishes. I love it, but I guess I'm more crazy about doing the table settings," said auburn-haired singer Abbe Lane. "I almost get more pleasure out of getting ready for the party than the actual affair.

"Let me tell you about my last bash. This time I chose a seashell motif. I used napkin holders made from real seashells. The place cards were shell-shaped and can be written on, erased and used again. With this I used an English Spode china decorated with a tiny floral design. I bought some special seafood forks for the occasion that look like mother of pearl and I found some real sea objects in an antique shop: small starfish enclosed in a crystal box, which I put on the table with sea shells and sea urchins arranged free-form," she said. "I love to look at a pretty table."

The menu for her seashell party included roast squab with wild rice and glazed carrots. "The dessert was fantastic – a gelatin bomb arranged on a huge platter with an assortment of fresh tropical fruits (guava, papayas, grapes, pineapples) served with whipped cream."

Abbe recited two of her favorite Italian recipes from memory, then added, "But please tell your readers not to forget the table setting."

# Abbe Lane's Zabaione

### Serves 4-6

6 egg yolks
¼ cup raw sugar
½ cup Marsala wine

1 tsp. pure vanilla extract
  or ½ tbsp. brandy
1 tbsp. cold water

1. *Combine egg yolks and sugar in top of double boiler. Place double boiler over heat, beating well.*
2. *Increase heat until mixture is slightly thickened.*
3. *Remove from heat.*
4. *Add wine, vanilla or brandy, beating well. Heat again.*
5. *Remove from heat.*
6. *Add water slowly; return double boiler to low heat, and beat and cook until thick and frothy. Do NOT boil.*
7. *Pour into wine glasses to serve. Can be served hot or cold.*

*NOTE: Cold zabaione is good poured over sponge or pound cake.*

# Kristy McNichol

Teenage Emmy winner Kristy McNichol says crêpes are a cinch to make with her electric crêpe maker. "I like to put a scoop of vanilla ice cream inside and roll it up like a cigar, then pour lots of chocolate sauce over the top. I never put things like chopped nuts or whipped cream on the top. In fact, I hate whipped cream unless it's on a chocolate sundae at Bob's Big Boy!"

A confirmed junk-food lover, Kristy says, "My number-one favorite food is a McDonald's hamburger. I could eat them morning, noon and night! Then, sometimes, I get cravings for weird things, like Mexican food – tacos with hot sauce. I won't try everything Mexican, though, because I hate cheese," she said, wrinkling her nose. "I adore anything chocolate – chocolate cake, chocolate brownies, chocolate anything."

Kristy's much like any other California girl; she dotes on her family, pets and friends, and she loves get-away weekends at the beach or in the mountains, where she can go skiing or snow-mobiling.

# Kristy McNichol's Dessert Crêpes

Makes 24 crêpes

1½ cups all-purpose flour
2 tbsps. sugar
scant ¼ tsp. salt
3 eggs

1½ cups milk
2 tbsps. melted butter or
　margarine
½ gallon vanilla ice cream

1. *Place all ingredients except ice cream in blender or mixer; beat well.*
2. *Cover; let stand at room temperature for 1 hour before using.*
3. *To cook crêpes, heat electric crêpe pan until ready light appears, or use regular crêpe pan, heated to the point where a drop of water skids across pan. Pour just enough batter to barely cover crêpe pan; cook only until crêpe no longer steams and bubbles and underside is delicately brown. This should take only 15-20 seconds. There is no need to brown both sides of crêpe.*
4. *Remove from pan carefully by inverting pan and using a fork or spatula to release crêpe.*
5. *Place crêpe, brown side down, on plate and fill lighter side with a scoop of the vanilla ice cream. Roll up like a cigar, top with chocolate sauce and serve immediately.*

NOTE: *There are three classic ways to fold crêpes: the roll (described above), the triangle and the pocket. Crêpes are fun to make, especially when everyone gets in on the act and fills his own. A half-gallon of ice cream and the crêpe recipe given here will serve at least 12 people, allowing 2 crêpes per person.*

# Juliet Mills

Movie stars, particularly women, have to go to almost any length these days to land plum roles, but seldom must they fatten up as much as British actress Juliet Mills did when she painfully added 25 pounds – a feat for the tiny, 97-pound actress – for her role of an English dumpling in the comedy, *Avanti*, opposite Jack Lemmon.

"The first 10 pounds were sorta fun," Juliet said. "I did that in three weeks. Then it started to become difficult, and I got very tired of stuffing myself. It's much more difficult than you think. Eating is very psychological. I notice I tend to eat more if I'm depressed or bored . . . I *et* (English vernacular for "ate") three proper good meals and tried not to eat candy, cakes or ice cream because I didn't want my skin to be ruined or my metabolism to really go."

It was John Mills, Juliet's father, and movie director Billy Wilder who finally helped her add the last poundage. "My father had me on English beer, and that did it until I got to Italy." By then, Juliet was well upholstered, but, she continued, "Mr. Wilder still said, 'It's really not enough.' I was like his own *pâté-de-fois-gras* goose, really being stuffed." Juliet laughed. Once the movie was completed, losing the added weight was even tougher. "I'd never go through that again."

Recently, Juliet prepared a special dinner for her parents. "I made my father's favorite dish – oxtail stew. I always make it ahead of time so all the flavors are absorbed. I can't bear entertaining and kind of dashing in and out of the kitchen, doing crêpes or soufflés at the last minute."

Her favorite dessert is carrot cake, a recipe from her brother.

# Juliet Mills's Carrot Cake

Makes one 9-inch cake

## For the cake

1½ cups vegetable oil
2 cups raw sugar or 1 cup
    white plus ½ cup light
    brown sugar
4 eggs
2 cups unbleached flour or
    1 cup white flour plus 1 cup
    whole wheat flour

2 tsps. baking soda
2 tsps. baking powder
2 tsps. cinnamon
1 tsp. salt
3 cups carrots, finely
    shredded
1 cup nuts, chopped

1. Combine vegetable oil and sugar, beating until well blended.
2. Add 1 egg at a time, mixing well after each addition.
3. Sift together all the dry ingredients. Add to cake batter, beating until smooth.
4. Stir in carrots and nuts. Beat batter ½ minute.
5. Pour mixture into 3 well-greased, lightly floured, round 9-inch layer tins. Bake in preheated 300° F. oven for 45 minutes, or until cake tester inserted in center comes out clean.
6. Cool in pans 10 minutes. Turn out onto wire racks to finish cooling.

## For the frosting

1 pkg. (8 oz.) cream cheese
1 stick margarine

4 tsps. pure vanilla extract
1 box confectioners' sugar

1. Cream together cream cheese and margarine until fluffy.
2. Add vanilla extract; gradually add confectioners' sugar, beating until very smooth.
3. Put layers together with frosting; frost outside of cake.

NOTE: For a delicious variation, make a 2-layer cake. Frost layers with date-nut filling; frost outside with brown sugar icing, flavored with ground mace.

# Jane Morgan

"I'm what you call a fantasy cook," said blonde singer Jane Morgan. "I'm never satisfied with a recipe so I do most of my cooking by ear, feel and taste! I love to cook. Generally it's steaks or chops, because Jerry is a meat-and-potatoes man."

Although Jane caters to the food whims of her husband, Jerry Weintraub – who is also her manager (as well as Frank Sinatra's) – she is always fascinated by new recipes and dishes. "The other day I prepared Sole *Bonne Femme*, the French fish classic, but I had to eat it all by myself because Jerry simply doesn't like French food." Jane's knowledge of French cuisine came about when she sang in Parisian *boîtes* (night clubs).

Jane's first attempts at cooking were in her mother's kitchen in their South Duxsbury (a Boston surburb) home. "I used to watch my father dig for clams every morning when they were in season." Through her late father, Bertram Currier, Jane is a direct descendent of Nathaniel Currier of Currier & Ives, and is deeply rooted in New England tradition.

"I bake bread, boil lobster, make baked beans, green corn muffins, boiled beef and cabbage and roast turkey. I like spicy things, and I make a turkey dressing with lots of nuts and spices. I like chicken soup made with oregano and basil, and I like spices and herbs in salad dressings. I can cook spur-of-the-moment menus, but I really like to have time to plan."

# Jane Morgan's Honey Cake

Serves 15-20

6 eggs
1 lb. honey
1½ cups sugar
1 cup cold coffee
1 tsp. lemon rind, grated

1 cup orange juice
5½ cups cake flour
3 tsps. baking powder
2 tsps. baking soda
¾ cup vegetable oil

1. *Beat eggs until lemon colored.*
2. *Add remaining ingredients, sifting cake flour and baking powder together. Blend well.*
3. *Pour batter into a large, well-greased, deep, square cake pan. Bake cake in preheated 350° F. oven about 1¼ hours, or until cake tests done when a toothpick comes out dry.*
4. *Let stand 10 minutes before turning out on cake rack.*

NOTE: *Jane's honey cake is very large. If preferred, bake in 2 small cake pans or 1 large spring cake pan.*

# Bess Myerson

"My mother fed us so carefully," said Bess Myerson, decked out in velvet jeans and beige shirt. "We always sat down to each meal and started with a plate of fresh, cleaned vegetables: a quarter head of lettuce, several stalks of celery, a couple of carrots, half a tomato and maybe a white radish, which we all loved!"

Bess is a very busy person who thinks about food more in terms of consumer needs and health than in terms of the culinary process, but she admires women "who are knowledgeable and into the whole cooking scene. It's a great skill; it shows discipline and it's vitally important!"

Bess tries to eat "intelligently, but simply." Her perennial good looks and svelte figure are a reflection of her preference for wholesome, simple foods. "I eat an awful lot, but my weight seems to stay fairly constant," said Bess, who is only five pounds heavier than she was in 1945 when she won the beauty pageant in Atlantic City.

Bess' greatest challenge and satisfaction began with her involvement in consumer affairs – an interest that constantly spills over into her own private life. "I'm constantly looking for unit prices and open dating, and being able to compare prices; I know how to buy. I always think of myself as going into a wonderful general store – some place in the country – with an open bucket where I could say, 'Give me 2 pounds of this and 4 ounces of that,' and not having to shop for packages in different sizes, mini-packages, six-packs. Familiar containers seem to somehow retain their shapes and yet contain less, because there is a lot of air in the tops of the boxes or bottles. The containers have been designed to tease the eye!"

# Bess Myerson's Baked Apples in Foil

Serves 4

4 baking apples
4 tbsps. honey or
   brown sugar

½ tsp. ground cinnamon
¼ tsp. ground nutmeg
2 tbsps. butter

1. *Remove core from each apple and peel halfway down from stem end.*
2. *Place each apple on large square of aluminum foil.*
3. *Fill center of each apple with honey, cinnamon, nutmeg and butter.*
4. *Bring foil over apples and loosely crumple ends of foil together. Some steam should escape as apples roast.*
5. *Place foil-wrapped apples in a shallow pan and bake in preheated 375° F. oven for 45 minutes.*
6. *About 10 minutes before apples are expected to be done, turn back foil. Baste apples several times with honey-spice mixture during remaining cooking time.*
7. *Serve warm, plain or with heavy cream.*

*NOTE: If desired, use raisins and/or chopped almonds to fill center of apples. Grated lemon or orange rind gives a delicate flavor to the apple.*

# Patrick O'Neal

Actor Patrick O'Neal and his wife, Cynthia, live in a remodeled brownstone on the West Side of New York. They dote on entertaining their friends at sit-down dinners. "I never cook for more than eight people," Cynthia said.

"And she's a marvelous cook, even studied at the Cordon Bleu," Patrick boasted, then went on to admit, "I have to say I'm a peculiar eater. I can go for days and won't eat deliberately. Then I can sit down and eat a detailed and enormous dinner. I seldom eat lunch when I'm working, but if it's a Friday night and we've invited a few friends in for dinner, I can go ape!"

Their mutual interest in food led to the establishment of "The Ginger Man," a restaurant Patrick owns and supervises in New York's Lincoln Center. "Obviously, our original motivation was to have a place to go so I could eat. We never anticipated the enormous response of our clients."

Their regulars include Angela Lansbury, George Segal and Leonard Bernstein. It's not unusual to see Andy Warhol in blue jeans or elegantly dressed Jackie Onassis with her children in the restaurant. The real secret at the Ginger Man is the choice of menu. "We have a nucleus of four or five things that people like," said Patrick. Top favorites include *coquilles St. Jacques, quenelles de brochet* (pike mousse with Natua sauce), and Patrick's favorite *ragout de boeuf Bourguignon*.

Patrick and his co-owner, actor Carroll O'Connor, also have a Ginger Man in Beverly Hills.

# The Ginger Man's Coeur à la Crème
# (Cream Cheese Hearts)

Serves 8

### For the hearts

½ lb. cream cheese
½ cup powdered sugar
pinch salt

1-inch piece vanilla bean
1 pint heavy cream
cheesecloth

8 heart-shaped wicker *coeur à la crème* baskets
(or perforated tin molds)

1. *Beat cream cheese until light and fluffy.*
2. *Gradually add powdered sugar, salt and vanilla bean (slit bean lengthwise with sharp knife, scraping small seeds into the mixture); blend well.*
3. *Whip heavy cream (place bowl in larger bowl filled with crushed ice) until cream holds its shape.*
4. *Add to cream cheese mixture, blending with whisk.*
5. *Cut 4 thicknesses of cheesecloth large enough to overlap edges of each heart-shaped basket. Wring out cheesecloth in ice water; carefully line each basket with layers of cheesecloth.*
6. *Fill each basket heaping full with cream cheese mixture. Overlap ends of cheesecloth. Refrigerate hearts overnight (or at least 6 hours), placing on plates to collect the whey.*

### For the sauce

¼ cup dry sherry or framboise
1½ ozs. Grand Marnier or
   orange liqueur
1½ ozs. dark sweet rum
¾ cup red currant jelly

1½ cups fresh, cleaned,
   sliced strawberries (or
   raspberries or sliced
   fresh peaches)
1 tbsp. fresh lemon juice

1. *Combine sherry, Grand Marnier, rum and currant jelly in saucepan. Heat over low heat to melt jelly, but do not cook.*
2. *Cool; add strawberries coated with lemon juice.*

### To serve

1. *Unfold ends of cheesecloth; turn each basket (or mold) upside down on glass dessert plate. Peel off cheesecloth and discard.*
2. *Outline "hearts" with whole, fresh strawberries; spoon sauce over "hearts."*

# Molly Picon

Molly Picon smiled fondly across the table at her husband, Jacob (Jonkel) Kalich. The scene was the 18th Street apartment the couple share with Molly's sister when they're in New York.

I asked if she had ever made her own pickles.

"Surely – the Jewish kind," Molly said, "with salt and garlic. . . ."

"I didn't know there were Gentile and Jewish pickles," Jonkel quipped, then went on. "I must tell you a story about Flo Ziegfield and his wife, Billie Burke. They came downtown to see Molly. I was trying to figure out where to take them to dinner. Across the street from the theater, on Second Avenue, was a very famous steak house called Moscowitz and Lupowitz, and the manager's name was Anselovitz. We thought all those waiters would be excited when they saw Ziegfield, but they had never seen or heard of him! When we came in, the waiters rushed over saying, 'Molly, Molly' and gave her the best table in the house. The first thing the waiter brought was a bowl of sour pickles, green pickles, sour tomatoes and seltzer. Billie Burke, being a very dainty person, said when she looked at the menu, 'Steak, steak, steak at midnight?' Then she called over the waiter and said, 'Pardon me, sir, have you any vegetables?' And the waiter looked at her and said, 'Lady, pickles aren't vegetables?'"

The Kaliches entertain in town mainly in restaurants. But in summer, they entertain in the country around their sixty-foot outdoor swimming pool. During Passover, the Kaliches often entertain the neighborhood children, passing out some of Molly's homemade farfel candy.

# Molly Picon's Pesach Farfel Candy

1 lb. strained clover honey        1 tbsp. ginger
1 cup sugar                        1 lb. matzo farfel

1 cup chopped nuts

1. *Boil honey and sugar until candy thermometer registers "soft crack" stage.*
2. *Add ginger, farfel and nuts.*
3. *Turn out on board dampened with ice water.*
4. *Wet hands with ice water and spread candy evenly to ¾ inch thickness.*
5. *Cool slightly. Cut into squares or diamonds with sharp knife.*

NOTE: *Molly says, "Farfel makes a nice nosh for young and older children."*

# Telly Savalas

As we talked, Aristotle (Telly) Savalas peered through dark glasses, looking the antithesis of the Hollywood star, decked out in a leaf-green printed open-neck shirt and grey suit. He often stroked his gleaming bald pate, which resembled a lopsided watermelon. From the start he emphasized his food tastes are strictly Spartan. His voice was like a big, booming bugle.

The New York-born actor, recalled some of "those Spartan" dishes from his childhood. "I would mention, not what you would call the exotic dishes, but more basic Greek dishes: fava beans, for example, boiled down to almost a pasty substance, flavored with a piece of onion, or *faki*, which is lentil soup. *Yaourti,* or yogurt, is, of course, a glass of milk for a Greek child.

"My mother (Christina Savalas) was the greatest swinger in the world. She's an artist and a beautiful woman (in 1938 she held the title of Miss Greece while being the mother of five children) and a great chick! But she can go into the kitchen and she's magic. Food for me is just to survive. As a Greek, I'm more concerned about things like beauty and romance," he said with malicious mirth.

"Every now and then I like the conceits of eating: dining out, to dress and have good service, but as a steady diet, that would drive me up the wall. I think my favorite thoroughly Greek food would be that delicacy *Kourambiethes*, that's a pastry. Or a great Greek spinach thing called *spanakapita* done in layers of feta cheese cooked like a pie all crisp and crusty. I love that," he said gleefully.

# Telly Savalas's Butter Cookies

Makes 4½ dozen cookies

1 lb. soft butter
½ cup vegetable oil
1 egg
½ cup sugar
1 tsp. baking powder

about 4½ cups all-purpose flour
good pinch ground cinnamon or cloves
confectioners' sugar

1 cup blanched almonds, ground

1. *Melt butter. Let it settle: discard milky white residue that forms in bottom of pan.*
2. *Put cooled drawn butter in mixing bowl with vegetable oil. Add egg and sugar; beat until light and fluffy.*
3. *Sift together flour, baking powder and cinnamon. Add to egg mixture, mixing well.*
4. *Add ground almonds; mix well.*
5. *Turn out on lightly floured board. Roll out with rolling pin; shape into diamond shapes or wedding bells.*
6. *Bake on ungreased baking sheets in preheated 350° F. oven about 25 minutes, or until lightly browned.*
7. *Remove from oven and roll in confectioners' sugar while still warm.*

NOTE: *Greeks are never without Kourambiethes (butter cookies)! Traditionally, they serve the confection with wine or coffee. For bridal feasts, the wedding bells are served; for Christmas, each cookie should be garnished with clove to represent the wise man who brought spices to the Christ child.*

# Millie Slavin

"I'm very down-to-earth, maybe what you'd call basic," said actress Millie Slavin, picking up with her fingers the fresh strawberries she'd ordered for dessert.

The attractive, transplanted New Yorker, who played Nurse Vera Wales on CBS-TV's "Rafferty," is refreshingly honest and unpretentious, with high cheekbones that clearly bespeak her Russian ancestry.

"My mother baked beautifully – things like the strudel that she stretched and stretched on the table and pirogi. She was a real artist. I remember as a child always hanging around the kitchen so I could lick out the pots and sample the fillings."

Millie gets a kick out of trying "things that are simple to prepare, but that look and taste exotic."

Two of her favorite recipes come from an old friend, New Yorker Elaine Feller, who still lives in Manhattan. "I had both dishes in her house one night," said Millie. "Her sweet and sour meat loaf is the best I've ever had, and I flipped over her fruit yogurt pie!"

# Millie Slavin's Fruit Yogurt Pie

Makes one 9-inch pie

1½ cups crushed graham
   crackers or vanilla wafers
¼ cup sugar
6 tbsps. melted butter
1 tsp. cinnamon

2 containers fruit-flavored
   yogurt
1½ pints heavy cream,
   whipped, or one 9-oz. container
   Cool Whip

2 cups prepared fruit: blueberries, strawberries,
peaches or bananas, or same amount
dry-pack frozen berries

1. *Combine graham cracker crumbs, sugar, butter and cinnamon.*
2. *Press mixture into bottom and sides of a 9-inch pie dish.*
3. *Spread half the fruit on bottom of crust.*
4. *Combine yogurt and whipped cream; spread over fruit layer.*
5. *Arrange remaining fruit over top of pie.*
6. *Chill at least 4 hours before serving. Serve very cold.*

NOTE: *Millie Slavin says, "This is an easy dessert. It's especially delicious if you use yogurt flavored with the same fruit as the fresh or frozen fruit, like strawberry yogurt and fresh strawberries." A mixture of strawberries and bananas also makes a delicious combination. Feel free to experiment!*

# Mark Spitz

"I'm not what you'd call a gourmet cook," said Mark Spitz between forkfuls of eggs Benedict at the Beverly Hills Hotel. "I fix basic things, like 'crummy hamburgers!' I never nosh between meals."

The lean super-swimmer of gold medals Olympics fame explained, "I cooked for myself while I was in college. I'm not a fancy cook, but I'm certainly not underfed!" Spitz's ideas about how to feed himself carry over from his days of training for the Olympics. His approach to diet, he said, is "more psychological than nutritional. I'm not a health food addict. I believe in doing what helps me feel good! My eating routine involves heavily loaded meals, like this one, early in the day. This way, my stomach feels full and I can get by on a light lunch. I used to compete around noon and eight o'clock at night. I'd have a big breakfast around nine. Then I'd warm up and compete at noon. I'd have a small lunch and a nap and eat some Jello just before my next competition. I never swim on a full stomach.

"When I was competing, I deliberately chose foods for variety because if I couldn't get a particular dish, like steak or eggs, then I could substitute easily. Some athletes are fanatics about vitamin pills. If that's what it takes to get them psyched up, terrific. But what would happen if I forgot my bottle of pills or couldn't get them in the drugstore on a Sunday? That would be disastrous!"

Mark enjoys the meals his wife, model Susie Weiner, prepares for him. "Susie's bundt cake is very good. I don't like chocolate cake, but I like her flecked cake. She is not a start-from-scratch cook! She'll frown a little and say, 'What does the box say to add next?'" Mark said, smiling.

# Susie Spitz's Flecked White Pound Cake

Serves 12-14

1 pkg. (about 18 ozs.) white
   cake mix
1 pkg. (7.2 ozs.) fluffy
   white frosting mix
4 eggs

1 container (8 ozs.) dairy
   sour cream
½ cup water
2 squares semi-sweet chocolate,
   coarsely grated

1. *Combine cake mix, frosting mix, eggs, sour cream and water. Beat 3 minutes at medium speed with electric mixer.*
2. *Add grated chocolate; mix 1 minute longer.*
3. *Pour batter into a greased, lightly floured 12-cup bundt cake pan. Bake in preheated 350° F. oven 50-60 minutes, or until toothpick inserted in center of cake comes out clean.*
4. *Cool cake in pan on wire rack 20 minutes.*
5. *Loosen cake carefully at edges with knife before turning out on wire rack to finish cooling. Slice to serve. Store in tightly covered cake box.*

NOTE: *Cake is very tender and similar to pound cake in texture. If desired, serve with confectioners' sugar or glaze with vanilla or chocolate icing.*

# Barbra Streisand

Take a gal who says, "I love a baked potato overcooked with a hard shell," favors a "diner hamburger" to a filet mignon, yet enjoys hostessing elegant sit-down dinners, and you have the basic ingredients of Barbra Streisand. "I love to eat, almost anything, but I like food that is cooked the day before. It tastes better warmed up the next day," Barbra said. "I'm a pretty good breakfast eater. I don't eat many eggs, but it's fun to break the top off a three-minute boiled egg and stuff it with toast and marmalade."

Barbra is a confirmed "nosher" and derives her greatest pleasure in late dining, preferably at home or in a diner. "You can get some of the best food in the world in a diner. I particularly love the kind of hamburgers you get there. The meat is fat, it's different and tastes better than what you can fix at home."

High on the list of Barbra's favorites are the riches of a Jewish delicatessen. Her favorites include *kishka* (sausage filled with a seasoned matzo meal mixture), stuffed cabbage and her favorite sandwich: bagels, lox, cream cheese and chopped onion.

"I'm a non-drinker," she explained. "I just don't like the taste of liquor. When I used to work in nightclubs and people would invite me to have a drink at the table, I'd ask for a plate of asparagus. I love it with melted butter or Hollandaise sauce."

Barbra, who adores Chinese food, is capable of ordering a complete meal in Chinese. She acquired this talent at 15, while working as a cashier in a Chinese restaurant.

"I love to eat cake and drink milk late at night. But I'm really mad about coffee ice cream — I used to eat it at the corner drugstore when I was a kid." Barbra measures her success in terms of food: "Success is having 10 honeydew melons and eating the top half-inch; it's sweet!"

# Barbra Streisand's Chocolate Fudge Sauce and Instant Coffee Ice Cream

Serves 4

## For the sauce

2 ozs. unsweetened chocolate
1 tbsp. butter
½ cup boiling water
1 cup sugar
dash salt

2 tbsps. light corn syrup
½ cup walnuts or toasted almonds, crushed
1 tsp. pure vanilla extract

1. *Melt chocolate and butter in double boiler; dilute with boiling water.*
2. *Add sugar, salt and corn syrup; stir to dissolve sugar.*
3. *Boil over direct heat 6 minutes, stirring often to prevent burning.*
4. *Cool to room temperature. Add walnuts and vanilla.*

## For the ice cream

1 cup milk
24 marshmallows
2 tsps. instant coffee

dash salt
1 cup heavy cream, chilled

1. *Heat milk slowly over low heat; add marshmallows a few at a time, stirring until marshmallows have melted.*
2. *Add instant coffee and salt; stir to dissolve.*
3. *Cool; pour into an ice cube tray. Dampen bottom of ice cube tray with water to hasten freezing.*
4. *Freeze until almost firm, stirring once to prevent large ice crystals from forming.*
5. *Beat cream until stiff, then fold into frozen mixture; return to freezer and freeze until firm.*
6. *Serve with chocolate fudge sauce drizzled over the top. Nuts may be sprinkled over the top.*

*NOTE: Barbra says, "Boil the sauce 8 minutes and pour over the ice cream to form a hard layer. Or serve the ice cream alone with pretzels because the salt is good with sweet."*

# Richard Thomas

"I'm basically just a throw-it-round cook: big roasts, salted and cooked in a 350° F. oven for an hour and a half, big green salads and baked potatoes," said actor Richard Thomas, John-Boy of TV's "The Waltons." "I'm definitely not a health food person, but then I'm not a steak eater but a roast man, beef or pork rib."

Richard ascribes his preference for simple fare to his parents, who are both dancers. "Coming from a ballet background, most of what we eat at our house is very basic: roasts, chops and vegetables – simple, hearty fare; certainly not a lot of fancy cooking. We don't like saucy foods, but I do wish I could make *criollas* the way my mother can. That's Cuban cooking: shredded beef and spices, chicken and rice, black beans and rice and fried bananas." His parents once danced in Havana and would like to return there someday.

Richard's newest recipe is an authentic applesauce cake, one from Appalachia, the locale of the Walton story. It's a recipe from Earl Hamner, the real John-Boy on whose life and family the series is based. It is Earl's mother who often baked the cake for her family.

"You can decorate it for the holiday season with holly," said Richard, "but don't eat the holly because it's awfully hard on your throat going down." He laughed at that one.

# Richard Thomas's Applesauce Cake
# with Whiskey Frosting

Serves 8-10

### For the cake

3½ cups sifted all-purpose
   flour
1 tsp. baking soda
2 tsps. nutmeg
1 tsp. cinnamon
½ tsp. cloves

pinch of salt
1 cup walnuts, chopped
2 cups light raisins
1 cup butter, softened
1 cup sugar
2 eggs

1 jar (16 ozs.) applesauce

1. *Sift flour with soda, spices and salt.*
2. *Combine nuts and raisins in bowl; stir in ½ cup of the flour mixture.*
3. *Cream butter and sugar in another bowl until light and fluffy.*
4. *Beat in eggs one at a time, beating thoroughly after each.*
5. *Alternately add flour mixture and applesauce, beginning and ending with the flour mixture.*
6. *Stir in raisin mixture.*
7. *Spoon into greased, floured 10-inch tube pan. Bake in preheated 350° F. oven for 1 hour and 20 minutes, or until cake tester inserted in center comes out clean.*
8. *Cool in pan for 15 minutes, then remove from pan and finish cooling on wire rack.*
9. *Spread with frosting. Cover until ready to serve. Cake keeps well; in fact, it's better several days after baking.*

### For the whiskey frosting

¼ cup butter, softened
1 tbsp. heavy cream or milk

1 lb. (4 cups) confectioners' sugar
3-4 tbsps. bourbon

1. *Stir together butter and cream; beat in 1 cup of the sugar.*
2. *Blend in remaining sugar and the bourbon until proper spreading consistency. Makes enough frosting to generously cover a 10-inch tube cake.*

# Mae West

Mae West was a startlingly beautiful woman with alabaster skin and wide-set sapphire blue eyes, framed with long black eyelashes and a trace of eyeshadow. In an interview before her death in 1980, she extended a soft manicured hand, with nails frosted a pearly pale pink, and seated herself, smoothing the folds of her floor-length, pale green peignoir. For a quick moment before she spoke, I wondered if I were faced with a stand-in, a lady some 40 years younger than Miss West's chronological age. Her low-pitched cadence seemed more befitting a Southern-bred woman than a native of Booklyn. I wondered if she had heard of the wine inspector who had said once, "The 1921 (vintages) were like Mae West, fully developed from the start."

"I don't drink and I don't smoke, but I think I should have tasted that," she said with a laugh. "I'm very health-minded. My father was once a fighter and had a gym in our house. All I've heard since before I could walk was the importance of maintaining good health and training.

"Real beauty and health come from within. It shows up in your skin or your face if you don't keep your system clean." Her favorite health tonic was carrot juice, which she consumed in quantity. "Think of all the nutrients you can get from one glass of uncooked carrots!" she exclaimed. "When I've been out to dinner and had a few little things that I shouldn't, I detoxicate. Our water is terrible. I've always washed my face and hair in bottled water. In the days when I was on the road, I carried Poland (purified) water with me. They even cooked my tea in it in the kitchens of the hotels where I stayed."

# Mae West's Diet Breakfast and/or Lunch Fruit Compote

Serves 1

1 large apple, chopped
1 large pear, chopped

1 large banana, chopped
2-3 almonds, grated

1. *Combine fruits; top with almonds.*
2. *If desired, apples may be sliced and combined with raisins and topped with syrup made of powdered almonds, milk and honey.*

*NOTE: Serious dieters, of course, should check their food intake with their doctors, Mae West says.*

# Bud Westmore

"I can make a movie star look glamorous, but it's her attitude towards life – an indefinable verve – that sets her apart from the rest of the human race," said the late Bud Westmore, a member of the famed Westmore family that has dominated the beauty scene in the film capital for more than half a century.

"When you feel well and eat well, that's part of the answer. Booze is an age-old destroyer of beauty. I've seen some great talents who made it halfway up the ladder of success only to be destroyed by excessive drinking." Bud, who judged many Miss America beauty contests, proudly pointed to a picture of his wife, the former Geanne Shores, whom he met when she was Miss California in the 1952 pageant. "Here's the real cook in our family," he said proudly.

In recent years, the Westmores spent much time on their 40-foot boat. "I'm really the upstairs cook while Geano works out in the galley below," said Bud. "We cook informally. I barbecue lobsters or steaks over briquettes in one of those swinging grills that project out over the water. While I finish off the barbecuing up on deck, Geano cooks up one of her favorite vegetable dishes on the alcohol stove in the galley.

"There is something I like to cook and that's tiger's milk cookies. After my heart attack, I had to stay away from certain foods and I happened on to this recipe. It's really delicious."

# Bud Westmore's Tiger's Milk Cookies

Makes 2 dozen cookies

1 cup raw sugar or light
  brown sugar
½ cup tiger's milk
1½ cups uncooked oatmeal
½ cup wheat germ
1½ tsp. cinnamon

½ tsp. cloves
½ tsp. salt
½ cup polyunsaturated
  oil
2 eggs
¾ cup raisins

¾ cup English walnuts, chopped

1. *Combine all ingredients except oil, eggs, nuts and raisins in large mixing bowl.*
2. *Add oil, mixing well.*
3. *In separate bowl, beat eggs until light; stir into sugar mixture, mixing well.*
4. *Stir in chopped walnuts and raisins.*
5. *You may bake at once, but for best results, wrap lightly in aluminum foil and refrigerate overnight.*
6. *To bake, rub hands lightly with flour. Break off bits of dough, forming balls the size of walnuts.*
7. *Place cookies on well-greased cookie sheet 1½ inches apart. Bake in preheated 350° F. oven 15 minutes, or until lightly browned.*

NOTE: *Raw sugar imparts a maple flavor to the cookies. Tiger's milk, a protein food supplement, is available at health food stores.*

# Nicol Williamson

"I *hope* this is the right mustard. Damn! It's English mustard! Oh well, it doesn't matter. I believe you shouldn't complain when you go elsewhere because you can't get what you're used to. You can't start ordering 'freshed-over' (fresh-caught) filet of sole, pulling a long face when nobody else has it," said Nicol Williamson, the ginger-haired thespian with the mutton-chop sideburns, as he suspiciously lathered his hamburger with the pungent condiment.

All this seemed an innocuous beginning to luncheon with the Scotsman in the King Cole Bar at New York's St. Regis Hotel.

"I eat sparsely, one meal a day," he said between sips of beer. "I hardly ever have fish here, but I eat chops and steaks because they're great. They make marvelous sandwiches in America (his favorites are club and corned beef with lots of mustard) like no where else in the world. The best hamburger I've had was at P.J. Clarke's."

Nicol's strictly a spectator cook and limits his entertaining in his Notting Hill Gate (London suburb) home to "sitting around and having a few drinks with friends. I have a one-story house with two bedrooms, a sitting and dining room, a kitchen – but the cooker (stove) doesn't work. When I go home (he was born in Hamilton, Scotland), I have these enormous breakfasts, and two hours later, an enormous lunch and a huge dinner. Their breakfasts are like 'girdle' scones. I suppose you'd call them griddle scones here. But they're made with soda. They're very large and sort of three-sided."

# Nicol Williamson's Griddle Scones

2 cups all-purpose flour
1 tsp. baking soda
1 tsp. baking powder
2 tbsp. sugar

pinch salt
3 tbsps. butter
1 egg, beaten
about 7 tbsps. milk

unsalted lard

1. Sift together dry ingredients in bowl. Cut in butter until the texture is like fine meal.
2. Combine egg with all but 1 tbsp. of the milk.
3. Make a well in the center of the dry ingredients. Add egg-milk mixture, mixing lightly with fork, to form fairly stiff dough. Add more milk if necessary.
4. Gather dough together gently with lightly floured hands to form a ball. Turn out on a lightly floured board. Roll out circle of dough about ½ inch thickness and cut into 8 pie-shaped wedges.
5. Rub griddle lightly with unsalted lard. Heat over medium heat.
6. Place scones on hot griddle, cook over medium heat, turn once to brown on both sides. Cooking directly on the griddle takes from 10-12 minutes. Watch closely so scones do not cook too rapidly.
6. To test for doneness, press down lightly with fingers to see that dough does not ooze out from the edges. Serve at once with butter and jam for breakfast or tea.

NOTE: American cooks can bake scones in the oven as you prepare biscuits. However, the texture is slightly different and not as crusty as the griddle-cooked scones. Some Scottish cooks prefer not to roll out the dough, but grab off small amounts of dough the size of a dessert spoon, shape the dough by pressing into triangle or diamond shapes on a lightly floured board and then toss the scones from one hand to the other to shake off excess flour before baking on the griddle.

# Holidays

# Richard Deacon

Actor Richard Deacon, who learned to cook as a boy in Binghamton, New York, has turned his favorite hobby – microwave cooking – into a book he believes helps cope with today's soaring food prices and energy shortage. Deacon's face is terribly familiar. So is his voice. He played Mel Cooley in the long-running "Dick Van Dyke" show.

While other boys had paper routes, Deacon, as a kid, baked banana bread and sold it in the neighborhood to raise a buck. "It was Andy Hardy time, a happy time," he said. "I'm by no means a gourmet cook. If anything, I'm a gourmand. I want things that are inexpensive, taste good and look like you've worked hard to prepare it when you haven't!"

Timing is the key to microwave success, according to Deacon. "It's what most cooks overlook. For years they have been looking at their roasts and saying, 'It's not ready yet. I'll leave it in another 20 minutes.' Microwave takes away the guess work. But if you don't read the directions and watch the timing, you'll get in trouble. Take, for example, people who say, 'I had a roast last night. It was tough!' It was tough because they didn't read in the book where it says 'allow roast to rest 15 minutes after you cook it.' If you don't, it's tough because the juices haven't gotten back into circulation again."

# Richard Deacon's Roast Capon with Pilgrim's Stuffing & Sauce

Serves 4

1 cleaned, dressed capon, weighing about 5 lbs.
¾ cup onion, chopped
liver from capon, chopped
8 tbsps. unsalted butter
⅓ cup celery, minced

2 tbsps. fresh parsley, chopped
1½ cups day-old bread, cut in cubes
2 cups prepared corn-bread stuffing

1 tsp. thyme leaves
1 tsp. tarragon
salt to taste
freshly ground pepper
watercress
crab apples

1. *Rinse and pat-dry capon; set aside.*
2. *Sauté onion and liver in 4 tbsps. butter until onion is transparent.*
3. *Add celery and parsley, stirring to blend. Cook 30 seconds.*
4. *In large mixing bowl, combine bread cubes, cornbread, thyme, tarragon, salt and pepper to taste. Add sautéed vegetables and mix well.*
5. *Pack cavities loosely with stuffing. Sew openings; truss tightly.*
6. *Place breast-side down on a trivet in baking dish and put in microwave oven. Allow 6 minutes per pound; turn 4 times while cooking.*
7. *After first 7½ minutes, rotate dish a half turn. After 15 minutes, turn capon over and cook another 7½ minutes.*
8. *Baste with remaining butter and brown for 6 minutes, or as desired. During cooking, if capon seems to be overcooking, cover with wax paper.*
9. *Test by pricking the skin of the thigh to see if juices run clear. Remove trussing. Garnish with watercress and crab apples.*

## For the sauce

1½ tsps. onion or shallots, minced
1½ tsps. butter
2 tbsps. flour

1 cup chicken broth
¾ cup cream
salt to taste
black pepper to taste

1. *Sauté onion in butter in shallow dish for 1 minute. Add flour; cook for 1½ minutes, stirring occasionally. Add ¾ cup chicken broth, blending well.*
2. *Cook sauce 5 minutes, stirring occasionally. Cover and reserve.*
3. *Pour fat from capon roasting pan into saucepan; add the rest of the chicken broth; cook 6-7 minutes, stirring occasionally.*
4. *Add reserved sauce; cook 3 minutes; add cream and cook 3 minutes.*
5. *Season with salt and pepper to taste; serve in heated gravy boat.*

# Jackie Gleason

"I love to eat, but if I eat the way I'd like to for one day, it means three days of dieting to get the weight off," said "The Great One," Jackie Gleason, glumly. Seated in his dressing room, he looked spiffy in a dark blue suit and ever-present red carnation.

"Bring the young lady some wine," he ordered his assistant, offering me some imported Italian vintage. "Eating is heaven," he added, "and dieting is sheer hell! Therefore, I can never really enjoy a meal!" He forgets dieting, however, when the holidays roll around. His wife, Marilyn Taylor Horwich, sister of June Taylor (she headed the famous dancing group that starred on Gleason's TV shows) is a great cook, according to her mate. "She makes me the greatest turkey, with three kinds of everything — dressing, cranberry dishes, potatoes," he said, smiling as though he'd just put away one of Marilyn's meals.

The Gleasons like to entertain in their palatial $400,000 pad in Inverrary, near Fort Lauderdale, Florida. Their house is designed exclusively for comfort. Jackie's three favorite areas of the house are the gargantuan billiards room, the game room and the book-lined library, which houses over 4,000 books. Gleason is a non-stop reader. He's particularly interested in books on Japanese and Turkish warfare. The airy and pretty formal dining room has yellow walls, a yellow Oriental rug, and four groups of tables and chairs. For snacks, they often eat in the kitchen or in the game room at the upholstered circular bar.

# Marilyn Gleason's Cranberry Relish Salad

Makes 2 quarts

6 cups fresh cranberries
2 cups sugar
2 cups water
½ cup almonds, chopped

1½ cups red apples,
unpeeled and finely
sliced
½ cup celery, chopped

3 envelopes unflavored gelatin
mixed with ½ cup water

1. Combine cranberries, sugar and water; bring to boil. Lower heat and simmer 10 minutes.
2. Stir in softened gelatin mixture. Stir until gelatin is dissolved.
3. Chill in refrigerator until slightly thickened.
4. Fold in apple, almonds and celery. Pour into 2-quart mold.
5. Chill overnight or 12 hours.
6. To unmold, dip into lukewarm water. Pat to loosen and invert on platter.
7. Serve alone or surrounded by frosted cranberries, candied kumquats, mandarin orange sections or holly leaves. Frost cranberries by dipping into slightly beaten egg white; then roll in granulated sugar. Dry cranberries in single layer on waxed paper at room temperature.

NOTE: A pretty, make-ahead delight for the Christmas dinner!

# Muriel Humphrey

When interviewed, silver-haired Muriel Humphrey, then the wife of the Vice President, greeted me on the balcony of their six-room apartment located high above midtown Washington. "Please come in and have some coffee," she said. The vice-presidential china, into which she poured coffee, was gold and white.

"Home is where we hang our hats!" she said, laughing. "We have two homes, here and Waverly (Minnesota). Thanksgiving in Minnesota means a big dinner for 12, 13, or more people. It means getting a 22-pound turkey and cooking like mad all day long, but I love it! The kitchen is the focal point in our family.

"By the way, I have a jim-dandy recipe for you," she added enthusiastically. "I started it this morning and when Hubert and I come tonight from a reception, we'll have it." It was chicken. She takes a five-pound roasting chicken, rubs it inside and out with Season-all (seasoned salt), places it breast-side up in a large piece of aluminum foil, rubs liberally with chunks of butter, and wraps it tightly before oven-roasting. "It can be started in the morning and finished off when we come home," she said.

"Asked if the Vice President ever spelled her in the kitchen, Muriel Humphrey said, "He used to do more. He would make special pancakes as a treat for the children. He's great on steaks and makes a great beef stew."

# Muriel Humphrey's Holiday Turkey and Dressing

Serves 12 - 16

### For bird and chicken stock

1 cleaned turkey, weighing 12-16 lbs.
with giblets and liver
seasoned salt
1 large bay leaf

½ tsp. salt
freshly ground black pepper
to taste
about 4 cups water

1 small white onion, peeled and chopped

1. Rub turkey inside and out with seasoned salt. Set aside.
2. Chop the heart, liver and gizzard, and put in saucepan with remaining ingredients. Simmer 2 hours. (Reserve stock for basting, dressing and gravy.)

### For the dressing

3 quarts bread cubes (day-old bread)
¾ cup onion, minced
1½ cups celery with leaves, chopped
1 cup butter, melted
2 tbsps. salt
1 tbsp. dried sage or thyme or
marjoram

1 tsp. seasoned salt
1 tsp. ground pepper
poultry seasoning to taste
1 or 2 eggs, beaten (optional)
chicken stock
flour
milk

water (from cooking mashed potatoes or other vegetables)

1. Sauté onion and celery in butter until vegetables soften; toss over bread cubes in large mixing bowl.
2. Add salt, sage, seasoned salt, pepper, poultry seasoning and eggs; mix well.
3. Moisten with chicken stock, mixing lightly with fork. Cool.
4. Fill neck and back cavities with dressing. Do not pack. Close with skewers or by sewing. Truss bird, and tie wings and legs to body.
5. Place turkey on aluminum foil in roasting pan, breast-side up. Dot plentifully with butter. Season liberally with seasoned salt. Bring ends of foil over breast to completely cover turkey. Do not cover with roasting pan lid.
6. Roast in preheated 450° F. oven for 1 hour.
7. Reduce temperature to 325° F. and roast for 5 or 6 additional hours.
8. Make gravy by adding flour, milk, water, and chicken stock to turkey pan drippings.

# Ed McMahon

Affable Ed McMahon suffers from the plague of many Americans. "Losing weight has been a constant battle." The super pitchman of "Tonight Show" fame looked fit and rested in his office here.

"When I cook, it's a leg of lamb, roast turkey or ham, even if it's not on the diet!" said Ed. "I used to bake bread and cakes, but I had to quit that." He blames his love for good food on his Irish paternal grandmother, Katie Fitzgerald McMahon. "The most arresting smell in this world is the aroma of fresh bread baking. That's how I woke up every morning I spent with my grandmother. She never heard of cereal. We'd have pork chops for breakfast. She was a wonderful cook and believed in serving potatoes at every meal!"

# Ed McMahon's Roast Turkey
# with Brandied Stuffing

### Serves 8

1 pkg. (8 ozs.) herb-seasoned
   stuffing mix
1 pkg. (8 ozs.) cornbread
   stuffing mix
1½ cups applesauce
½ cup canned crushed
   pineapple, drained
handful fresh mushrooms,
   chopped

1 cup orange or lemon
   marmalade
½ tsp. ground sage
1 cup brandy
½ cup cooked pork sausage,
   crumbled (optional)
1 cup butter, melted
10-12 lbs. dressed turkey
6 strips bacon

1. *Combine stuffing mixes, applesauce, pineapple, mushrooms, marmalade, sage, brandy, sausage and butter.*
2. *Stuff turkey; close with skewers or by stitching; truss bird.*
3. *Place on rack, breast-side up, in roasting pan. Place bacon strips over breast.*
4. *Roast in preheated 325° F. oven for 1 hour.*
5. *Cover loosely with a foil tent and continue roasting about 3 hours longer, or until well-browned and tender, basting occasionally.*
6. *Remove bacon when it is crisp; crumble it into dressing after bird is removed from the oven. (Omit if sausage has been added to stuffing.)*

NOTE: *Additional brandy can be brushed on bird as it cooks to give it color and flavor.*

# Pat Nixon

"I learned to cook from my mother who knew what a pinch of this or a dash of that can do to food," Pat Nixon said. The former First Lady chatted in girl-talk fashion about cooking, one of her favorite pursuits.

"I never taste food when I cook, but my daughters don't understand when I say use a pinch of salt or add a dash of pepper. They are much more successful when they follow recipes," said Pat.

The Nixons like to entertain at small sitdown dinners for 12. "We like 3-course dinners because Dick doesn't like those long drawn-out affairs with six or seven courses."

The Nixons have a decided sweet tooth. Top dessert choices include angel pie (hard meringue filled with a rich chocolate cream), almond mocha torte and vanilla soufflé.

"I've gotten recipes from our travels all over the world. Dick's always been fond of Brazilian rice and all of us like Mexican food." This is probably a carryover from their California days. "We've always liked a variety of different cuisine," she said. "When we visited the USSR in 1959, we did the return dinner in the American Embassy and brought along our own food (frozen steaks, corn on the cob and potatoes for baking). We wanted to serve the Russians a typically American meal. I was the only woman at the Kremlin dinner and I said, 'I would like to meet your wives.' The women came and the dinner was so well received, particularly the baked potatoes. The Russians enjoy eating hearty foods."

A private family dinner at home with their daughters is a happy occasion for the Nixons. "We have candlelight and music," she explained, a smile lighting up her brown eyes. "It's so important when you lead a busy life. The family meal is the one time in the day when we can all be together."

# Pat Nixon's White House Christmas Cookies

Makes 10 dozen cookies

1 cup sugar
2 cups butter, at room temperature
1 tsp. pure vanilla extract

½ tbsp. lemon rind, grated
2 eggs
6-7 cups cake flour

1. *Cream together sugar and butter in an electric mixer. When fluffy, add vanilla and lemon rind, blending well. Add eggs, one at a time, mixing well.*
2. *Remove from mixer and add cake flour, blending with a heavy mixing spoon.*
3. *Chill dough in refrigerator for 1 hour or overnight.*
4. *Roll out dough to ⅛-inch thickness and cut out with favorite Christmas cookie cutters.*
5. *Bake in preheated 375° F. oven until brown, approximately 7-8 minutes.*

*NOTE: If colored granulated sugar is to be used for decoration, prepare an egg wash (1 well-beaten egg with 1 tsp. milk added) and brush over the cut-out dough. Sprinkle with sugar before baking.*

# Beverly Sills

Soprano Beverly Sills is a gourmet cook, but she quickly admits with a smile, "Everything I know about cooking, I learned from my husband. He's a graduate of the Cordon Bleu. I'm impressed by his cooking." She is married to retired journalist Peter Greenough. The couple live in a big, rambling apartment overlooking New York's Central Park.

Thanksgiving dinner in the Sills-Greenough *ménage* is always strictly traditional, with everyone getting into the cooking act, including Peter, Beverly and her mother. "We start out with Peter's oysters Rockefeller. I make the stuffing for the turkey with apricots, chestnuts and, when I have them, truffles. Basically, I'm a thrower-inner. I just keep adding things to the dressing until it tastes right.

"My mother always brings the dessert. She makes four or five different kinds of pie, usually including fresh apple or peach, but never pumpkin, because nobody in this family will eat it. She also makes a marvelous cake – it has seven different layers, including one of graham crackers and one of chocolate pudding. The whole thing is frosted with whipped cream. It's awfully rich and awfully good! We usually have a centerpiece of a huge mound of fruit, and that finishes off the meal."

# Beverly Sills's Oysters Rockefeller

### Serves 6

3 dozen oysters
1 lb. fresh spinach, washed
 and chopped
⅔ cup butter
1 small onion, peeled and minced
1 stalk celery, minced
1 leek (white part only), minced
½ tsp. oregano

salt to taste
freshly ground black
 pepper to taste
2 tbsps. flour
1 cup milk
1 cup Parmesan cheese,
 freshly grated
rock salt

1 small clove garlic, pressed

1. Scrub oysters thoroughly, then rinse in several changes of ice water. Insert a knife with a thin, strong blade between the shells and pry open by twisting. Discard the flatter shell, allowing oysters to remain in the curved shells. Reserve.
2. Wash spinach thoroughly; pick over carefully, discarding stems; pat-dry.
3. Cook spinach in a minimal amount of salted boiling water until barely tender. Drain and reserve.
4. Melt half the butter in a saucepan. Add onion, celery, leek, garlic, oregano, salt and pepper to taste. Sauté vegetables.
5. Melt 2 tbsps. butter in separate saucepan; add flour, stirring with a wire whisk until smooth.
6. Heat milk until boiling; add to flour-butter mixture, stirring constantly until smooth and thickened.
7. Combine sautéed vegetables, spinach, sauce and ½ cup Parmesan cheese. Mix well.
8. Arrange oysters in their shells in shallow baking pan on a bed of rock salt. Spoon sauce over them. Sprinkle with remaining cheese and dot with remaining butter. Bake in preheated 350° F. oven 12 minutes, or until lightly browned.
9. Serve piping hot. Delicious for first course.

# K.T. Stevens

"I love making all the traditional holiday foods and big dinners," said tall, blonde actress K.T. Stevens. "I've always cooked for anywhere from 20 to 27 people. I'm famous for my oyster dressing. Everyone loves it." Fans know K.T. best as Vanessa Prentiss in the popular CBS-TV soap, "The Young and the Restless."

Christmas dinner for K.T. takes place in her Brentwood house. "I serve buffet, of course, because my house is too small for a sit-down dinner. I usually have a green salad and fix yams, peas and onions and roast turkey and oyster dressing. I started making oyster dressing when I was married. My ex-husband (actor Hugh Marlowe) suggested it. He had it once and liked it. I invented my own version. My boys, who were always finicky about exotic foods, just loved it. They're grown now, but if they have turkey any time and there is no oyster dressing, forget it," she said, laughing. "I used to cook much more when the boys were home. I've gotten a little lazy.

"I'm very health conscious and getting more so. Fortunately, I've always enjoyed eating foods that are good for me. I love vegetables and salads. I eat very little red meat. I often have turkey and chicken, and feel great."

A second-generation show business personality, K.T. is the daughter of the late, famous director Sam Wood. "I can remember when Rudolph Valentino came to visit when I was very tiny. My father directed several of his films."

# K. T. Stevens's Oyster Dressing

### Enough to stuff a 25-lb. turkey

10 ribs of celery, chopped
2 medium-size onions, peeled
   and chopped
1 lb. butter
2 loaves white bread, toasted
   and cut into small cubes
1 tbsp. salt
½ tsp. freshly ground
   black pepper (more
   if desired)

1 tbsp. poultry seasoning
½ tbsp. ground sage
   (more if desired)
4 cups liquid (turkey stock
   or oyster liquor)
1½ quarts oysters, freshly
   shucked and chopped
1 cup fresh parsley,
   chopped

1. *Sauté celery and onion in melted butter until onion is transparent.*
2. *Add bread cubes, salt, pepper, poultry seasoning, and sage; mix thoroughly.*
3. *Add enough liquid to moisten bread.*
4. *Add oysters and parsley; mix well.*

# Jerry Stiller &
# Anne Meara

*"Corned beef and cabbage and Irish potatoes,
Chanukah, Christmas and Passover Seders,
Shamrocks and blintzes and nuns that have wings,
These are a few of our favorite things."*

These were the opening words of Stiller and Meara, the husband and wife comedy team who sang this parody to the tune from *Sound of Music* as they talked about Chanukah and Christmas. Their humor, largely based on their own experiences, trades heavily on the fact that she's Irish Catholic and he's Jewish. Even so, it's a happy blending of opposites, a successful distillation of tastes, particularly when it comes to food.

"When Anne makes Irish soda bread, she uses Dr. Brown's celery tonic," Jerry interjected, referring to a soda found in Jewish delicatessens.

"Then, there's an Irish boiled dinner and boiled cabbage," Anne said. "Just give the guests a fifth of Irish and they all get boiled. Brendan Behan always called it a 'touch of the sauce,' " she added in Gaelic dialect.

The Stillers observe both holidays in the classic manner with appropriate decorations and foods. Menorah and Christmas tree stand side by side in their living room. Chanukah usually comes first. "We usually start off with chicken soup with kreplach," Jerry said. "After soup comes stuffed derma and a vegetable like peas and carrots. *Latkes* (potato pancakes) and applesauce is a traditional Chanukah dish and can be served alone or as a dessert."

"Luckily, Christmas only comes one day a year – after all that eating! We love turkey and dressing made from deviled matzoh balls," Anne joked. "I go ape over sweet potato casserole made with marshmallows."

# Jerry Stiller's Chicken Soup with Kreplach

Serves 6

### For the chicken soup

1 tender young cleaned hen,
  weighing about 4½ lbs.
3 quarts water
1 small yellow onion, peeled
  and chopped
handful fresh parsley

2 small ribs celery with leaves
2 carrots, peeled and
  chopped
1 large bay leaf
1 tbsp. salt
4 peppercorns, bruised

1. *Wash chicken carefully; trim excess fat. Cut chicken into fourths.*
2. *Place chicken in large stock pot with rest of ingredients. Bring to simmer; cook, uncovered, about 3 hours or until tender. Skim off scum and fat.*
3. *Cool to room temperature. Refrigerate; discard layer of congealed fat that forms on the top.*
4. *Reheat soup; correct seasonings.*
5. *Drop in kreplach and cook about 15 minutes, or until they rise to the top.*

### For the kreplach filling

1 cup chicken livers, boiled
1 hard-cooked egg
1 small onion, peeled
1 tsp. fresh parsley, minced

salt to taste
freshly ground pepper to taste
1 generous tsp. schmaltz
  (rendered chicken fat)

1. *Chop livers, egg and onion together; season with salt and pepper to taste.*
2. *Add parsley and enough schmaltz to hold the mixture together.*

### For the noodle dough

2 small eggs, beaten          ½ tsp. salt          2 cups all-purpose flour

1. *Mix eggs, salt, and half the flour with a fork. Add more flour, mixing well until the dough leaves the sides of the bowl.*
2. *Turn out on lightly floured board; knead until dough is smooth and elastic.*
3. *Roll out paper-thin on clean, lightly floured cloth. Cut into 3-inch squares.*
4. *Place about 1 tsp. of filling in center of each square. Fold over, forming triangles. Seal all edges with floured tines of a fork.*

# Andy Warhol

Seated in his office, "The Factory," in the lower reaches of Manhattan, Andy Warhol looked like he could play the part of a ghost at the Dracula-inspired party he was cooking up. He is slightly built, pallid, bespectacled, and has a prominent streak of white-on-black hair. Warhol, the psychedelic pioneer many people still associate with the soup can pop art culture of the 60s, is a serious-minded person with an eye for the exquisite as well as the unusual.

"At my party, Bloody Marys and Vampire canapés are a perfect beginning!" said Andy. Although he doesn't like blood sausage, the main ingredient in Vampire canapés (rounds of sausage and cherry tomatoes, speared with toothpicks), he said, "It's really the prettiest processed meat available. Steak tartar on black bread is the best! I always thought steak tartar was made by putting raw meat through a meat grinder, but in good restaurants, they hand-cut the meat with a sharp knife into a very fine mince. I like to flavor the meat with condiments to make it look red and gory! What about some catsup and Escoffier sauce? And, to decorate the top, raw duck eggs or dove eggs."

For the main course, Andy selected something "ghoulish, like goulash! I love to make stuffed cabbage. I flavor the meat like goulash. My filling is flavored with ginger, stuffed and wrapped in red cabbage leaves. The sauce is similar to borscht." Aside from being a better-than-average cook, Andy is busy these days with many different projects, including his newspaper, movies, television and painting. "Now, I just do portraits and flowers. I suppose because nobody really thought I knew how to draw! Some people still think of me in terms of soup cans. And they still hate it. I'm trying to make up for it now by painting flowers."

# Andy Warhol's Ghoulish Goulash
# (Stuffed Cabbage)

### Serves 6

2 medium heads red cabbage
boiling salted water
½ lb. lean ground beef
2 cups cooked rice
1 egg, beaten
2 tbsps. parsley,
  chopped
2 tbsps. fresh lemon juice

1 tsp. salt
freshly ground black
  pepper to taste
½ tsp. ground ginger or ¼
  tsp. ginger root,
  finely grated
4 tbsps. butter
½ cup beef broth

2 cups ripe, fresh tomatoes, peeled

1. *Remove core from cabbages. Separate six of the largest leaves from each head by holding cabbage under running water to loosen leaves.*
2. *Plunge leaves in boiling salted water. Cover and cook 3 minutes, or until leaves are wilted.*
3. *Mix together beef, rice, egg, parsley, lemon juice, salt, pepper and ginger.*
4. *Place about 2-3 tbsps. meat-rice mixture in center of each leaf. Fold in corners to form rectangle; roll up and secure with toothpicks or string. Repeat, filling all the leaves.*
5. *Cook stuffed cabbage in butter until browned on all sides.*
6. *Place cabbage rolls in casserole.*
7. *Stir broth and tomatoes into pan drippings; bring to boil. Pour over cabbage rolls.*
8. *Cover and bake in preheated 350° F. oven 1 hour. Serve at once.*

*NOTE: For a "goulash" effect, add sour cream to pan drippings and season to taste. Or, for "redder" effect, use tomato sauce! Use remaining cabbage in slaw. If desired, more meat may be used.*

# NOTES

SL-3201-1/S139